THE DIVINE COMEDY

THE DIVINE COMEDY
INFERNO
PURGATORIO
PARADISO

DANTE

TRANSLATED BY
HENRY WADSWORTH LONGFELLOW

WITH ILLUSTRATIONS BY
GUSTAVE DORÉ

FALL RIVER PRESS

New York

FALL RIVER PRESS

New York

An Imprint of Sterling Publishing
387 Park Avenue South
New York, NY 10016

Introduction by Melinda Corey © 2008 by Barnes & Noble.

This 2013 edition published by Fall River Press

The Fell Types are digitally reproduced by Igino Marini. www.iginomarini.com

ISBN: 978-1-4351-4691-4

Manufactured in the United States of America

5 7 9 10 8 6

Contents

Inferno

Purgatorio

PARADISO

INTRODUCTION

NEARLY SEVEN HUNDRED YEARS OLD, *THE DIVINE COMEDY* OF DANTE ALIGHIERI still impresses with its ambitious scope and vision. The three-volume work takes for its grand theme the experience of life after death, and explores its possibilities in the three metaphysical settings alluded to in each book's title: *Inferno*, *Purgatorio*, and *Paradiso*. The poem's execution in *terza rima*, the rhyme scheme invented for it, has never been duplicated. It is acknowledged as the main epic poem of modern Italian literature and the foremost epic poem of the Christian religion. It has influenced writers ever since its publication. As the Argentinian writer Jorge Luis Borges says, "[A]s soon as I open it tomorrow, I will discover things I did not see before. I know this book will go on, beyond my waking life, and beyond ours."

GENESIS

Dante Alighieri was born in Florence, Italy, between May and June 1265. His ancestry was noteworthy, though his family was of modest means. Both his parents died when he was young. Dante was betrothed in marriage to Gemma di Manetto Donati and was married in 1285. Together they had three children. Yet Gemma was never the love of his life and Dante never wrote about her. That prize he reserved for the object of his highest esteem, the beloved and unobtainable Beatrice Portinari.

Dante began writing *The Divine Comedy* around 1306, after he had been convicted of barratry (the selling of offices) by a pro-papacy political faction, the Black Guelphs. The conviction occurred *in absentia* on January 27, 1302, and was based on trumped-up charges. It resulted in Dante, a member of the opposing anti-papacy White Guelphs, being stripped of his property and banished from his native Florence. Later he was threatened with death should he ever return. Dante completed the *Comedy* in 1321.

Dante never returned to Florence. For the two decades following his banishment, he wandered through various towns in Italy, including Verona, Forlì, Arezzo, Treviso, and Ravenna, where he died of malaria on September 13, 1321.

ORGANIZATION

The three books of the *Divine Comedy* comprise 100 cantos, divided into thirty-three cantos each in *Purgatorio* and *Paradiso* and thirty-four in *Inferno*. The additional canto in *Inferno* serves as an introduction to the entire *Divine Comedy*.

Inferno, the first book, is set during April 1300, when Dante was 35. He was halfway through his biblically appointed life of three score years and ten, and so fit the pronouncement in Canto I that he, Dante, the narrator, is "[M]idway upon the journey of our life." The year 1300 also marks the beginning of Dante's public service in Florence, from which he would be barred.

Numbers are strongly symbolic in the *Divine Comedy*, particularly the number three. The *Comedy's* verse scheme, *terza rima*, is an eleven-syllable (or hendecasyllable) line that falls into three-line tercets that follow the interlinking rhyme scheme aba bcb cdc, dede or aba bcb cdc ded ee.

Dante invented this three-line stanza to serve as the basic unit of his narrative. Each unit expresses a thought; the units join together in the larger canto through the interlinking rhyme scheme. The middle line rhymes with the outer two of the next stanza; the pattern continues throughout the poem.

The architecture of the worlds Dante writes about is equally elegant and complex, and also is shaped by the number three. The world of *Inferno* divides into nine levels, which further divide in descending order along lines consistent with the three Aristotelian classes of sin: (1) sins of incontinence, due to the inability to control natural desire; (2) sins of brutishness or violence, characterized by turning the naturally repulsive into something appealing; and (3) sins of malice or fraud, i.e., wrong actions caused by abusing reason. Above these three divisions is an anteroom, home to the Neutrals, who did nothing with their lives.

After encountering the Neutrals, Dante and Virgil are ferried across the river Acheron. Once on the other side, they begin their journey through the concentric circles of Hell. The first circle is home to the virtuous heathen. The circles that follow are for incontinent sinners: the second is for the lascivious, the third for the gluttonous, the fourth for the avaricious and prodigal, the fifth for the wrathful, and the sixth for heretics.

Violent sinners follow: the seventh circle is home to those who committed violence against others, violence against themselves, and violence against nature and art. Next are fraudulent sinners: the eighth circle is the realm of panderers and seducers, flatterers, simonists, diviners, barrators, hypocrites, thieves, fraudulent counselors, makers of discord, and falsifiers. The ninth circle has sinners who are treacherous to kindred, country and cause, guests, and lords and benefactors.

The world of *Purgatorio* is a place of transition and hope. Unlike the eternities of Hell and Heaven, Purgatory is a place where inhabitants make acts of penance and gain absolution. Dante depicts Purgatory as a mountain, built when Satan was thrown from Heaven to the center of the earth and the earth closed behind him. Through Purgatory, ordinary sinners such as Dante may climb back spiritually and physically to the garden that humans once enjoyed as Eden.

Purgatory is divided into three parts defined by different types of love: perverse, defective, and excessive. Perverse love derives from the taking of delight in others' misfortunes and wrong acts. Inadequate love is practiced by those who half-heartedly pursue God's love. Excessive love is felt by those who exceed the limits for love of earthly pleasures. Additionally, Purgatory is divided into seven circles, for purging the seven deadly sins.

The ten heavens of *Paradiso* are arranged in order of increasing proximity to God. Architecturally, Paradise follows the Ptolemaic model, consisting of seven concentric planetary spheres that circle the earth. Dante ascends these seven planets, each one providing different moral and spiritual meanings from inconstancy to temperance.

Afterward, Dante encounters the souls in the Stellar Heaven, the Angels in the Primum Mobile, and finally the Heaven beyond space and time, where God, his angels, and the most blessed humans live. In *The Divine Comedy*, this is Dante's ultimate goal.

CHRONOLOGY

The events of the *Comedy* take place over seven days in April 1300. The night on which Dante loses himself in the forest is Good Friday. Dante and Virgil pass through the chasms of Hell during Saturday. On Saturday evening the two descend Satan's sides to the center of the earth. By dawn on Easter Sunday, they ascend to the foot of Mount Purgatory. The two traverse Purgatory and Dante enters Paradise. The journey ends on Thursday evening.

LITERARY FORM

Dante's *Divine Comedy* is, at its most basic level, a comedy. Dante called it the *Commedia* because he wrote it in the low and middle styles, not the "lofty verses" of works such as Virgil's *Aeneid*. Further, Dante calls his work a comedy because it ends happily: it allows those who desire salvation to be saved.

COSMOLOGY

In the scheme of *The Divine Comedy*, the earth is the center of the universe. Hell is under the city of Jerusalem in the Northern Hemisphere. It appears as a vast reversed cone reaching from near the earth's surface to the center, the farthest point from God. The sides of the cone form diminishing concentric circles where the different classes of the impenitent reside. Each level is set aside for a worse type of sinner. Jerusalem, where Christ was crucified, is the center of Hell. Mount Purgatory is in the Southern Hemisphere. The highest Heaven is beyond time and space.

THEOLOGY

Much of the theology of the *Comedy* derives from the teachings of theologian Thomas Aquinas. Born in 1225 near Naples, Italy, Aquinas studied at a Benedictine monastery, then went on to study at the University of Naples, where he received his doctorate in theology. For the rest of his life, he lectured in philosophy and theology. His principal subject of study was Aristotle, whose philosophy was central to Aquinas's main work, *Summa Theologica*, which he completed by 1273. He died near Rome in 1274.

Through his studies of Aristotle, Aquinas confirmed the soundness of logical argument, using it to prove the existence of God and to investigate His nature. Aquinas fashioned a world view that conveyed the divinity and truth of Christianity with logical rigor.

Dante follows this rigorous logical thinking throughout *The Divine Comedy*. The conception of Hell, the concentric spheres, the heavenly bodies, the angelic visions, and the vision of the Prime Mover are all informed by Aquinas. Both men join reason and faith at the center of the human quest for truth. The truth they find is God's will.

Personae

On his journey, Dante encounters a mix of historic and topically relevant personalities: statesmen (Brutus), nobles (Count Ugolino), popes (Boniface), lovers (Paolo and Francesca), and legendary figures (Ulysses). Together, they illustrate the philosophy, theology, politics, and drama of the Middle Ages. Of those characters, the most important are the two guides who accompany Dante through his travels: Virgil and Beatrice.

Virgil, the poet who leads Dante through the many levels of Hell and Purgatory, was hardly a random choice as guide. Dante selected Virgil because, in part, he represents what Dante wanted to be—the greatest Roman poet of his time. He also chose Virgil because Dante knew that he and Virgil were both just earthly sinners. Their encounter is a great artistic moment, what critic Ernst Curtius refers to as "the meeting of the great Latins."

Virgil (Publius Vergilius Maro, 70–19 B.C.) lived his adult life amidst the political chaos following the assassination of Julius Caesar in 44 B.C. He had survived dispossession because his collection of eclogues, the *Bucolics*, was well received by the minister of culture, Maecenas. Between 37 and 30 B.C., Virgil wrote *The Georgics*, a wish for peace under Octavius (Augustus) Caesar. From then until he died, Virgil wrote his greatest work, the *Aeneid*. This twelve-volume *homage* to the *Iliad* and the *Odyssey* told of Trojan prince Aeneas and expressed faith in Rome's future under Augustus. The poem was considered a great triumph for the Roman people and government.

Dante was strongly influenced by the *Aeneid* and borrowed from it for *The*

Divine Comedy. He uses the construct of traversing the underworld (as Virgil does) to frame his journeys through Hell and Purgatory. Yet he did not accept all the thinking of the day about Virgil. He also found limitations to Virgil, whom he felt lacked understanding of the Roman empire's political and religious greatness.

Because he is a pagan, Virgil is not allowed into Heaven. For that journey, Dante needs Beatrice. In addition to being his ideal object of affection, Beatrice is Dante's incarnation of holiness; in the *Purgatorio* he refers to her as "holy and alert." In reality, Beatrice was most likely Beatrice Portinari (1266–1290), a wealthy Florentine girl whom Dante first encountered when he was nine. From then until the end of his life, Dante was enraptured by Beatrice. They met once again, nine years later, but because the two were already otherwise betrothed, Dante could love Beatrice only from afar. In this, he followed the medieval practice of courtly love. Dante tells the history of his love for Beatrice in his collection of love poems and prose, *La Vita Nuova* (c. 1293–1294).

After Beatrice's death in 1290, Dante dedicated the rest of his life to his love for her. But a later vision told him that he was still unworthy of understanding her ultimate spiritual significance. For that he had to gain the inner enlightenment and intellectual improvement learned on his journey through Hell and Purgatory. Only then could he experience the Divine Love of Beatrice and Paradise.

TRANSLATIONS

Henry Wadsworth Longfellow (1807–1882) was already one of America's leading poets by the mid-nineteenth century when he began composing his English translation of *The Divine Comedy*. Completed between 1865 and 1867, Longfellow's translation reflects the poet's gifts as a creator of demotic, accessible works. Just as his own hugely popular poems developed an American interest in poetry, Longfellow's translation increased American interest in Dante by linking the Italian poet to a national American voice. While Longfellow's translation of *The Divine Comedy* became a standard for nineteenth-century English-language editions, it is but part of a long, distinguished line of literary translations of Dante.

Given that no original transcript of *The Divine Comedy* exists, all Dante volumes are in some form a translation. Among the earliest was that of Italian writer Giovanni Boccaccio (1313–1375), in 1348. Modern English language translations include those by scholars Charles Eliot Norton, Carlyle-Okey-Wicksteed, Laurence Binyon, Allen Mandelbaum, and John Sinclair. Novelist translators include Dorothy Sayers; poets include William Blake, John Ciardi, and Robert Pinsky. All have wrestled with the work in various ways. Unable to reproduce the *terza rima* rhyme scheme without damaging the movement of the text, translators have accommodated themselves with off-rhyme, blank verse, free rhyme, and prose.

The vivid imagery in *The Divine Comedy* has inspired artists and led to many distinguished illustrations of the text. Among the most highly esteemed are those by William Blake and Gustave Doré. Artists inspired by Dante include Spanish painter Salvador Dali, who created a series of paintings from the *Divine Comedy*.

LEGACY

The Divine Comedy was immediately acknowledged as an original masterwork. One index to interest in it is the many manuscripts of the *Comedy* that were prepared during the fourteenth and fifteenth centuries.

By the eighteenth century, however, *The Divine Comedy* had fallen from critical esteem. In his *Philosophical Dictionary* (1764), French writer Voltaire dismissed Dante: "His reputation will go on increasing, because scarce anybody reads him." Eighteenth-century British novelist Horace Walpole sloughed him off as a mouthpiece of the Catholic church.

By the late eighteenth and early nineteenth centuries, romantic writers such as William Blake rediscovered the text. Literary interest blossomed in the twentieth century. Dante was honored by writers including James Joyce, T. S. Eliot, Ezra Pound, and Samuel Beckett, all of whom were inspired by his writing. Portions of Eliot's *The Waste Land* draw from the *Comedy*.

The Divine Comedy has been and will remain a staple of the college curriculum. Like Plato, Aristotle, Virgil, and Shakespeare, Dante will be taught at school and promoted to readers who yearn to learn of the world's best thinking and writing.

—MELINDA COREY

Melinda Corey is the author or coauthor of over 30 books of non-fiction, including the New York Public Library's *Book of Answers*, *The American Film Institute Desk Reference*, *Facts about the 20th Century*, and several literary calendars. She also contributed to *The New York Public Library Literature Companion* and the *Eyewitness Companion to Film*. She is a graduate of the University of Chicago and holds an MFA from Columbia University. She lives in Westchester County with her husband and daughter, and teaches at Mercy College in New York.

DANTE ALIGHIERI

The
Divine Comedy

Inferno

⇥ CANTO I ⇤

Midway upon the journey of our life
    I found myself within a forest dark,
For the straightforward pathway had been lost.

Ah me! how hard a thing it is to say
    What was this forest savage, rough, and stern,   5
    Which in the very thought renews the fear.

So bitter is it, death is little more;
    But of the good to treat, which there I found,
    Speak will I of the other things I saw there.

I cannot well repeat how there I entered,   10
    So full was I of slumber at the moment
    In which I had abandoned the true way.

But after I had reached a mountain's foot,
    At that point where the valley terminated,
    Which had with consternation pierced my heart,   15

Upward I looked, and I beheld its shoulders,
    Vested already with that planet's rays
    Which leadeth others right by every road.

Then was the fear a little quieted
    That in my heart's lake had endured throughout   20
    The night, which I had passed so piteously.

Midway upon the journey of our life
I found myself within a forest dark,
For the straightforward pathway had been lost.

Inferno I, lines 1–3

And even as he, who, with distressful breath,
    Forth issued from the sea upon the shore,
    Turns to the water perilous and gazes;

So did my soul, that still was fleeing onward,   25
    Turn itself back to re-behold the pass
    Which never yet a living person left.

After my weary body I had rested,
    The way resumed I on the desert slope,
    So that the firm foot ever was the lower.   30

And lo! almost where the ascent began,
    A panther light and swift exceedingly,
    Which with a spotted skin was covered o'er!

And never moved she from before my face,
    Nay, rather did impede so much my way,   35
    That many times I to return had turned.

The time was the beginning of the morning,
    And up the sun was mounting with those stars
    That with him were, what time the Love Divine

At first in motion set those beauteous things;   40
    So were to me occasion of good hope,
    The variegated skin of that wild beast,

The hour of time, and the delicious season;
    But not so much, that did not give me fear
    A lion's aspect which appeared to me.   45

He seemed as if against me he were coming
    With head uplifted, and with ravenous hunger,
    So that it seemed the air was afraid of him;

And lo! almost where the ascent began,
A panther light and swift exceedingly,
Which with a spotted skin was covered o'er!

Inferno I, lines 31–33

He seemed as if against me he were coming
With head uplifted, and with ravenous hunger

Inferno I, lines 46–47

And a she-wolf, that with all hungerings
    Seemed to be laden in her meagerness,   50
    And many folk has caused to live forlorn!

She brought upon me so much heaviness,
    With the affright that from her aspect came,
    That I the hope relinquished of the height.

And as he is who willingly acquires,   55
    And the time comes that causes him to lose,
    Who weeps in all his thoughts and is despondent,

E'en such made me that beast withouten peace,
    Which, coming on against me by degrees
    Thrust me back thither where the sun is silent.   60

While I was rushing downward to the lowland,
    Before mine eyes did one present himself,
    Who seemed from long-continued silence hoarse.

When I beheld him in the desert vast,
    "Have pity on me," unto him I cried,   65
    "Whiche'er thou art, or shade or real man!"

He answered me: "Not man; man once I was,
    And both my parents were of Lombardy,
    And Mantuans by country both of them.

Sub Julio was I born, though it was late,   70
    And lived at Rome under the good Augustus,
    During the time of false and lying gods.

A poet was I, and I sang that just
    Son of Anchises, who came forth from Troy,
    After that Ilion the superb was burned.   75

But thou, why goest thou back to such annoyance?
    Why climb'st thou not the Mount Delectable,
    Which is the source and cause of every joy?"

"Now, art thou that Virgilius and that fountain
    Which spreads abroad so wide a river of speech?"   80
    I made response to him with bashful forehead.

"O, of the other poets honor and light,
    Avail me the long study and great love
    That have impelled me to explore thy volume!

Thou art my master, and my author thou,   85
    Thou art alone the one from whom I took
    The beautiful style that has done honor to me.

Behold the beast, for which I have turned back;
    Do thou protect me from her, famous Sage,
    For she doth make my veins and pulses tremble."   90

"Thee it behoves to take another road,"
    Responded he, when he beheld me weeping,
    "If from this savage place thou wouldst escape;

Because this beast, at which thou criest out,
    Suffers not any one to pass her way,   95
    But so doth harass him, that she destroys him;

And has a nature so malign and ruthless,
    That never doth she glut her greedy will,
    And after food is hungrier than before.

Many the animals with whom she weds,   100
    And more they shall be still, until the Greyhound
    Comes, who shall make her perish in her pain.

"Behold the beast, for which I have turned back;
   Do thou protect me from her, famous Sage"

Inferno I, lines 88–89

He shall not feed on either earth or pelf,
   But upon wisdom, and on love and virtue;
   'Twixt Feltro and Feltro shall his nation be;   105

Of that low Italy shall he be the savior,
   On whose account the maid Camilla died,
   Euryalus, Turnus, Nisus, of their wounds;

Through every city shall he hunt her down,
   Until he shall have driven her back to Hell,   110
   There from whence envy first did let her loose.

Therefore I think and judge it for thy best
   Thou follow me, and I will be thy guide,
   And lead thee hence through the eternal place,

Where thou shalt hear the desperate lamentations,   115
   Shalt see the ancient spirits disconsolate,
   Who cry out each one for the second death;

And thou shalt see those who contented are
   Within the fire, because they hope to come,
   Whene'er it may be, to the blessed people;   120

To whom, then, if thou wishest to ascend,
   A soul shall be for that than I more worthy;
   With her at my departure I will leave thee;

Because that Emperor, who reigns above,
   In that I was rebellious to his law,   125
   Wills that through me none come into his city.

He governs everywhere, and there he reigns;
   There is his city and his lofty throne;
   O happy he whom thereto he elects!"

And I to him: "Poet, I thee entreat,   130
    By that same God whom thou didst never know,
    So that I may escape this woe and worse,

Thou wouldst conduct me there where thou hast said,
    That I may see the portal of Saint Peter,
    And those thou makest so disconsolate."   135

Then he moved on, and I behind him followed.

⚔ CANTO II ⚔

The Descent—Dante's Protest and Virgil's Appeal—
The Intercession of the Three Ladies Benedight

D ay was departing, and the embrowned air
    Released the animals that are on earth
From their fatigues; and I the only one

Made myself ready to sustain the war,
    Both of the way and likewise of the woe,   5
    Which memory that errs not shall retrace.

O Muses, O high genius, now assist me!
    O memory, that didst write down what I saw,
    Here thy nobility shall be manifest!

And I began: "Poet, who guidest me,   10
    Regard my manhood, if it be sufficient,
    Ere to the arduous pass thou dost confide me.

Thou sayest, that of Silvius the parent,
    While yet corruptible, unto the world
    Immortal went, and was there bodily.   15

Then he moved on, and I behind him followed.

Inferno I, line 136

Day was departing

Inferno II, line 1

But if the adversary of all evil
    Was courteous, thinking of the high effect
    That issue would from him, and who, and what,

To men of intellect unmeet it seems not;
    For he was of great Rome, and of her empire   20
    In the empyreal heaven as father chosen;

The which and what, wishing to speak the truth,
    Were stablished as the holy place, wherein
    Sits the successor of the greatest Peter.

Upon this journey, whence thou givest him vaunt,   25
    Things did he hear, which the occasion were
    Both of his victory and the papal mantle.

Thither went afterwards the Chosen Vessel,
    To bring back comfort thence unto that Faith,
    Which of salvation's way is the beginning.   30

But I, why thither come, or who concedes it?
    I not Æneas am, I am not Paul,
    Nor I, nor others, think me worthy of it.

Therefore, if I resign myself to come,
    I fear the coming may be ill-advised;   35
    Thou'rt wise, and knowest better than I speak."

And as he is, who unwills what he willed,
    And by new thoughts doth his intention change,
    So that from his design he quite withdraws,

Such I became, upon that dark hillside,   40
    Because, in thinking, I consumed the emprise,
    Which was so very prompt in the beginning.

"If I have well thy language understood,"
  Replied that shade of the Magnanimous,
  "Thy soul attainted is with cowardice,   45

Which many times a man encumbers so,
  It turns him back from honored enterprise,
  As false sight doth a beast, when he is shy.

That thou mayst free thee from this apprehension,
  I'll tell thee why I came, and what I heard   50
  At the first moment when I grieved for thee.

Among those was I who are in suspense,
  And a fair, saintly Lady called to me
  In such wise, I besought her to command me.

Her eyes where shining brighter than the Star;   55
  And she began to say, gentle and low,
  With voice angelical, in her own language:

'O spirit courteous of Mantua,
  Of whom the fame still in the world endures,
  And shall endure, long-lasting as the world;   60

A friend of mine, and not the friend of fortune,
  Upon the desert slope is so impeded
  Upon his way, that he has turned through terror,

And may, I fear, already be so lost,
  That I too late have risen to his succor,   65
  From that which I have heard of him in Heaven.

Bestir thee now, and with thy speech ornate,
  And with what needful is for his release,
  Assist him so, that I may be consoled.

Beatrice am I, who do bid thee go;   70
    I come from there, where I would fain return;
    Love moved me, which compelleth me to speak.

When I shall be in presence of my Lord,
    Full often will I praise thee unto him.'
    Then paused she, and thereafter I began: 75

'O Lady of virtue, thou alone through whom
    The human race exceedeth all contained
    Within the heaven that has the lesser circles,

So grateful unto me is thy commandment,
    To obey, if 'twere already done, were late;   80
    No farther need'st thou ope to me thy wish.

But the cause tell me why thou dost not shun
    The here descending down into this center,
    From the vast place thou burnest to return to.'

'Since thou wouldst fain so inwardly discern,   85
    Briefly will I relate,' she answered me,
    'Why I am not afraid to enter here.

Of those things only should one be afraid
    Which have the power of doing others harm;
    Of the rest, no; because they are not fearful.   90

God in his mercy such created me
    That misery of yours attains me not,
    Nor any flame assails me of this burning.

A gentle Lady is in Heaven, who grieves
    At this impediment, to which I send thee,   95
    So that stern judgment there above is broken.

"Beatrice am I, who do bid thee go"

Inferno II, line 70

In her entreaty she besought Lucìa,
   And said, "Thy faithful one now stands in need
   Of thee, and unto thee I recommend him."

Lucìa, foe of all that cruel is,   100
   Hastened away, and came unto the place
   Where I was sitting with the ancient Rachel.

"Beatrice," said she, "the true praise of God,
   Why succorest thou not him, who loved thee so,
   For thee he issued from the vulgar herd?   105

Dost thou not hear the pity of his plaint?
   Dost thou not see the death that combats him
   Beside that flood, where ocean has no vaunt?"

Never were persons in the world so swift
   To work their weal and to escape their woe,   110
   As I, after such words as these were uttered,

Came hither downward from my blessed seat,
   Confiding in thy dignified discourse,
   Which honors thee, and those who've listened to it.'

After she thus had spoken unto me,   115
   Weeping, her shining eyes she turned away;
   Whereby she made me swifter in my coming;

And unto thee I came, as she desired;
   I have delivered thee from that wild beast,
   Which barred the beautiful mountain's short ascent. 120

What is it, then? Why, why dost thou delay?
   Why is such baseness bedded in thy heart?
   Daring and hardihood why hast thou not,

Seeing that three such Ladies benedight
    Are caring for thee in the court of Heaven,   125
    And so much good my speech doth promise thee?"

Even as the flowerets, by nocturnal chill,
    Bowed down and closed, when the sun whitens them,
    Uplift themselves all open on their stems;

Such I became with my exhausted strength,   130
    And such good courage to my heart there coursed,
    That I began, like an intrepid person:

"O she compassionate, who succored me,
    And courteous thou, who hast obeyed so soon
    The words of truth which she addressed to thee!   135

Thou hast my heart so with desire disposed
    To the adventure, with these words of thine,
    That to my first intent I have returned.

Now go, for one sole will is in us both,
    Thou Leader, and thou Lord, and Master thou."   140
    Thus said I to him; and when he had moved,

I entered on the deep and savage way.

⊰ Canto III ⊱

The Gate of Hell—The Inefficient or Indifferent—Pope Celestine V—
The Shores of Acheron—Charon—The Earthquake and the Swoon

"Through me the way is to the city dolent;
    Through me the way is to eternal dole;
Through me the way among the people lost.

Justice incited my sublime Creator;
    Created me divine Omnipotence,   5
    The highest Wisdom and the primal Love.

Before me there were no created things,
    Only eterne, and I eternal last.
    All hope abandon, ye who enter in!"

These words in somber color I beheld   10
    Written upon the summit of a gate;
    Whence I: "Their sense is, Master, hard to me!"

And he to me, as one experienced:
    "Here all suspicion needs must be abandoned,
    All cowardice must needs be here extinct.   15

We to the place have come, where I have told thee
    Thou shalt behold the people dolorous
    Who have foregone the good of intellect."

And after he had laid his hand on mine
    With joyful mien, whence I was comforted,   20
    He led me in among the secret things.

"All hope abandon, ye who enter in!"

Inferno III, line 9

There sighs, complaints, and ululations loud
   Resounded through the air without a star,
   Whence I, at the beginning, wept thereat.

Languages diverse, horrible dialects,   25
   Accents of anger, words of agony,
   And voices high and hoarse, with sound of hands,

Made up a tumult that goes whirling on
   For ever in that air for ever black,
   Even as the sand doth, when the whirlwind breathes. 30

And I, who had my head with horror bound,
   Said: "Master, what is this which now I hear?
   What folk is this, which seems by pain so vanquished?"

And he to me: "This miserable mode
   Maintain the melancholy souls of those   35
   Who lived withouten infamy or praise.

Commingled are they with that caitiff choir
   Of Angels, who have not rebellious been,
   Nor faithful were to God, but were for self.

The heavens expelled them, not to be less fair;   40
   Nor them the nethermore abyss receives,
   For glory none the damned would have from them."

And I: "O Master, what so grievous is
   To these, that maketh them lament so sore?"
   He answered: "I will tell thee very briefly.   45

These have no longer any hope of death;
   And this blind life of theirs is so debased,
   They envious are of every other fate.

No fame of them the world permits to be;
   Misericord and Justice both disdain them.   50
   Let us not speak of them, but look, and pass."

And I, who looked again, beheld a banner,
   Which, whirling round, ran on so rapidly,
   That of all pause it seemed to me indignant;

And after it there came so long a train   55
   Of people, that I ne'er would have believed
   That ever Death so many had undone.

When some among them I had recognized,
   I looked, and I beheld the shade of him
   Who made through cowardice the great refusal.   60

Forthwith I comprehended, and was certain,
   That this the sect was of the caitiff wretches
   Hateful to God and to his enemies.

These miscreants, who never were alive,
   Were naked, and were stung exceedingly   65
   By gadflies and by hornets that were there.

These did their faces irrigate with blood,
   Which, with their tears commingled, at their feet
   By the disgusting worms was gathered up.

And when to gazing farther I betook me.   70
   People I saw on a great river's bank;
   Whence said I: "Master, now vouchsafe to me,

That I may know who these are, and what law
   Makes them appear so ready to pass over,
   As I discern athwart the dusky light."   75

And he to me: "These things shall all be known
    To thee, as soon as we our footsteps stay
    Upon the dismal shore of Acheron."

Then with mine eyes ashamed and downward cast,
    Fearing my words might irksome be to him,   80
    From speech refrained I till we reached the river.

And lo! towards us coming in a boat
    An old man, hoary with the hair of eld,
    Crying: "Woe unto you, ye souls depraved!

Hope nevermore to look upon the heavens;   85
    I come to lead you to the other shore,
    To the eternal shades in heat and frost.

And thou, that yonder standest, living soul,
    Withdraw thee from these people, who are dead!"
    But when he saw that I did not withdraw,   90

He said: "By other ways, by other ports
    Thou to the shore shalt come, not here, for passage;
    A lighter vessel needs must carry thee."

And unto him the Guide: "Vex thee not, Charon;
    It is so willed there where is power to do   95
    That which is willed; and farther question not."

Thereat were quieted the fleecy cheeks
    Of him the ferryman of the livid fen,
    Who round about his eyes had wheels of flame.

But all those souls who weary were and naked   100
    Their color changed and gnashed their teeth together,
    As soon as they had heard those cruel words.

And lo! towards us coming in a boat
An old man, hoary with the hair of eld,
Crying: "Woe unto you, ye souls depraved!"

Inferno III, lines 82–84

God they blasphemed and their progenitors,
    The human race, the place, the time, the seed
    Of their engendering and of their birth!   105

Thereafter all together they drew back,
    Bitterly weeping, to the accursed shore,
    Which waiteth every man who fears not God.

Charon the demon, with the eyes of glede,
    Beckoning to them, collects them all together,   110
    Beats with his oar whoever lags behind.

As in the autumn-time the leaves fall off,
    First one and then another, till the branch
    Unto the earth surrenders all its spoils;

In similar wise the evil seed of Adam   115
    Throw themselves from that margin one by one,
    At signals, as a bird unto its lure.

So they depart across the dusky wave,
    And ere upon the other side they land,
    Again on this side a new troop assembles.   120

"My son," the courteous Master said to me,
    "All those who perish in the wrath of God
    Here meet together out of every land;

And ready are they to pass o'er the river,
    Because celestial Justice spurs them on,   125
    So that their fear is turned into desire.

This way there never passes a good soul;
    And hence if Charon doth complain of thee,
    Well mayst thou know now what his speech imports."

Charon the demon, with the eyes of glede,
Beckoning to them, collects them all together,
Beats with his oar whoever lags behind.

Inferno III, lines 109–111

This being finished, all the dusk champaign 130
    Trembled so violently, that of that terror
    The recollection bathes me still with sweat.

The land of tears gave forth a blast of wind,
    And fulminated a vermilion light,
    Which overmastered in me every sense, 135

And as a man whom sleep hath seized I fell.

⊰ CANTO IV ⊱

The First Circle, Limbo: Virtuous Pagans and the Unbaptized—
The Four Poets, Homer, Horace, Ovid, and Lucan—
The Noble Castle of Philosophy

Broke the deep lethargy within my head
    A heavy thunder, so that I upstarted,
Like to a person who by force is wakened;

And round about I moved my rested eyes,
    Uprisen erect, and steadfastly I gazed, 5
    To recognize the place wherein I was.

True is it, that upon the verge I found me
    Of the abysmal valley dolorous,
    That gathers thunder of infinite ululations.

Obscure, profound it was, and nebulous, 10
    So that by fixing on its depths my sight
    Nothing whatever I discerned therein.

"Let us descend now into the blind world,"
  Began the Poet, pallid utterly;
  "I will be first, and thou shalt second be."   15

And I, who of his color was aware,
  Said: "How shall I come, if thou art afraid,
  Who'rt wont to be a comfort to my fears?"

And he to me: "The anguish of the people
  Who are below here in my face depicts   20
  That pity which for terror thou hast taken.

Let us go on, for the long way impels us."
  Thus he went in, and thus he made me enter
  The foremost circle that surrounds the abyss.

There, as it seemed to me from listening,   25
  Were lamentations none, but only sighs,
  That tremble made the everlasting air.

And this arose from sorrow without torment,
  Which the crowds had, that many were and great,
  Of infants and of women and of men.   30

To me the Master good: "Thou dost not ask
  What spirits these, which thou beholdest, are?
  Now will I have thee know, ere thou go farther,

That they sinned not; and if they merit had,
  'Tis not enough, because they had not baptism   35
  Which is the portal of the Faith thou holdest;

And if they were before Christianity,
  In the right manner they adored not God;
  And among such as these am I myself.

For such defects, and not for other guilt,   40
    Lost are we, and are only so far punished,
    That without hope we live on in desire."

Great grief seized on my heart when this I heard,
    Because some people of much worthiness
    I knew, who in that Limbo were suspended.   45

"Tell me, my Master, tell me, thou my Lord,"
    Began I, with desire of being certain
    Of that Faith which o'ercometh every error,

"Came any one by his own merit hence,
    Or by another's, who was blessed thereafter?"   50
    And he, who understood my covert speech,

Replied: "I was a novice in this state,
    When I saw hither come a Mighty One,
    With sign of victory incoronate.

Hence he drew forth the shade of the First Parent,   55
    And that of his son Abel, and of Noah,
    Of Moses the lawgiver, and the obedient

Abraham, patriarch, and David, king,
    Israel with his father and his children,
    And Rachel, for whose sake he did so much,   60

And others many, and he made them blessed;
    And thou must know, that earlier than these
    Never were any human spirits saved."

We ceased not to advance because he spake,
    But still were passing onward through the forest,   65
    The forest, say I, of thick-crowded ghosts.

"Lost are we, and are only so far punished,
That without hope we live on in desire."

Inferno IV, lines 41–42

Not very far as yet our way had gone
    This side the summit, when I saw a fire
    That overcame a hemisphere of darkness.

We were a little distant from it still,   70
    But not so far that I in part discerned not
    That honorable people held that place.

"O thou who honorest every art and science,
    Who may these be, which such great honor have,
    That from the fashion of the rest it parts them?"   75

And he to me: "The honorable name,
    That sounds of them above there in thy life,
    Wins grace in Heaven, that so advances them."

In the meantime a voice was heard by me:
    "All honor be to the preeminent Poet;   80
    His shade returns again, that was departed."

After the voice had ceased and quiet was,
    Four mighty shades I saw approaching us;
    Semblance had they nor sorrowful nor glad.

To say to me began my gracious Master: 85
    "Him with that falchion in his hand behold,
    Who comes before the three, even as their lord.

That one is Homer, Poet sovereign;
    He who comes next is Horace, the satirist;
    The third is Ovid, and the last is Lucan.   90

Because to each of these with me applies
    The name that solitary voice proclaimed,
    They do me honor, and in that do well."

Thus I beheld assemble the fair school
   Of that lord of the song preeminent,   95
   Who o'er the others like an eagle soars.

When they together had discoursed somewhat,
   They turned to me with signs of salutation,
   And on beholding this, my Master smiled;

And more of honor still, much more, they did me,   100
   In that they made me one of their own band;
   So that the sixth was I, 'mid so much wit.

Thus we went on as far as to the light,
   Things saying 'tis becoming to keep silent,
   As was the saying of them where I was.   105

We came unto a noble castle's foot,
   Seven times encompassëd with lofty walls,
   Defended round by a fair rivulet;

This we passed over even as firm ground;
   Through portals seven I entered with these Sages;   110
   We came into a meadow of fresh verdure.

People were there with solemn eyes and slow,
   Of great authority in their countenance;
   They spake but seldom, and with gentle voices.

Thus we withdrew ourselves upon one side   115
   Into an opening luminous and lofty,
   So that they all of them were visible.

There opposite, upon the green enamel,
   Were pointed out to me the mighty spirits,
   Whom to have seen I feel myself exalted.   120

Thus I beheld assemble the fair school
Of that lord of the song preeminent,
Who o'er the others like an eagle soars.

Inferno IV, lines 94–96

I saw Electra with companions many,
   'Mongst whom I knew both Hector and Æneas,
   Cæsar in armor with gerfalcon eyes;

I saw Camilla and Penthesilea
   On the other side, and saw the King Latinus,   125
   Who with Lavinia his daughter sat;

I saw that Brutus who drove Tarquin forth,
   Lucretia, Julia, Marcia, and Cornelia,
   And saw alone, apart, the Saladin.

When I had lifted up my brows a little,   130
   The Master I beheld of those who know,
   Sit with his philosophic family.

All gaze upon him, and all do him honor.
   There I beheld both Socrates and Plato,
   Who nearer him before the others stand;   135

Democritus, who puts the world on chance,
   Diogenes, Anaxagoras, and Thales,
   Zeno, Empedocles, and Heraclitus;

Of qualities I saw the good collector,
   Hight Dioscorides; and Orpheus saw I,   140
   Tully and Livy, and moral Seneca,

Euclid, geometrician, and Ptolemy,
   Galen, Hippocrates, and Avicenna,
   Averroes, who the great Comment made.

I cannot all of them portray in full,   145
   Because so drives me onward the long theme,
   That many times the word comes short of fact.

The sixfold company in two divides;
    Another way my sapient Guide conducts me
    Forth from the quiet to the air that trembles;   150

And to a place I come where nothing shines.

⊰ CANTO V ⊱

The Second Circle: The Wanton—Minos—
The Infernal Hurricane—Francesca da Rimini

Thus I descended out of the first circle
    Down to the second, that less space begirds,
And so much greater dole, that goads to wailing.

There standeth Minos horribly, and snarls;
    Examines the transgressions at the entrance;   5
    Judges, and sends according as he girds him.

I say, that when the spirit evil-born
    Cometh before him, wholly it confesses;
    And this discriminator of transgressions

Seeth what place in Hell is meet for it;   10
    Girds himself with his tail as many times
    As grades he wishes it should be thrust down.

Always before him many of them stand;
    They go by turns each one unto the judgment;
    They speak, and hear, and then are downward hurled. 15

"O thou, that to this dolorous hostelry
    Comest," said Minos to me, when he saw me,
    Leaving the practice of so great an office,

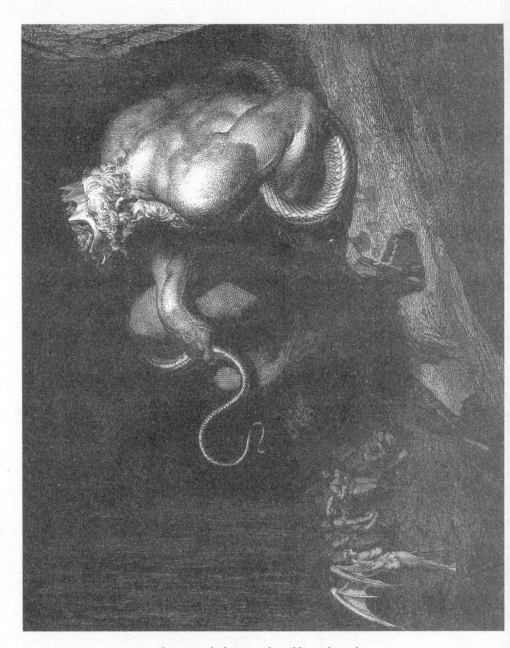

There standeth Minos horribly, and snarls;
Examines the transgressions at the entrance;
Judges, and sends according as he girds him.

Inferno V, lines 4–6

"Look how thou enterest, and in whom thou trustest;
    Let not the portal's amplitude deceive thee."   20
    And unto him my Guide: "Why criest thou too?

Do not impede his journey fate-ordained;
    It is so willed there where is power to do
    That which is willed; and ask no further question."

And now begin the dolesome notes to grow   25
    Audible unto me; now am I come
    There where much lamentation strikes upon me.

I came into a place mute of all light,
    Which bellows as the sea does in a tempest,
    If by opposing winds 't is combated.   30

The infernal hurricane that never rests
    Hurtles the spirits onward in its rapine;
    Whirling them round, and smiting, it molests them.

When they arrive before the precipice,
    There are the shrieks, the plaints, and the laments,   35
    There they blaspheme the puissance divine.

I understood that unto such a torment
    The carnal malefactors were condemned,
    Who reason subjugate to appetite.

And as the wings of starlings bear them on   40
    In the cold season in large band and full,
    So doth that blast the spirits maledict;

It hither, thither, downward, upward, drives them;
    No hope doth comfort them for evermore,
    Not of repose, but even of lesser pain.   45

The infernal hurricane that never rests
Hurtles the spirits onward in its rapine

Inferno V, lines 31–32

And as the cranes go chanting forth their lays,
    Making in air a long line of themselves,
    So saw I coming, uttering lamentations,

Shadows borne onward by the aforesaid stress.
    Whereupon said I: "Master, who are those   50
    People, whom the black air so castigates?"

"The first of those, of whom intelligence
    Thou fain wouldst have," then said he unto me,
    "The empress was of many languages.

To sensual vices she was so abandoned,   55
    That lustful she made licit in her law,
    To remove the blame to which she had been led.

She is Semiramis, of whom we read
    That she succeeded Ninus, and was his spouse;
    She held the land which now the Sultan rules.   60

The next is she who killed herself for love,
    And broke faith with the ashes of Sichæus;
    Then Cleopatra the voluptuous."

Helen I saw, for whom so many ruthless
    Seasons revolved; and saw the great Achilles,   65
    Who at the last hour combated with Love.

Paris I saw, Tristan; and more than a thousand
    Shades did he name and point out with his finger,
    Whom Love had separated from our life.

After that I had listened to my Teacher,   70
    Naming the dames of eld and cavaliers,
    Pity prevailed, and I was nigh bewildered.

And I began: "O Poet, willingly
   Speak would I to those two, who go together,
   And seem upon the wind to be so light."   75

And he to me: "Thou'lt mark, when they shall be
   Nearer to us; and then do thou implore them
   By love which leadeth them, and they will come."

Soon as the wind in our direction sways them,
   My voice uplift I: "O ye weary souls!   80
   Come speak to us, if no one interdicts it."

As turtledoves, called onward by desire,
   With open and steady wings to the sweet nest
   Fly through the air by their volition borne,

So came they from the band where Dido is,   85
   Approaching us athwart the air malign,
   So strong was the affectionate appeal.

"O living creature gracious and benignant,
   Who visiting goest through the purple air
   Us, who have stained the world incarnadine,   90

If were the King of the Universe our friend,
   We would pray unto him to give thee peace,
   Since thou hast pity on our woe perverse.

Of what it pleases thee to hear and speak,
   That will we hear, and we will speak to you,   95
   While silent is the wind, as it is now.

Sitteth the city, wherein I was born,
   Upon the seashore where the Po descends
   To rest in peace with all his retinue.

"O Poet, willingly
Speak would I to those two, who go together,
And seem upon the wind to be so light."

Inferno V, lines 73–75

Love, that on gentle heart doth swiftly seize,   100
    Seized this man for the person beautiful
    That was ta'en from me, and still the mode offends me.

Love, that exempts no one beloved from loving,
    Seized me with pleasure of this man so strongly,
    That, as thou seest, it doth not yet desert me;   105

Love has conducted us unto one death;
    Caina waiteth him who quenched our life!"
    These words were borne along from them to us.

As soon as I had heard those souls tormented,
    I bowed my face, and so long held it down   110
    Until the Poet said to me: "What thinkest?"

When I made answer, I began: "Alas!
    How many pleasant thoughts, how much desire,
    Conducted these unto the dolorous pass!"

Then unto them I turned me, and I spake,   115
    And I began: "Thine agonies, Francesca,
    Sad and compassionate to weeping make me.

But tell me, at the time of those sweet sighs,
    By what and in what manner Love conceded,
    That you should know your dubious desires?"   120

And she to me: "There is no greater sorrow
    Than to be mindful of the happy time
    In misery, and that thy Teacher knows.

But, if to recognize the earliest root
    Of love in us thou hast so great desire,   125
    I will do even as he who weeps and speaks.

"Love has conducted us unto one death;
Caina waiteth him who quenched our life!"
These words were borne along from them to us.

Inferno V, lines 106–108

One day we reading were for our delight
    Of Launcelot, how Love did him enthrall.
    Alone we were and without any fear.

Full many a time our eyes together drew   130
    That reading, and drove the color from our faces;
    But one point only was it that o'ercame us.

When as we read of the much-longed-for smile
    Being by such a noble lover kissed,
    This one, who ne'er from me shall be divided,   135

Kissed me upon the mouth all palpitating.
    Galeotto was the book and he who wrote it.
    That day no farther did we read therein."

And all the while one spirit uttered this,
    The other one did weep so, that, for pity,   140
    I swooned away as if I had been dying,

And fell, even as a dead body falls.

⊰ Canto VI ⊱

The Third Circle: The Gluttonous — Cerberus —
The Eternal Rain — Ciacco — Florence

At the return of consciousness, that closed
    Before the pity of those two relations,
Which utterly with sadness had confused me,

New torments I behold, and new tormented
    Around me, whichsoever way I move,   5
    And whichsoever way I turn, and gaze.

"That day no farther did we read therein."

Inferno V, line 138

I swooned away as if I had been dying,
And fell, even as a dead body falls.

Inferno V, lines 141–142

In the third circle am I of the rain
 Eternal, maledict, and cold, and heavy;
 Its law and quality are never new.

Huge hail, and water somber-hued, and snow,   10
 Athwart the tenebrous air pour down amain;
 Noisome the earth is, that receiveth this.

Cerberus, monster cruel and uncouth,
 With his three gullets like a dog is barking
 Over the people that are there submerged.   15

Red eyes he has, and unctuous beard and black,
 And belly large, and armed with claws his hands;
 He rends the spirits, flays, and quarters them.

Howl the rain maketh them like unto dogs;
 One side they make a shelter for the other;   20
 Oft turn themselves the wretched reprobates.

When Cerberus perceived us, the great worm!
 His mouths he opened, and displayed his tusks;
 Not a limb had he that was motionless.

And my Conductor, with his spans extended,   25
 Took of the earth, and with his fists well filled,
 He threw it into those rapacious gullets.

Such as that dog is, who by barking craves,
 And quiet grows soon as his food he gnaws,
 For to devour it he but thinks and struggles,   30

The like became those muzzles filth-begrimed
 Of Cerberus the demon, who so thunders
 Over the souls that they would fain be deaf.

And my Conductor, with his spans extended,
Took of the earth, and with his fists well-filled,
He threw it into those rapacious gullets.

Inferno VI, lines 25–27

We passed across the shadows, which subdues
  The heavy rainstorm, and we placed our feet   35
  Upon their vanity that person seems.

They all were lying prone upon the earth,
  Excepting one, who sat upright as soon
  As he beheld us passing on before him.

"O thou that art conducted through this Hell,"   40
  He said to me, "recall me, if thou canst;
  Thyself wast made before I was unmade."

And I to him: "The anguish which thou hast
  Perhaps doth draw thee out of my remembrance,
  So that it seems not I have ever seen thee.   45

But tell me who thou art, that in so doleful
  A place art put, and in such punishment,
  If some are greater, none is so displeasing."

And he to me: "Thy city, which is full
  Of envy so that now the sack runs over,   50
  Held me within it in the life serene.

You citizens were wont to call me Ciacco;
  For the pernicious sin of gluttony
  I, as thou seest, am battered by this rain.

And I, sad soul, am not the only one,   55
  For all these suffer the like penalty
  For the like sin"; and word no more spake he.

I answered him: "Ciacco, thy wretchedness
  Weighs on me so that it to weep invites me;
  But tell me, if thou knowest, to what shall come   60

"For the pernicious sin of gluttony
I, as thou seest, am battered by this rain."

Inferno VI, lines 53–54

The citizens of the divided city;
   If any there be just; and the occasion
   Tell me why so much discord has assailed it."

And he to me: "They, after long contention,
   Will come to bloodshed; and the rustic party   65
   Will drive the other out with much offense.

Then afterwards behoves it this one fall
   Within three suns, and rise again the other
   By force of him who now is on the coast.

High will it hold its forehead a long while,   70
   Keeping the other under heavy burdens,
   Howe'er it weeps thereat and is indignant.

The just are two, and are not understood there;
   Envy and Arrogance and Avarice
   Are the three sparks that have all hearts enkindled." 75

Here ended he his tearful utterance;
   And I to him: "I wish thee still to teach me,
   And make a gift to me of further speech.

Farinata and Tegghiaio, once so worthy,
   Jacopo Rusticucci, Arrigo, and Mosca,   80
   And others who on good deeds set their thoughts,

Say where they are, and cause that I may know them;
   For great desire constraineth me to learn
   If Heaven doth sweeten them, or Hell envenom."

And he: "They are among the blacker souls;   85
   A different sin downweighs them to the bottom;
   If thou so far descendest, thou canst see them.

But when thou art again in the sweet world,
   I pray thee to the mind of others bring me;
   No more I tell thee and no more I answer."   90

Then his straightforward eyes he turned askance,
   Eyed me a little, and then bowed his head;
   He fell therewith prone like the other blind.

And the Guide said to me: "He wakes no more
   This side the sound of the angelic trumpet;   95
   When shall approach the hostile Potentate,

Each one shall find again his dismal tomb,
   Shall reassume his flesh and his own figure,
   Shall hear what through eternity re-echoes."

So we passed onward o'er the filthy mixture   100
   Of shadows and of rain with footsteps slow,
   Touching a little on the future life.

Wherefore I said: "Master, these torments here,
   Will they increase after the mighty sentence,
   Or lesser be, or will they be as burning?"   105

And he to me: "Return unto thy science,
   Which wills, that as the thing more perfect is,
   The more it feels of pleasure and of pain.

Albeit that this people maledict
   To true perfection never can attain,   110
   Hereafter more than now they look to be."

Round in a circle by that road we went,
   Speaking much more, which I do not repeat;
   We came unto the point where the descent is;

There we found Plutus the great enemy.   115

⊰ CANTO VII ⊱

The Fourth Circle: The Avaricious and the Prodigal—Plutus—
Fortune and Her Wheel—The Fifth Circle: The Irascible and the Sullen—Styx

"Papë Satàn, Papë Satàn, Aleppë!"
   Thus Plutus with his clucking voice began;
And that benignant Sage, who all things knew,

Said, to encourage me: "Let not thy fear
   Harm thee; for any power that he may have   5
   Shall not prevent thy going down this crag."

Then he turned round unto that bloated lip,
   And said: "Be silent, thou accursed wolf;
   Consume within thyself with thine own rage.

Not causeless is this journey to the abyss;   10
   Thus is it willed on high, where Michael wrought
   Vengeance upon the proud adultery."

Even as the sails inflated by the wind
   Involved together fall when snaps the mast,
   So fell the cruel monster to the earth.   15

Thus we descended into the fourth chasm,
   Gaining still farther on the dolesome shore
   Which all the woe of the universe insacks.

Justice of God, ah! who heaps up so many
   New toils and sufferings as I beheld?   20
   And why doth our transgression waste us so?

"Be silent, thou accursed wolf;
Consume within thyself with thine own rage."

Inferno VII, lines 8–9

As doth the billow there upon Charybdis,
    That breaks itself on that which it encounters,
    So here the folk must dance their roundelay.

Here saw I people, more than elsewhere, many,   25
    On one side and the other, with great howls,
    Rolling weights forward by main force of chest.

They clashed together, and then at that point
    Each one turned backward, rolling retrograde,
    Crying, "Why keepest?" and, "Why squanderest
      thou?"   30

Thus they returned along the lurid circle
    On either hand unto the opposite point,
    Shouting their shameful meter evermore.

Then each, when he arrived there, wheeled about
    Through his half-circle to another joust;   35
    And I, who had my heart pierced as it were,

Exclaimed: "My Master, now declare to me
    What people these are, and if all were clerks,
    These shaven crowns upon the left of us."

And he to me: "All of them were asquint   40
    In intellect in the first life, so much
    That there with measure they no spending made.

Clearly enough their voices bark it forth,
    Whene'er they reach the two points of the circle,
    Where sunders them the opposite defect.   45

Clerks those were who no hairy covering
    Have on the head, and Popes and Cardinals,
    In whom doth Avarice practice its excess."

And I: "My Master, among such as these
    I ought forsooth to recognize some few,   50
    Who were infected with these maladies."

And he to me: "Vain thought thou entertainest;
    The undiscerning life which made them sordid
    Now makes them unto all discernment dim.

Forever shall they come to these two buttings;   55
    These from the sepulcher shall rise again
    With the fist closed, and these with tresses shorn.

Ill giving and ill keeping the fair world
    Have ta'en from them, and placed them in this scuffle;
    Whate'er it be, no words adorn I for it.   60

Now canst thou, Son, behold the transient farce
    Of goods that are committed unto Fortune,
    For which the human race each other buffet;

For all the gold that is beneath the moon,
    Or ever has been, of these weary souls   65
    Could never make a single one repose."

"Master," I said to him, "now tell me also
    What is this Fortune which thou speakest of,
    That has the world's goods so within its clutches?"

And he to me: "O creatures imbecile,   70
    What ignorance is this which doth beset you?
    Now will I have thee learn my judgment of her.

He whose omniscience everything transcends
    The heavens created, and gave who should guide them,
    That every part to every part may shine,   75

"For all the gold that is beneath the moon,
Or ever has been, of these weary souls
Could never make a single one repose."

Inferno VII, lines 64–66

Distributing the light in equal measure;
    He in like manner to the mundane splendors
    Ordained a general ministress and guide,

That she might change at times the empty treasures
    From race to race, from one blood to another,   80
    Beyond resistance of all human wisdom.

Therefore one people triumphs, and another
    Languishes, in pursuance of her judgment,
    Which hidden is, as in the grass a serpent.

Your knowledge has no counterstand against her;   85
    She makes provision, judges, and pursues
    Her governance, as theirs the other gods.

Her permutations have not any truce;
    Necessity makes her precipitate,
    So often cometh who his turn obtains.   90

And this is she who is so crucified
    Even by those who ought to give her praise,
    Giving her blame amiss, and bad repute.

But she is blissful, and she hears it not;
    Among the other primal creatures gladsome   95
    She turns her sphere, and blissful she rejoices.

Let us descend now unto greater woe;
    Already sinks each star that was ascending
    When I set out, and loitering is forbidden."

We crossed the circle to the other bank,   100
    Near to a fount that boils, and pours itself
    Along a gully that runs out of it.

The water was more somber far than perse;
    And we, in company with the dusky waves,
        Made entrance downward by a path uncouth.   105

A marsh it makes, which has the name of Styx,
    This tristful brooklet, when it has descended
        Down to the foot of the malign gray shores.

And I, who stood intent upon beholding,
    Saw people mud-besprent in that lagoon,   110
        All of them naked and with angry look.

They smote each other not alone with hands,
    But with the head and with the breast and feet,
        Tearing each other piecemeal with their teeth.

Said the good Master: "Son, thou now beholdest   115
    The souls of those whom anger overcame;
        And likewise I would have thee know for certain

Beneath the water people are who sigh
    And make this water bubble at the surface,
        As the eye tells thee wheresoe'er it turns.   120

Fixed in the mire they say, 'We sullen were
    In the sweet air, which by the sun is gladdened,
        Bearing within ourselves the sluggish reek;

Now we are sullen in this sable mire.'
    This hymn do they keep gurgling in their throats,   125
        For with unbroken words they cannot say it."

Thus we went circling round the filthy fen
    A great arc 'twixt the dry bank and the swamp,
        With eyes turned unto those who gorge the mire;

Unto the foot of a tower we came at last.   130

"Son, thou now beholdest
The souls of those whom anger overcame"

Inferno VII, lines 115–116

⊰ CANTO VIII ⊱

Phlegyas—Philippo Argenti—The Gate of the City of Dis

I say, continuing, that long before
　　We to the foot of that high tower had come,
Our eyes went upward to the summit of it,

By reason of two flamelets we saw placed there,
　　And from afar another answer them,　　　　5
　　So far, that hardly could the eye attain it.

And, to the sea of all discernment turned,
　　I said: "What sayeth this, and what respondeth
　　That other fire? and who are they that made it?"

And he to me: "Across the turbid waves　　　　10
　　What is expected thou canst now discern,
　　If reek of the morass conceal it not."

Cord never shot an arrow from itself
　　That sped away athwart the air so swift,
　　As I beheld a very little boat　　　　15

Come o'er the water tow'rds us at that moment,
　　Under the guidance of a single pilot,
　　Who shouted, "Now art thou arrived, fell soul?"

"Phlegyas, Phlegyas, thou criest out in vain
　　For this once," said my Lord; "thou shalt not have us　20
　　Longer than in the passing of the slough."

As he who listens to some great deceit
　　That has been done to him, and then resents it,
　　Such became Phlegyas, in his gathered wrath.

My Guide descended down into the boat,   25
    And then he made me enter after him,
    And only when I entered seemed it laden.

Soon as the Guide and I were in the boat,
    The antique prow goes on its way, dividing
    More of the water than 'tis wont with others.   30

While we were running through the dead canal,
    Uprose in front of me one full of mire,
    And said, "Who 'rt thou that comest ere the hour?"

And I to him: "Although I come, I stay not;
    But who art thou that hast become so squalid?"   35
    "Thou seest that I am one who weeps," he answered.

And I to him: "With weeping and with wailing,
    Thou spirit maledict, do thou remain;
    For thee I know, though thou art all defiled."

Then stretched he both his hands unto the boat;   40
    Whereat my wary Master thrust him back,
    Saying, "Away there with the other dogs!"

Thereafter with his arms he clasped my neck;
    He kissed my face, and said: "Disdainful soul,
    Blessed be she who bore thee in her bosom.   45

That was an arrogant person in the world;
    Goodness is none, that decks his memory;
    So likewise here his shade is furious.

How many are esteemed great kings up there,
    Who here shall be like unto swine in mire,   50
    Leaving behind them horrible dispraises!"

The antique prow goes on its way, dividing
More of the water than 'tis wont with others.

Inferno VIII, lines 29–30

Then stretched he both his hands unto the boat;
Whereat my wary Master thrust him back

Inferno VIII, lines 40–41

And I: "My Master, much should I be pleased,
   If I could see him soused into this broth,
   Before we issue forth out of the lake."

And he to me: "Ere unto thee the shore   55
   Reveal itself, thou shalt be satisfied;
   Such a desire 'tis meet thou shouldst enjoy."

A little after that, I saw such havoc
   Made of him by the people of the mire,
   That still I praise and thank my God for it.   60

They all were shouting, "At Philippo Argenti!"
   And that exasperate spirit Florentine
   Turned round upon himself with his own teeth.

We left him there, and more of him I tell not;
   But on mine ears there smote a lamentation,   65
   Whence forward I intent unbar mine eyes.

And the good Master said: "Even now, my Son,
   The city draweth near whose name is Dis,
   With the grave citizens, with the great throng."

And I: "Its mosques already, Master, clearly   70
   Within there in the valley I discern
   Vermilion, as if issuing from the fire

They were." And he to me: "The fire eternal
   That kindles them within makes them look red,
   As thou beholdest in this nether Hell."   75

Then we arrived within the moats profound,
   That circumvallate that disconsolate city;
   The walls appeared to me to be of iron.

Not without making first a circuit wide,
We came unto a place where loud the pilot   80
Cried out to us, "Debark, here is the entrance."

More than a thousand at the gates I saw
Out of the Heavens rained down, who angrily
Were saying, "Who is this that without death

Goes through the kingdom of the people dead?"   85
And my sagacious Master made a sign
Of wishing secretly to speak with them.

A little then they quelled their great disdain,
And said: "Come thou alone, and he begone
Who has so boldly entered these dominions.   90

Let him return alone by his mad road;
Try, if he can; for thou shalt here remain,
Who hast escorted him through such dark regions."

Think, Reader, if I was discomforted
At utterance of the accursed words;   95
For never to return here I believed.

"O my dear Guide, who more than seven times
Hast rendered me security, and drawn me
From imminent peril that before me stood,

Do not desert me," said I, "thus undone;   100
And if the going farther be denied us,
Let us retrace our steps together swiftly."

And that Lord, who had led me thitherward,
Said unto me: "Fear not; because our passage
None can take from us, it by Such is given.   105

But here await me, and thy weary spirit
    Comfort and nourish with a better hope;
    For in this nether world I will not leave thee."

So onward goes and there abandons me
    My Father sweet, and I remain in doubt,   110
    For No and Yes within my head contend.

I could not hear what he proposed to them;
    But with them there he did not linger long,
    Ere each within in rivalry ran back.

They closed the portals, those our adversaries,   115
    On my Lord's breast, who had remained without
    And turned to me with footsteps far between.

His eyes cast down, his forehead shorn had he
    Of all its boldness, and he said, with sighs,
    "Who has denied to me the dolesome houses?"   120

And unto me: "Thou, because I am angry,
    Fear not, for I will conquer in the trial,
    Whatever for defense within be planned.

This arrogance of theirs is nothing new;
    For once they used it at less secret gate,   125
    Which finds itself without a fastening still.

O'er it didst thou behold the dead inscription;
    And now this side of it descends the steep,
    Passing across the circles without escort,

One by whose means the city shall be opened."   130

I could not hear what he proposed to them;
But with them there he did not linger long,
Ere each within in rivalry ran back.

Inferno VIII, lines 112–114

⊰ CANTO IX ⊱

The Furies and Medusa—The Angel—The City of Dis—
The Sixth Circle: Heresiarchs

T hat hue which cowardice brought out on me,
 Beholding my Conductor backward turn,
Sooner repressed within him his new color.

He stopped attentive, like a man who listens,
 Because the eye could not conduct him far   5
 Through the black air, and through the heavy fog.

"Still it behoveth us to win the fight,"
 Began he; "Else . . . Such offered us herself . . .
 O how I long that some one here arrive!"

Well I perceived, as soon as the beginning   10
 He covered up with what came afterward,
 That they were words quite different from the first;

But nonetheless his saying gave me fear,
 Because I carried out the broken phrase,
 Perhaps to a worse meaning than he had.   15

"Into this bottom of the doleful conch
 Doth any e'er descend from the first grade,
 Which for its pain has only hope cut off?"

This question put I; and he answered me:
 "Seldom it comes to pass that one of us   20
 Maketh the journey upon which I go.

True is it, once before I here below
  Was conjured by that pitiless Erictho,
  Who summoned back the shades unto their bodies.

Naked of me short while the flesh had been,   25
  Before within that wall she made me enter,
  To bring a spirit from the circle of Judas;

That is the lowest region and the darkest,
  And farthest from the heaven which circles all.
  Well know I the way; therefore be reassured.   30

This fen, which a prodigious stench exhales,
  Encompasses about the city dolent,
  Where now we cannot enter without anger."

And more he said, but not in mind I have it;
  Because mine eye had altogether drawn me   35
  Tow'rds the high tower with the red-flaming summit,

Where in a moment saw I swift uprisen
  The three infernal Furies stained with blood,
  Who had the limbs of women and their mien,

And with the greenest hydras were begirt;   40
  Small serpents and cerastes were their tresses,
  Wherewith their horrid temples were entwined.

And he who well the handmaids of the Queen
  Of everlasting lamentation knew,
  Said unto me: "Behold the fierce Erinnys.   45

This is Megæra, on the left-hand side;
  She who is weeping on the right, Alecto;
  Tisiphone is between"; and then was silent.

"This is Megæra, on the left-hand side;
She who is weeping on the right, Alecto;
Tisiphone is between"

Inferno IX, lines 46–48

Each one her breast was rending with her nails;
    They beat them with their palms, and cried so loud, 50
    That I for dread pressed close unto the Poet.

"Medusa come, so we to stone will change him!"
    All shouted looking down; "in evil hour
    Avenged we not on Theseus his assault!"

"Turn thyself round, and keep thine eyes close shut, 55
    For if the Gorgon appear, and thou shouldst see it,
    No more returning upward would there be."

Thus said the Master; and he turned me round
    Himself, and trusted not unto my hands
    So far as not to blind me with his own. 60

O ye who have undistempered intellects,
    Observe the doctrine that conceals itself
    Beneath the veil of the mysterious verses!

And now there came across the turbid waves
    The clangor of a sound with terror fraught, 65
    Because of which both of the margins trembled;

Not otherwise it was than of a wind
    Impetuous on account of adverse heats,
    That smites the forest, and, without restraint,

The branches rends, beats down, and bears away; 70
    Right onward, laden with dust, it goes superb,
    And puts to flight the wild beasts and the shepherds.

Mine eyes he loosed, and said: "Direct the nerve
    Of vision now along that ancient foam,
    There yonder where that smoke is most intense." 75

Even as the frogs before the hostile serpent
   Across the water scatter all abroad,
   Until each one is huddled in the earth.

More than a thousand ruined souls I saw,
   Thus fleeing from before one who on foot   80
   Was passing o'er the Styx with soles unwet.

From off his face he fanned that unctuous air,
   Waving his left hand oft in front of him,
   And only with that anguish seemed he weary.

Well I perceived one sent from Heaven was he,   85
   And to the Master turned; and he made sign
   That I should quiet stand, and bow before him.

Ah! how disdainful he appeared to me!
   He reached the gate, and with a little rod
   He opened it, for there was no resistance.   90

"O banished out of Heaven, people despised!"
   Thus he began upon the horrid threshold;
   "Whence is this arrogance within you couched?

Wherefore recalcitrate against that will,
   From which the end can never be cut off,   95
   And which has many times increased your pain?

What helpeth it to butt against the fates?
   Your Cerberus, if you remember well,
   For that still bears his chin and gullet peeled."

Then he returned along the miry road,   100
   And spake no word to us, but had the look
   Of one whom other care constrains and goads

He reached the gate, and with a little rod
He opened it, for there was no resistance.

Inferno IX, lines 89–90

Than that of him who in his presence is;
   And we our feet directed tow'rds the city,
   After those holy words all confident.   105

Within we entered without any contest;
   And I, who inclination had to see
   What the condition such a fortress holds,

Soon as I was within, cast round mine eye,
   And see on every hand an ample plain,   110
   Full of distress and torment terrible.

Even as at Arles, where stagnant grows the Rhone,
   Even as at Pola near to the Quarnaro,
   That shuts in Italy and bathes its borders,

The sepulchers make all the place uneven;   115
   So likewise did they there on every side,
   Saving that there the manner was more bitter;

For flames between the sepulchers were scattered,
   By which they so intensely heated were,
   That iron more so asks not any art.   120

All of their coverings uplifted were,
   And from them issued forth such dire laments,
   Sooth seemed they of the wretched and tormented.

And I: "My Master, what are all those people
   Who, having sepulture within those tombs,   125
   Make themselves audible by doleful sighs?"

And he to me: "Here are the Heresiarchs,
   With their disciples of all sects, and much
   More than thou thinkest laden are the tombs.

"My Master, what are all those people
Who, having sepulture within those tombs,
Make themselves audible by doleful sighs?"

Inferno IX, lines 124–126

Here like together with its like is buried;   130
    And more and less the monuments are heated."
    And when he to the right had turned, we passed

Between the torments and high parapets.

⊰ CANTO X ⊱

*Farinata and Cavalcante de' Cavalcanti—
Discourse on the Knowledge of the Damned*

Now onward goes, along a narrow path
    Between the torments and the city wall,
My Master, and I follow at his back.

"O power supreme, that through these impious circles
    Turnest me," I began, "as pleases thee,   5
    Speak to me, and my longings satisfy;

The people who are lying in these tombs,
    Might they be seen? already are uplifted
    The covers all, and no one keepeth guard."

And he to me: "They all will be closed up   10
    When from Jehoshaphat they shall return
    Here with the bodies they have left above.

Their cemetery have upon this side
    With Epicurus all his followers,
    Who with the body mortal make the soul;   15

But in the question thou dost put to me,
    Within here shalt thou soon be satisfied,
    And likewise in the wish thou keepest silent."

And I: "Good Leader, I but keep concealed
    From thee my heart, that I may speak the less,   20
    Nor only now hast thou thereto disposed me."

"O Tuscan, thou who through the city of fire
    Goest alive, thus speaking modestly,
    Be pleased to stay thy footsteps in this place.

Thy mode of speaking makes thee manifest   25
    A native of that noble fatherland,
    To which perhaps I too molestful was."

Upon a sudden issued forth this sound
    From out one of the tombs; wherefore I pressed,
    Fearing, a little nearer to my Leader.   30

And unto me he said: "Turn thee; what dost thou?
    Behold there Farinata who has risen;
    From the waist upwards wholly shalt thou see him."

I had already fixed mine eyes on his,
    And he uprose erect with breast and front   35
    E'en as if Hell he had in great despite.

And with courageous hands and prompt my Leader
    Thrust me between the sepulchers towards him,
    Exclaiming, "Let thy words explicit be."

As soon as I was at the foot of his tomb,   40
    Somewhat he eyed me, and, as if disdainful,
    Then asked of me, "Who were thine ancestors?"

I, who desirous of obeying was,
    Concealed it not, but all revealed to him;
    Whereat he raised his brows a little upward.   45

As soon as I was at the foot of his tomb,
Somewhat he eyed me, and, as if disdainful,
Then asked of me, "Who were thine ancestors?"

Inferno X, lines 40–42

Then said he: "Fiercely adverse have they been
    To me, and to my fathers, and my party;
    So that two several times I scattered them."

"If they were banished, they returned on all sides,"
    I answered him, "the first time and the second;   50
    But yours have not acquired that art aright."

Then there uprose upon the sight, uncovered
    Down to the chin, a shadow at his side;
    I think that he had risen on his knees.

Round me he gazed, as if solicitude   55
    He had to see if someone else were with me,
    But after his suspicion was all spent,

Weeping, he said to me: "If through this blind
    Prison thou goest by loftiness of genius,
    Where is my son? and why is he not with thee?"   60

And I to him: "I come not of myself;
    He who is waiting yonder leads me here,
    Whom in disdain perhaps your Guido had."

His language and the mode of punishment
    Already unto me had read his name;   65
    On that account my answer was so full.

Up starting suddenly, he cried out: "How
    Saidst thou—he had? Is he not still alive?
    Does not the sweet light strike upon his eyes?"

When he became aware of some delay,   70
    Which I before my answer made, supine
    He fell again, and forth appeared no more.

But the other, magnanimous, at whose desire
   I had remained, did not his aspect change,
   Neither his neck he moved, nor bent his side.   75

"And if," continuing his first discourse,
   "They have that art," he said, "not learned aright,
   That more tormenteth me, than doth this bed.

But fifty times shall not rekindled be
   The countenance of the Lady who reigns here,   80
   Ere thou shalt know how heavy is that art;

And as thou wouldst to the sweet world return,
   Say why that people is so pitiless
   Against my race in each one of its laws?"

Whence I to him: "The slaughter and great carnage   85
   Which have with crimson stained the Arbia, cause
   Such orisons in our temple to be made."

After his head he with a sigh had shaken,
   "There I was not alone," he said, "nor surely
   Without a cause had with the others moved.   90

But there I was alone, where every one
   Consented to the laying waste of Florence,
   He who defended her with open face."

"Ah! so hereafter may your seed repose,"
   I him entreated, "solve for me that knot,   95
   Which has entangled my conceptions here.

It seems that you can see, if I hear rightly,
   Beforehand whatsoe'er time brings with it,
   And in the present have another mode."

"We see, like those who have imperfect sight,   100
    The things," he said, "that distant are from us;
    So much still shines on us the Sovereign Ruler.

When they draw near, or are, is wholly vain
    Our intellect, and if none brings it to us,
    Not anything know we of your human state.   105

Hence thou canst understand, that wholly dead
    Will be our knowledge from the moment when
    The portal of the future shall be closed."

Then I, as if compunctious for my fault,
    Said: "Now, then, you will tell that fallen one,   110
    That still his son is with the living joined.

And if just now, in answering, I was dumb,
    Tell him I did it because I was thinking
    Already of the error you have solved me."

And now my Master was recalling me,   115
    Wherefore more eagerly I prayed the spirit
    That he would tell me who was with him there.

He said: "With more than a thousand here I lie;
    Within here is the second Frederick,
    And the Cardinal, and of the rest I speak not."   120

Thereon he hid himself; and I towards
    The ancient poet turned my steps, reflecting
    Upon that saying, which seemed hostile to me.

He moved along; and afterward, thus going,
    He said to me, "Why art thou so bewildered?"   125
    And I in his inquiry satisfied him.

"Let memory preserve what thou hast heard
    Against thyself," that Sage commanded me,
    "And now attend here"; and he raised his finger.

"When thou shalt be before the radiance sweet   130
    Of her whose beauteous eyes all things behold,
    From her thou'lt know the journey of thy life."

Unto the left hand then he turned his feet;
    We left the wall, and went towards the middle,
    Along a path that strikes into a valley,   135

Which even up there unpleasant made its stench.

⊰ CANTO XI ⊱

The Broken Rocks — Pope Anastasius —
General Description of the Inferno and Its Divisions

U pon the margin of a lofty bank
    Which great rocks broken in a circle made,
We came upon a still more cruel throng;

And there, by reason of the horrible
    Excess of stench the deep abyss throws out,   5
    We drew ourselves aside behind the cover

Of a great tomb, whereon I saw a writing,
    Which said: "Pope Anastasius I hold,
    Whom out of the right way Photinus drew."

"Slow it behoveth our descent to be,   10
    So that the sense be first a little used
    To the sad blast, and then we shall not heed it."

We drew ourselves aside behind the cover
Of a great tomb, whereon I saw a writing,
Which said: "Pope Anastasius I hold"

Inferno XI, lines 6–8

The Master thus; and unto him I said,
  "Some compensation find, that the time pass not
    Idly"; and he: "Thou seest I think of that.   15

My son, upon the inside of these rocks,"
  Began he then to say, "are three small circles,
    From grade to grade, like those which thou art leaving.

They all are full of spirits maledict;
  But that hereafter sight alone suffice thee,   20
    Hear how and wherefore they are in constraint.

Of every malice that wins hate in Heaven,
  Injury is the end; and all such end
    Either by force or fraud afflicteth others.

But because fraud is man's peculiar vice,   25
  More it displeases God; and so stand lowest
    The fraudulent, and greater dole assails them.

All the first circle of the Violent is;
  But since force may be used against three persons,
    In three rounds 'tis divided and constructed.   30

To God, to ourselves, and to our neighbor can we
  Use force; I say on them and on their things,
    As thou shalt hear with reason manifest.

A death by violence, and painful wounds,
  Are to our neighbor given; and in his substance   35
    Ruin, and arson, and injurious levies;

Whence homicides, and he who smites unjustly,
  Marauders, and freebooters, the first round
    Tormenteth all in companies diverse.

Man may lay violent hands upon himself   40
    And his own goods; and therefore in the second
    Round must perforce without avail repent

Whoever of your world deprives himself,
    Who games, and dissipates his property,
    And weepeth there, where he should jocund be.   45

Violence can be done the Deity,
    In heart denying and blaspheming Him,
    And by disdaining Nature and her bounty.

And for this reason doth the smallest round
    Seal with its signet Sodom and Cahors,   50
    And who, disdaining God, speaks from the heart.

Fraud, wherewithal is every conscience stung,
    A man may practice upon him who trusts,
    And him who doth no confidence imburse.

This latter mode, it would appear, dissevers   55
    Only the bond of love which Nature makes;
    Wherefore within the second circle nestle

Hypocrisy, flattery, and who deals in magic,
    Falsification, theft, and simony,
    Panders, and barrators, and the like filth.   60

By the other mode, forgotten is that love
    Which Nature makes, and what is after added,
    From which there is a special faith engendered.

Hence in the smallest circle, where the point is
    Of the Universe, upon which Dis is seated,   65
    Whoe'er betrays forever is consumed."

And I: "My Master, clear enough proceeds
   Thy reasoning, and full well distinguishes
   This cavern and the people who possess it.

But tell me, those within the fat lagoon,   70
   Whom the wind drives, and whom the rain doth beat,
   And who encounter with such bitter tongues,

Wherefore are they inside of the red city
   Not punished, if God has them in his wrath,
   And if he has not, wherefore in such fashion?"   75

And unto me he said: "Why wanders so
   Thine intellect from that which it is wont?
   Or, sooth, thy mind where is it elsewhere looking?

Hast thou no recollection of those words
   With which thine Ethics thoroughly discusses   80
   The dispositions three, that Heaven abides not—

Incontinence, and Malice, and insane
   Bestiality? and how Incontinence
   Less God offendeth, and less blame attracts?

If thou regardest this conclusion well,   85
   And to thy mind recallest who they are
   That up outside are undergoing penance,

Clearly wilt thou perceive why from these felons
   They separated are, and why less wroth
   Justice divine doth smite them with its hammer."   90

"O Sun, that healest all distempered vision,
   Thou dost content me so, when thou resolvest,
   That doubting pleases me no less than knowing!

Once more a little backward turn thee," said I,
　　"There where thou sayest that usury offends　　95
　　Goodness divine, and disengage the knot."

"Philosophy," he said, "to him who heeds it,
　　Noteth, not only in one place alone,
　　After what manner Nature takes her course

From Intellect Divine, and from its art;　　100
　　And if thy Physics carefully thou notest,
　　After not many pages shalt thou find,

That this your art as far as possible
　　Follows, as the disciple doth the master;
　　So that your art is, as it were, God's grandchild.　　105

From these two, if thou bringest to thy mind
　　Genesis at the beginning, it behoves
　　Mankind to gain their life and to advance;

And since the usurer takes another way,
　　Nature herself and in her follower　　110
　　Disdains he, for elsewhere he puts his hope.

But follow, now, as I would fain go on,
　　For quivering are the Fishes on the horizon,
　　And the Wain wholly over Caurus lies,

And far beyond there we descend the crag."　　115

⚔ CANTO XII ⚓

The Minotaur—The Seventh Circle: The Violent—The River Phlegethon—
The Violent against Their Neighbors—The Centaurs—Tyrants

T he place where to descend the bank we came
    Was alpine, and from what was there, moreover,
Of such a kind that every eye would shun it.

Such as that ruin is which in the flank
    Smote, on this side of Trent, the Adige,   5
    Either by earthquake or by failing stay,

For from the mountain's top, from which it moved,
    Unto the plain the cliff is shattered so,
    Some path 'twould give to him who was above;

Even such was the descent of that ravine,   10
    And on the border of the broken chasm
    The infamy of Crete was stretched along,

Who was conceived in the fictitious cow;
    And when he us beheld, he bit himself,
    Even as one whom anger racks within.   15

My Sage towards him shouted: "Peradventure
    Thou think'st that here may be the Duke of Athens,
    Who in the world above brought death to thee?

Get thee gone, beast, for this one cometh not
    Instructed by thy sister, but he comes   20
    In order to behold your punishments."

And on the border of the broken chasm
The infamy of Crete was stretched along,
Who was conceived in the fictitious cow

Inferno XII, lines 11–13

As is that bull who breaks loose at the moment
   In which he has received the mortal blow,
   Who cannot walk, but staggers here and there,

The Minotaur beheld I do the like;   25
   And he, the wary, cried: "Run to the passage;
   While he wroth, 'tis well thou shouldst descend."

Thus down we took our way o'er that discharge
   Of stones, which oftentimes did move themselves
   Beneath my feet, from the unwonted burden.   30

Thoughtful I went; and he said: "Thou art thinking
   Perhaps upon this ruin, which is guarded
   By that brute anger which just now I quenched.

Now will I have thee know, the other time
   I here descended to the nether Hell,   35
   This precipice had not yet fallen down.

But truly, if I well discern, a little
   Before His coming who the mighty spoil
   Bore off from Dis, in the supernal circle,

Upon all sides the deep and loathsome valley   40
   Trembled so, that I thought the Universe
   Was thrilled with love, by which there are who think

The world ofttimes converted into chaos;
   And at that moment this primeval crag
   Both here and elsewhere made such overthrow.   45

But fix thine eyes below; for draweth near
   The river of blood, within which boiling is
   Whoe'er by violence doth injure others."

O blind cupidity, O wrath insane,
 That spurs us onward so in our short life, 50
 And in the eternal then so badly steeps us!

I saw an ample moat bent like a bow,
 As one which all the plain encompasses,
 Conformable to what my Guide had said.

And between this and the embankment's foot 55
 Centaurs in file were running, armed with arrows,
 As in the world they used the chase to follow.

Beholding us descend, each one stood still,
 And from the squadron three detached themselves,
 With bows and arrows in advance selected; 60

And from afar one cried: "Unto what torment
 Come ye, who down the hillside are descending?
 Tell us from there; if not, I draw the bow."

My Master said: "Our answer will we make
 To Chiron, near you there; in evil hour, 65
 That will of thine was evermore so hasty."

Then touched he me, and said: "This one is Nessus,
 Who perished for the lovely Dejanira,
 And for himself, himself did vengeance take.

And he in the midst, who at his breast is gazing, 70
 Is the great Chiron, who brought up Achilles;
 That other Pholus is, who was so wrathful.

Thousands and thousands go about the moat
 Shooting with shafts whatever soul emerges
 Out of the blood, more than his crime allots." 75

Beholding us descend, each one stood still,
And from the squadron three detached themselves,
With bows and arrows in advance selected

Inferno XII, lines 58–60

Chiron an arrow took, and with the notch
Backward upon his jaws he put his beard.

Inferno XII, lines 77–78

Near we approached unto those monsters fleet;
　　Chiron an arrow took, and with the notch
　　Backward upon his jaws he put his beard.

After he had uncovered his great mouth,
　　He said to his companions: "Are you ware　　　80
　　That he behind moveth whate'er he touches?

Thus are not wont to do the feet of dead men."
　　And my good Guide, who now was at his breast,
　　Where the two natures are together joined,

Replied: "Indeed he lives, and thus alone　　　85
　　Me it behoves to show him the dark valley;
　　Necessity, and not delight, impels us.

Someone withdrew from singing Halleluja,
　　Who unto me committed this new office;
　　No thief is he, nor I a thievish spirit.　　　90

But by that virtue through which I am moving
　　My steps along this savage thoroughfare,
　　Give us someone of thine, to be with us,

And who may show us where to pass the ford,
　　And who may carry this one on his back;　　　95
　　For 'tis no spirit that can walk the air."

Upon his right breast Chiron wheeled about,
　　And said to Nessus: "Turn and do thou guide them,
　　And warn aside, if other band may meet you."

We with our faithful escort onward moved　　　100
　　Along the brink of the vermilion boiling,
　　Wherein the boiled were uttering loud laments.

People I saw within up to the eyebrows,
    And the great Centaur said: "Tyrants are these,
    Who dealt in bloodshed and in pillaging.   105

Here they lament their pitiless mischiefs; here
    Is Alexander, and fierce Dionysius
    Who upon Sicily brought dolorous years.

That forehead there which has the hair so black
    Is Azzolin; and the other who is blond,   110
    Obizzo is of Esti, who, in truth,

Up in the world was by his stepson slain."
    Then turned I to the Poet; and he said,
    "Now he be first to thee, and second I."

A little farther on the Centaur stopped   115
    Above a folk, who far down as the throat
    Seemed from that boiling stream to issue forth.

A shade he showed us on one side alone,
    Saying: "He cleft asunder in God's bosom
    The heart that still upon the Thames is honored."   120

Then people saw I, who from out the river
    Lifted their heads and also all the chest;
    And many among these I recognized.

Thus ever more and more grew shallower
    That blood, so that the feet alone it covered;   125
    And there across the moat our passage was.

"Even as thou here upon this side beholdest
    The boiling stream, that aye diminishes,"
    The Centaur said, "I wish thee to believe

That on this other more and more declines   130
    Its bed, until it reunites itself
    Where it behoveth tyranny to groan.

Justice divine, upon this side, is goading
    That Attila, who was a scourge on earth,
    And Pyrrhus, and Sextus; and forever milks   135

The tears which with the boiling it unseals
    In Rinier da Corneto and Rinier Pazzo,
    Who made upon the highways so much war."

Then back he turned, and passed again the ford.

⊰ CANTO XIII ⊱

The Wood of Thorns—The Harpies—The Violent against Themselves—
Suicides—Pier della Vigna—Lano and Jacopo da Sant' Andrea

Not yet had Nessus reached the other side,
    When we had put ourselves within a wood,
That was not marked by any path whatever.

Not foliage green, but of a dusky color,
    Not branches smooth, but gnarled and intertangled,   5
    Not appletrees were there, but thorns with poison.

Such tangled thickets have not, nor so dense,
    Those savage wild beasts, that in hatred hold
    'Twixt Cecina and Corneto the tilled places.

There do the hideous Harpies make their nests,   10
    Who chased the Trojans from the Strophades,
    With sad announcement of impending doom;

They make laments upon the wondrous trees.

Inferno XIII, line 15

Broad wings have they, and necks and faces human,
  And feet with claws, and their great bellies fledged;
  They make laments upon the wondrous trees.   15

And the good Master: "Ere thou enter farther,
  Know that thou art within the second round,"
  Thus he began to say, "and shalt be, till

Thou comest out upon the horrible sand;
  Therefore look well around, and thou shalt see   20
  Things that will credence give unto my speech."

I heard on all sides lamentations uttered,
  And person none beheld I who might make them,
  Whence, utterly bewildered, I stood still.

I think he thought that I perhaps might think   25
  So many voices issued through those trunks
  From people who concealed themselves from us;

Therefore the Master said: "If thou break off
  Some little spray from any of these trees,
  The thoughts thou hast will wholly be made vain."   30

Then stretched I forth my hand a little forward,
  And plucked a branchlet off from a great thorn;
  And the trunk cried, "Why dost thou mangle me?"

After it had become embrowned with blood,
  It recommenced its cry: "Why dost thou rend me?   35
  Hast thou no spirit of pity whatsoever?

Men once we were, and now are changed to trees;
  Indeed, thy hand should be more pitiful,
  Even if the souls of serpents we had been."

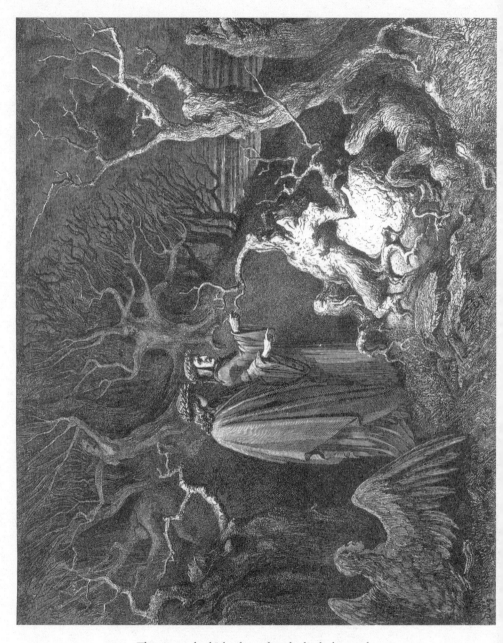

Then stretched I forth my hand a little forward,
And plucked a branchlet off from a great thorn;
And the trunk cried, "Why dost thou mangle me?"

Inferno XIII, lines 31–33

As out of a green brand, that is on fire   40
    At one of the ends, and from the other drips
    And hisses with the wind that is escaping;

So from that splinter issued forth together
    Both words and blood; whereat I let the tip
    Fall, and stood like a man who is afraid.   45

"Had he been able sooner to believe,"
    My Sage made answer, "O thou wounded soul,
    What only in my verses he has seen,

Not upon thee had he stretched forth his hand;
    Whereas the thing incredible has caused me   50
    To put him to an act which grieveth me.

But tell him who thou wast, so that by way
    Of some amends thy fame he may refresh
    Up in the world, to which he can return."

And the trunk said: "So thy sweet words allure me,   55
    I cannot silent be; and you be vexed not,
    That I a little to discourse am tempted.

I am the one who both keys had in keeping
    Of Frederick's heart, and turned them to and fro
    So softly in unlocking and in locking,   60

That from his secrets most men I withheld;
    Fidelity I bore the glorious office
    So great, I lost thereby my sleep and pulses.

The courtesan who never from the dwelling
    Of Cæsar turned aside her strumpet eyes,   65
    Death universal and the vice of courts,

Inflamed against me all the other minds,
 And they, inflamed, did so inflame Augustus,
 That my glad honors turned to dismal mournings.

My spirit, in disdainful exultation,   70
 Thinking by dying to escape disdain,
 Made me unjust against myself, the just.

I, by the roots unwonted of this wood,
 Do swear to you that never broke I faith
 Unto my lord, who was so worthy of honor;   75

And to the world if one of you return,
 Let him my memory comfort, which is lying
 Still prostrate from the blow that envy dealt it."

Waited awhile, and then: "Since he is silent,"
 The Poet said to me, "lose not the time,   80
 But speak, and question him, if more may please thee."

Whence I to him: "Do thou again inquire
 Concerning what thou thinks't will satisfy me;
 For I cannot, such pity is in my heart."

Therefore he recommenced: "So may the man   85
 Do for thee freely what thy speech implores,
 Spirit incarcerate, again be pleased

To tell us in what way the soul is bound
 Within these knots; and tell us, if thou canst,
 If any from such members e'er is freed."   90

Then blew the trunk amain, and afterward
 The wind was into such a voice converted:
 "With brevity shall be replied to you.

When the exasperated soul abandons
    The body whence it rent itself away,   95
    Minos consigns it to the seventh abyss.

It falls into the forest, and no part
    Is chosen for it; but where Fortune hurls it,
    There like a grain of spelt it germinates.

It springs a sapling, and a forest tree;   100
    The Harpies, feeding then upon its leaves,
    Do pain create, and for the pain an outlet.

Like others for our spoils shall we return;
    But not that any one may them revest,
    For 'tis not just to have what one casts off.   105

Here we shall drag them, and along the dismal
    Forest our bodies shall suspended be,
    Each to the thorn of his molested shade."

We were attentive still unto the trunk,
    Thinking that more it yet might wish to tell us,   110
    When by a tumult we were overtaken,

In the same way as he is who perceives
    The boar and chase approaching to his stand,
    Who hears the crashing of the beasts and branches;

And two behold! upon our left-hand side,   115
    Naked and scratched, fleeing so furiously,
    That of the forest every fan they broke.

He who was in advance: "Now help, Death, help!"
    And the other one, who seemed to lag too much,
    Was shouting: "Lano, were not so alert   120

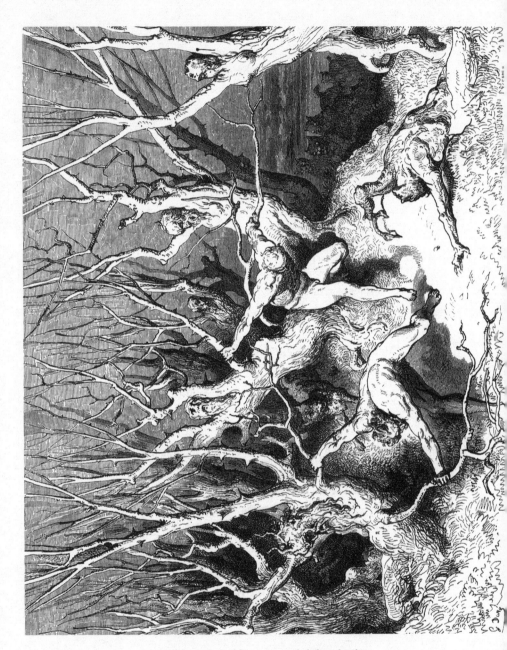

And two behold! upon our left-hand side,
Naked and scratched, fleeing so furiously,
That of the forest every fan they broke.

Inferno XIII, lines 115–117

Those legs of thine at joustings of the Toppo!"
   And then, perchance because his breath was failing,
   He grouped himself together with a bush.

Behind them was the forest full of black
   She-mastiffs, ravenous, and swift of foot   125
   As greyhounds, who are issuing from the chain.

On him who had crouched down they set their teeth,
   And him they lacerated piece by piece,
   Thereafter bore away those aching members.

Thereat my Escort took me by the hand,   130
   And led me to the bush, that all in vain
   Was weeping from its bloody lacerations.

"O Jacopo," it said, "of Sant' Andrea,
   What helped it thee of me to make a screen?
   What blame have I in thy nefarious life?"   135

When near him had the Master stayed his steps,
   He said: "Who wast thou, that through wounds so many
   Art blowing out with blood thy dolorous speech?"

And he to us: "O souls, that hither come
   To look upon the shameful massacre   140
   That has so rent away from me my leaves,

Gather them up beneath the dismal bush;
   I of that city was which to the Baptist
   Changed its first patron, wherefore he for this

Forever with his art will make it sad.   145
   And were it not that on the pass of Arno
   Some glimpses of him are remaining still,

Those citizens, who afterwards rebuilt it
  Upon the ashes left by Attila,
  In vain had caused their labor to be done.   150

Of my own house I made myself a gibbet."

⊣ CANTO XIV ⊢

*The Sand Waste and the Rain of Fire—The Violent against God—
Capaneus—The Statue of Time, and the Four Infernal Rivers*

Because the charity of my native place
    Constrained me, gathered I the scattered leaves,
And gave them back to him, who now was hoarse.

Then came we to the confine, where disparted
  The second round is from the third, and where   5
  A horrible form of Justice is beheld.

Clearly to manifest these novel things,
  I say that we arrived upon a plain,
  Which from its bed rejecteth every plant;

The dolorous forest is a garland to it   10
  All round about, as the sad moat to that;
  There close upon the edge we stayed our feet.

The soil was of an arid and thick sand,
  Not of another fashion made than that
  Which by the feet of Cato once was pressed.   15

Vengeance of God, O how much oughtest thou
  By each one to be dreaded, who doth read
  That which was manifest unto mine eyes!

Of naked souls beheld I many herds,
    Who all were weeping very miserably,   20
    And over them seemed set a law diverse.

Supine upon the ground some folk were lying;
    And some were sitting all drawn up together,
    And others went about continually.

Those who were going round were far the more,   25
    And those were less who lay down to their torment,
    But had their tongues more loosed to lamentation.

O'er all the sand-waste, with a gradual fall,
    Were raining down dilated flakes of fire,
    As of the snow on Alp without a wind.   30

As Alexander, in those torrid parts
    Of India, beheld upon his host
    Flames fall unbroken till they reached the ground.

Whence he provided with his phalanxes
    To trample down the soil, because the vapor   35
    Better extinguished was while it was single;

Thus was descending the eternal heat,
    Whereby the sand was set on fire, like tinder
    Beneath the steel, for doubling of the dole.

Without repose forever was the dance   40
    Of miserable hands, now there, now here,
    Shaking away from off them the fresh gleeds.

"Master," began I, "thou who overcomest
    All things except the demons dire, that issued
    Against us at the entrance of the gate,   45

O'er all the sand-waste, with a gradual fall,
Were raining down dilated flakes of fire.

Inferno XIV, lines 28–29

Who is that mighty one who seems to heed not
   The fire, and lieth lowering and disdainful,
   So that the rain seems not to ripen him?"

And he himself, who had become aware
   That I was questioning my Guide about him,   50
   Cried: "Such as I was living, am I, dead.

If Jove should weary out his smith, from whom
   He seized in anger the sharp thunderbolt,
   Wherewith upon the last day I was smitten,

And if he wearied out by turns the others   55
   In Mongibello at the swarthy forge,
   Vociferating, 'Help, good Vulcan, help!'

Even as he did there at the fight of Phlegra,
   And shot his bolts at me with all his might,
   He would not have thereby a joyous vengeance."   60

Then did my Leader speak with such great force,
   That I had never heard him speak so loud:
   "O Capaneus, in that is not extinguished

Thine arrogance, thou punished art the more;
   Not any torment, saving thine own rage,   65
   Would be unto thy fury pain complete."

Then he turned round to me with better lip,
   Saying: "One of the Seven Kings was he
   Who Thebes besieged, and held, and seems to hold

God in disdain, and little seems to prize him;   70
   But, as I said to him, his own despites
   Are for his breast the fittest ornaments.

Now follow me, and mind thou do not place
   As yet thy feet upon the burning sand,
   But always keep them close unto the wood."   75

Speaking no word, we came to where there gushes
   Forth from the wood a little rivulet,
   Whose redness makes my hair still stand on end.

As from the Bulicamë springs the brooklet,
   The sinful women later share among them,   80
   So downward through the sand it went its way.

The bottom of it, and both sloping banks,
   Were made of stone, and the margins at the side;
   Whence I perceived that there the passage was.

"In all the rest which I have shown to thee   85
   Since we have entered in within the gate
   Whose threshold unto no one is denied,

Nothing has been discovered by thine eyes
   So notable as is the present river,
   Which all the little flames above it quenches."   90

These words were of my Leader; whence I prayed him
   That he would give me largess of the food,
   For which he had given me largess of desire.

"In the mid-sea there sits a wasted land,"
   Said he thereafterward, "whose name is Crete,   95
   Under whose king the world of old was chaste.

There is a mountain there, that once was glad
   With waters and with leaves, which was called Ida;
   Now 'tis deserted, as a thing worn out.

Rhea once chose it for the faithful cradle   100
    Of her own son; and to conceal him better,
    Whene'er he cried, she there had clamors made.

A grand old man stands in the mount erect,
    Who holds his shoulders turned tow'rds Damietta,
    And looks at Rome as if it were his mirror.   105

His head is fashioned of refined gold,
    And of pure silver are the arms and breast;
    Then he is brass as far down as the fork.

From that point downward all is chosen iron,
    Save that the right foot is of kiln-baked clay,   110
    And more he stands on that than on the other.

Each part, except the gold, is by a fissure
    Asunder cleft, that dripping is with tears,
    Which gathered together perforate that cavern.

From rock to rock they fall into this valley;   115
    Acheron, Styx, and Phlegethon they form;
    Then downward go along this narrow sluice

Unto that point where is no more descending.
    They form Cocytus; what that pool may be
    Thou shalt behold, so here 'tis not narrated."   120

And I to him: "If so the present runnel
    Doth take its rise in this way from our world,
    Why only on this verge appears it to us?"

And he to me: "Thou knowest the place is round,
    And notwithstanding thou hast journeyed far,   125
    Still to the left descending to the bottom,

Thou hast not yet through all the circle turned.
    Therefore if something new appear to us,
    It should not bring amazement to thy face."

And I again: "Master, where shall be found   130
    Lethe and Phlegethon, for of one thou'rt silent,
    And sayest the other of this rain is made?"

"In all thy questions truly thou dost please me,"
    Replied he; "but the boiling of the red
    Water might well solve one of them thou makest.   135

Thou shalt see Lethe, but outside this moat,
    There where the souls repair to lave themselves,
    When sin repented of has been removed."

Then said he: "It is time now to abandon
    The wood; take heed that thou come after me;   140
    A way the margins make that are not burning,

And over them all vapors are extinguished."

⊰ CANTO XV ⊱

The Violent against Nature — Brunetto Latini

Now bears us onward one of the hard margins,
    And so the brooklet's mist o'ershadows it,
From fire it saves the water and the dikes.

Even as the Flemings, 'twixt Cadsand and Bruges,
    Fearing the flood that tow'rds them hurls itself,   5
    Their bulwarks build to put the sea to flight;

And as the Paduans along the Brenta,
    To guard their villas and their villages,
    Or ever Chiarentana feel the heat;

In such similitude had those been made,   10
    Albeit not so lofty nor so thick,
    Whoever he might be, the master made them.

Now were we from the forest so remote,
    I could not have discovered where it was,
    Even if backward I had turned myself,   15

When we a company of souls encountered,
    Who came beside the dike, and every one
    Gazed at us, as at evening we are wont

To eye each other under a new moon,
    And so towards us sharpened they their brows   20
    As an old tailor at the needle's eye.

Thus scrutinized by such a family,
    By someone I was recognized, who seized
    My garment's hem, and cried out, "What a marvel!"

And I, when he stretched forth his arm to me,   25
    On his baked aspect fastened so mine eyes,
    That the scorched countenance prevented not

His recognition by my intellect;
    And bowing down my face unto his own,
    I made reply, "Are you here, Ser Brunetto?"   30

And he: "May't not displease thee, O my son,
    If a brief space with thee Brunetto Latini
    Backward return and let the trail go on."

"Are you here, Ser Brunetto?"

Inferno XV, line 30

I said to him: "With all my power I ask it;
    And if you wish me to sit down with you,   35
    I will, if he please, for I go with him."

"O son," he said, "whoever of this herd
    A moment stops, lies then a hundred years,
    Nor fans himself when smiteth him the fire.

Therefore go on; I at thy skirts will come,   40
    And afterward will I rejoin my band,
    Which goes lamenting its eternal doom."

I did not dare to go down from the road
    Level to walk with him; but my head bowed
    I held as one who goeth reverently.   45

And he began: "What fortune or what fate
    Before the last day leadeth thee down here?
    And who is this that showeth thee the way?"

"Up there above us in the life serene,"
    I answered him, "I lost me in a valley,   50
    Or ever yet my age had been completed.

But yestermorn I turned my back upon it;
    This one appeared to me, returning thither,
    And homeward leadeth me along this road."

And he to me: "If thou thy star do follow,   55
    Thou canst not fail thee of a glorious port,
    If well I judged in the life beautiful.

And if I had not died so prematurely,
    Seeing Heaven thus benignant unto thee,
    I would have given thee comfort in the work.   60

But that ungrateful and malignant people,
    Which of old time from Fesole descended,
    And smacks still of the mountain and the granite,

Will make itself, for thy good deeds, thy foe;
    And it is right; for among crabbed sorbs   65
    It ill befits the sweet fig to bear fruit.

Old rumor in the world proclaims them blind;
    A people avaricious, envious, proud;
    Take heed that of their customs thou do cleanse thee.

Thy fortune so much honor doth reserve thee,   70
    One party and the other shall be hungry
    For thee; but far from goat shall be the grass.

Their litter let the beasts of Fesole
    Make of themselves, nor let them touch the plant,
    If any still upon their dunghill rise,   75

In which may yet revive the consecrated
    Seed of those Romans, who remained there when
    The nest of such great malice it became."

"If my entreaty wholly were fulfilled,"
    Replied I to him, "not yet would you be   80
    In banishment from human nature placed;

For in my mind is fixed, and touches now
    My heart the dear and good paternal image
    Of you, when in the world from hour to hour

You taught me how a man becomes eternal;   85
    And how much I am grateful, while I live
    Behoves that in my language be discerned.

What you narrate of my career I write,
    And keep it to be glossed with other text
    By a Lady who can do it, if I reach her.   90

This much will I have manifest to you;
    Provided that my conscience do not chide me,
    For whatsoever Fortune I am ready.

Such handsel is not new unto mine ears;
    Therefore let Fortune turn her wheel around   95
    As it may please her, and the churl his mattock."

My Master thereupon on his right cheek
    Did backward turn himself, and looked at me;
    Then said: "He listeneth well who noteth it."

Nor speaking less on that account, I go   100
    With Ser Brunetto, and I ask who are
    His most known and most eminent companions.

And he to me: "To know of some is well;
    Of others it were laudable to be silent,
    For short would be the time for so much speech.   105

Know them in sum, that all of them were clerks,
    And men of letters great and of great fame,
    In the world tainted with the selfsame sin.

Priscian goes yonder with that wretched crowd,
    And Francis of Accorso; and thou hadst seen there,   110
    If thou hadst had a hankering for such scurf,

That one, who by the Servant of the Servants
    From Arno was transferred to Bacchiglione,
    Where he has left his sin-excited nerves.

More would I say, but coming and discoursing   115
    Can be no longer; for that I behold
    New smoke uprising yonder from the sand.

A people comes with whom I may not be;
    Commended unto thee be my Tesoro,
    In which I still live, and no more I ask."   120

Then he turned round, and seemed to be of those
    Who at Verona run for the Green Mantle
    Across the plain; and seemed to be among them

The one who wins, and not the one who loses.

⊰ CANTO XVI ⊱

Guidoguerra, Aldobrandi, and Rusticucci—Cataract of the River of Blood

Now was I where was heard the reverberation
    Of water falling into the next round,
Like to that humming which the beehives make,

When shadows three together started forth,
    Running, from out a company that passed   5
    Beneath the rain of the sharp martyrdom.

Towards us came they, and each one cried out:
    "Stop, thou; for by thy garb to us thou seemest
    To be someone of our depraved city."

Ah me! what wounds I saw upon their limbs,   10
    Recent and ancient by the flames burnt in!
    It pains me still but to remember it.

Unto their cries my Teacher paused attentive;
　　He turned his face towards me, and "Now wait,"
　　He said; "to these we should be courteous.　　15

And if it were not for the fire that darts
　　The nature of this region, I should say
　　That haste were more becoming thee than them."

As soon as we stood still, they recommenced
　　The old refrain, and when they overtook us,　　20
　　Formed of themselves a wheel, all three of them.

As champions stripped and oiled are wont to do,
　　Watching for their advantage and their hold,
　　Before they come to blows and thrusts between them,

Thus, wheeling round, did every one his visage　　25
　　Direct to me, so that in opposite wise
　　His neck and feet continual journey made.

And, "If the misery of this soft place
　　Bring in disdain ourselves and our entreaties,"
　　Began one, "and our aspect black and blistered,　　30

Let the renown of us thy mind incline
　　To tell us who thou art, who thus securely
　　Thy living feet dost move along through Hell.

He in whose footprints thou dost see me treading,
　　Naked and skinless though he now may go,　　35
　　Was of a greater rank than thou dost think;

He was the grandson of the good Gualdrada;
　　His name was Guidoguerra, and in life
　　Much did he with his wisdom and his sword.

The other, who close by me treads the sand,   40
    Tegghiaio Aldobrandi is, whose fame
    Above there in the world should welcome be.

And I, who with them on the cross am placed,
    Jacopo Rusticucci was; and truly
    My savage wife, more than aught else, doth
        harm me."   45

Could I have been protected from the fire,
    Below I should have thrown myself among them,
    And think the Teacher would have suffered it;

But as I should have burned and baked myself,
    My terror overmastered my good will,   50
    Which made me greedy of embracing them.

Then I began: "Sorrow and not disdain
    Did your condition fix within me so,
    That tardily it wholly is stripped off,

As soon as this my Lord said unto me   55
    Words, on account of which I thought within me
    That people such as you are were approaching.

I of your city am; and evermore
    Your labors and your honorable names
    I with affection have retraced and heard.   60

I leave the gall, and go for the sweet fruits
    Promised to me by the veracious Leader;
    But to the center first I needs must plunge."

"So may the soul for a long while conduct
    Those limbs of thine," did he make answer then,   65
    "And so may thy renown shine after thee,

Valor and courtesy, say if they dwell
  Within our city, as they used to do,
  Or if they wholly have gone out of it;

For Guglielmo Borsier, who is in torment   70
  With us of late, and goes there with his comrades,
  Doth greatly mortify us with his words."

"The new inhabitants and the sudden gains,
  Pride and extravagance have in thee engendered,
  Florence, so that thou weep'st thereat already!"   75

In this wise I exclaimed with face uplifted;
  And the three, taking that for my reply,
  Looked at each other, as one looks at truth.

"If other times so little it doth cost thee,"
  Replied they all, "to satisfy another,   80
  Happy art thou, thus speaking at thy will!

Therefore, if thou escape from these dark places,
  And come to rebehold the beauteous stars,
  When it shall pleasure thee to say, 'I was,'

See that thou speak of us unto the people."   85
  Then they broke up the wheel, and in their flight
  It seemed as if their agile legs were wings.

Not an Amen could possibly be said
  So rapidly as they had disappeared;
  Wherefore the Master deemed best to depart.   90

I followed him, and little had we gone,
  Before the sound of water was so near us,
  That speaking we should hardly have been heard.

Even as that stream which holdeth its own course
    The first from Monte Veso tow'rds the East,   95
    Upon the left-hand slope of Apennine,

Which is above called Acquacheta, ere
    It down descendeth into its low bed,
    And at Forlì is vacant of that name,

Reverberates there above San Benedetto   100
    From Alps, by falling at a single leap,
    Where for a thousand there were room enough;

Thus downward from a bank precipitate,
    We found resounding that dark-tinted water,
    So that it soon the ear would have offended.   105

I had a cord around about me girt,
    And therewithal I whilom had designed
    To take the panther with the painted skin.

After I this had all from me unloosed,
    As my Conductor had commanded me,   110
    I reached it to him, gathered up and coiled,

Whereat he turned himself to the right side,
    And at a little distance from the verge,
    He cast it down into that deep abyss.

"It must needs be some novelty respond,"   115
    I said within myself, "to the new signal
    The Master with his eye is following so."

Ah me! how very cautious men should be
    With those who not alone behold the act,
    But with their wisdom look into the thoughts!   120

He said to me: "Soon there will upward come
    What I await; and what thy thought is dreaming
    Must soon reveal itself unto thy sight."

Aye to that truth which has the face of falsehood,
    A man should close his lips as far as may be,   125
    Because without his fault it causes shame;

But here I cannot; and, Reader, by the notes
    Of this my Comedy to thee I swear,
    So may they not be void of lasting favor,

Athwart that dense and darksome atmosphere   130
    I saw a figure swimming upward come,
    Marvelous unto every steadfast heart,

Even as he returns who goeth down
    Sometimes to clear an anchor, which has grappled
    Reef, or aught else that in the sea is hidden,   135

Who upward stretches, and draws in his feet.

⊰ CANTO XVII ⊱

*Geryon—The Violent against Art—Usurers—
Descent into the Abyss of Malebolge*

"Behold the monster with the pointed tail,
    Who cleaves the hills, and breaketh walls and weapons,
Behold him who infecteth all the world."

Thus unto me my Guide began to say,
    And beckoned him that he should come to shore,   5
    Near to the confine of the trodden marble;

And that uncleanly image of deceit
Came up and thrust ashore its head and bust

Inferno XVII, lines 7–8

And that uncleanly image of deceit
   Came up and thrust ashore its head and bust,
   But on the border did not drag its tail.

The face was as the face of a just man,   10
   Its semblance outwardly was so benign,
   And of a serpent all the trunk beside.

Two paws it had, hairy unto the armpits;
   The back, and breast, and both the sides it had
   Depicted o'er with nooses and with shields.   15

With colors more, groundwork or broidery
   Never in cloth did Tartars make nor Turks,
   Nor were such tissues by Arachne laid.

As sometimes wherries lie upon the shore,
   That part are in the water, part on land;   20
   And as among the guzzling Germans there,

The beaver plants himself to wage his war;
   So that vile monster lay upon the border,
   Which is of stone, and shutteth in the sand.

His tail was wholly quivering in the void,   25
   Contorting upwards the envenomed fork,
   That in the guise of scorpion armed its point.

The Guide said: "Now perforce must turn aside
   Our way a little, even to that beast
   Malevolent, that yonder coucheth him."   30

We therefore on the right side descended,
   And made ten steps upon the outer verge,
   Completely to avoid the sand and flame;

And after we are come to him, I see
    A little farther off upon the sand   35
    A people sitting near the hollow place.

Then said to me the Master: "So that full
    Experience of this round thou bear away,
    Now go and see what their condition is.

There let thy conversation be concise;   40
    Till thou returnest I will speak with him,
    That he concede to us his stalwart shoulders."

Thus farther still upon the outermost
    Head of that seventh circle all alone
    I went, where sat the melancholy folk.   45

Out of their eyes was gushing forth their woe;
    This way, that way, they helped them with their hands
    Now from the flames and now from the hot soil.

Not otherwise in summer do the dogs,
    Now with the foot, now with the muzzle, when   50
    By fleas, or flies, or gadflies, they are bitten.

When I had turned mine eyes upon the faces
    Of some, on whom the dolorous fire is falling,
    Not one of them I knew; but I perceived

That from the neck of each there hung a pouch,   55
    Which certain color had, and certain blazon;
    And thereupon it seems their eyes are feeding.

And as I gazing round me come among them,
    Upon a yellow pouch I azure saw
    That had the face and posture of a lion.   60

Proceeding then the current of my sight,
    Another of them saw I, red as blood,
    Display a goose more white than butter is.

And one, who with an azure sow and gravid
    Emblazoned had his little pouch of white,   65
    Said unto me: "What dost thou in this moat?

Now get thee gone; and since thou'rt still alive,
    Know that a neighbor of mine, Vitaliano,
    Will have his seat here on my left-hand side.

A Paduan am I with these Florentines;   70
    Full many a time they thunder in mine ears,
    Exclaiming, 'Come the sovereign cavalier,

He who shall bring the satchel with three goats' ";
    Then twisted he his mouth, and forth he thrust
    His tongue, like to an ox that licks its nose.   75

And fearing lest my longer stay might vex
    Him who had warned me not to tarry long,
    Backward I turned me from those weary souls.

I found my Guide, who had already mounted
    Upon the back of that wild animal,   80
    And said to me: "Now be both strong and bold.

Now we descend by stairways such as these;
    Mount thou in front, for I will be midway,
    So that the tail may have no power to harm thee."

Such as he is who has so near the ague   85
    Of quartan that his nails are blue already,
    And trembles all, but looking at the shade;

Even such became I at those proffered words;
 But shame in me his menaces produced,
 Which maketh servant strong before good master.   90

I seated me upon those monstrous shoulders;
 I wished to say, and yet the voice came not
 As I believed, "Take heed that thou embrace me."

But he, who other times had rescued me
 In other peril, soon as I had mounted,   95
 Within his arms encircled and sustained me,

And said: "Now, Geryon, bestir thyself;
 The circles large, and the descent be little;
 Think of the novel burden which thou hast."

Even as the little vessel shoves from shore,   100
 Backward, still backward, so he thence withdrew;
 And when he wholly felt himself afloat,

There where his breast had been he turned his tail,
 And that extended like an eel he moved,
 And with his paws drew to himself the air.   105

A greater fear I do not think there was
 What time abandoned Phaeton the reins,
 Whereby the heavens, as still appears, were scorched;

Nor when the wretched Icarus his flanks
 Felt stripped of feathers by the melting wax,   110
 His father crying, "An ill way thou takest!"

Than was my own, when I perceived myself
 On all sides in the air, and saw extinguished
 The sight of everything but of the monster.

Onward he goeth, swimming slowly, slowly;
Wheels and descends

Inferno XVII, lines 115–116

Onward he goeth, swimming slowly, slowly;   115
   Wheels and descends, but I perceive it only
   By wind upon my face and from below.

I heard already on the right the whirlpool
   Making a horrible crashing under us;
   Whence I thrust out my head with eyes cast
      downward.   120

Then was I still more fearful of the abyss;
   Because I fires beheld, and heard laments,
   Whereat I, trembling, all the closer cling.

I saw then, for before I had not seen it,
   The turning and descending, by great horrors   125
   That were approaching upon divers sides.

As falcon who has long been on the wing,
   Who, without seeing either lure or bird,
   Maketh the falconer say, "Ah me, thou stoopest,"

Descendeth weary, whence he started swiftly,   130
   Thorough a hundred circles, and alights
   Far from his master, sullen and disdainful;

Even thus did Geryon place us on the bottom,
   Close to the bases of the rough-hewn rock,
   And being disencumbered of our persons,   135

He sped away as arrow from the string.

⊰ CANTO XVIII ⊱

The Eighth Circle, Malebolge: The Fraudulent and the Malicious—
The First Bolgia: Seducers and Panders—Venedico Caccianimico—Jason—
The Second Bolgia: Flatterers—Allessio Interminelli—Thais

There is a place in Hell called Malebolge,
   Wholly of stone and of an iron color,
As is the circle that around it turns.

Right in the middle of the field malign
   There yawns a well exceeding wide and deep,   5
   Of which its place the structure will recount.

Round, then, is that enclosure which remains
   Between the well and foot of the high, hard bank,
   And has distinct in valleys ten its bottom.

As where for the protection of the walls   10
   Many and many moats surround the castles,
   The part in which they are a figure forms,

Just such an image those presented there;
   And as about such strongholds from their gates
   Unto the outer bank are little bridges,   15

So from the precipice's base did crags
   Project, which intersected dikes and moats,
   Unto the well that truncates and collects them.

Within this place, down shaken from the back
   Of Geryon, we found us; and the Poet   20
   Held to the left, and I moved on behind.

Upon my right hand I beheld new anguish,
New torments, and new wielders of the lash,
Wherewith the foremost Bolgia was replete.

Down at the bottom were the sinners naked;   25
This side the middle came they facing us,
Beyond it, with us, but with greater steps;

Even as the Romans, for the mighty host,
The year of Jubilee, upon the bridge,
Have chosen a mode to pass the people over;   30

For all upon one side towards the Castle
Their faces have, and go unto Saint Peter's;
On the other side they go towards the Mountain.

This side and that, along the livid stone
Beheld I hornëd demons with great scourges,   35
Who cruelly were beating them behind.

Ah me! how they did make them lift their legs
At the first blows! and sooth not any one
The second waited for, nor for the third.

While I was going on, mine eyes by one   40
Encountered were; and straight I said: "Already
With sight of this one I am not unfed."

Therefore I stayed my feet to make him out,
And with me the sweet Guide came to a stand,
And to my going somewhat back assented;   45

And he, the scourged one, thought to hide himself,
Lowering his face, but little it availed him;
For said I: "Thou that castest down thine eyes,

Ah me! how they did make them lift their legs
At the first blows!

Inferno XVIII, lines 37–38

If false are not the features which thou bearest,
    Thou art Venedico Caccianimico;   50
    But what doth bring thee to such pungent sauces?"

And he to me: "Unwillingly I tell it;
    But forces me thine utterance distinct,
    Which makes me recollect the ancient world.

I was the one who the fair Ghisola   55
    Induced to grant the wishes of the Marquis,
    Howe'er the shameless story may be told.

Not the sole Bolognese am I who weeps here;
    Nay, rather is this place so full of them,
    That not so many tongues today are taught   60

'Twixt Reno and Savena to say *sipa*;
    And if thereof thou wishest pledge or proof,
    Bring to thy mind our avaricious heart."

While speaking in this manner, with his scourge
    A demon smote him, and said: "Get thee gone   65
    Pander, there are no women here for coin."

I joined myself again unto mine Escort;
    Thereafterward with footsteps few we came
    To where a crag projected from the bank.

This very easily did we ascend,   70
    And turning to the right along its ridge,
    From those eternal circles we departed.

When we were there, where it is hollowed out
    Beneath, to give a passage to the scourged,
    The Guide said: "Wait, and see that on thee strike   75

The vision of those others evil-born,
    Of whom thou hast not yet beheld the faces,
    Because together with us they have gone."

From the old bridge we looked upon the train
    Which tow'rds us came upon the other border,   80
    And which the scourges in like manner smite.

And the good Master, without my inquiring,
    Said to me: "See that tall one who is coming,
    And for his pain seems not to shed a tear;

Still what a royal aspect he retains!   85
    That Jason is, who by his heart and cunning
    The Colchians of the Ram made destitute.

He by the isle of Lemnos passed along
    After the daring women pitiless
    Had unto death devoted all their males.   90

There with his tokens and with ornate words
    Did he deceive Hypsipyle, the maiden
    Who first, herself, had all the rest deceived.

There did he leave her pregnant and forlorn;
    Such sin unto such punishment condemns him,   95
    And also for Medea is vengeance done.

With him go those who in such wise deceive;
    And this sufficient be of the first valley
    To know, and those that in its jaws it holds."

We were already where the narrow path   100
    Crosses athwart the second dike, and forms
    Of that a buttress for another arch.

Thence we heard people, who are making moan
    In the next Bolgia, snorting with their muzzles,
    And with their palms beating upon themselves   105

The margins were encrusted with a mold
    By exhalation from below, that sticks there,
    And with the eyes and nostrils wages war.

The bottom is so deep, no place suffices
    To give us sight of it, without ascending   110
    The arch's back, where most the crag impends.

Thither we came, and thence down in the moat
    I saw a people smothered in a filth
    That out of human privies seemed to flow;

And whilst below there with mine eye I search,   115
    I saw one with his head so foul with ordure,
    It was not clear if he were clerk or layman.

He screamed to me: "Wherefore art thou so eager
    To look at me more than the other foul ones?"
    And I to him: "Because, if I remember,   120

I have already seen thee with dry hair,
    And thou'rt Alessio Interminei of Lucca;
    Therefore I eye thee more than all the others."

And he thereon, belaboring his pumpkin:
    "The flatteries have submerged me here below,   125
    Wherewith my tongue was never surfeited."

Then said to me the Guide: "See that thou thrust
    Thy visage somewhat farther in advance,
    That with thine eyes thou well the face attain

I saw a people smothered in a filth
That out of human privies seemed to flow

Inferno XVIII, lines 113–114

"Thais the harlot is it, who replied
Unto her paramour, when he said, 'Have I
Great gratitude from thee?'—'Nay, marvelous' "

Inferno XVIII, lines 133–135

Of that uncleanly and disheveled drab,   130
    Who there doth scratch herself with filthy nails,
    And crouches now, and now on foot is standing.

Thais the harlot is it, who replied
    Unto her paramour, when he said, 'Have I
    Great gratitude from thee?'—'Nay, marvelous';   135

And herewith let our sight be satisfied."

⊰ CANTO XIX ⊱

The Third Bolgia: Simoniacs—Pope Nicholas III—
Dante's Reproof of Corrupt Prelates

O Simon Magus, O forlorn disciples,
    Ye who the things of God, which ought to be
The brides of holiness, rapaciously

For silver and for gold do prostitute,
    Now it behoves for you the trumpet sound,   5
    Because in this third Bolgia ye abide.

We had already on the following tomb
    Ascended to that portion of the crag
    Which o'er the middle of the moat hangs plumb.

Wisdom supreme, O how great art thou showest   10
    In heaven, in earth, and in the evil world,
    And with what justice doth thy power distribute!

I saw upon the sides and on the bottom
    The livid stone with perforations filled,
    All of one size, and every one was round.   15

To me less ample seemed they not, nor greater
    Than those that in my beautiful Saint John
    Are fashioned for the place of the baptizers,

And one of which, not many years ago,
    I broke for someone, who was drowning in it;   20
    Be this a seal all men to undeceive.

Out of the mouth of each one there protruded
    The feet of a transgressor, and the legs
    Up to the calf, the rest within remained.

In all of them the soles were both on fire;   25
    Wherefore the joints so violently quivered,
    They would have snapped asunder withes and bands.

Even as the flame of unctuous things is wont
    To move upon the outer surface only,
    So likewise was it there from heel to point.   30

"Master, who is that one who writhes himself,
    More than his other comrades quivering,"
    I said, "and whom a redder flame is sucking?"

And he to me: "If thou wilt have me bear thee
    Down there along that bank which lowest lies,   35
    From him thou'lt know his errors and himself."

And I: "What pleases thee, to me is pleasing;
    Thou art my Lord, and knowest that I depart not
    From thy desire, and knowest what is not spoken."

Straightway upon the fourth dike we arrived;   40
    We turned, and on the left-hand side descended
    Down to the bottom full of holes and narrow.

And the good Master yet from off his haunch
   Deposed me not, till to the hole he brought me
   Of him who so lamented with his shanks.   45

"Whoe'er thou art, that standest upside down,
   O doleful soul, implanted like a stake,"
   To say began I, "if thou canst, speak out."

I stood even as the friar who is confessing
   The false assassin, who, when he is fixed,   50
   Recalls him, so that death may be delayed.

And he cried out: "Dost thou stand there already,
   Dost thou stand there already, Boniface?
   By many years the record lied to me.

Art thou so early satiate with that wealth,   55
   For which thou didst not fear to take by fraud
   The beautiful Lady, and then work her woe?"

Such I became, as people are who stand,
   Not comprehending what is answered them,
   As if bemocked, and know not how to answer.   60

Then said Virgilius: "Say to him straightway,
   'I am not he, I am not he thou thinkest.' "
   And I replied as was imposed on me.

Whereat the spirit writhed with both his feet,
   Then, sighing, with a voice of lamentation   65
   Said to me: "Then what wantest thou of me?

If who I am thou carest so much to know,
   That thou on that account hast crossed the bank,
   Know that I vested was with the great mantle;

"O doleful soul, implanted like a stake,"
To say began I, "if thou canst, speak out."

Inferno XIX, lines 47–48

And truly was I son of the She-bear,   70
    So eager to advance the cubs, that wealth
    Above, and here myself, I pocketed.

Beneath my head the others are dragged down
    Who have preceded me in simony,
    Flattened along the fissure of the rock.   75

Below there I shall likewise fall, whenever
    That one shall come who I believed thou wast,
    What time the sudden question I proposed.

But longer I my feet already toast,
    And here have been in this way upside down,   80
    Than he will planted stay with reddened feet;

For after him shall come of fouler deed
    From tow'rds the west a Pastor without law,
    Such as befits to cover him and me.

New Jason will he be, of whom we read   85
    In Maccabees; and as his king was pliant,
    So he who governs France shall be to this one."

I do not know if I were here too bold,
    That him I answered only in this meter:
    "I pray thee tell me now how great a treasure   90

Our Lord demanded of Saint Peter first,
    Before he put the keys into his keeping?
    Truly he nothing asked but 'Follow me.'

Nor Peter nor the rest asked of Matthias
    Silver or gold, when he by lot was chosen   95
    Unto the place the guilty soul had lost.

Therefore stay here, for thou art justly punished,
    And keep safe guard o'er the ill-gotten money,
    Which caused thee to be valiant against Charles.

And were it not that still forbids it me   100
    The reverence for the keys superlative
    Thou hadst in keeping in the gladsome life,

I would make use of words more grievous still;
    Because your avarice afflicts the world,
    Trampling the good and lifting the depraved.   105

The Evangelist you Pastors had in mind,
    When she who sitteth upon many waters
    To fornicate with kings by him was seen;

The same who with the seven heads was born,
    And power and strength from the ten horns received, 110
    So long as virtue to her spouse was pleasing.

Ye have made yourselves a god of gold and silver;
    And from the idolater how differ ye,
    Save that he one, and ye a hundred worship?

Ah, Constantine! of how much ill was mother,   115
    Not thy conversion, but that marriage dower
    Which the first wealthy Father took from thee!"

And while I sang to him such notes as these,
    Either that anger or that conscience stung him,
    He struggled violently with both his feet.   120

I think in sooth that it my Leader pleased,
    With such contented lip he listened ever
    Unto the sound of the true words expressed.

Therefore with both his arms he took me up,
    And when he had me all upon his breast,   125
    Remounted by the way where he descended.

Nor did he tire to have me clasped to him;
    But bore me to the summit of the arch
    Which from the fourth dike to the fifth is passage.

There tenderly he laid his burden down,   130
    Tenderly on the crag uneven and steep,
    That would have been hard passage for the goats:

Thence was unveiled to me another valley.

✠ CANTO XX ✠

The Fourth Bolgia: Soothsayers—Amphiaraus, Tiresias, Aruns, Manto,
Eryphylus, Michael Scott, Guido Bonatti, and Asdente—
Virgil Reproaches Dante's Pity—Mantua's Foundation

O f a new pain behoves me to make verses
    And give material to the twentieth canto
Of the first song, which is of the submerged.

I was already thoroughly disposed
    To peer down into the uncovered depth,   5
    Which bathed itself with tears of agony;

And people saw I through the circular valley,
    Silent and weeping, coming at the pace
    Which in this world the Litanies assume.

As lower down my sight descended on them,   10
   Wondrously each one seemed to be distorted
   From chin to the beginning of the chest;

For tow'rds the reins the countenance was turned,
   And backward it behoved them to advance,
   As to look forward had been taken from them.   15

Perchance indeed by violence of palsy
   Someone has been thus wholly turned awry;
   But I ne'er saw it, nor believe it can be.

As God may let thee, Reader, gather fruit
   From this thy reading, think now for thyself   20
   How I could ever keep my face unmoistened,

When our own image near me I beheld
   Distorted so, the weeping of the eyes
   Along the fissure bathed the hinder parts.

Truly I wept, leaning upon a peak   25
   Of the hard crag, so that my Escort said
   To me: "Art thou, too, of the other fools?

Here pity lives when it is wholly dead;
   Who is a greater reprobate than he
   Who feels compassion at the doom divine?   30

Lift up, lift up thy head, and see for whom
   Opened the earth before the Thebans' eyes;
   Wherefore they all cried: 'Whither rushest thou,

Amphiaraus? Why dost leave the war?'
   And downward ceased he not to fall amain   35
   As far as Minos, who lays hold on all.

See, he has made a bosom of his shoulders!
   Because he wished to see too far before him
   Behind he looks, and backward goes his way:

Behold Tiresias, who his semblance changed,   40
   When from a male a female he became,
   His members being all of them transformed;

And afterwards was forced to strike once more
   The two entangled serpents with his rod,
   Ere he could have again his manly plumes.   45

That Aruns is, who backs the other's belly,
   Who in the hills of Luni, there where grubs
   The Carrarese who houses underneath,

Among the marbles white a cavern had
   For his abode; whence to behold the stars   50
   And sea, the view was not cut off from him.

And she there, who is covering up her breasts,
   Which thou beholdest not, with loosened tresses,
   And on that side has all the hairy skin,

Was Manto, who made quest through many lands,   55
   Afterwards tarried there where I was born;
   Whereof I would thou list to me a little.

After her father had from life departed,
   And the city of Bacchus had become enslaved,
   She a long season wandered through the world.   60

Above in beauteous Italy lies a lake
   At the Alp's foot that shuts in Germany
   Over Tyrol, and has the name Benaco.

By a thousand springs, I think, and more, is bathed,
   'Twixt Garda and Val Camonica, Pennino,   65
   With water that grows stagnant in that lake.

Midway a place is where the Trentine Pastor,
   And he of Brescia, and the Veronese
   Might give his blessing, if he passed that way.

Sitteth Peschiera, fortress fair and strong,   70
   To front the Brescians and the Bergamasks,
   Where round about the bank descendeth lowest.

There of necessity must fall whatever
   In bosom of Benaco cannot stay,
   And grows a river down through verdant pastures.   75

Soon as the water doth begin to run,
   No more Benaco is it called, but Mincio,
   Far as Governo, where it falls in Po.

Not far it runs before it finds a plain
   In which it spreads itself, and makes it marshy,   80
   And oft 'tis wont in summer to be sickly.

Passing that way the virgin pitiless
   Land in the middle of the fen descried,
   Untilled and naked of inhabitants;

There to escape all human intercourse,   85
   She with her servants stayed, her arts to practice
   And lived, and left her empty body there.

The men, thereafter, who were scattered round,
   Collected in that place, which was made strong
   By the lagoon it had on every side;   90

They built their city over those dead bones,
    And, after her who first the place selected,
    Mantua named it, without other omen.

Its people once within more crowded were,
    Ere the stupidity of Casalodi   95
    From Pinamonte had received deceit.

Therefore I caution thee, if e'er thou hearest
    Originate my city otherwise,
    No falsehood may the verity defraud."

And I: "My Master, thy discourses are   100
    To me so certain, and so take my faith,
    That unto me the rest would be spent coals.

But tell me of the people who are passing,
    If any one noteworthy thou beholdest,
    For only unto that my mind reverts."   105

Then said he to me: "He who from the cheek
    Thrusts out his beard upon his swarthy shoulders
    Was, at the time when Greece was void of males,

So that there scarce remained one in the cradle,
    An augur, and with Calchas gave the moment,   110
    In Aulis, when to sever the first cable.

Eryphylus his name was, and so sings
    My lofty Tragedy in some part or other;
    That knowest thou well, who knowest the whole of it.

The next, who is so slender in the flanks,   115
    Was Michael Scott, who of a verity
    Of magical illusions knew the game.

Behold Guido Bonatti, behold Asdente,
   Who now unto his leather and his thread
   Would fain have stuck, but he too late repents.   120

Behold the wretched ones, who left the needle,
   The spool and rock, and made them fortune-tellers;
   They wrought their magic spells with herb and image.

But come now, for already holds the confines
   Of both the hemispheres, and under Seville   125
   Touches the ocean-wave, Cain and the thorns,

And yesternight the moon was round already;
   Thou shouldst remember well it did not harm thee
   From time to time within the forest deep."

Thus spake he to me, and we walked the while.   130

⊰ Canto XXI ⊱

The Fifth Bolgia: Peculators—The Elder of Santa Zita—
Malacoda and Other Devils

From bridge to bridge thus, speaking other things
   Of which my Comedy cares not to sing,
We came along, and held the summit, when

We halted to behold another fissure
   Of Malebolge and other vain laments;   5
   And I beheld it marvelously dark.

As in the Arsenal of the Venetians
   Boils in the winter the tenacious pitch
   To smear their unsound vessels o'er again,

For sail they cannot; and instead thereof   10
　　One makes his vessel new, and one recaulks
　　The ribs of that which many a voyage has made;

One hammers at the prow, one at the stern,
　　This one makes oars, and that one cordage twists,
　　Another mends the mainsail and the mizzen;   15

Thus, not by fire, but by the art divine,
　　Was boiling down below there a dense pitch
　　Which upon every side the bank belimed.

I saw it, but I did not see within it
　　Aught but the bubbles that the boiling raised,   20
　　And all swell up and resubside compressed.

The while below there fixedly I gazed,
　　My Leader, crying out: "Beware, beware!"
　　Drew me unto himself from where I stood.

Then I turned round, as one who is impatient   25
　　To see what it behoves him to escape,
　　And whom a sudden terror doth unman,

Who, while he looks, delays not his departure;
　　And I beheld behind us a black devil,
　　Running along upon the crag, approach.   30

Ah, how ferocious was he in his aspect!
　　And how he seemed to me in action ruthless,
　　With open wings and light upon his feet!

His shoulders, which sharp-pointed were and high,
　　A sinner did encumber with both haunches,   35
　　And he held clutched the sinews of the feet.

From off our bridge, he said: "O Malebranche,
   Behold one of the elders of Saint Zita;
   Plunge him beneath, for I return for others

Unto that town, which is well furnished with them.   40
   All there are barrators, except Bonturo;
   No into Yes for money there is changed."

He hurled him down, and over the hard crag
   Turned round, and never was a mastiff loosened
   In so much hurry to pursue a thief.   45

The other sank, and rose again face downward;
   But the demons, under cover of the bridge,
   Cried: "Here the Santo Volto has no place!

Here swims one otherwise than in the Serchio;
   Therefore, if for our gaffs thou wishest not,   50
   Do not uplift thyself above the pitch."

They seized him then with more than a hundred rakes;
   They said: "It here behoves thee to dance covered,
   That, if thou canst, thou secretly mayest pilfer."

Not otherwise the cooks their scullions make   55
   Immerse into the middle of the caldron
   The meat with hooks, so that it may not float.

Said the good Master to me: "That it be not
   Apparent thou art here, crouch thyself down
   Behind a jag, that thou mayest have some screen;   60

And for no outrage that is done to me
   Be thou afraid, because these things I know,
   For once before was I in such a scuffle."

They seized him then with more than a hundred rakes

Inferno XXI, line 52

Then he passed on beyond the bridge's head,
    And as upon the sixth bank he arrived,   65
    Need was for him to have a steadfast front.

With the same fury, and the same uproar,
    As dogs leap out upon a mendicant,
    Who on a sudden begs, where'er he stops,

They issued from beneath the little bridge,   70
    And turned against him all their grappling-irons;
    But he cried out: "Be none of you malignant!

Before those hooks of yours lay hold of me,
    Let one of you step forward, who may hear me,
    And then take counsel as to grappling me."   75

They all cried out: "Let Malacoda go";
    Whereat one started, and the rest stood still,
    And he came to him, saying: "What avails it?"

"Thinkest thou, Malacoda, to behold me
    Advanced into this place," my Master said,   80
    "Safe hitherto from all your skill of fence,

Without the will divine, and fate auspicious?
    Let me go on, for it in Heaven is willed
    That I another show this savage road."

Then was his arrogance so humbled in him,   85
    That he let fall his grapnel at his feet,
    And to the others said: "Now strike him not."

And unto me my Guide: "O thou, who sittest
    Among the splinters of the bridge crouched down,
    Securely now return to me again."   90

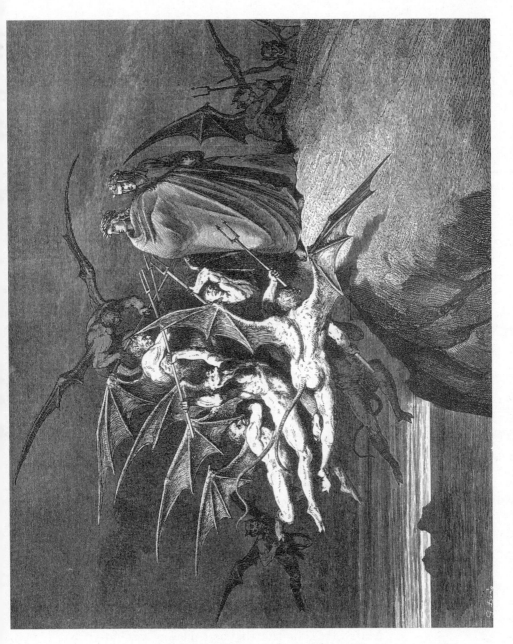

But he cried out: "Be none of you malignant!"

Inferno XXI, line 72

Wherefore I started and came swiftly to him;
   And all the devils forward thrust themselves,
   So that I feared they would not keep their compact.

And thus beheld I once afraid the soldiers
   Who issued under safeguard from Caprona,   95
   Seeing themselves among so many foes.

Close did I press myself with all my person
   Beside my Leader, and turned not mine eyes
   From off their countenance, which was not good.

They lowered their rakes, and "Wilt thou have me
      hit him,"   100
   They said to one another, "on the rump?"
   And answered: "Yes; see that thou nick him with it."

But the same demon who was holding parley
   With my Conductor turned him very quickly,
   And said: "Be quiet, be quiet, Scarmiglione";   105

Then said to us: "You can no farther go
   Forward upon this crag, because is lying
   All shattered, at the bottom, the sixth arch.

And if it still doth please you to go onward,
   Pursue your way along upon this rock;   110
   Near is another crag that yields a path.

Yesterday, five hours later than this hour,
   One thousand and two hundred sixty-six
   Years were complete, that here the way was broken.

I send in that direction some of mine   115
   To see if any one doth air himself;
   Go ye with them; for they will not be vicious.

Step forward, Alichino and Calcabrina,"
    Began he to cry out, "and thou, Cagnazzo;
    And Barbariccia, do thou guide the ten.   120

Come forward, Libicocco and Draghignazzo,
    And tuskèd Ciriatto and Graffiacane,
    And Farfarello and mad Rubicante;

Search ye all round about the boiling pitch;
    Let these be safe as far as the next crag,   125
    That all unbroken passes o'er the dens."

"O me! what is it, Master, that I see?
    Pray let us go," I said, "without an escort,
    If thou knowest how, since for myself I ask none.

If thou art as observant as thy wont is,   130
    Dost thou not see that they do gnash their teeth,
    And with their brows are threatening woe to us?"

And he to me: "I will not have thee fear;
    Let them gnash on, according to their fancy,
    Because they do it for those boiling wretches."   135

Along the left-hand dike they wheeled about;
    But first had each one thrust his tongue between
    His teeth towards their leader for a signal;

And he had made a trumpet of his rump.

⇥ CANTO XXII ⇤

Ciampolo, Friar Gomita, and Michael Zanche—The Malebranche Quarrel

I have erewhile seen horsemen moving camp,
  Begin the storming, and their muster make,
And sometimes starting off for their escape;

Vaunt-couriers have I seen upon your land,
  O Aretines, and foragers go forth,   5
  Tournaments stricken, and the joustings run,

Sometimes with trumpets and sometimes with bells,
  With kettle-drums, and signals of the castles,
  And with our own, and with outlandish things,

But never yet with bagpipe so uncouth   10
  Did I see horsemen move, nor infantry,
  Nor ship by any sign of land or star.

We went upon our way with the ten demons;
  Ah, savage company! but in the church
  With saints, and in the tavern with the gluttons!   15

Ever upon the pitch was my intent,
  To see the whole condition of that Bolgia,
  And of the people who therein were burned.

Even as the dolphins, when they make a sign
  To mariners by arching of the back,   20
  That they should counsel take to save their vessel,

Thus sometimes, to alleviate his pain,
  One of the sinners would display his back,
  And in less time conceal it than it lightens.

As on the brink of water in a ditch   25
   The frogs stand only with their muzzles out,
   So that they hide their feet and other bulk,

So upon every side the sinners stood;
   But ever as Barbariccia near them came,
   Thus underneath the boiling they withdrew.   30

I saw, and still my heart doth shudder at it,
   One waiting thus, even as it comes to pass
   One frog remains, and down another dives;

And Graffiacan, who most confronted him,
   Grappled him by his tresses smeared with pitch,   35
   And drew him up, so that he seemed an otter.

I knew, before, the names of all of them,
   So had I noted them when they were chosen,
   And when they called each other, listened how.

"O Rubicante, see that thou do lay   40
   Thy claws upon him, so that thou mayst flay him,"
   Cried all together the accursed ones.

And I: "My Master, see to it, if thou canst,
   That thou mayst know who is the luckless wight,
   Thus come into his adversaries' hands."   45

Near to the side of him my Leader drew,
   Asked of him whence he was; and he replied:
   "I in the kingdom of Navarre was born;

My mother placed me servant to a lord,
   For she had borne me to a ribald knave,   50
   Destroyer of himself and of his things.

Then I domestic was of good King Thibault;
   I set me there to practice barratry,
   For which I pay the reckoning in this heat."

And Ciriatto, from whose mouth projected,   55
   On either side, a tusk, as in a boar,
   Caused him to feel how one of them could rip.

Among malicious cats the mouse had come;
   But Barbariccia clasped him in his arms,
   And said: "Stand ye aside, while I enfork him."   60

And to my Master he turned round his head;
  "Ask him again," he said, "if more thou wish
   To know from him, before someone destroy him."

The Guide: "Now tell then of the other culprits;
   Knowest thou any one who is a Latian,   65
   Under the pitch?" And he: "I separated

Lately from one who was a neighbor to it;
   Would that I still were covered up with him,
   For I should fear not either claw nor hook!"

And Libicocco: "We have borne too much";   70
   And with his grapnel seized him by the arm,
   So that, by rending, he tore off a tendon.

Eke Draghignazzo wished to pounce upon him
   Down at the legs; whence their Decurion
   Turned round and round about with evil look.   75

When they again somewhat were pacified,
   Of him, who still was looking at his wound,
   Demanded my Conductor without stay:

"Who was that one, from whom a luckless parting
  Thou sayest thou hast made, to come ashore?"   80
  And he replied: "It was the Friar Gomita,

He of Gallura, vessel of all fraud,
  Who had the enemies of his Lord in hand,
  And dealt so with them each exults thereat;

Money he took, and let them smoothly off,   85
  As he says; and in other offices
  A barrator was he, not mean but sovereign.

Foregathers with him one Don Michel Zanche
  Of Logodoro; and of Sardinia
  To gossip never do their tongues feel tired.   90

O me! see that one, how he grinds his teeth;
  Still farther would I speak, but am afraid
  Lest he to scratch my itch be making ready."

And the grand Provost, turned to Farfarello,
  Who rolled his eyes about as if to strike,   95
  Said: "Stand aside there, thou malicious bird."

"If you desire either to see or hear,"
  The terror-stricken recommenced thereon,
  "Tuscans or Lombards, I will make them come.

But let the Malebranche cease a little,   100
  So that these may not their revenges fear,
  And I, down sitting in this very place,

For one that I am will make seven come,
  When I shall whistle, as our custom is
  To do whenever one of us comes out."   105

Cagnazzo at these words his muzzle lifted,
　Shaking his head, and said: "Just hear the trick
　Which he has thought of, down to throw himself!"

Whence he, who snares in great abundance had,
　Responded: "I by far too cunning am,   110
　When I procure for mine a greater sadness."

Alichin held not in, but running counter
　Unto the rest, said to him: "If thou dive,
　I will not follow thee upon the gallop,

But I will beat my wings above the pitch;   115
　The height be left, and be the bank a shield
　To see if thou alone dost countervail us."

O thou who readest, thou shalt hear new sport!
　Each to the other side his eyes averted;
　He first, who most reluctant was to do it.   120

The Navarrese selected well his time;
　Planted his feet on land, and in a moment
　Leaped, and released himself from their design.

Whereat each one was suddenly stung with shame,
　But he most who was cause of the defeat;   125
　Therefore he moved, and cried: "Thou art o'ertaken."

But little it availed, for wings could not
　Outstrip the fear; the other one went under,
　And, flying, upward he his breast directed;

Not otherwise the duck upon a sudden   130
　Dives under, when the falcon is approaching,
　And upward he returneth cross and weary.

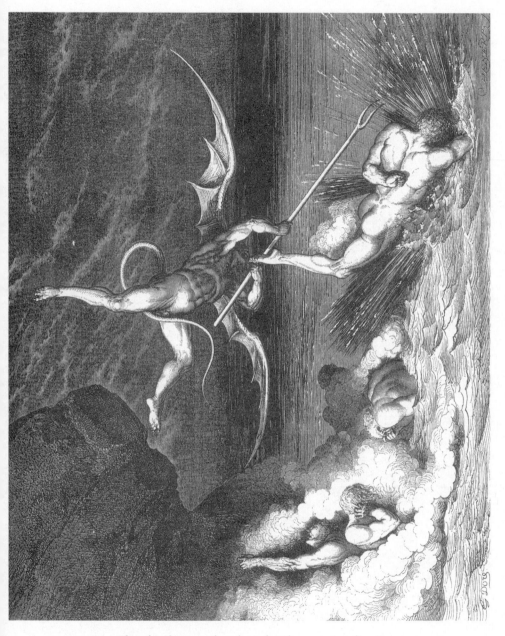

Therefore he moved, and cried: "Thou art o'ertaken."

Inferno XXII, line 126

But sooth the other was a doughty sparhawk
To clapperclaw him well; and both of them
Fell in the middle of the boiling pond.

Inferno XXII, lines 139–141

Infuriate at the mockery, Calcabrina
　　Flying behind him followed close, desirous
　　The other should escape, to have a quarrel.   135

And when the barrator had disappeared,
　　He turned his talons upon his companion,
　　And grappled with him right above the moat.

But sooth the other was a doughty sparhawk
　　To clapperclaw him well; and both of them   140
　　Fell in the middle of the boiling pond.

A sudden intercessor was the heat;
　　But ne'ertheless of rising there was naught,
　　To such degree they had their wings belimed.

Lamenting with the others, Barbariccia   145
　　Made four of them fly to the other side
　　With all their gaffs, and very speedily

This side and that they to their posts descended;
　　They stretched their hooks towards the pitch-ensnared,
　　Who were already baked within the crust,   150

And in this manner busied did we leave them.

⊰ Canto XXIII ⊱

Escape from the Malebranche—The Sixth Bolgia: Hypocrites—
Catalano and Loderingo—Caiaphas

Silent, alone, and without company
We went, the one in front, the other after,
As go the Minor Friars along their way.

Upon the fable of Æsop was directed
My thought, by reason of the present quarrel,   5
Where he has spoken of the frog and mouse;

For *mo* and *issa* are not more alike
Than this one is to that, if well we couple
End and beginning with a steadfast mind.

And even as one thought from another springs,   10
So afterward from that was born another,
Which the first fear within me double made.

Thus did I ponder: "These on our account
Are laughed to scorn, with injury and scoff
So great, that much I think it must annoy them.   15

If anger be engrafted on ill will,
They will come after us more merciless
Than dog upon the leveret which he seizes,"

I felt my hair stand all on end already
With terror, and stood backwardly intent,   20
When said I: "Master, if thou hidest not

Thyself and me forthwith, of Malebranche
   I am in dread; we have them now behind us;
   I so imagine them, I already feel them."

And he: "If I were made of leaded glass,   25
   Thine outward image I should not attract
   Sooner to me than I imprint the inner.

Just now thy thoughts came in among my own,
   With similar attitude and similar face,
   So that of both one counsel sole I made.   30

If peradventure the right bank so slope
   That we to the next Bolgia can descend,
   We shall escape from the imagined chase."

Not yet he finished rendering such opinion,
   When I beheld them come with outstretched wings, 35
   Not far remote, with will to seize upon us.

My Leader on a sudden seized me up,
   Even as a mother who by noise is wakened,
   And close beside her sees the enkindled flames,

Who takes her son, and flies, and does not stop,   40
   Having more care of him than of herself,
   So that she clothes her only with a shift;

And downward from the top of the hard bank
   Supine he gave him to the pendent rock,
   That one side of the other Bolgia walls.   45

Ne'er ran so swiftly water through a sluice
   To turn the wheel of any land-built mill,
   When nearest to the paddles it approaches,

As did my Master down along that border,
  Bearing me with him on his breast away,   50
  As his own son, and not as a companion.

Hardly the bed of the ravine below
  His feet had reached, ere they had reached the hill
  Right over us; but he was not afraid;

For the high Providence, which had ordained   55
  To place them ministers of the fifth moat,
  The power of thence departing took from all.

A painted people there below we found,
  Who went about with footsteps very slow,
  Weeping and in their semblance tired and
    vanquished.   60

They had on mantles with the hoods low down
  Before their eyes, and fashioned of the cut
  That in Cologne they for the monks are made.

Without, they gilded are so that it dazzles;
  But inwardly all leaden and so heavy   65
  That Frederick used to put them on of straw.

O everlastingly fatiguing mantle!
  Again we turned us, still to the left hand
  Along with them, intent on their sad plaint;

But owing to the weight, that weary folk   70
  Came on so tardily, that we were new
  In company at each motion of the haunch.

Whence I unto my Leader: "See thou find
  Someone who may by deed or name be known,
  And thus in going move thine eye about."   75

Hardly the bed of the ravine below
His feet had reached, ere they had reached the hill
Right over us

Inferno XXIII, lines 52–54

They had on mantles with the hoods low down
Before their eyes

Inferno XXIII, lines 61–62

And one, who understood the Tuscan speech,
  Cried to us from behind: "Stay ye your feet,
  Ye, who so run athwart the dusky air!

Perhaps thou'lt have from me what thou demandest."
  Whereat the Leader turned him, and said: "Wait,   80
  And then according to his pace proceed."

I stopped, and two beheld I show great haste
  Of spirit, in their faces, to be with me;
  But the burden and the narrow way delayed them.

When they came up, long with an eye askance   85
  They scanned me without uttering a word.
  Then to each other turned, and said together:

"He by the action of his throat seems living;
  And if they dead are, by what privilege
  Go they uncovered by the heavy stole?"   90

Then said to me: "Tuscan, who to the college
  Of miserable hypocrites art come,
  Do not disdain to tell us who thou art."

And I to them: "Born was I, and grew up
  In the great town on the fair river of Arno,   95
  And with the body am I've always had.

But who are ye, in whom there trickles down
  Along your cheeks such grief as I behold?
  And what pain is upon you, that so sparkles?"

And one replied to me: "These orange cloaks   100
  Are made of lead so heavy, that the weights
  Cause in this way their balances to creak.

Frati Gaudenti were we, and Bolognese;
    I Catalano, and he Loderingo
    Named, and together taken by thy city,   105

As the wont is to take one man alone,
    For maintenance of its peace; and we were such
    That still it is apparent round Gardingo."

"O Friars," began I, "your iniquitous . . ."
    But said no more; for to mine eyes there rushed   110
    One crucified with three stakes on the ground.

When me he saw, he writhed himself all over,
    Blowing into his beard with suspirations;
    And the Friar Catalan, who noticed this,

Said to me: "This transfixed one, whom thou seest,   115
    Counselled the Pharisees that it was meet
    To put one man to torture for the people.

Crosswise and naked is he on the path,
    As thou perceivest; and he needs must feel,
    Whoever passes, first how much he weighs;   120

And in like mode his father-in-law is punished
    Within this moat, and the others of the council,
    Which for the Jews was a malignant seed."

And thereupon I saw Virgilius marvel
    O'er him who was extended on the cross   125
    So vilely in eternal banishment.

Then he directed to the Friar this voice:
    "Be not displeased, if granted thee, to tell us
    If to the right hand any pass slope down

"This transfixed one, whom thou seest,
Counseled the Pharisees that it was meet
To put one man to torture for the people."

Inferno XXIII, lines 115–117

By which we two may issue forth from here,   130
    Without constraining some of the black angels
    To come and extricate us from this deep."

Then he made answer: "Nearer than thou hopest
    There is a rock, that forth from the great circle
    Proceeds, and crosses all the cruel valleys,   135

Save that at this 'tis broken, and does not bridge it;
    You will be able to mount up the ruin,
    That sidelong slopes and at the bottom rises."

The Leader stood awhile with head bowed down;
    Then said: "The business badly he recounted   140
    Who grapples with his hook the sinners yonder."

And the Friar: "Many of the Devil's vices
    Once heard I at Bologna, and among them,
    That he's a liar and the father of lies."

Thereat my Leader with great strides went on,   145
    Somewhat disturbed with anger in his looks;
    Whence from the heavy-laden I departed

After the prints of his beloved feet.

⊰ CANTO XXIV ⊱

The Seventh Bolgia: Thieves—Vanni Fucci—Serpents

In that part of the youthful year wherein
    The Sun his locks beneath Aquarius tempers,
And now the nights draw near to half the day,

What time the hoar-frost copies on the ground
   The outward semblance of her sister white,   5
   But little lasts the temper of her pen,

The husbandman, whose forage faileth him,
   Rises, and looks, and seeth the champaign
   All gleaming white, whereat he beats his flank,

Returns in doors, and up and down laments,   10
   Like a poor wretch, who knows not what to do;
   Then he returns and hope revives again,

Seeing the world has changed its countenance
   In little time, and takes his shepherd's crook,
   And forth the little lambs to pasture drives.   15

Thus did the Master fill me with alarm,
   When I beheld his forehead so disturbed,
   And to the ailment came as soon the plaster.

For as we came unto the ruined bridge,
   The Leader turned to me with that sweet look   20
   Which at the mountain's foot I first beheld.

His arms he opened, after some advisement
   Within himself elected, looking first
   Well at the ruin, and laid hold of me.

And even as he who acts and meditates,   25
   For aye it seems that he provides beforehand,
   So upward lifting me towards the summit

Of a huge rock, he scanned another crag,
   Saying: "To that one grapple afterwards,
   But try first if 'tis such that it will hold thee."   30

This was no way for one clothed with a cloak;
    For hardly we, he light, and I pushed upward,
    Were able to ascend from jag to jag.

And had it not been, that upon that precinct
    Shorter was the ascent than on the other,   35
    He I know not, but I had been dead beat.

But because Malebolge tow'rds the mouth
    Of the profoundest well is all inclining,
    The structure of each valley doth import

That one bank rises and the other sinks.   40
    Still we arrived at length upon the point
    Wherefrom the last stone breaks itself asunder.

The breath was from my lungs so milked away,
    When I was up, that I could go no farther,
    Nay, I sat down upon my first arrival.   45

"Now it behoves thee thus to put off sloth,"
    My Master said; "for sitting upon down,
    Or under quilt, one cometh not to fame,

Withouten which whoso his life consumes
    Such vestige leaveth of himself on earth,   50
    As smoke in air or in the water foam.

And therefore raise thee up, o'ercome the anguish
    With spirit that o'ercometh every battle,
    If with its heavy body it sink not.

A longer stairway it behoves thee mount;   55
    'Tis not enough from these to have departed;
    Let it avail thee, if thou understand me."

Then I uprose, showing myself provided
   Better with breath than I did feel myself,
   And said: "Go on, for I am strong and bold."   60

Upward we took our way along the crag,
   Which jagged was, and narrow, and difficult,
   And more precipitous far than that before.

Speaking I went, not to appear exhausted;
   Whereat a voice from the next moat came forth,   65
   Not well adapted to articulate words.

I know not what it said, though o'er the back
   I now was of the arch that passes there;
   But he seemed moved to anger who was speaking.

I was bent downward, but my living eyes   70
   Could not attain the bottom, for the dark;
   Wherefore I: "Master, see that thou arrive

At the next round, and let us descend the wall;
   For as from hence I hear and understand not,
   So I look down and nothing I distinguish."   75

"Other response," he said, "I make thee not,
   Except the doing; for the modest asking
   Ought to be followed by the deed in silence."

We from the bridge descended at its head,
   Where it connects itself with the eighth bank,   80
   And then was manifest to me the Bolgia;

And I beheld therein a terrible throng
   Of serpents, and of such a monstrous kind,
   That the remembrance still congeals my blood

Let Libya boast no longer with her sand;   85
    For if Chelydri, Jaculi, and Pharæ
    She breeds, with Cenchri and with Amphisbæna,

Neither so many plagues nor so malignant
    E'er showed she with all Ethiopia,
    Nor with whatever on the Red Sea is!   90

Among this cruel and most dismal throng
    People were running naked and affrighted.
    Without the hope of hole or heliotrope.

They had their hands with serpents bound behind them;
    These riveted upon their reins the tail   95
    And head, and were in front of them entwined.

And lo! at one who was upon our side
    There darted forth a serpent, which transfixed him
    There where the neck is knotted to the shoulders.

Nor O so quickly e'er, nor I was written,   100
    As he took fire, and burned; and ashes wholly
    Behoved it that in falling he became.

And when he on the ground was thus destroyed,
    The ashes drew together, and of themselves
    Into himself they instantly returned.   105

Even thus by the great sages 'tis confessed
    The phoenix dies, and then is born again,
    When it approaches its five-hundredth year;

On herb or grain it feeds not in its life,
    But only on tears of incense and amomum,   110
    And nard and myrrh are its last winding-sheet.

Among this cruel and most dismal throng
People were running naked and affrighted.

Inferno XXIV, lines 91–92

And as he is who falls, and knows not how,
    By force of demons who to earth down drag him,
    Or other oppilation that binds man,

When he arises and around him looks,   115
    Wholly bewildered by the mighty anguish
    Which he has suffered, and in looking sighs;

Such was that sinner after he had risen.
    Justice of God! O how severe it is,
    That blows like these in vengeance poureth down! 120

The Guide thereafter asked him who he was;
    Whence he replied: "I rained from Tuscany
    A short time since into this cruel gorge.

A bestial life, and not a human, pleased me,
    Even as the mule I was; I'm Vanni Fucci,   125
    Beast, and Pistoia was my worthy den."

And I unto the Guide: "Tell him to stir not,
    And ask what crime has thrust him here below,
    For once a man of blood and wrath I saw him."

And the sinner, who had heard, dissembled not,   130
    But unto me directed mind and face,
    And with a melancholy shame was painted.

Then said: "It pains me more that thou hast caught me
    Amid this misery where thou seest me,
    Than when I from the other life was taken.   135

What thou demandest I cannot deny;
    So low am I put down because I robbed
    The sacristy of the fair ornaments,

And falsely once 'twas laid upon another;
 But that thou mayst not such a sight enjoy, 140
 If thou shalt e'er be out of the dark places,

Thine ears to my announcement ope and hear:
 Pistoia first of Neri groweth meager;
 Then Florence doth renew her men and manners;

Mars draws a vapor up from Val di Magra, 145
 Which is with turbid clouds enveloped round,
 And with impetuous and bitter tempest

Over Campo Picen shall be the battle;
 When it shall suddenly rend the mist asunder,
 So that each Bianco shall thereby be smitten. 150

And this I've said that it may give thee pain."

⊰ Canto XXV ⊱

*Vanni Fucci's Punishment—Agnello Brunelleschi, Buoso degli Abati,
Puccio Sciancato, Cianfa de' Donati, and Guercio Cavalcanti*

At the conclusion of his words, the thief
 Lifted his hands aloft with both the figs,
Crying: "Take that, God, for at thee I aim them."

From that time forth the serpents were my friends;
 For one entwined itself about his neck 5
 As if it said: "I will not thou speak more";

And round his arms another, and rebound him,
 Clinching itself together so in front,
 That with them he could not a motion make.

Pistoia, ah, Pistoia! why resolve not   10
    To burn thyself to ashes and so perish,
    Since in ill-doing thou thy seed excellest?

Through all the somber circles of this Hell,
    Spirit I saw not against God so proud,
    Not he who fell at Thebes down from the walls!   15

He fled away, and spake no further word;
    And I beheld a Centaur full of rage
    Come crying out: "Where is, where is the scoffer?"

I do not think Maremma has so many
    Serpents as he had all along his back,
    As far as where our countenance begins.   20

Upon the shoulders, just behind the nape,
    With wings wide open was a dragon lying,
    And he sets fire to all that he encounters.

My Master said: "That one is Cacus, who   25
    Beneath the rock upon Mount Aventine
    Created oftentimes a lake of blood.

He goes not on the same road with his brothers,
    By reason of the fraudulent theft he made
    Of the great herd, which he had near to him;   30

Whereat his tortuous actions ceased beneath
    The mace of Hercules, who peradventure
    Gave him a hundred, and he felt not ten."

While he was speaking thus, he had passed by,
    And spirits three had underneath us come,   35
    Of which nor I aware was, nor my Leader,

Until what time they shouted: "Who are you?"
   On which account our story made a halt,
   And then we were intent on them alone.

I did not know them; but it came to pass,   40
   As it is wont to happen by some chance,
   That one to name the other was compelled,

Exclaiming: "Where can Cianfa have remained?"
   Whence I, so that the Leader might attend,
   Upward from chin to nose my finger laid.   45

If thou art, Reader, slow now to believe
   What I shall say, it will no marvel be,
   For I who saw it hardly can admit it.

As I was holding raised on them my brows,
   Behold! a serpent with six feet darts forth   50
   In front of one, and fastens wholly on him.

With middle feet it bound him round the paunch,
   And with the forward ones his arms it seized;
   Then thrust its teeth through one cheek and the other;

The hindermost it stretched upon his thighs,   55
   And put its tail through in between the two,
   And up behind along the reins outspread it.

Ivy was never fastened by its barbs
   Unto a tree so, as this horrible reptile
   Upon the other's limbs entwined its own.   60

Then they stuck close, as if of heated wax
   They had been made, and intermixed their color;
   Nor one nor other seemed now what he was;

E'en as proceedeth on before the flame
 Upward along the paper a brown color,   65
 Which is not black as yet, and the white dies.

The other two looked on, and each of them
 Cried out: "O me, Agnello, how thou changest!
 Behold, thou now art neither two nor one."

Already the two heads had one become,   70
 When there appeared to us two figures mingled
 Into one face, wherein the two were lost.

Of the four lists were fashioned the two arms,
 The thighs and legs, the belly and the chest
 Members became that never yet were seen.   75

Every original aspect there was canceled;
 Two and yet none did the perverted image
 Appear, and such departed with slow pace.

Even as a lizard, under the great scourge
 Of days canicular, exchanging hedge,   80
 Lightning appeareth if the road it cross;

Thus did appear, coming towards the bellies
 Of the two others, a small fiery serpent,
 Livid and black as is a peppercorn.

And in that part whereat is first received   85
 Our aliment, it one of them transfixed;
 Then downward fell in front of him extended.

The one transfixed looked at it, but said naught;
 Nay, rather with feet motionless he yawned,
 Just as if sleep or fever had assailed him.   90

"O me, Agnello, how thou changest!
Behold, thou now art neither two nor one."

Inferno XXV, lines 68–69

He at the serpent gazed, and it at him;
    One through the wound, the other through the mouth
    Smoked violently, and the smoke commingled.

Henceforth be silent Lucan, where he mentions
    Wretched Sabellus and Nassidius,   95
    And wait to hear what now shall be shot forth.

Be silent Ovid, of Cadmus and Arethusa;
    For if him to a snake, her to fountain,
    Converts he fabling, that I grudge him not;

Because two natures never front to front   100
    Has he transmuted, so that both the forms
    To interchange their matter ready were.

Together they responded in such wise,
    That to a fork the serpent cleft his tail,
    And eke the wounded drew his feet together.   105

The legs together with the thighs themselves
    Adhered so, that in little time the juncture
    No sign whatever made that was apparent.

He with the cloven tail assumed the figure
    The other one was losing, and his skin   110
    Became elastic, and the other's hard.

I saw the arms draw inward at the armpits,
    And both feet of the reptile, that were short,
    Lengthen as much as those contracted were.

Thereafter the hind feet, together twisted,   115
    Became the member that a man conceals,
    And of his own the wretch had two created.

While both of them the exhalation veils
   With a new color, and engenders hair
   On one of them and depilates the other,   120

The one uprose and down the other fell,
   Though turning not away their impious lamps,
   Underneath which each one his muzzle changed.

He who was standing drew it tow'rds the temples,
   And from excess of matter, which came thither,   125
   Issued the ears from out the hollow cheeks;

What did not backward run and was retained
   Of that excess made to the face a nose,
   And the lips thickened far as was befitting.

He who lay prostrate thrusts his muzzle forward,   130
   And backward draws the ears into his head,
   In the same manner as the snail its horns;

And so the tongue, which was entire and apt
   For speech before, is cleft, and the bi-forked
   In the other closes up, and the smoke ceases.   135

The soul, which to a reptile had been changed,
   Along the valley hissing takes to flight,
   And after him the other speaking sputters.

Then did he turn upon him his new shoulders,
   And said to the other: "I'll have Buoso run,   140
   Crawling as I have done, along this road."

In this way I beheld the seventh ballast
   Shift and reshift, and here be my excuse
   The novelty, if aught my pen transgress.

And notwithstanding that mine eyes might be   145
　　Somewhat bewildered, and my mind dismayed,
　　They could not flee away so secretly

But that I plainly saw Puccio Sciancato;
　　And he it was who sole of three companions,
　　Which came in the beginning, was not changed;   150

The other was he whom thou, Gaville, weepest.

⊰ Canto XXVI ⊱

The Eighth Bolgia: Evil Counselors—Ulysses and Diomed—
Ulysses' Last Voyage

Rejoice, O Florence, since thou art so great,
　　That over sea and land thou beatest thy wings,
And throughout Hell thy name is spread abroad!

Among the thieves five citizens of thine
　　Like these I found, whence shame comes unto me,   5
　　And thou thereby to no great honor risest.

But if when morn is near our dreams are true,
　　Feel shalt thou in a little time from now
　　What Prato, if none other, craves for thee.

And if it now were, it were not too soon;   10
　　Would that it were, seeing it needs must be,
　　For 'twill aggrieve me more the more I age.

We went our way, and up along the stairs
　　The bourns had made us to descend before,
　　Remounted my Conductor and drew me.   15

And following the solitary path
   Among the rocks and ridges of the crag,
   The foot without the hand sped not at all.

Then sorrowed I, and sorrow now again,
   When I direct my mind to what I saw,   20
   And more my genius curb than I am wont,

That it may run not unless virtue guide it;
   So that if some good star, or better thing,
   Have given me good, I may myself not grudge it.

As many as the hind (who on the hill   25
   Rests at the time when he who lights the world
   His countenance keeps least concealed from us,

While as the fly gives place unto the gnat)
   Seeth the glow-worms down along the valley,
   Perchance there where he ploughs and makes his
      vintage;   30

With flames as manifold resplendent all
   Was the eighth Bolgia, as I grew aware
   As soon as I was where the depth appeared.

And such as he who with the bears avenged him
   Beheld Elijah's chariot at departing,   35
   What time the steeds to heaven erect uprose,

For with his eye he could not follow it
   So as to see aught else than flame alone,
   Even as a little cloud ascending upward,

Thus each along the gorge of the intrenchment   40
   Was moving; for not one reveals the theft,
   And every flame a sinner steals away.

I stood upon the bridge uprisen to see,
    So that, if I had seized not on a rock,
    Down had I fallen without being pushed.   45

And the Leader, who beheld me so attent,
    Exclaimed: "Within the fires the spirits are;
    Each swathes himself with that wherewith he burns."

"My Master," I replied, "by hearing thee
    I am more sure; but I surmised already   50
    It might be so, and already wished to ask thee

Who is within that fire, which comes so cleft
    At top, it seems uprising from the pyre
    Where was Eteocles with his brother placed."

He answered me: "Within there are tormented   55
    Ulysses and Diomed, and thus together
    They unto vengeance run as unto wrath.

And there within their flame do they lament
    The ambush of the horse, which made the door
    Whence issued forth the Romans' gentle seed;   60

Therein is wept the craft, for which being dead
    Deidamia still deplores Achilles,
    And pain for the Palladium there is borne."

"If they within those sparks possess the power
    To speak," I said, "thee, Master, much I pray,   65
    And re-pray, that the prayer be worth a thousand,

That thou make no denial of awaiting
    Until the hornëd flame shall hither come;
    Thou seest that with desire I lean towards it."

"Within the fires the spirits are;
Each swathes himself with that wherewith he burns."

Inferno XXVI, lines 47–48

And he to me: "Worthy is thy entreaty   70
    Of much applause, and therefore I accept it;
    But take heed that thy tongue restrain itself.

Leave me to speak, because I have conceived
    That which thou wishest; for they might disdain
    Perchance, since they were Greeks, discourse
        of thine."   75

When now the flame had come unto that point,
    Where to my Leader it seemed time and place,
    After this fashion did I hear him speak:

"O ye, who are twofold within one fire,
    If I deserved of you, while I was living,   80
    If I deserved of you or much or little

When in the world I wrote the lofty verses,
    Do not move on, but one of you declare
    Whither, being lost, he went away to die."

Then of the antique flame the greater horn,   85
    Murmuring, began to wave itself about
    Even as a flame doth which the wind fatigues.

Thereafterward, the summit to and fro
    Moving as if it were the tongue that spake,
    It uttered forth a voice, and said: "When I   90

From Circe had departed, who concealed me
    More than a year there near unto Gaëta,
    Or ever yet Æneas named it so,

Nor fondness for my son, nor reverence
    For my old father, nor the due affection   95
    Which joyous should have made Penelope,

Could overcome within me the desire
   I had to be experienced of the world,
   And of the vice and virtue of mankind;

But I put forth on the high open sea   100
   With one sole ship, and that small company
   By which I never had deserted been.

Both of the shores I saw as far as Spain,
   Far as Morocco, and the isle of Sardes,
   And the others which that sea bathes round about. 105

I and my company were old and slow
   When at that narrow passage we arrived
   Where Hercules his landmarks set as signals,

That man no farther onward should adventure.
   On the right hand behind me left I Seville,   110
   And on the other already had left Ceuta.

'O brothers, who amid a hundred thousand
   Perils,' I said, 'have come unto the West,
   To this so inconsiderable vigil

Which is remaining of your senses still   115
   Be ye unwilling to deny the knowledge,
   Following the sun, of the unpeopled world.

Consider ye the seed from which ye sprang;
   Ye were not made to live like unto brutes,
   But for pursuit of virtue and of knowledge.'   120

So eager did I render my companions,
   With this brief exhortation, for the voyage,
   That then I hardly could have held them back.

And having turned our stern unto the morning,
 We of the oars made wings for our mad flight, 125
 Evermore gaining on the larboard side.

Already all the stars of the other pole
 The night beheld, and ours so very low
 It did not rise above the ocean floor.

Five times rekindled and as many quenched 130
 Had been the splendor underneath the moon,
 Since we had entered into the deep pass,

When there appeared to us a mountain, dim
 From distance, and it seemed to me so high
 As I had never any one beheld. 135

Joyful were we, and soon it turned to weeping;
 For out of the new land a whirlwind rose,
 And smote upon the fore part of the ship.

Three times it made her whirl with all the waters,
 At the fourth time it made the stern uplift, 140
 And the prow downward go, as pleased Another,

Until the sea above us closed again."

⊰ Canto XXVII ⊱

Guido da Montefeltro—His Deception by Pope Boniface VIII

Already was the flame erect and quiet,
 To speak no more, and now departed from us
With the permission of the gentle Poet;

When yet another, which behind it came,
    Caused us to turn our eyes upon its top   5
    By a confusëd sound that issued from it.

As the Sicilian bull (that bellowed first
    With the lament of him, and that was right,
    Who with his file had modulated it)

Bellowed so with the voice of the afflicted,   10
    That, notwithstanding it was made of brass,
    Still it appeared with agony transfixed;

Thus, by not having any way or issue
    At first from out the fire, to its own language
    Converted were the melancholy words.   15

But afterwards, when they had gathered way
    Up through the point, giving it that vibration
    The tongue had given them in their passage out,

We heard it said: "O thou, at whom I aim
    My voice, and who but now wast speaking Lombard, 20
    Saying, 'Now go thy way, no more I urge thee,'

Because I come perchance a little late,
    To stay and speak with me let it not irk thee;
    Thou seest it irks not me, and I am burning.

If thou but lately into this blind world   25
    Hast fallen down from that sweet Latian land,
    Wherefrom I bring the whole of my transgression,

Say, if the Romagnuols have peace or war,
    For I was from the mountains there between
    Urbino and the yoke whence Tiber bursts."   30

I still was downward bent and listening,
    When my Conductor touched me on the side,
    Saying: "Speak thou: this one a Latian is."

And I, who had beforehand my reply
    In readiness, forthwith began to speak: 35
    "O soul, that down below there art concealed,

Romagna thine is not and never has been
    Without war in the bosom of its tyrants;
    But open war I none have left there now.

Ravenna stands as it long years has stood;   40
    The Eagle of Polenta there is brooding,
    So that she covers Cervia with her vans.

The city which once made the long resistance,
    And of the French a sanguinary heap,
    Beneath the Green Paws finds itself again;   45

Verrucchio's ancient Mastiff and the new,
    Who made such bad disposal of Montagna,
    Where they are wont make wimbles of their teeth.

The cities of Lamone and Santerno
    Governs the Lioncel of the white lair,   50
    Who changes sides 'twixt summertime and winter;

And that of which the Savio bathes the flank,
    Even as it lies between the plain and mountain,
    Lives between tyranny and a free state.

Now I entreat thee tell us who thou art;   55
    Be not more stubborn than the rest have been,
    So may thy name hold front there in the world."

After the fire a little more had roared
    In its own fashion, the sharp point it moved
    This way and that, and then gave forth such breath: 60

"If I believed that my reply were made
    To one who to the world would e'er return,
    This flame without more flickering would stand still;

But inasmuch as never from this depth
    Did any one return, if I hear true, 65
    Without the fear of infamy I answer,

I was a man of arms, then Cordelier,
    Believing thus begirt to make amends;
    And truly my belief had been fulfilled

But for the High Priest, whom may ill betide, 70
    Who put me back into my former sins;
    And how and wherefore I will have thee hear.

While I was still the form of bone and pulp
    My mother gave to me, the deeds I did
    Were not those of a lion, but a fox. 75

The machinations and the covert ways
    I knew them all, and practiced so their craft,
    That to the ends of earth the sound went forth.

When now unto that portion of mine age
    I saw myself arrived, when each one ought 80
    To lower the sails, and coil away the ropes,

That which before had pleased me then displeased me;
    And penitent and confessing I surrendered,
    Ah woe is me! and it would have bestead me;

The Leader of the modern Pharisees   85
   Having a war near unto Lateran,
   And not with Saracens nor with the Jews,

For each one of his enemies was Christian,
   And none of them had been to conquer Acre,
   Nor merchandising in the Sultan's land,   90

Nor the high office, nor the sacred orders,
   In him regarded, nor in me that cord
   Which used to make those girt with it more meager;

But even as Constantine sought out Sylvester
   To cure his leprosy, within Soracte,   95
   So this one sought me out as an adept

To cure him of the fever of his pride.
   Counsel he asked of me, and I was silent,
   Because his words appeared inebriate.

And then he said: 'Be not thy heart afraid;   100
   Henceforth I thee absolve; and thou instruct me
   How to raze Palestrina to the ground.

Heaven have I power to lock and to unlock,
   As thou dost know; therefore the keys are two,
   The which my predecessor held not dear.'   105

Then urged me on his weighty arguments
   There, where my silence was the worst advice;
   And said I: 'Father, since thou washest me

Of that sin into which I now must fall,
   The promise long with the fulfillment short   110
   Will make thee triumph in thy lofty seat.'

Francis came afterward, when I was dead,
　　For me; but one of the black Cherubim
　　Said to him: 'Take him not; do me no wrong;

He must come down among my servitors,　　115
　　Because he gave the fraudulent advice
　　From which time forth I have been at his hair;

For who repents not cannot be absolved,
　　Nor can one both repent and will at once,
　　Because of the contradiction which consents not.'　　120

O miserable me! how I did shudder
　　When he seized on me, saying: 'Peradventure
　　Thou didst not think that I was a logician!'

He bore me unto Minos, who entwined
　　Eight times his tail about his stubborn back,　　125
　　And after he had bitten it in great rage,

Said: 'Of the thievish fire a culprit this';
　　Wherefore, here where thou seest, am I lost,
　　And vested thus in going I bemoan me."

When it had thus completed its recital,　　130
　　The flame departed uttering lamentations,
　　Writhing and flapping its sharp-pointed horn.

Onward we passed, both I and my Conductor,
　　Up o'er the crag above another arch,
　　Which the moat covers, where is paid the fee　　135

By those who, sowing discord, win their burden.

⊰ CANTO XXVIII ⊱

The Ninth Bolgia: Schismatics—Mahomet and Ali—
Pier da Medicina, Curio, Mosca, and Bertrand de Born

W̲ho ever could, e'en with untrammelled words,
  Tell of the blood and of the wounds in full
Which now I saw, by many times narrating?

Each tongue would for a certainty fall short
  By reason of our speech and memory,   5
  That have small room to comprehend so much.

If were again assembled all the people
  Which formerly upon the fateful land
  Of Puglia were lamenting for their blood

Shed by the Romans and the lingering war   10
  That of the rings made such illustrious spoils,
  As Livy has recorded, who errs not,

With those who felt the agony of blows
  By making counterstand to Robert Guiscard,
  And all the rest, whose bones are gathered still   15

At Ceperano, where a renegade
  Was each Apulian, and at Tagliacozzo,
  Where without arms the old Alardo conquered,

And one his limb transpierced, and one lopped off,
  Should show, it would be nothing to compare   20
  With the disgusting mode of the ninth Bolgia.

A cask by losing center-piece or cant
   Was never shattered so, as I saw one
   Rent from the chin to where one breaketh wind.

Between his legs were hanging down his entrails;   25
   His heart was visible, and the dismal sack
   That maketh excrement of what is eaten.

While I was all absorbed in seeing him,
   He looked at me, and opened with his hands
   His bosom, saying: "See now how I rend me;   30

How mutilated, see, is Mahomet;
   In front of me doth Ali weeping go,
   Cleft in the face from forelock unto chin;

And all the others whom thou here beholdest,
   Disseminators of scandal and of schism   35
   While living were, and therefore are cleft thus.

A devil is behind here, who doth cleave us
   Thus cruelly, unto the falchion's edge
   Putting again each one of all this ream,

When we have gone around the doleful road;   40
   By reason that our wounds are closed again
   Ere any one in front of him repass.

But who art thou, that musest on the crag,
   Perchance to postpone going to the pain
   That is adjudged upon thine accusations?"   45

"Nor death hath reached him yet, nor guilt doth bring him,"
   My Master made reply, "to be tormented;
   But to procure him full experience,

He looked at me, and opened with his hands
His bosom, saying: "See now how I rend me"

Inferno XXVIII, lines 29–30

Me, who am dead, behoves it to conduct him
    Down here through Hell, from circle unto circle;   50
    And this is true as that I speak to thee."

More than a hundred were there when they heard him,
    Who in the moat stood still to look at me,
    Through wonderment oblivious of their torture.

"Now say to Fra Dolcino, then, to arm him,   55
    Thou, who perhaps wilt shortly see the sun,
    If soon he wish not here to follow me,

So with provisions, that no stress of snow
    May give the victory to the Novarese,
    Which otherwise to gain would not be easy."   60

After one foot to go away he lifted,
    This word did Mahomet say unto me,
    Then to depart upon the ground he stretched it.

Another one, who had his throat pierced through,
    And nose cut off close underneath the brows,   65
    And had no longer but a single ear,

Staying to look in wonder with the others,
    Before the others did his gullet open,
    Which outwardly was red in every part,

And said: "O thou, whom guilt doth not condemn,   70
    And whom I once saw up in Latian land,
    Unless too great similitude deceive me,

Call to remembrance Pier da Medicina,
    If e'er thou see again the lovely plain
    That from Vercelli slopes to Marcabò,   75

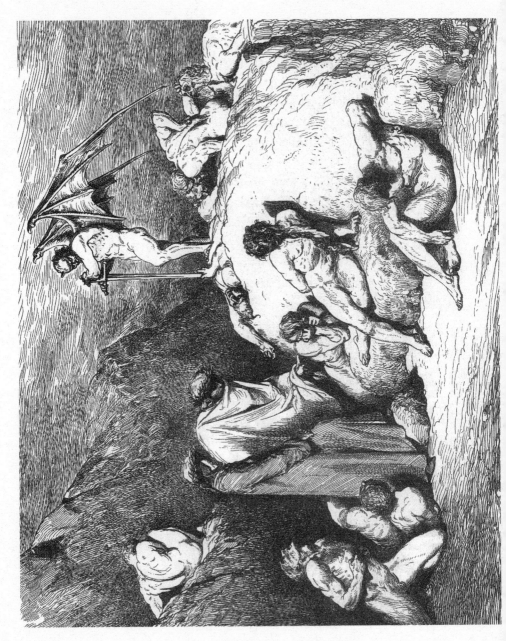

"Call to remembrance Pier da Medicina"

Inferno XXVIII, line 73

And make it known to the best two of Fano,
　　To Messer Guido and Angiolello likewise,
　　That if foreseeing here be not in vain,

Cast over from their vessel shall they be,
　　And drowned near unto the Cattolica,　　　　　80
　　By the betrayal of a tyrant fell.

Between the isles of Cyprus and Majorca
　　Neptune ne'er yet beheld so great a crime,
　　Neither of pirates nor Argolic people.

That traitor, who sees only with one eye,　　　　85
　　And holds the land, which someone here with me
　　Would fain be fasting from the vision of,

Will make them come unto a parley with him;
　　Then will do so, that to Focara's wind
　　They will not stand in need of vow or prayer."　　90

And I to him: "Show to me and declare,
　　If thou wouldst have me bear up news of thee,
　　Who is this person of the bitter vision."

Then did he lay his hand upon the jaw
　　Of one of his companions, and his mouth　　　　95
　　Oped, crying: "This is he, and he speaks not.

This one, being banished, every doubt submerged
　　In Cæsar by affirming the forearmed
　　Always with detriment allowed delay."

O how bewildered unto me appeared,　　　　　　100
　　With tongue asunder in his windpipe slit,
　　Curio, who in speaking was so bold!

And one, who both his hands dissevered had,
    The stumps uplifting through the murky air,
    So that the blood made horrible his face,   105

Cried out: "Thou shalt remember Mosca also,
    Who said, alas! 'A thing done has an end!'
    Which was an ill seed for the Tuscan people."

"And death unto thy race," thereto I added;
    Whence he, accumulating woe on woe,   110
    Departed, like a person sad and crazed.

But I remained to look upon the crowd;
    And saw a thing which I should be afraid,
    Without some further proof, even to recount,

If it were not that conscience reassures me,   115
    That good companion which emboldens man
    Beneath the hauberk of its feeling pure.

I truly saw, and still I seem to see it,
    A trunk without a head walk in like manner
    As walked the others of the mournful herd.   120

And by the hair it held the head dissevered,
    Hung from the hand in fashion of a lantern,
    And that upon us gazed and said: "O me!"

It of itself made to itself a lamp,
    And they were two in one, and one in two;   125
    How that can be, He knows who so ordains it.

When it was come close to the bridge's foot,
    It lifted high its arm with all the head,
    To bring more closely unto us its words,

By the hair it held the head dissevered,
Hung from the hand in fashion of a lantern,
And that upon us gazed and said: "O me!"

Inferno XXVIII, lines 121–123

Which were: "Behold now the sore penalty,   130
 Thou, who dost breathing go the dead beholding;
 Behold if any be as great as this.

And so that thou may carry news of me,
 Know that Bertram de Born am I, the same
 Who gave to the Young King the evil comfort.   135

I made the father and the son rebellious;
 Achitophel not more with Absalom
 And David did with his accursed goadings.

Because I parted persons so united,
 Parted do I now bear my brain, alas!   140
 From its beginning, which is in this trunk.

Thus is observed in me the counterpoise."

⊰ Canto XXIX ⊱

Geri del Bello — The Tenth Bolgia: Alchemists —
Griffolino d' Arezzo and Capocchio

The many people and the divers wounds
 These eyes of mine had so inebriated,
That they were wishful to stand still and weep;

But said Virgilius: "What dost thou still gaze at?
 Why is thy sight still riveted down there   5
 Among the mournful, mutilated shades?

Thou hast not done so at the other Bolge;
 Consider, if to count them thou believest,
 That two-and-twenty miles the valley winds,

But said Virgilius: "What dost thou still gaze at?
Why is thy sight still riveted down there
Among the mournful, mutilated shades?"

Inferno XXIX, lines 4–6

And now the moon is underneath our feet;   10
   Henceforth the time allotted us is brief,
   And more is to be seen than what thou seest."

"If thou hadst," I made answer thereupon,
   "Attended to the cause for which I looked,
   Perhaps a longer stay thou wouldst have pardoned."   15

Meanwhile my Guide departed, and behind him
   I went, already making my reply,
   And superadding: "In that cavern where

I held mine eyes with such attention fixed,
   I think a spirit of my blood laments   20
   The sin which down below there costs so much."

Then said the Master: "Be no longer broken
   Thy thought from this time forward upon him;
   Attend elsewhere, and there let him remain;

For him I saw below the little bridge,   25
   Pointing at thee, and threatening with his finger
   Fiercely, and heard him called Geri del Bello.

So wholly at that time wast thou impeded
   By him who formerly held Altaforte,
   Thou didst not look that way; so he departed."   30

"O my Conductor, his own violent death,
   Which is not yet avenged for him," I said,
   "By any who is sharer in the shame,

Made him disdainful; whence he went away,
   As I imagine, without speaking to me,   35
   And thereby made me pity him the more."

Thus did we speak as far as the first place
  Upon the crag, which the next valley shows
  Down to the bottom, if there were more light.

When we were now right over the last cloister   40
  Of Malebolge, so that its lay-brothers
  Could manifest themselves unto our sight,

Divers lamentings pierced me through and through,
  Which with compassion had their arrows barbed,
  Whereat mine ears I covered with my hands.   45

What pain would be, if from the hospitals
  Of Valdichiana, 'twixt July and September,
  And of Maremma and Sardinia

All the diseases in one moat were gathered,
  Such was it here, and such a stench came from it   50
  As from putrescent limbs is wont to issue.

We had descended on the furthest bank
  From the long crag, upon the left hand still,
  And then more vivid was my power of sight

Down tow'rds the bottom, where the ministress   55
  Of the high Lord, Justice infallible,
  Punishes forgers, which she here records.

I do not think a sadder sight to see
  Was in Ægina the whole people sick,
  (When was the air so full of pestilence,   60

The animals, down to the little worm,
  All fell, and afterwards the ancient people,
  According as the poets have affirmed,

Such a stench came from it
As from putrescent limbs is wont to issue.

Inferno XXIX, lines 50–51

Were from the seed of ants restored again)
    Than was it to behold through that dark valley   65
    The spirits languishing in divers heaps.

This on the belly, that upon the back
    One of the other lay, and others crawling
    Shifted themselves along the dismal road.

We step by step went onward without speech,   70
    Gazing upon and listening to the sick
    Who had not strength enough to lift their bodies.

I saw two sitting leaned against each other,
    As leans in heating platter against platter,
    From head to foot bespotted o'er with scabs;   75

And never saw I plied a currycomb
    By stable-boy for whom his master waits,
    Or him who keeps awake unwillingly,

As every one was plying fast the bite
    Of nails upon himself, for the great rage   80
    Of itching which no other succor had.

And the nails downward with them dragged the scab,
    In fashion as a knife the scales of bream,
    Or any other fish that has them largest.

"O thou, that with thy fingers dost dismail thee,"   85
    Began my Leader unto one of them,
    "And makest of them pincers now and then,

Tell me if any Latian is with those
    Who are herein; so may thy nails suffice thee
    To all eternity unto this work."   90

Every one was plying fast the bite
Of nails upon himself, for the great rage
Of itching which no other succor had.

Inferno XXIX, lines 79–81

"Latians are we, whom thou so wasted seest,
   Both of us here," one weeping made reply;
   "But who art thou, that questionest about us?"

And said the Guide: "One am I who descends
   Down with this living man from cliff to cliff,   95
   And I intend to show Hell unto him."

Then broken was their mutual support,
   And trembling each one turned himself to me,
   With others who had heard him by rebound.

Wholly to me did the good Master gather,   100
   Saying: "Say unto them whate'er thou wishest."
   And I began, since he would have it so:

"So may your memory not steal away
   In the first world from out the minds of men,
   But so may it survive 'neath many suns,   105

Say to me who ye are, and of what people;
   Let not your foul and loathsome punishment
   Make you afraid to show yourselves to me."

"I of Arezzo was," one made reply,
   "And Albert of Siena had me burned;   110
   But what I died for does not bring me here.

'Tis true I said to him, speaking in jest,
   That I could rise by flight into the air,
   And he who had conceit, but little wit,

Would have me show to him the art; and only   115
   Because no Dædalus I made him, made me
   Be burned by one who held him as his son.

But unto the last Bolgia of the ten,
    For alchemy, which in the world I practiced,
    Minos, who cannot err, has me condemned."   120

And to the Poet said I: "Now was ever
    So vain a people as the Sienese?
    Not for a certainty the French by far."

Whereat the other leper, who had heard me,
    Replied unto my speech: "Taking out Stricca,   125
    Who knew the art of moderate expenses,

And Niccolò, who the luxurious use
    Of cloves discovered earliest of all
    Within that garden where such seed takes root;

And taking out the band, among whom squandered   130
    Caccia d'Ascian his vineyards and vast woods,
    And where his wit the Abbagliato proffered!

But, that thou know who thus doth second thee
    Against the Sienese, make sharp thine eye
    Tow'rds me, so that my face well answer thee,   135

And thou shalt see I am Capocchio's shade,
    Who metals falsified by alchemy;
    Thou must remember, if I well descry thee,

How I a skilful ape of nature was."

❧ CANTO XXX ❧

Other Falsifiers or Forgers—Gianni Schicchi, Myrrha, Adam of Brescia,
Potiphar's Wife, and Sinon of Troy

'Twas at the time when Juno was enraged,
     For Semele, against the Theban blood,
As she already more than once had shown,

So reft of reason Athamas became,
     That, seeing his own wife with children twain   5
     Walking encumbered upon either hand,

He cried: "Spread out the nets, that I may take
     The lioness and her whelps upon the passage";
     And then extended his unpitying claws,

Seizing the first, who had the name Learchus,   10
     And whirled him round, and dashed him on a rock;
     And she, with the other burthen, drowned herself—

And at the time when fortune downward hurled
     The Trojan's arrogance, that all things dared,
     So that the king was with his kingdom crushed,   15

Hecuba sad, disconsolate, and captive,
     When lifeless she beheld Polyxena,
     And of her Polydorus on the shore

Of ocean was the dolorous one aware,
     Out of her senses like a dog she barked,   20
     So much the anguish had her mind distorted;

But not of Thebes the furies nor the Trojan
   Were ever seen in any one so cruel
   In goading beasts, and much more human members,

As I beheld two shadows pale and naked,   25
   Who, biting, in the manner ran along
   That a boar does, when from the sty turned loose.

One to Capocchio came, and by the nape
   Seized with its teeth his neck, so that in dragging
   It made his belly grate the solid bottom.   30

And the Aretine, who trembling had remained,
   Said to me: "That mad sprite is Gianni Schicchi,
   And raving goes thus harrying other people."

"O," said I to him, "so may not the other
   Set teeth on thee, let it not weary thee   35
   To tell us who it is, ere it dart hence."

And he to me: "That is the ancient ghost
   Of the nefarious Myrrha, who became
   Beyond all rightful love her father's lover.

She came to sin with him after this manner,   40
   By counterfeiting of another's form;
   As he who goeth yonder undertook,

That he might gain the lady of the herd,
   To counterfeit in himself Buoso Donati,
   Making a will and giving it due form."   45

And after the two maniacs had passed
   On whom I held mine eye, I turned it back
   To look upon the other evil-born.

"That mad sprite is Gianni Schicchi,
And raving goes thus harrying other people."

Inferno XXX, lines 32–33

"That is the ancient ghost
Of the nefarious Myrrha, who became
Beyond all rightful love her father's lover."

Inferno XXX, lines 37–39

I saw one made in fashion of a lute,
    If he had only had the groin cut off   50
    Just at the point at which a man is forked.

The heavy dropsy, that so disproportions
    The limbs with humors, which it ill concocts,
    That the face corresponds not to the belly,

Compelled him so to hold his lips apart   55
    As does the hectic, who because of thirst
    One tow'rds the chin, the other upward turns.

"O ye, who without any torment are,
    And why I know not, in the world of woe,"
    He said to us, "behold, and be attentive   60

Unto the misery of Master Adam;
    I had while living much of what I wished,
    And now, alas! a drop of water crave.

The rivulets, that from the verdant hills
    Of Cassentin descend down into Arno,   65
    Making their channels to be cold and moist,

Ever before me stand, and not in vain;
    For far more doth their image dry me up
    Than the disease which strips my face of flesh.

The rigid justice that chastizes me   70
    Draweth occasion from the place in which
    I sinned, to put the more my sighs in flight.

There is Romena, where I counterfeited
    The currency imprinted with the Baptist,
    For which I left my body burned above.   75

But if I here could see the tristful soul
    Of Guido, or Alessandro, or their brother,
    For Branda's fount I would not give the sight.

One is within already, if the raving
    Shades that are going round about speak truth;   80
    But what avails it me, whose limbs are tied?

If I were only still so light, that in
    A hundred years I could advance one inch,
    I had already started on the way,

Seeking him out among this squalid folk,   85
    Although the circuit be eleven miles,
    And be not less than half a mile across.

For them am I in such a family;
    They did induce me into coining florins,
    Which had three carats of impurity."   90

And I to him: "Who are the two poor wretches
    That smoke like unto a wet hand in winter,
    Lying there close upon thy right-hand confines?"

"I found them here," replied he, "when I rained
    Into this chasm, and since they have not turned,   95
    Nor do I think they will for evermore.

One the false woman is who accused Joseph,
    The other the false Sinon, Greek of Troy;
    From acute fever they send forth such reek."

And one of them, who felt himself annoyed   100
    At being, peradventure, named so darkly,
    Smote with the fist upon his hardened paunch.

It gave a sound, as if it were a drum;
   And Master Adam smote him in the face,
   With arm that did not seem to be less hard,   105

Saying to him: "Although be taken from me
   All motion, for my limbs that heavy are,
   I have an arm unfettered for such need."

Whereat he answer made: "When thou didst go
   Unto the fire, thou hadst it not so ready: 110
   But hadst it so and more when thou wast coining."

The dropsical: "Thou sayest true in that;
   But thou wast not so true a witness there,
   Where thou wast questioned of the truth at Troy."

"If I spake false, thou falsifiedst the coin,"   115
   Said Sinon; "and for one fault I am here,
   And thou for more than any other demon."

"Remember, perjurer, about the horse,"
   He made reply who had the swollen belly,
   "And rueful be it thee the whole world knows it."   120

"Rueful to thee the thirst be wherewith cracks
   Thy tongue," the Greek said, "and the putrid water
   That hedges so thy paunch before thine eyes."

Then the false-coiner: "So is gaping wide
   Thy mouth for speaking evil, as 'tis wont;   125
   Because if I have thirst, and humor stuff me

Thou hast the burning and the head that aches,
   And to lick up the mirror of Narcissus
   Thou wouldst not want words many to invite thee."

In listening to them was I wholly fixed,   130
    When said the Master to me: "Now just look,
    For little wants it that I quarrel with thee."

When him I heard in anger speak to me,
    I turned me round towards him with such shame
    That still it eddies through my memory.   135

And as he is who dreams of his own harm,
    Who dreaming wishes it may be a dream,
    So that he craves what is, as if it were not;

Such I became, not having power to speak,
    For to excuse myself I wished, and still   140
    Excused myself, and did not think I did it.

"Less shame doth wash away a greater fault,"
    The Master said, "than this of thine has been;
    Therefore thyself disburden of all sadness,

And make account that I am aye beside thee,   145
    If e'er it come to pass that fortune bring thee
    Where there are people in a like dispute;

For a base wish it is to wish to hear it."

⊰ CANTO XXXI ⊱

The Giants, Nimrod, Ephialtes, and Antæus—
Descent to Cocytus

One and the selfsame tongue first wounded me,
  So that it tinged the one cheek and the other,
And then held out to me the medicine;

Thus do I hear that once Achilles' spear,
  His and his father's, used to be the cause   5
  First of a sad and then a gracious boon.

We turned our backs upon the wretched valley,
  Upon the bank that girds it round about,
  Going across it without any speech.

There it was less than night, and less than day,   10
  So that my sight went little in advance;
  But I could hear the blare of a loud horn,

So loud it would have made each thunder faint,
  Which, counter to it following its way,
  Mine eyes directed wholly to one place.   15

After the dolorous discomfiture
  When Charlemagne the holy emprise lost,
  So terribly Orlando sounded not.

Short while my head turned thitherward I held
  When many lofty towers I seemed to see,   20
  Whereat I: "Master, say, what town is this?"

And he to me: "Because thou peerest forth
    Athwart the darkness at too great a distance,
    It happens that thou errest in thy fancy.

Well shalt thou see, if thou arrivest there,   25
    How much the sense deceives itself by distance;
    Therefore a little faster spur thee on."

Then tenderly he took me by the hand,
    And said: "Before we farther have advanced,
    That the reality may seem to thee   30

Less strange, know that these are not towers, but giants,
    And they are in the well, around the bank,
    From navel downward, one and all of them."

As, when the fog is vanishing away,
    Little by little doth the sight refigure   35
    Whate'er the mist that crowds the air conceals,

So, piercing through the dense and darksome air,
    More and more near approaching tow'rd the verge,
    My error fled, and fear came over me;

Because as on its circular parapets   40
    Montereggione crowns itself with towers,
    E'en thus the margin which surrounds the well

With one half of their bodies turreted
    The horrible giants, whom Jove menaces
    E'en now from out the heavens when he thunders.   45

And I of one already saw the face,
    Shoulders, and breast, and great part of the belly,
    And down along his sides both of the arms.

Certainly Nature, when she left the making
    Of animals like these, did well indeed,   50
    By taking such executors from Mars;

And if of elephants and whales she doth not
    Repent her, whosoever looketh subtly
    More just and more discreet will hold her for it;

For where the argument of intellect   55
    Is added unto evil will and power,
    No rampart can the people make against it.

His face appeared to me as long and large
    As is at Rome the pinecone of Saint Peter's,
    And in proportion were the other bones;   60

So that the margin, which an apron was
    Down from the middle, showed so much of him
    Above it, that to reach up to his hair

Three Frieslanders in vain had vaunted them;
    For I beheld thirty great palms of him   65
    Down from the place where man his mantle buckles.

"Raphael mai amech izabi almi,"
    Began to clamor the ferocious mouth,
    To which were not befitting sweeter psalms.

And unto him my Guide: "Soul idiotic,   70
    Keep to thy horn, and vent thyself with that,
    When wrath or other passion touches thee.

Search round thy neck, and thou wilt find the belt
    Which keeps it fastened, O bewildered soul,
    And see it, where it bars thy mighty breast."   75

"Soul idiotic,
Keep to thy horn, and vent thyself with that,
When wrath or other passion touches thee."

Inferno XXXI, lines 70–72

Then said to me: "He doth himself accuse;
    This one is Nimrod, by whose evil thought
    One language in the world is not still used.

Here let us leave him and not speak in vain;
    For even such to him is every language   80
    As his to others, which to none is known."

Therefore a longer journey did we make,
    Turned to the left, and a crossbow-shot oft
    We found another far more fierce and large.

In binding him, who might the master be   85
    I cannot say; but he had pinioned close
    Behind the right arm, and in front the other,

With chains, that held him so begirt about
    From the neck down, that on the part uncovered
    It wound itself as far as the fifth gyre.   90

"This proud one wished to make experiment
    Of his own power against the Supreme Jove,"
    My Leader said, "whence he has such a guerdon.

Ephialtes is his name; he showed great prowess.
    What time the giants terrified the gods;   95
    The arms he wielded never more he moves."

And I to him: "If possible, I should wish
    That of the measureless Briareus
    These eyes of mine might have experience."

Whence he replied: "Thou shalt behold Antæus   100
    Close by here, who can speak and is unbound,
    Who at the bottom of all crime shall place us.

"This proud one wished to make experiment
Of his own power against the Supreme Jove"

Inferno XXXI, lines 91–92

Much farther yon is he whom thou wouldst see,
 And he is bound, and fashioned like to this one,
 Save that he seems in aspect more ferocious." 105

There never was an earthquake of such might
 That it could shake a tower so violently,
 As Ephialtes suddenly shook himself.

Then was I more afraid of death than ever,
 For nothing more was needful than the fear, 110
 If I had not beheld the manacles.

Then we proceeded farther in advance,
 And to Antæus came, who, full five ells
 Without the head, forth issued from the cavern.

"O thou, who in the valley fortunate, 115
 Which Scipio the heir of glory made,
 When Hannibal turned back with all his hosts,

Once brought'st a thousand lions for thy prey,
 And who, hadst thou been at the mighty war
 Among thy brothers, some it seems still think 120

The sons of Earth the victory would have gained:
 Place us below, nor be disdainful of it,
 There where the cold doth lock Cocytus up.

Make us not go to Tityus nor Typhœus;
 This one can give of that which here is longed for; 125
 Therefore stoop down, and do not curl thy lip.

Still in the world can he restore thy fame;
 Because he lives, and still expects long life,
 If to itself Grace call him not untimely."

But lightly in the abyss, which swallows up
Judas with Lucifer, he put us down

Inferno XXXI, lines 142–143

So said the Master; and in haste the other   130
    His hands extended and took up my Guide—
    Hands whose great pressure Hercules once felt.

Virgilius, when he felt himself embraced,
    Said unto me: "Draw nigh, that I may take thee";
    Then of himself and me one bundle made.   135

As seems the Carisenda, to behold
    Beneath the leaning side, when goes a cloud
    Above it so that opposite it hangs;

Such did Antæus seem to me, who stood
    Watching to see him stoop, and then it was   140
    I could have wished to go some other way.

But lightly in the abyss, which swallows up
    Judas with Lucifer, he put us down;
    Nor thus bowed downward made he there delay,

But, as a mast does in a ship, uprose.   145

⊰ CANTO XXXII ⊱

The Ninth Circle: Traitors—The Frozen Lake of Cocytus—First Division, Caïna:
Traitors to Their Kindred—Camicion de' Pazzi—Second Division, Antenora:
Traitors to Their Country—Dante Questions Bocca degli Abati—Buoso da Duera

I f I had rhymes both rough and stridulous,
    As were appropriate to the dismal hole
Down upon which thrust all the other rocks,

I would press out the juice of my conception
    More fully; but because I have them not,   5
    Not without fear I bring myself to speak;

For 'tis no enterprise to take in jest,
    To sketch the bottom of all the universe,
    Nor for a tongue that cries Mamma and Babbo.

But may those Ladies help this verse of mine,   10
    Who helped Amphion in enclosing Thebes,
    That from the fact the word be not diverse.

O rabble ill-begotten above all,
    Who're in the place to speak of which is hard,
    'Twere better ye had here been sheep or goats!   15

When we were down within the darksome well,
    Beneath the giant's feet, but lower far,
    And I was scanning still the lofty wall,

I heard it said to me: "Look how thou steppest!
    Take heed thou do not trample with thy feet   20
    The heads of the tired, miserable brothers!"

Whereat I turned me round, and saw before me
    And underfoot a lake, that from the frost
    The semblance had of glass, and not of water.

So thick a veil ne'er made upon its current   25
    In wintertime Danube in Austria,
    Nor there beneath the frigid sky the Don,

As there was here; so that if Tambernich
    Had fallen upon it, or Pietrapana,
    E'en at the edge 'twould not have given a creak.   30

"Look how thou steppest!
Take heed thou do not trample with thy feet
The heads of the tired, miserable brothers!"

Inferno XXXII, lines 19–21

And as to croak the frog doth place himself
  With muzzle out of water—when is dreaming
  Of gleaning oftentimes the peasant-girl—

Livid, as far down as where shame appears,
  Were the disconsolate shades within the ice,   35
  Setting their teeth unto the note of storks.

Each one his countenance held downward bent;
  From mouth the cold, from eyes the doleful heart
  Among them witness of itself procures.

When round about me somewhat I had looked,   40
  I downward turned me, and saw two so close,
  The hair upon their heads together mingled.

"Ye who so strain your breasts together, tell me,"
  I said, "who are you"; and they bent their necks,
  And when to me their faces they had lifted,   45

Their eyes, which first were only moist within,
  Gushed o'er the eyelids, and the frost congealed
  The tears between, and locked them up again.

Clamp never bound together wood with wood
  So strongly; whereat they, like two he-goats,   50
  Butted together, so much wrath o'ercame them.

And one, who had by reason of the cold
  Lost both his ears, still with his visage downward,
  Said: "Why dost thou so mirror thyself in us?

If thou desire to know who these two are,   55
  The valley whence Bisenzio descends
  Belonged to them and to their father Albert.

They from one body came, and all Caïna
    Thou shalt search through, and shalt not find a shade
    More worthy to be fixed in gelatine;   60

Not he in whom were broken breast and shadow
    At one and the same blow by Arthur's hand;
    Focaccia not; not he who me encumbers

So with his head I see no farther forward,
    And bore the name of Sassol Mascheroni;   65
    Well knowest thou who he was, if thou art Tuscan.

And that thou put me not to further speech,
    Know that I Camicion de' Pazzi was,
    And wait Carlino to exonerate me."

Then I beheld a thousand faces, made   70
    Purple with cold; whence o'er me comes a shudder,
    And evermore will come, at frozen ponds.

And while we were advancing tow'rds the middle,
    Where everything of weight unites together,
    And I was shivering in the eternal shade,   75

Whether 'twere will, or destiny, or chance,
    I know not; but in walking 'mong the heads
    I struck my foot hard in the face of one.

Weeping he growled: "Why dost thou trample me?
    Unless thou comest to increase the vengeance   80
    of Montaperti, why dost thou molest me?"

And I: "My Master, now wait here for me,
    That I through him may issue from a doubt;
    Then thou mayst hurry me, as thou shalt wish."

The Leader stopped; and to that one I said   85
  Who was blaspheming vehemently still:
  "Who art thou, that thus reprehendest others?"

"Now who art thou, that goest through Antenora
  Smiting," replied he, "other people's cheeks,
  So that, if thou wert living, 'twere too much?"   90

"Living I am, and dear to thee it may be,"
  Was my response, "if thou demandest fame,
  That 'mid the other notes thy name I place."

And he to me: "For the reverse I long;
  Take thyself hence, and give me no more trouble;   95
  For ill thou knowest to flatter in this hollow."

Then by the scalp behind I seized upon him,
  And said: "It must needs be thou name thyself,
  Or not a hair remain upon thee here."

Whence he to me: "Though thou strip off my hair,   100
  I will not tell thee who I am, nor show thee,
  If on my head a thousand times thou fall."

I had his hair in hand already twisted,
  And more than one shock of it had pulled out,
  He barking, with his eyes held firmly down,   105

When cried another: "What doth ail thee, Bocca?
  Is't not enough to clatter with thy jaws,
  But thou must bark? what devil touches thee?"

"Now," said I, "I care not to have thee speak,
  Accursed traitor; for unto thy shame   110
  I will report of thee veracious news."

Then by the scalp behind I seized upon him,
And said: "It must needs be thou name thyself,
Or not a hair remain upon thee here."

Inferno **XXXII**, lines 97–99

"Begone," replied he, "and tell what thou wilt,
But be not silent, if thou issue hence,
Of him who had just now his tongue so prompt;

He weepeth here the silver of the French;   115
'I saw,' thus canst thou phrase it, 'him of Duera
There where the sinners stand out in the cold.'

If thou shouldst questioned be who else was there,
Thou hast beside thee him of Beccaria,
Of whom the gorget Florence slit asunder;   120

Gianni del Soldanier, I think, may be
Yonder with Ganellon, and Tebaldello
Who oped Faenza when the people slep."

Already we had gone away from him,
When I beheld two frozen in one hole,   125
So that one head a hood was to the other;

And even as bread through hunger is devoured,
The uppermost on the other set his teeth,
There where the brain is to the nape united.

Not in another fashion Tydeus gnawed   130
The temples of Menalippus in disdain,
Than that one did the skull and the other things.

"O thou, who showest by such bestial sign
Thy hatred against him whom thou art eating,
Tell me the wherefore," said I, "with this compact,   135

That if thou rightfully of him complain,
In knowing who ye are, and his transgression,
I in the world above repay thee for it,

If that wherewith I speak be not dried up."

The uppermost on the other set his teeth,
There where the brain is to the nape united.

Inferno **XXXII**, lines 128–129

⊰ Canto XXXIII ⊱

Count Ugolino and the Archbishop Ruggieri—The Death of Count Ugolino's Sons—
Third Division of the Ninth Circle, Ptolomæa: Traitors to Their Friends—
Friar Alberigo, Branco d' Oria

His mouth uplifted from his grim repast,
 That sinner, wiping it upon the hair
Of the same head that he behind had wasted.

Then he began: "Thou wilt that I renew
 The desperate grief, which wrings my heart already 5
 To think of only, ere I speak of it;

But if my words be seed that may bear fruit
 Of infamy to the traitor whom I gnaw,
 Speaking and weeping shalt thou see together.

I know not who thou art, nor by what mode 10
 Thou hast come down here; but a Florentine
 Thou seemest to me truly, when I hear thee.

Thou hast to know I was Count Ugolino,
 And this one was Ruggieri the Archbishop;
 Now I will tell thee why I am such a neighbor. 15

That, by effect of his malicious thoughts,
 Trusting in him I was made prisoner,
 And after put to death, I need not say;

But ne'ertheless what thou canst not have heard,
 That is to say, how cruel was my death, 20
 Hear shalt thou, and shalt know if he has wronged me.

A narrow perforation in the mew,
    Which bears because of me the title of Famine,
    And in which others still must be locked up,

Had shown me through its opening many moons   25
    Already, when I dreamed the evil dream
    Which of the future rent for me the veil.

This one appeared to me as lord and master,
    Hunting the wolf and whelps upon the mountain
    For which the Pisans cannot Lucca see.   30

With sleuth-hounds gaunt, and eager, and well trained,
    Gualandi with Sismondi and Lanfianchi
    He had sent out before him to the front.

After brief course seemed unto me forespent
    The father and the sons, and with sharp tushes   35
    It seemed to me I saw their flanks ripped open.

When I before the morrow was awake,
    Moaning amid their sleep I heard my sons
    Who with me were, and asking after bread.

Cruel indeed art thou, if yet thou grieve not,   40
    Thinking of what my heart foreboded me,
    And weep'st thou not, what art thou wont to weep at?

They were awake now, and the hour drew nigh
    At which our food used to be brought to us,
    And through his dream was each one apprehensive;   45

And I heard locking up the under door
    Of the horrible tower; whereat without a word
    I gazed into the faces of my sons.

"I calmed me then, not to make them more sad."

Inferno XXXIII, line 64

I wept not, I within so turned to stone;
    They wept; and darling little Anselm mine   50
    Said: 'Thou dost gaze so, father, what doth ail thee?'

Still not a tear I shed, nor answer made
    All of that day, nor yet the night thereafter,
    Until another sun rose on the world.

As now a little glimmer made its way   55
    Into the dolorous prison, and I saw
    Upon four faces my own very aspect,

Both of my hands in agony I bit;
    And, thinking that I did it from desire
    Of eating, on a sudden they uprose,   60

And said they: 'Father, much less pain 'twill give us
    If thou do eat of us; thyself didst clothe us
    With this poor flesh, and do thou strip it off.'

I calmed me then, not to make them more sad.
    That day we all were silent, and the next.   65
    Ah! obdurate earth, wherefore didst thou not open?

When we had come unto the fourth day, Gaddo
    Threw himself down outstretched before my feet,
    Saying, 'My father, why dost thou not help me?'

And there he died; and, as thou seest me,   70
    I saw the three fall, one by one, between
    The fifth day and the sixth; whence I betook me,

Already blind, to groping over each,
    And three days called them after they were dead;
    Then hunger did what sorrow could not do."   75

"When we had come unto the fourth day, Gaddo
Threw himself down outstretched before my feet,
Saying, 'My father, why dost thou not help me?' "

Inferno XXXIII, lines 67–69

"Then hunger did what sorrow could not do."

Inferno XXXIII, line 75

When he had said this, with his eyes distorted,
  The wretched skull resumed he with his teeth,
  Which, as a dog's, upon the bone were strong.

Ah! Pisa, thou opprobrium of the people
  Of the fair land there where the *Sì* doth sound,   80
  Since slow to punish thee thy neighbors are,

Let the Capraia and Gorgona move,
  And make a hedge across the mouth of Arno
  That every person in thee it may drown!

For if Count Ugolino had the fame   85
  Of having in thy castles thee betrayed,
  Thou shouldst not on such cross have put his sons.

Guiltless of any crime, thou modern Thebes!
  Their youth made Uguccione and Brigata,
  And the other two my song doth name above!   90

We passed still farther onward, where the ice
  Another people ruggedly enswathes,
  Not downward turned, but all of them reversed.

Weeping itself there does not let them weep,
  And grief that finds a barrier in the eyes   95
  Turns itself inward to increase the anguish;

Because the earliest tears a cluster form,
  And, in the manner of a crystal visor,
  Fill all the cup beneath the eyebrow full.

And notwithstanding that, as in a callus,   100
  Because of cold all sensibility
  Its station had abandoned in my face,

Still it appeared to me I felt some wind;
   Whence I: "My Master, who sets this in motion?
   Is not below here every vapor quenched?"   105

Whence he to me: "Full soon shalt thou be where
   Thine eye shall answer make to thee of this,
   Seeing the cause which raineth down the blast."

And one of the wretches of the frozen crust
   Cried out to us: "O souls so merciless   110
   That the last post is given unto you,

Lift from mine eyes the rigid veils, that I
   May vent the sorrow which impregns my heart
   A little, e'er the weeping recongeal."

Whence I to him: "If thou wouldst have me help thee 115
   Say who thou wast; and if I free thee not,
   May I go to the bottom of the ice."

Then he replied: "I am Friar Alberigo;
   He am I of the fruit of the bad garden,
   Who here a date am getting for my fig."   120

"O," said I to him, "now art thou, too, dead?"
   And he to me: "How may my body fare
   Up in the world, no knowledge I possess.

Such an advantage has this Ptolomæa,
   That oftentimes the soul descendeth here   125
   Sooner than Atropos in motion sets it.

And, that thou mayest more willingly remove
   From off my countenance these glassy tears,
   Know that as soon as any soul betrays

As I have done, his body by a demon   130
    Is taken from him, who thereafter rules it,
    Until his time has wholly been revolved.

Itself down rushes into such a cistern;
    And still perchance above appears the body
    Of yonder shade, that winters here behind me.   135

This thou shouldst know, if thou hast just come down;
    It is Ser Branca d' Oria, and many years
    Have passed away since he was thus locked up."

"I think," said I to him, "thou dost deceive me;
    For Branca d' Oria is not dead as yet,   140
    And eats, and drinks, and sleeps, and puts on clothes."

"In moat above," said he, "of Malebranche,
    There where is boiling the tenacious pitch,
    As yet had Michel Zanche not arrived,

When this one left a devil in his stead   145
    In his own body and one near of kin,
    Who made together with him the betrayal.

But hitherward stretch out thy hand forthwith,
    Open mine eyes"—and open them I did not,
    And to be rude to him was courtesy.   150

Ah, Genoese! ye men at variance
    With every virtue, full of every vice
    Wherefore are ye not scattered from the world?

For with the vilest spirit of Romagna
    I found of you one such, who for his deeds   155
    In soul already in Cocytus bathes,

And still above in body seems alive!

⊰ CANTO XXXIV ⊱

Fourth Division of the Ninth Circle, the Judecca:
Traitors to Their Lords and Benefactors—
Lucifer, Judas Iscariot, Brutus, and Cassius—
The Chasm of Lethe—The Ascent

" '*Vexilla Regis prodeunt Inferni*'
   Towards us; therefore look in front of thee,"
My Master said, "if thou discernest him."

As, when there breathes a heavy fog, or when
   Our hemisphere is darkening into night,   5
   Appears far off a mill the wind is turning,

Methought that such a building then I saw;
   And, for the wind, I drew myself behind
   My Guide, because there was no other shelter.

Now was I, and with fear in verse I put it,   10
   There where the shades were wholly covered up,
   And glimmered through like unto straws in glass.

Some prone are lying, others stand erect,
   This with the head, and that one with the soles;
   Another, bow-like, face to feet inverts.   15

When in advance so far we had proceeded,
   That it my Master pleased to show to me
   The creature who once had the beauteous semblance,

He from before me moved and made me stop,
   Saying: "Behold Dis, and behold the place   20
   Where thou with fortitude must arm thyself."

"Behold Dis, and behold the place
Where thou with fortitude must arm thyself."

Inferno XXXIV, lines 20–21

How frozen I became and powerless then,
    Ask it not, Reader, for I write it not,
    Because all language would be insufficient.

I did not die, and I alive remained not;   25
    Think for thyself now, hast thou aught of wit,
    What I became, being of both deprived.

The Emperor of the kingdom dolorous
    From his mid-breast forth issued from the ice;
    And better with a giant I compare   30

Than do the giants with those arms of his;
    Consider now how great must be that whole,
    Which unto such a part conforms itself.

Were he as fair once, as he now is foul,
    And lifted up his brow against his Maker,   35
    Well may proceed from him all tribulation.

O, what a marvel it appeared to me,
    When I beheld three faces on his head!
    The one in front, and that vermilion was;

Two were the others, that were joined with this   40
    Above the middle part of either shoulder,
    And they were joined together at the crest;

And the right-hand one seemed 'twixt white and yellow;
    The left was such to look upon as those
    Who come from where the Nile falls valley-ward.   45

Underneath each came forth two mighty wings,
    Such as befitting were so great a bird;
    Sails of the sea I never saw so large.

No feathers had they, but as of a bat
   Their fashion was; and he was waving them,   50
   So that three winds proceeded forth therefrom.

Thereby Cocytus wholly was congealed.
   With six eyes did he weep, and down three chins
   Trickled the teardrops and the bloody drivel.

At every mouth he with his teeth was crunching   55
   A sinner, in the manner of a brake,
   So that he three of them tormented thus.

To him in front the biting was as naught
   Unto the clawing, for sometimes the spine
   Utterly stripped of all the skin remained.   60

"That soul up there which has the greatest pain,"
   The Master said, "is Judas Iscariot;
   With head inside, he plies his legs without.

Of the two others, who head downward are,
   The one who hangs from the black jowl is Brutus;   65
   See how he writhes himself, and speaks no word.

And the other, who so stalwart seems, is Cassius.
   But night is reascending, and 'tis time
   That we depart, for we have seen the whole."

As seemed him good, I clasped him round the neck,   70
   And he the vantage seized of time and place,
   And when the wings were opened wide apart,

He laid fast hold upon the shaggy sides;
   From fell to fell descended downward then
   Between the thick hair and the frozen crust.   75

When we were come to where the thigh revolves
Exactly on the thickness of the haunch,
The Guide, with labor and with hard-drawn breath,

Turned round his head where he had had his legs,
And grappled to the hair, as one who mounts,   80
So that to Hell I thought we were returning.

"Keep fast thy hold, for by such stairs as these,"
The Master said, panting as one fatigued,
"Must we perforce depart from so much evil."

Then through the opening of a rock he issued,   85
And down upon the margin seated me;
Then tow'rds me he outstretched his wary step.

I lifted up mine eyes and thought to see
Lucifer in the same way I had left him;
And I beheld him upward hold his legs.   90

And if I then became disquieted,
Let stolid people think who do not see
What the point is beyond which I had passed.

"Rise up," the Master said, "upon thy feet;
The way is long, and difficult the road,   95
And now the sun to middle-tierce returns."

It was not any palace corridor
There where we were, but dungeon natural,
With floor uneven and unease of light.

"Ere from the abyss I tear myself away,   100
My Master," said I when I had arisen,
"To draw me from an error speak a little;

Where is the ice? and how is this one fixed
   Thus upside down? and how in such short time
   From eve to morn has the sun made his transit?"   105

And he to me: "Thou still imaginest
   Thou art beyond the center, where I grasped
   The hair of the fell worm, who mines the world.

That side thou wast, so long as I descended;
   When round I turned me, thou didst pass the point   110
   To which things heavy draw from every side,

And now beneath the hemisphere art come
   Opposite that which overhangs the vast
   Dry-land, and 'neath whose cope was put to death

The Man who without sin was born and lived.   115
   Thou hast thy feet upon the little sphere
   Which makes the other face of the Judecca.

Here it is morn when it is evening there;
   And he who with his hair a stairway made us
   Still fixed remaineth as he was before.   120

Upon this side he fell down out of heaven;
   And all the land, that whilom here emerged,
   For fear of him made of the sea a veil,

And came to our hemisphere; and peradventure
   To flee from him, what on this side appears   125
   Left the place vacant here, and back recoiled."

A place there is below, from Beelzebub
   As far receding as the tomb extends,
   Which not by sight is known, but by the sound

The Guide and I into that hidden road
Now entered, to return to the bright world

Inferno XXXIV, lines 133–134

Thence we came forth to rebehold the stars.

Inferno XXXIV, line 139

Of a small rivulet, that there descendeth   130
   Through chasm within the stone, which it has gnawed
   With course that winds about and slightly falls.

The Guide and I into that hidden road
   Now entered, to return to the bright world;
   And without care of having any rest   135

We mounted up, he first and I the second,
   Till I beheld through a round aperture
   Some of the beauteous things that Heaven doth bear;

Thence we came forth to rebehold the stars.

⊰ CANTO I ⊱

*The Shores of Purgatory — The Four Stars —
Cato of Utica — The Rush*

To run o'er better waters hoists its sail
   The little vessel of my genius now,
That leaves behind itself a sea so cruel;

And of that second kingdom will I sing
   Wherein the human spirit doth purge itself,   5
   And to ascend to heaven becometh worthy.

But let dead Poesy here rise again,
   O holy Muses, since that I am yours,
   And here Calliope somewhat ascend,

My song accompanying with that sound,   10
   Of which the miserable magpies felt
   The blow so great, that they despaired of pardon.

Sweet color of the oriental sapphire,
   That was upgathered in the cloudless aspect
   Of the pure air, as far as the first circle,   15

Unto mine eyes did recommence delight
   Soon as I issued forth from the dead air,
   Which had with sadness filled mine eyes and breast.

The beauteous planet, that to love incites,
   Was making all the orient to laugh,   20
   Veiling the Fishes that were in her escort.

The beauteous planet, that to love incites,
Was making all the orient to laugh,
Veiling the Fishes that were in her escort.

Purgatorio I, lines 19–21

To the right hand I turned, and fixed my mind
   Upon the other pole, and saw four stars
   Ne'er seen before save by the primal people.

Rejoicing in their flamelets seemed the heaven.   25
   O thou septentrional and widowed site,
   Because thou art deprived of seeing these!

When from regarding them I had withdrawn,
   Turning a little to the other pole,
   There where the Wain had disappeared already,   30

I saw beside me an old man alone,
   Worthy of so much reverence in his look,
   That more owes not to father any son.

A long beard and with white hair intermingled
   He wore, in semblance like unto the tresses,   35
   Of which a double list fell on his breast.

The rays of the four consecrated stars
   Did so adorn his countenance with light,
   That him I saw as were the sun before him.

"Who are you? ye who, counter the blind river,   40
   Have fled away from the eternal prison?"
   Moving those venerable plumes, he said:

"Who guided you? or who has been your lamp
   In issuing forth out of the night profound,
   That ever black makes the infernal valley?   45

The laws of the abyss, are they thus broken?
   Or is there changed in heaven some council new,
   That being damned ye come unto my crags?"

I saw beside me an old man alone,
Worthy of so much reverence in his look,
That more owes not to father any son.

Purgatorio I, lines 31–33

Then did my Leader lay his grasp upon me,
>   And with his words, and with his hands and signs,   50
>   Reverent he made in me my knees and brow;

Then answered him: "I came not of myself;
>   A Lady from Heaven descended, at whose prayers
>   I aided this one with my company.

But since it is thy will more be unfolded   55
>   Of our condition, how it truly is,
>   Mine cannot be that this should be denied thee.

This one has never his last evening seen,
>   But by his folly was so near to it
>   That very little time was there to turn.   60

As I have said, I unto him was sent
>   To rescue him, and other way was none
>   Than this to which I have myself betaken.

I've shown him all the people of perdition,
>   And now those spirits I intend to show   65
>   Who purge themselves beneath thy guardianship.

How I have brought him would be long to tell thee.
>   Virtue descendeth from on high that aids me
>   To lead him to behold thee and to hear thee.

Now may it please thee to vouchsafe his coming;   70
>   He seeketh Liberty, which is so dear,
>   As knoweth he who life for her refuses.

Thou know'st it; since, for her, to thee not bitter
>   Was death in Utica, where thou didst leave
>   The vesture, that will shine so, the great day.   75

By us the eternal edicts are not broken;
　　Since this one lives, and Minos binds not me;
　　But of that circle I, where are the chaste

Eyes of thy Marcia, who in looks still prays thee,
　　O holy breast, to hold her as thine own;　　　80
　　For her love, then, incline thyself to us.

Permit us through thy sevenfold realm to go;
　　I will take back this grace from thee to her,
　　If to be mentioned there below thou deignest."

"Marcia so pleasing was unto mine eyes　　　85
　　While I was on the other side," then said he,
　　"That every grace she wished of me I granted;

Now that she dwells beyond the evil river,
　　She can no longer move me, by that law
　　Which, when I issued forth from there, was made.　　90

But if a Lady of Heaven do move and rule thee,
　　As thou dost say, no flattery is needful;
　　Let it suffice thee that for her thou ask me.

Go, then, and see thou gird this one about
　　With a smooth rush, and that thou wash his face,　　95
　　So that thou cleanse away all stain therefrom,

For 'twere not fitting that the eye o'ercast
　　By any mist should go before the first
　　Angel, who is of those of Paradise.

This little island round about its base　　　100
　　Below there, yonder, where the billow beats it,
　　Doth rushes bear upon its washy ooze;

No other plant that putteth forth the leaf,
   Or that doth indurate, can there have life,
   Because it yieldeth not unto the shocks.   105

Thereafter be not this way your return;
   The sun, which now is rising, will direct you
   To take the mount by easier ascent."

With this he vanished; and I raised me up
   Without a word, and wholly drew myself   110
   Unto my Guide, and turned mine eyes to him.

And he began: "Son, follow thou my steps;
   Let us turn back, for on this side declines
   The plain unto its lower boundaries."

The dawn was vanquishing the matin hour   115
   Which fled before it, so that from afar
   I recognized the trembling of the sea.

Along the solitary plain we went
   As one who unto the lost road returns,
   And till he finds it seems to go in vain.   120

As soon as we were come to where the dew
   Fights with the sun, and, being in a part
   Where shadow falls, little evaporates,

Both of his hands upon the grass outspread
   In gentle manner did my Master place;   125
   Whence I, who of his action was aware,

Extended unto him my tearful cheeks;
   There did he make in me uncovered wholly
   That hue which Hell had covered up in me.

Then came we down upon the desert shore   130
    Which never yet saw navigate its waters
    Any that afterward had known return.

There he begirt me as the other pleased;
    O marvelous! for even as he culled
    The humble plant, such it sprang up again   135

Suddenly there where he uprooted it.

⊰ Canto II ⊱

The Celestial Pilot — Casella — The Departure

Already had the sun the horizon reached
    Whose circle of meridian covers o'er
Jerusalem with its most lofty point,

And night that opposite to him revolves
    Was issuing forth from Ganges with the Scales   5
    That fall from out her hand when she exceedeth;

So that the white and the vermilion cheeks
    Of beautiful Aurora, where I was,
    By too great age were changing into orange.

We still were on the border of the sea,   10
    Like people who are thinking of their road,
    Who go in heart, and with the body stay;

And lo! as when, upon the approach of morning,
    Through the gross vapors Mars grows fiery red
    Down in the West upon the ocean floor,   15

Appeared to me—may I again behold it!—
  A light along the sea so swiftly coming,
  Its motion by no flight of wing is equaled;

From which when I a little had withdrawn
  Mine eyes, that I might question my Conductor,   20
  Again I saw it brighter grown and larger.

Then on each side of it appeared to me
  I knew not what of white, and underneath it
  Little by little there came forth another.

My Master yet had uttered not a word   25
  While the first whiteness into wings unfolded;
  But when he clearly recognized the pilot,

He cried: "Make haste, make haste to bow the knee!
  Behold the Angel of God! fold thou thy hands!
  Henceforward shalt thou see such officers!   30

See how he scorneth human arguments,
  So that nor oar he wants, nor other sail
  Than his own wings, between so distant shores.

See how he holds them pointed up to heaven,
  Fanning the air with the eternal pinions,   35
  That do not moult themselves like mortal hair!"

Then as still nearer and more near us came
  The Bird Divine, more radiant he appeared,
  So that nearby the eye could not endure him,

But down I cast it; and he came to shore   40
  With a small vessel, very swift and light,
  So that the water swallowed naught thereof.

But when he clearly recognized the pilot,
He cried: "Make haste, make haste to bow the knee!
Behold the Angel of God!"

Purgatorio II, lines 27–29

Upon the stern stood the Celestial Pilot;
    Beatitude seemed written in his face,
    And more than a hundred spirits sat within.   45

"In exitu Israel de Ægypto!"
    They chanted all together in one voice,
    With whatso in that psalm is after written.

Then made he sign of holy rood upon them,
    Whereat all cast themselves upon the shore,   50
    And he departed swiftly as he came.

The throng which still remained there unfamiliar
    Seemed with the place, all round about them gazing,
    As one who in new matters makes essay.

On every side was darting forth the day   55
    The sun, who had with his resplendent shafts
    From the mid-heaven chased forth the Capricorn,

When the new people lifted up their faces
    Towards us, saying to us: "If ye know,
    Show us the way to go unto the mountain."   60

And answer made Virgilius: "Ye believe
    Perchance that we have knowledge of this place,
    But we are strangers even as yourselves.

Just now we came, a little while before you,
    Another way, which was so rough and steep,   65
    That mounting will henceforth seem sport to us."

The souls who had, from seeing me draw breath,
    Become aware that I was still alive,
    Pallid in their astonishment became;

Beatitude seemed written in his face

Purgatorio II, line 44

And as to messenger who bears the olive   70
    The people throng to listen to the news,
    And no one shows himself afraid of crowding,

So at the sight of me stood motionless
    Those fortunate spirits, all of them, as if
    Oblivious to go and make them fair.   75

One from among them saw I coming forward,
    As to embrace me, with such great affection,
    That it incited me to do the like.

O empty shadows, save in aspect only!
    Three times behind it did I clasp my hands,   80
    As oft returned with them to my own breast!

I think with wonder I depicted me;
    Whereat the shadow smiled and backward drew;
    And I, pursuing it, pressed farther forward.

Gently it said that I should stay my steps;   85
    Then knew I who it was, and I entreated
    That it would stop awhile to speak with me.

It made reply to me: "Even as I loved thee
    In mortal body, so I love thee free;
    Therefore I stop; but wherefore goest thou?"   90

"My own Casella! to return once more
    There where I am, I make this journey," said I;
    "But how from thee has so much time be taken?"

And he to me: "No outrage has been done me,
    If he who takes both when and whom he pleases   95
    Has many times denied to me this passage,

For of a righteous will his own is made.
    He, sooth to say, for three months past has taken
    Whoever wished to enter with all peace;

Whence I, who now had turned unto that shore   100
    Where salt the waters of the Tiber grow,
    Benignantly by him have been received.

Unto that outlet now his wing is pointed,
    Because for evermore assemble there
    Those who tow'rds Acheron do not descend."   105

And I: "If some new law take not from thee
    Memory or practice of the song of love,
    Which used to quiet in me all my longings,

Thee may it please to comfort therewithal
    Somewhat this soul of mine, that with its body   110
    Hitherward coming is so much distressed."

"Love, that within my mind discourses with me,"
    Forthwith began he so melodiously,
    The melody within me still is sounding.

My Master, and myself, and all that people   115
    Which with him were, appeared as satisfied
    As if naught else might touch the mind of any.

We all of us were moveless and attentive
    Unto his notes; and lo! the grave old man,
    Exclaiming: "What is this, ye laggard spirits?   120

What negligence, what standing still is this?
    Run to the mountain to strip off the slough,
    That lets not God be manifest to you."

Even as when, collecting grain or tares,
    The doves, together at their pasture met,   125
    Quiet, nor showing their accustomed pride,

If aught appear of which they are afraid,
    Upon a sudden leave their food alone,
    Because they are assailed by greater care;

So that fresh company did I behold   130
    The song relinquish, and go tow'rds the hill,
    As one who goes, and knows not whitherward;

Nor was our own departure less in haste.

⇥ CANTO III ⇤

Discourse on the Limits of Reason—The Foot of the Mountain—
Those Who Died in Contumacy of Holy Church—Manfredi

Inasmuch as the instantaneous flight
    Had scattered them asunder o'er the plain,
Turned to the mountain whither reason spurs us,

I pressed me close unto my faithful comrade,
    And how without him had I kept my course?   5
    Who would have led me up along the mountain?

He seemed to me within himself remorseful;
    O noble conscience, and without a stain,
    How sharp a sting is trivial fault to thee!

After his feet had laid aside the haste   10
    Which mars the dignity of every act,
    My mind, that hitherto had been restrained,

Let loose its faculties as if delighted,
    And I my sight directed to the hill
    That highest tow'rds the heaven uplifts itself.   15

The sun, that in our rear was flaming red,
    Was broken in front of me into the figure
    Which had in me the stoppage of its rays;

Unto one side I turned me, with the fear
    Of being left alone, when I beheld   20
    Only in front of me the ground obscured.

"Why dost thou still mistrust?" my Comforter
    Began to say to me turned wholly round;
    "Dost thou not think me with thee, and that I guide thee?

'Tis evening there already where is buried   25
    The body within which I cast a shadow;
    'Tis from Brundusium ta'en, and Naples has it.

Now if in front of me no shadow fall,
    Marvel not at it more than at the heavens,
    Because one ray impedeth not another   30

To suffer torments, both of cold and heat,
    Bodies like this that Power provides, which wills
    That how it works be not unveiled to us.

Insane is he who hopeth that our reason
    Can traverse the illimitable way,   35
    Which the one Substance in three Persons follows!

Mortals, remain contented at the *Quia*;
    For if ye had been able to see all,
    No need there were for Mary to give birth;

And ye have seen desiring without fruit,   40
    Those whose desire would have been quieted,
    Which evermore is given them for a grief.

I speak of Aristotle and of Plato,
    And many others"—and here bowed his head,
    And more he said not, and remained disturbed.   45

We came meanwhile unto the mountain's foot;
    There so precipitate we found the rock,
    That nimble legs would there have been in vain.

'Twixt Lerici and Turbìa, the most desert,
    The most secluded pathway is a stair   50
    Easy and open, if compared with that.

"Who knoweth now upon which hand the hill
    Slopes down," my Master said, his footsteps staying,
    "So that who goeth without wings may mount?"

And while he held his eyes upon the ground   55
    Examining the nature of the path,
    And I was looking up around the rock,

On the left hand appeared to me a throng
    Of souls, that moved their feet in our direction,
    And did not seem to move, they came so slowly.   60

"Lift up thine eyes," I to the Master said;
    "Behold, on this side, who will give us counsel,
    If thou of thine own self can have it not."

Then he looked at me, and with frank expression
    Replied: "Let us go there, for they come slowly,   65
    And thou be steadfast in thy hope, sweet son."

On the left hand appeared to me a throng
Of souls, that moved their feet in our direction,
And did not seem to move

Purgatorio III, lines 58–60

Still was that people as far off from us,
    After a thousand steps of ours I say,
    As a good thrower with his hand would reach,

When they all crowded unto the hard masses   70
    Of the high bank, and motionless stood and close,
    As he stands still to look who goes in doubt.

"O happy dead! O spirits elect already!"
    Virgilius made beginning, "by that peace
    Which I believe is waiting for you all,   75

Tell us upon what side the mountain slopes,
    So that the going up be possible,
    For to lose time irks him most who most knows."

As sheep come issuing forth from out the fold
    By ones and twos and threes, and the others stand   80
    Timidly, holding down their eyes and nostrils,

And what the foremost does the others do,
    Huddling themselves against her, if she stop,
    Simple and quiet and the wherefore know not;

So moving to approach us thereupon   85
    I saw the leader of that fortunate flock,
    Modest in face and dignified in gait.

As soon as those in the advance saw broken
    The light upon the ground at my right side,
    So that from me the shadow reached the rock,   90

They stopped, and backward drew themselves somewhat;
    And all the others, who came after them,
    Not knowing why nor wherefore, did the same.

"Without your asking, I confess to you
 This is a human body which you see,   95
 Whereby the sunshine on the ground is cleft.

Marvel ye not thereat, but be persuaded
 That not without a power which comes from Heaven
 Doth he endeavor to surmount this wall."

The Master thus; and said those worthy people: 100
 "Return ye then, and enter in before us,"
 Making a signal with the back o' the hand

And one of them began: "Whoe'er thou art,
 Thus going turn thine eyes, consider well
 If e'er thou saw me in the other world."   105

I turned me tow'rds him, and looked at him closely;
 Blond was he, beautiful, and of noble aspect,
 But one of his eyebrows had a blow divided.

When with humility I had disclaimed
 E'er having seen him, "Now behold!" he said, 110
 And showed me high upon his breast a wound.

Then said he with a smile: "I am Manfredi,
 The grandson of the Empress Costanza;
 Therefore, when thou returnest, I beseech thee

Go to my daughter beautiful, the mother   115
 Of Sicily's honor and of Aragon's,
 And the truth tell her, if aught else be told.

After I had my body lacerated
 By these two mortal stabs, I gave myself
 Weeping to Him, who willingly doth pardon. 120

Horrible my iniquities had been;
    But Infinite Goodness hath such ample arms,
    That it receives whatever turns to it.

Had but Cosenza's pastor, who in chase
    Of me was sent by Clement at that time,   125
    In God read understandingly this page,

The bones of my dead body still would be
    At the bridge-head, near unto Benevento,
    Under the safeguard of the heavy cairn.

Now the rain bathes and moveth them the wind,   130
    Beyond the realm, almost beside the Verde,
    Where he transported them with tapers quenched.

By malison of theirs is not so lost
    Eternal Love, that it cannot return,
    So long as hope has anything of green.   135

True is it, who in contumacy dies
    Of Holy Church, though penitent at last,
    Must wait upon the outside this bank

Thirty times told the time that he has been
    In his presumption, unless such decree   140
    Shorter by means of righteous prayers become.

See now if thou hast power to make me happy,
    By making known unto my good Costanza
    How thou hast seen me, and this ban beside,

For those on earth can much advance us here."   145

⊰ Canto IV ⊱

Farther Ascent—Nature of the Mountain—
The Negligent, Who Postponed Repentance Till the Last Hour—Belacqua

Whenever by delight or else by pain,
　　That seizes any faculty of ours,
Wholly to that the soul collects itself,

It seemeth that no other power it heeds;
　　And this against that error is which thinks   5
　　One soul above another kindles in us.

And hence, whenever aught is heard or seen
　　Which keeps the soul intently bent upon it,
　　Time passes on, and we perceive it not,

Because one faculty is that which listens,   10
　　And other that which the soul keeps entire;
　　This is as if in bonds, and that is free.

Of this I had experience positive
　　In hearing and in gazing at that spirit;
　　For fifty full degrees uprisen was   15

The sun, and I had not perceived it, when
　　We came to where those souls with one accord
　　Cried out unto us: "Here is what you ask."

A greater opening ofttimes hedges up
　　With but a little forkful of his thorns   20
　　The villager, what time the grape imbrowns,

Than was the passageway through which ascended
　　Only my Leader and myself behind him,
　　After that company departed from us.

One climbs Sanleo and descends in Noli,   25
    And mounts the summit of Bismantova,
    With feet alone; but here one needs must fly;

With the swift pinions and the plumes I say
    Of great desire, conducted after him
    Who gave me hope, and made a light for me.   30

We mounted upward through the rifted rock,
    And on each side the border pressed upon us,
    And feet and hands the ground beneath required.

When we were come upon the upper rim
    Of the high bank, out on the open slope,   35
    "My Master," said I, "what way shall we take?"

And he to me: "No step of thine descend;
    Still up the mount behind me win thy way,
    Till some sage escort shall appear to us."

The summit was so high it vanquished sight,   40
    And the hillside precipitous far more
    Than line from middle quadrant to the center.

Spent with fatigue was I, when I began:
    "O my sweet Father! turn thee and behold
    How I remain alone, unless thou stay!"   45

"O son," he said, "up yonder drag thyself,"
    Pointing me to a terrace somewhat higher,
    Which on that side encircles all the hill.

These words of his so spurred me on, that I
    Strained every nerve, behind him scrambling up,   50
    Until the circle was beneath my feet.

We mounted upward through the rifted rock,
And on each side the border pressed upon us

Purgatorio IV, lines 31–32

Thereon ourselves we seated both of us
 Turned to the East, from which we had ascended,
 For all men are delighted to look back.

To the low shores mine eyes I first directed,   55
 Then to the sun uplifted them, and wondered
 That on the left hand we were smitten by it.

The Poet well perceived that I was wholly
 Bewildered at the chariot of the light,
 Where 'twixt us and the Aquilon it entered.   60

Whereon he said to me: "If Castor and Pollux
 Were in the company of yonder mirror,
 That up and down conducteth with its light,

Thou wouldst behold the zodiac's jagged wheel
 Revolving still more near unto the Bears,   65
 Unless it swerved aside from its old track.

How that may be wouldst thou have power to think,
 Collected in thyself, imagine Zion
 Together with this mount on earth to stand,

So that they both one sole horizon have,   70
 And hemispheres diverse; whereby the road
 Which Phaeton, alas! knew not to drive,

Thou'lt see how of necessity must pass
 This on one side, when that upon the other,
 If thine intelligence right clearly heed."   75

"Truly, my Master," said I, "never yet
 Saw I so clearly as I now discern,
 There where my wit appeared incompetent,

That the mid-circle of supernal motion,
    Which in some art is the Equator called,   80
    And aye remains between the Sun and Winter,

For reason which thou sayest, departeth hence
    Tow'rds the Septentrion, what time the Hebrews
    Beheld it tow'rds the region of the heat.

But, if it pleaseth thee, I fain would learn   85
    How far we have to go; for the hill rises
    Higher than eyes of mine have power to rise."

And he to me: "This mount is such, that ever
    At the beginning down below 'tis tiresome,
    And aye the more one climbs, the less it hurts.   90

Therefore, when it shall seem so pleasant to thee,
    That going up shall be to thee as easy
    As going down the current in a boat,

Then at this pathway's ending thou wilt be;
    There to repose thy panting breath expect;   95
    No more I answer; and this I know for true."

And as he finished uttering these words,
    A voice close by us sounded: "Peradventure
    Thou wilt have need of sitting down ere that."

At sound thereof each one of us turned round,   100
    And saw upon the left hand a great rock,
    Which neither I nor he before had noticed.

Thither we drew; and there were persons there
    Who in the shadow stood behind the rock,
    As one through indolence is wont to stand.   105

Thither we drew; and there were persons there
Who in the shadow stood behind the rock,
As one through indolence is wont to stand.

Purgatorio IV, lines 103–105

And one of them, who seemed to me fatigued,
　　Was sitting down, and both his knees embraced,
　　Holding his face low down between them bowed.

"O my sweet Lord," I said, "do turn thine eye
　　On him who shows himself more negligent　　110
　　Then even Sloth herself his sister were."

Then he turned round to us, and he gave heed,
　　Just lifting up his eyes above his thigh,
　　And said: "Now go thou up, for thou art valiant."

Then knew I who he was; and the distress,　　115
　　That still a little did my breathing quicken,
　　My going to him hindered not; and after

I came to him he hardly raised his head,
　　Saying: "Hast thou seen clearly how the sun
　　O'er thy left shoulder drives his chariot?"　　120

His sluggish attitude and his curt words
　　A little unto laughter moved my lips;
　　Then I began: "Belacqua, I grieve not

For thee henceforth; but tell me, wherefore seated
　　In this place art thou? Waitest thou an escort?　　125
　　Or has thy usual habit seized upon thee?"

And he: "O brother, what's the use of climbing?
　　Since to my torment would not let me go
　　The Angel of God, who sitteth at the gate.

First heaven must needs so long revolve me round　　130
　　Outside thereof, as in my life it did,
　　Since the good sighs I to the end postponed,

Unless, e'er that, some prayer may bring me aid
 Which rises from a heart that lives in grace;
 What profit others that in heaven are heard not?" 135

Meanwhile the Poet was before me mounting,
 And saying: "Come now; see the sun has touched
 Meridian, and from the shore the night

Covers already with her foot Morocco."

⇥ CANTO V ⇤

Those Who Died by Violence, but Repentant—
Buonconte di Monfeltro—La Pia

I had already from those shades departed,
 And followed in the footsteps of my Guide,
When from behind, pointing his finger at me,

One shouted: "See, it seems as if shone not
 The sunshine on the left of him below, 5
 And like one living seems he to conduct him."

Mine eyes I turned at utterance of these words,
 And saw them watching with astonishment
 But me, but me, and the light which was broken!

"Why doth thy mind so occupy itself," 10
 The Master said, "that thou thy pace dost slacken?
 What matters it to thee what here is whispered?

Come after me, and let the people talk;
 Stand like a steadfast tower, that never wags
 Its top for all the blowing of the winds; 15

For evermore the man in whom is springing
    Thought upon thought, removes from him the mark,
    Because the force of one the other weakens."

What could I say in answer but "I come"?
    I said it somewhat with that color tinged   20
    Which makes a man of pardon sometimes worthy.

Meanwhile along the mountain-side across
    Came people in advance of us a little,
    Singing the *Miserere* verse by verse.

When they became aware I gave no place   25
    For passage of the sunshine through my body,
    They changed their song into a long, hoarse "Oh!"

And two of them, in form of messengers,
    Ran forth to meet us, and demanded of us,
    "Of your condition make us cognizant."   30

And said my Master: "Ye can go your way
    And carry back again to those who sent you,
    That this one's body is of very flesh.

If they stood still because they saw his shadow,
    As I suppose, enough is answered them;   35
    Him let them honor, it may profit them."

Vapors enkindled saw I ne'er so swiftly
    At early nightfall cleave the air serene,
    Nor, at the set of sun, the clouds of August,

But upward they returned in briefer time,   40
    And, on arriving, with the others wheeled
    Tow'rds us, like troops that run without a rein.

Meanwhile along the mountain-side across
Came people in advance of us a little,
Singing the *Miserere* verse by verse.

Purgatorio V, lines 22–24

"This folk that presses unto us is great,
    And cometh to implore thee," said the Poet;
    "So still go onward, and in going listen."   45

"O soul that goest to beatitude
    With the same members wherewith thou wast born,"
    Shouting they came, "a little stay thy steps,

Look, if thou e'er hast any of us seen,
    So that o'er yonder thou bear news of him;   50
    Ah, why dost thou go on? Ah, why not stay?

Long since we all were slain by violence,
    And sinners even to the latest hour;
    Then did a light from heaven admonish us,

So that, both penitent and pardoning, forth   55
    From life we issued reconciled to God,
    Who with desire to see Him stirs our hearts."

And I: "Although I gaze into your faces,
    No one I recognize; but if may please you
    Aught I have power to do, ye well-born spirits,   60

Speak ye, and I will do it, by that peace
    Which, following the feet of such a Guide,
    From world to world makes itself sought by me."

And one began: "Each one has confidence
    In thy good offices without an oath,   65
    Unless the I cannot cut off the I will;

Whence I, who speak alone before the others,
    Pray thee, if ever thou dost see the land
    That 'twixt Romagna lies and that of Charles,

Thou be so courteous to me of thy prayers   70
   In Fano, that they pray for me devoutly,
   That I may purge away my grave offenses.

From thence was I; but the deep wounds, through which
   Issued the blood wherein I had my seat,
   Were dealt me in bosom of the Antenori,   75

There where I thought to be the most secure;
   'Twas he of Este had it done, who held me
   In hatred far beyond what justice willed.

But if towards the Mira I had fled,
   When I was overtaken at Oriaco,   80
   I still should be o'er yonder where men breathe.

I ran to the lagoon, and reeds and mire
   Did so entangle me I fell, and saw there
   A lake made from my veins upon the ground."

Then said another: "Ah, be that desire   85
   Fulfilled that draws thee to the lofty mountain,
   As thou with pious pity aidest mine.

I was of Montefeltro, and am Buonconte;
   Giovanna, nor none other cares for me;
   Hence among these I go with downcast front."   90

And I to him: "What violence or what chance
   Led thee astray so far from Campaldino,
   That never has thy sepulture been known?"

"Oh," he replied, "at Casentino's foot
   A river crosses named Archiano, born   95
   Above the Hermitage in Apennine.

There where the name thereof becometh void
    Did I arrive, pierced through and through the throat,
    Fleeing on foot, and bloodying the plain;

There my sight lost I, and my utterance   100
    Ceased in the name of Mary, and thereat
    I fell, and tenantless my flesh remained.

Truth will I speak, repeat it to the living;
    God's Angel took me up, and he of hell
    Shouted: 'O thou from heaven, why dost thou
        rob me?   105

Thou bearest away the eternal part of him,
    For one poor little tear, that takes him from me;
    But with the rest I'll deal in other fashion!'

Well knowest thou how in the air is gathered
    That humid vapor which to water turns,   110
    Soon as it rises where the cold doth grasp it.

He joined that evil will, which aye seeks evil,
    To intellect, and moved the mist and wind
    By means of power, which his own nature gave;

Thereafter, when the day was spent, the valley   115
    From Pratomagno to the great yoke covered
    With fog, and made the heaven above intent,

So that the pregnant air to water changed;
    Down fell the rain, and to the gullies came
    Whate'er of it earth tolerated not;   120

And as it mingled with the mighty torrents,
    Towards the royal river with such speed
    It headlong rushed, that nothing held it back.

"God's Angel took me up, and he of hell
Shouted: 'O thou from heaven, why dost thou rob me?' "

Purgatorio V, lines 104–105

"Do thou remember me who am the Pia;
Siena made me, unmade me Maremma"

Purgatorio V, lines 133–134

My frozen body near unto its outlet
    The robust Archian found, and into Arno   125
    Thrust it, and loosened from my breast the cross

I made of me, when agony o'ercame me;
    It rolled me on the banks and on the bottom,
    Then with its booty covered and begirt me."

"Ah, when thou hast returned unto the world,   130
    And rested thee from thy long journeying,"
    After the second followed the third spirit,

"Do thou remember me who am the Pia;
    Siena made me, unmade me Maremma;
    He knoweth it, who had encircled first,   135

Espousing me, my finger with his gem."

⊰ CANTO VI ⊱

Dante's Inquiry on Prayers for the Dead — Sordello — Italy

W hene'er is broken up the game of Zara,
    He who has lost remains behind despondent,
The throws repeating, and in sadness learns;

The people with the other all depart;
    One goes in front, and one behind doth pluck him,   5
    And at his side one brings himself to mind;

He pauses not, and this and that one hears;
    They crowd no more to whom his hand he stretches,
    And from the throng he thus defends himself.

Even such was I in that dense multitude,   10
　　Turning to them this way and that my face,
　　And, promising, I freed myself therefrom.

There was the Aretine, who from the arms
　　Untamed of Ghin di Tacco had his death,
　　And he who fleeing from pursuit was drowned.   15

There was imploring with his hands outstretched
　　Frederick Novello, and that one of Pisa
　　Who made the good Marzucco seem so strong.

I saw Count Orso; and the soul divided
　　By hatred and by envy from its body,   20
　　As it declared, and not for crime committed,

Pierre de la Brosse I say; and here provide
　　While still on earth the Lady of Brabant,
　　So that for this she be of no worse flock!

As soon as I was free from all those shades   25
　　Who only prayed that someone else may pray,
　　So as to hasten their becoming holy,

Began I: "It appears that thou deniest,
　　O light of mine, expressly in some text,
　　That orison can bend decree of Heaven;   30

And ne'ertheless these people pray for this.
　　Might then their expectation bootless be?
　　Or is to me thy saying not quite clear?"

And he to me: "My writing is explicit,
　　And not fallacious is the hope of these,   35
　　If with sane intellect 'tis well regarded;

For top of judgment doth not vail itself,
    Because the fire of love fulfills at once
    What he must satisfy who here installs him.

And there, where I affirmed that proposition,   40
    Defect was not amended by a prayer,
    Because the prayer from God was separate.

Verily, in so deep a questioning
    Do not decide, unless she tell it thee,
    Who light 'twixt truth and intellect shall be.   45

I know not if thou understand; I speak
    Of Beatrice; her shalt thou see above,
    Smiling and happy, on this mountain's top."

And I: "Good Leader, let us make more haste,
    For I no longer tire me as before;   50
    And see, e'en now the hill a shadow casts."

"We will go forward with this day," he answered,
    "As far as now is possible for us;
    But otherwise the fact is than thou thinkest.

Ere thou art up there, thou shalt see return   55
    Him, who now hides himself behind the hill,
    So that thou dost not interrupt his rays.

But yonder there behold! a soul that stationed
    All, all alone is looking hitherward;
    It will point out to us the quickest way."   60

We came up unto it; O Lombard soul,
    How lofty and disdainful thou didst bear thee,
    And grand and slow in moving of thine eyes!

Nothing whatever did it say to us,
But let us go our way, eying us only   65
After the manner of a couchant lion;

Still near to it Virgilius drew, entreating
That it would point us out the best ascent;
And it replied not unto his demand,

But of our native land and of our life   70
It questioned us; and the sweet Guide began:
"Mantua,"—and the shade, all in itself recluse,

Rose tow'rds him from the place where first it was,
Saying: "O Mantuan, I am Sordello
Of thine own land!" and one embraced the other.   75

Ah! servile Italy, grief's hostelry!
A ship without a pilot in great tempest!
No Lady thou of Provinces, but brothel!

That noble soul was so impatient, only
At the sweet sound of his own native land,   80
To make its citizen glad welcome there;

And now within thee are not without war
Thy living ones, and one doth gnaw the other
Of those whom one wall and one fosse shut in!

Search, wretched one, all round about the shores   85
Thy seaboard, and then look within thy bosom,
If any part of thee enjoyeth peace!

What boots it, that for thee Justinian
The bridle mend, if empty be the saddle?
Withouten this the shame would be the less.   90

Ah! people, thou that oughtest to be devout,
    And to let Cæsar sit upon the saddle,
    If well thou hearest what God teacheth thee,

Behold how fell this wild beast has become,
    Being no longer by the spur corrected,   95
    Since thou hast laid thy hand upon the bridle.

O German Albert! who abandonest
    Her that has grown recalcitrant and savage,
    And oughtest to bestride her saddlebow,

May a just judgment from the stars down fall   100
    Upon thy blood, and be it new and open,
    That thy successor may have fear thereof;

Because thy father and thyself have suffered,
    By greed of those transalpine lands distrained,
    The garden of the empire to be waste.   105

Come and behold Montecchi and Cappelletti,
    Monaldi and Fillippeschi, careless man!
    Those sad already, and these doubt-depressed!

Come, cruel one! come and behold the oppression
    Of thy nobility, and cure their wounds,   110
    And thou shalt see how safe is Santafiore!

Come and behold thy Rome, that is lamenting,
    Widowed, alone, and day and night exclaims,
    "My Cæsar, why hast thou forsaken me?"

Come and behold how loving are the people;   115
    And if for us no pity moveth thee,
    Come and be made ashamed of thy renown!

And if it lawful be, O Jove Supreme!
  Who upon earth for us wast crucified,
  Are thy just eyes averted otherwhere?   120

Or preparation is't, that, in the abyss
  Of thine own counsel, for some good thou makest
  From our perception utterly cut off?

For all the towns of Italy are full
  Of tyrants, and becometh a Marcellus   125
  Each peasant churl who plays the partisan!

My Florence! well mayst thou contented be
  With this digression, which concerns thee not,
  Thanks to thy people who such forethought take!

Many at heart have justice, but shoot slowly,   130
  That unadvised they come not to the bow,
  But on their very lips thy people have it!

Many refuse to bear the common burden;
  But thy solicitous people answereth
  Without being asked, and crieth: "I submit."   135

Now be thou joyful, for thou hast good reason;
  Thou affluent, thou in peace, thou full of wisdom!
  If I speak true, the event conceals it not.

Athens and Lacedæmon, they who made
  The ancient laws, and were so civilized,   140
  Made towards living well a little sign

Compared with thee, who makest such finespun
  Provisions, that to middle of November
  Reaches not what thou in October spinnest.

How oft, within the time of thy remembrance,   145
   Laws, money, offices, and usages
   Hast thou remodeled, and renewed thy members?

And if thou mind thee well, and see the light,
   Thou shalt behold thyself like a sick woman,
   Who cannot find repose upon her down,   150

But by her tossing wardeth off her pain.

⊰ CANTO VII ⊱

The Valley of Flowers — Negligent Princes

After the gracious and glad salutations
   Had three and four times been reiterated,
Sordello backward drew and said, "Who are you?"

"Or ever to this mountain were directed
   The souls deserving to ascend to God,   5
   My bones were buried by Octavian.

I am Virgilius; and for no crime else
   Did I lose heaven, than for not having faith";
   In this wise then my Leader made reply.

As one who suddenly before him sees   10
   Something whereat he marvels, who believes
   And yet does not, saying, "It is! it is not!"

So he appeared; and then bowed down his brow,
   And with humility returned towards him,
   And, where inferiors embrace, embraced him.   15

So he appeared; and then bowed down his brow,
And with humility returned towards him,
And, where inferiors embrace, embraced him.

Purgatorio VII, lines 13–15

"O glory of the Latians, thou," he said,
   "Through whom our language showed what it could do
   O pride eternal of the place I came from,

What merit or what grace to me reveals thee?
   If I to hear thy words be worthy, tell me   20
   If thou dost come from Hell, and from what cloister."

"Through all the circles of the doleful realm,"
   Responded he, "have I come hitherward;
   Heaven's power impelled me, and with that I come.

I by not doing, not by doing, lost   25
   The sight of that high sun which thou desirest,
   And which too late by me was recognized.

A place there is below not sad with torments,
   But darkness only, where the lamentations
   Have not the sound of wailing, but are sighs.   30

There dwell I with the little innocents
   Snatched by the teeth of Death, or ever they
   Were from our human sinfulness exempt.

There dwell I among those who the three saintly
   Virtues did not put on, and without vice   35
   The others knew and followed all of them.

But if thou know and can, some indication
   Give us by which we may the sooner come
   Where Purgatory has its right beginning."

He answered: "No fixed place has been assigned us;   40
   'Tis lawful for me to go up and round;
   So far as I can go, as guide I join thee.

But see already how the day declines,
    And to go up by night we are not able;
    Therefore 'tis well to think of some fair sojourn.   45

Souls are there on the right hand here withdrawn;
    If thou permit me I will lead thee to them,
    And thou shalt know them not without delight."

"How is this?" was the answer; "should one wish
    To mount by night would he prevented be   50
    By others? or mayhap would not have power?"

And on the ground the good Sordello drew
    His finger, saying, "See, this line alone
    Thou couldst not pass after the sun is gone;

Not that aught else would hindrance give, however,   55
    To going up, save the nocturnal darkness;
    This with the want of power the will perplexes.

We might indeed therewith return below,
    And, wandering, walk the hillside round about,
    While the horizon holds the day imprisoned."   60

Thereon my Lord, as if in wonder, said:
    "Do thou conduct us thither, where thou sayest
    That we can take delight in tarrying."

Little had we withdrawn us from that place,
    When I perceived the mount was hollowed out   65
    In fashion as the valleys here are hollowed.

"Thitherward," said that shade, "will we repair,
    Where of itself the hillside makes a lap,
    And there for the new day will we await."

'Twixt hill and plain there was a winding path   70
　　Which led us to the margin of that dell,
　　Where dies the border more than half away.

Gold and fine silver, and scarlet and pearl-white,
　　The Indian wood resplendent and serene,
　　Fresh emerald the moment it is broken,   75

By herbage and by flowers within that hollow
　　Planted, each one in color would be vanquished,
　　As by its greater vanquished is the less.

Nor in that place had nature painted only,
　　But of the sweetness of a thousand odors   80
　　Made there a mingled fragrance and unknown.

"*Salve Regina*," on the green and flowers
　　There seated, singing, spirits I beheld,
　　Which were not visible outside the valley.

"Before the scanty sun now seeks his nest,"   85
　　Began the Mantuan who had led us thither,
　　"Among them do not wish me to conduct you.

Better from off this ledge the acts and faces
　　Of all of them will you discriminate,
　　Than in the plain below received among them.   90

He who sits highest, and the semblance bears
　　Of having what he should have done neglected,
　　And to the others' song moves not his lips,

Rudolph the Emperor was, who had the power
　　To heal the wounds that Italy have slain,   95
　　So that through others slowly she revives.

"*Salve Regina*," on the green and flowers
There seated, singing, spirits I beheld

Purgatorio VII, lines 82–83

The other, who in look doth comfort him,
    Governed the region where the water springs,
    The Moldau bears the Elbe, and Elbe the sea.

His name was Ottocar; and in swaddling-clothes   100
    Far better he than bearded Winceslaus
    His son, who feeds in luxury and ease.

And the small-nosed, who close in council seems
    With him that has an aspect so benign,
    Died fleeing and disflowering the lily;   105

Look there, how he is beating at his breast!
    Behold the other one, who for his cheek
    Sighing has made of his own palm a bed;

Father and father-in-law of France's Pest
    Are they, and know his vicious life and lewd,   110
    And hence proceeds the grief that so doth pierce them.

He who appears so stalwart, and chimes in,
    Singing, with that one of the manly nose,
    The cord of every valor wore begirt;

And if as King had after him remained   115
    The stripling who in rear of him is sitting,
    Well had the valor passed from vase to vase,

Which cannot of the other heirs be said.
    Frederick and Jacomo possess the realms,
    But none the better heritage possesses.   120

Not oftentimes upriseth through the branches
    The probity of man; and this He wills
    Who gives it, so that we may ask of Him.

Eke to the large-nosed reach my words, no less
 Than to the other, Pier, who with him sings;   125
 Whence Provence and Apulia grieve already

The plant is as inferior to its seed,
 As more than Beatrice and Margaret
 Costanza boasteth of her husband still.

Behold the monarch of the simple life,   130
 Harry of England, sitting there alone;
 He in his branches has a better issue.

He who the lowest on the ground among them
 Sits looking upward, is the Marquis William,
 For whose sake Alessandria and her war   135

Make Monferrat and Canavese weep."

⊰ Canto VIII ⊱

*The Guardian Angels and the Serpent — Nino di Gallura —
The Three Stars — Currado Malaspina.*

'Twas now the hour that turneth back desire
 In those who sail the sea, and melts the heart,
The day they've said to their sweet friends farewell,

And the new pilgrim penetrates with love,
 If he doth hear from far away a bell   5
 That seemeth to deplore the dying day,

When I began to make of no avail
 My hearing, and to watch one of the souls
 Uprisen, that begged attention with its hand.

It joined and lifted upward both its palms,   10
    Fixing its eyes upon the orient,
    As if it said to God, "Naught else I care for."

"Te lucis ante" so devoutly issued
    Forth from its mouth, and with such dulcet notes,
    It made me issue forth from my own mind.   15

And then the others, sweetly and devoutly,
    Accompanied it through all the hymn entire,
    Having their eyes on the supernal wheels.

Here, Reader, fix thine eyes well on the truth,
    For now indeed so subtile is the veil,   20
    Surely to penetrate within is easy.

I saw that army of the gentle-born
    Thereafterward in silence upward gaze,
    As if in expectation, pale and humble;

And from on high come forth and down descend,   25
    I saw two Angels with two flaming swords,
    Truncated and deprivëd of their points.

Green as the little leaflets just now born
    Their garments were, which, by their verdant pinions
    Beaten and blown abroad, they trailed behind.   30

One just above us came to take his station,
    And one descended to the opposite bank,
    So that the people were contained between them.

Clearly in them discerned I the blond head;
    But in their faces was the eye bewildered,   35
    As faculty confounded by excess.

"From Mary's bosom both of them have come,"
  Sordello said, "as guardians of the valley
  Against the serpent, that will come anon."

Whereupon I, who knew not by what road,   40
  Turned round about, and closely drew myself,
  Utterly frozen, to the faithful shoulders.

And once again Sordello: "Now descend we
  'Mid the grand shades, and we will speak to them;
  Right pleasant will it be for them to see you."   45

Only three steps I think that I descended,
  And was below, and saw one who was looking
  Only at me, as if he fain would know me.

Already now the air was growing dark,
  But not so that between his eyes and mine   50
  It did not show what it before locked up.

Tow'rds me he moved, and I tow'rds him did move;
  Noble Judge Nino! how it me delighted,
  When I beheld thee not among the damned!

No greeting fair was left unsaid between us;   55
  Then asked he: "How long is it since thou camest
  O'er the far waters to the mountain's foot?"

"Oh!" said I to him, "through the dismal places
  I came this morn; and am in the first life,
  Albeit the other, going thus, I gain."   60

And on the instant my reply was heard,
  He and Sordello both shrank back from me,
  Like people who are suddenly bewildered.

One to Virgilius, and the other turned
    To one who sat there, crying, "Up, Currado!   65
    Come and behold what God in grace has willed!"

Then, turned to me: "By that especial grace
    Thou owest unto Him, who so conceals
    His own first wherefore, that it has no ford,

When thou shalt be beyond the waters wide,   70
    Tell my Giovanna that she pray for me,
    Where answer to the innocent is made.

I do not think her mother loves me more,
    Since she has laid aside her wimple white,
    Which she, unhappy, needs must wish again.   75

Through her full easily is comprehended
    How long in woman lasts the fire of love,
    If eye or touch do not relight it often.

So fair a hatchment will not make for her
    The Viper marshalling the Milanese   80
    A-field, as would have made Gallura's Cock."

In this wise spake he, with the stamp impressed
    Upon his aspect of that righteous zeal
    Which measurably burneth in the heart.

My greedy eyes still wandered up to heaven,   85
    Still to that point where slowest are the stars,
    Even as a wheel the nearest to its axle.

And my Conductor: "Son, what dost thou gaze at
    Up there?" And I to him: "At those three torches
    With which this hither pole is all on fire."   90

And he to me: "The four resplendent stars
    Thou sawest this morning are down yonder low,
    And these have mounted up to where those were."

As he was speaking, to himself Sordello
    Drew him, and said, "Lo there our Adversary!"   95
    And pointed with his finger to look thither.

Upon the side on which the little valley
    No barrier hath, a serpent was; perchance
    The same which gave to Eve the bitter food.

'Twixt grass and flowers came on the evil streak,   100
    Turning at times its head about, and licking
    Its back like to a beast that smoothes itself.

I did not see, and therefore cannot say
    How the celestial falcons 'gan to move,
    But well I saw that they were both in motion.   105

Hearing the air cleft by their verdant wings,
    The serpent fled, and round the Angels wheeled,
    Up to their stations flying back alike.

The shade that to the Judge had near approached
    When he had called, throughout that whole assault 110
    Had not a moment loosed its gaze on me.

"So may the light that leadeth thee on high
    Find in thine own freewill as much of wax
    As needful is up to the highest azure,"

Began it, "if some true intelligence   115
    Of Valdimagra or its neighborhood
    Thou knowest, tell it me, who once was great there.

Hearing the air cleft by their verdant wings,
The serpent fled, and round the Angels wheeled

Purgatorio VIII, lines 106–107

Currado Malaspina was I called;
    I'm not the elder, but from him descended;
    To mine I bore the love which here refineth."   120

"O," said I unto him, "through your domains
    I never passed, but where is there a dwelling
    Throughout all Europe, where they are not known?

That fame, which doeth honor to your house,
    Proclaims its Signors and proclaims its land,   125
    So that he knows of them who ne'er was there.

And, as I hope for heaven, I swear to you
    Your honored family in naught abates
    The glory of the purse and of the sword.

It is so privileged by use and nature,   130
    That though a guilty head misguide the world,
    Sole it goes right, and scorns the evil way."

And he: "Now go; for the sun shall not lie
    Seven times upon the pillow which the Ram
    With all his four feet covers and bestrides,   135

Before that such a courteous opinion
    Shall in the middle of thy head be nailed
    With greater nails than of another's speech,

Unless the course of justice standeth still."

ᵈᕇ CANTO IX ᕈᵉ

Dante's Dream of the Eagle — The Gate of Purgatory and the Angel —
Seven P's — The Keys

The concubine of old Tithonus now
   Gleamed white upon the eastern balcony,
Forth from the arms of her sweet paramour;

With gems her forehead all relucent was,
   Set in the shape of that cold animal   5
   Which with its tail doth smite amain the nations,

And of the steps, with which she mounts, the Night
   Had taken two in that place where we were,
   And now the third was bending down its wings;

When I, who something had of Adam in me,   10
   Vanquished by sleep, upon the grass reclined,
   There were all five of us already sat.

Just at the hour when her sad lay begins
   The little swallow, near unto the morning,
   Perchance in memory of her former woes,   15

And when the mind of man, a wanderer
   More from the flesh, and less by thought imprisoned,
   Almost prophetic in its visions is,

In dreams it seemed to me I saw suspended
   An eagle in the sky, with plumes of gold,   20
   With wings wide open, and intent to stoop,

And this, it seemed to me, was where had been
   By Ganymede his kith and kin abandoned,
   When to the high consistory he was rapt.

The concubine of old Tithonus now
Gleamed white upon the eastern balcony

Purgatorio IX, lines 1–2

I thought within myself, perchance he strikes   25
    From habit only here, and from elsewhere
    Disdains to bear up any in his feet.

Then wheeling somewhat more, it seemed to me,
    Terrible as the lightning he descended,
    And snatched me upward even to the fire.   30

Therein it seemed that he and I were burning,
    And the imagined fire did scorch me so,
    That of necessity my sleep was broken.

Not otherwise Achilles started up,
    Around him turning his awakened eyes,   35
    And knowing not the place in which he was,

What time from Chiron stealthily his mother
    Carried him sleeping in her arms to Scyros,
    Wherefrom the Greeks withdrew him afterwards,

Than I upstarted, when from off my face   40
    Sleep fled away; and pallid I became,
    As doth the man who freezes with affright.

Only my Comforter was at my side,
    And now the sun was more than two hours high,
    And turned towards the seashore was my face.   45

"Be not intimidated," said my Lord,
    "Be reassured, for all is well with us;
    Do not restrain, but put forth all thy strength.

Thou hast at length arrived at Purgatory;
    See there the cliff that closes it around;   50
    See there the entrance, where it seems disjoined.

Terrible as the lightning he descended,
And snatched me upward even to the fire.

Purgatorio IX, lines 29–30

Whilom at dawn, which doth precede the day,
    When inwardly thy spirit was asleep
    Upon the flowers that deck the land below,

There came a Lady and said: 'I am Lucìa;   55
    Let me take this one up, who is asleep;
    So will I make his journey easier for him.'

Sordello and the other noble shapes
    Remained; she took thee, and, as day grew bright,
    Upward she came, and I upon her footsteps.   60

She laid thee here; and first her beauteous eyes
    That open entrance pointed out to me;
    Then she and sleep together went away."

In guise of one whose doubts are reassured,
    And who to confidence his fear doth change,   65
    After the truth has been discovered to him,

So did I change; and when without disquiet
    My Leader saw me, up along the cliff
    He moved, and I behind him, tow'rd the height.

Reader, thou seest well how I exalt   70
    My theme, and therefore if with greater art
    I fortify it, marvel not thereat.

Nearer approached we, and were in such place,
    That there, where first appeared to me a rift
    Like to a crevice that disparts a wall,   75

I saw a portal, and three stairs beneath,
    Diverse in color, to go up to it,
    And a gatekeeper, who yet spake no word.

I saw him seated on the highest stair,
Such in the face that I endured it not.
And in his hand he had a naked sword

Purgatorio IX, lines 80–82

And as I opened more and more mine eyes,
    I saw him seated on the highest stair,   80
    Such in the face that I endured it not.

And in his hand he had a naked sword,
    Which so reflected back the sunbeams tow'rds us,
    That oft in vain I lifted up mine eyes.

"Tell it from where you are, what is't you wish?"   85
    Began he to exclaim; "where is the escort?
    Take heed your coming hither harm you not!"

"A Lady of Heaven, with these things conversant,"
    My Master answered him, "but even now
    Said to us, 'Thither go; there is the portal.' "   90

"And may she speed your footsteps in all good,"
    Again began the courteous janitor;
    "Come forward then unto these stairs of ours."

Thither did we approach; and the first stair
    Was marble white, so polished and so smooth,   95
    I mirrored myself therein as I appear.

The second, tinct of deeper hue than perse,
    Was of a calcined and uneven stone,
    Cracked all asunder lengthwise and across.

The third, that uppermost rests massively,   100
    Porphyry seemed to me, as flaming red
    As blood that from a vein is spirting forth.

Both of his feet was holding upon this
    The Angel of God, upon the threshold seated,
    Which seemed to me a stone of diamond.   105

Along the three stairs upward with good will
  Did my Conductor draw me, saying: "Ask
  Humbly that he the fastening may undo."

Devoutly at the holy feet I cast me,
  For mercy's sake besought that he would open,   110
  But first upon my breast three times I smote.

Seven P's upon my forehead he described
  With the sword's point, and, "Take heed that thou wash
  These wounds, when thou shalt be within," he said.

Ashes, or earth that dry is excavated,   115
  Of the same color were with his attire,
  And from beneath it he drew forth two keys.

One was of gold, and the other was of silver;
  First with the white, and after with the yellow,
  Plied he the door, so that I was content.   120

"Whenever faileth either of these keys
  So that it turn not rightly in the lock,"
  He said to us, "this entrance doth not open.

More precious one is, but the other needs
  More art and intellect ere it unlock,   125
  For it is that which doth the knot unloose.

From Peter I have them; and he bade me err
  Rather in opening than in keeping shut,
  If people but fall down before my feet."

Then pushed the portals of the sacred door,   130
  Exclaiming: "Enter; but I give you warning
  That forth returns whoever looks behind."

And when upon their hinges were turned round
   The swivels of that consecrated gate,
   Which are of metal, massive and sonorous,   135

Roared not so loud, nor so discordant seemed
   Tarpeia, when was ta'en from it the good
   Metellus, wherefore meager it remained.

At the first thunder-peal I turned attentive,
   And *"Te Deum laudamus"* seemed to hear   140
   In voices mingled with sweet melody.

Exactly such an image rendered me
   That which I heard, as we are wont to catch,
   When people singing with the organ stand;

For now we hear, and now hear not, the words.   145

⊰ CANTO X ⊱

The Needle's Eye — The First Circle: The Proud — The Sculptures on the Wall

When we had crossed the threshold of the door
   Which the perverted love of souls disuses,
Because it makes the crooked way seem straight,

Re-echoing I heard it closed again;
   And if I had turned back mine eyes upon it,   5
   What for my failing had been fit excuse?

We mounted upward through a rifted rock,
   Which undulated to this side and that,
   Even as a wave receding and advancing.

"Here it behoves us use a little art,"   10
   Began my Leader, "to adapt ourselves
   Now here, now there, to the receding side."

And this our footsteps so infrequent made,
   That sooner had the moon's decreasing disk
   Regained its bed to sink again to rest,   15

Than we were forth from out that needle's eye;
   But when we free and in the open were,
   There where the mountain backward piles itself,

I wearied out, and both of us uncertain
   About our way, we stopped upon a plain   20
   More desolate than roads across the deserts.

From where its margin borders on the void,
   To foot of the high bank that ever rises,
   A human body three times told would measure;

And far as eye of mine could wing its flight,   25
   Now on the left, and on the right flank now,
   The same this cornice did appear to me.

Thereon our feet had not been moved as yet,
   When I perceived the embankment round about,
   Which all right of ascent had interdicted,   30

To be of marble white, and so adorned
   With sculptures, that not only Polycletus,
   But Nature's self, had there been put to shame.

The Angel, who came down to earth with tidings
   Of peace, that had been wept for many a year,   35
   And opened Heaven from its long interdict,

In front of us appeared so truthfully
    There sculptured in a gracious attitude,
    He did not seem an image that is silent.

One would have sworn that he was saying, *"Ave"*;   40
    For she was there in effigy portrayed
    Who turned the key to ope the exalted love,

And in her mien this language had impressed,
    "Ecce ancilla Dei," as distinctly
    As any figure stamps itself in wax.   45

"Keep not thy mind upon one place alone,"
    The gentle Master said, who had me standing
    Upon that side where people have their hearts;

Whereat I moved mine eyes, and I beheld
    In rear of Mary, and upon that side   50
    Where he was standing who conducted me,

Another story on the rock imposed;
    Wherefore I passed Virgilius and drew near,
    So that before mine eyes it might be set.

There sculptured in the selfsame marble were   55
    The cart and oxen, drawing the holy ark,
    Wherefore one dreads an office not appointed.

People appeared in front, and all of them
    In seven choirs divided, of two senses
    Made one say "No," the other, "Yes, they sing."   60

Likewise unto the smoke of the frankincense,
    Which there was imaged forth, the eyes and nose
    Were in the yes and no discordant made.

Preceded there the vessel benedight,
  Dancing with girded loins, the humble Psalmist,   65
  And more and less than King was he in this.

Opposite, represented at the window
  Of a great palace, Michal looked upon him,
  Even as a woman scornful and afflicted.

I moved my feet from where I had been standing,   70
  To examine near at hand another story,
  Which after Michal glimmered white upon me.

There the high glory of the Roman Prince
  Was chronicled, whose great beneficence
  Moved Gregory to his great victory;   75

'Tis of the Emperor Trajan I am speaking;
  And a poor widow at his bridle stood,
  In attitude of weeping and of grief.

Around about him seemed it thronged and full
  Of cavaliers, and the eagles in the gold   80
  Above them visibly in the wind were moving.

The wretched woman in the midst of these
  Seemed to be saying: "Give me vengeance, Lord,
  For my dead son, for whom my heart is breaking."

And he to answer her: "Now wait until   85
  I shall return." And she: "My Lord," like one
  In whom grief is impatient, "shouldst thou not

Return?" And he: "Who shall be where I am
  Will give it thee." And she: "Good deed of others
  What boots it thee, if thou neglect thine own?"   90

The wretched woman in the midst of these
Seemed to be saying: "Give me vengeance, Lord,
For my dead son, for whom my heart is breaking."

Purgatorio X, lines 82–84

Whence he: "Now comfort thee, for it behoves me
   That I discharge my duty ere I move;
   Justice so wills, and pity doth retain me."

He who on no new thing has ever looked
   Was the creator of this visible language,   95
   Novel to us, for here it is not found.

While I delighted me in contemplating
   The images of such humility,
   And dear to look on for their Maker's sake,

"Behold, upon this side, but rare they make   100
   Their steps," the Poet murmured, "many people;
   These will direct us to the lofty stairs."

Mine eyes, that in beholding were intent
   To see new things, of which they curious are,
   In turning round towards him were not slow.   105

But still I wish not, Reader, thou shouldst swerve
   From thy good purposes, because thou hearest
   How God ordaineth that the debt be paid;

Attend not to the fashion of the torment,
   Think of what follows; think that at the worst   110
   It cannot reach beyond the mighty sentence.

"Master," began I, "that which I behold
   Moving towards us seems to me not persons,
   And what I know not, so in sight I waver."

And he to me: "The grievous quality   115
   Of this their torment bows them so to earth,
   That my own eyes at first contended with it;

But look there fixedly, and disentangle
  By sight what cometh underneath those stones;
  Already canst thou see how each is stricken."   120

O ye proud Christians! wretched, weary ones!
  Who, in the vision of the mind infirm
  Confidence have in your backsliding steps,

Do ye not comprehend that we are worms,
  Born to bring forth the angelic butterfly   125
  That flieth unto judgment without screen?

Why floats aloft your spirit high in air?
  Like are ye unto insects undeveloped,
  Even as the worm in whom formation fails!

As to sustain a ceiling or a roof,   130
  In place of corbel, oftentimes a figure
  Is seen to join its knees unto its breast,

Which makes of the unreal real anguish
  Arise in him who sees it; fashioned thus
  Beheld I those, when I had ta'en good heed.   135

True is it, they were more or less bent down,
  According as they more or less were laden;
  And he who had most patience in his looks

Weeping did seem to say, "I can no more!"

⊰ CANTO XI ⊱

The Humble Prayer — Omberto di Santafiore —
Oderisi d' Agobbio — Provenzan Salvani

"Our Father, thou who dwellest in the heavens,
　　Not circumscribed, but from the greater love
Thou bearest to the first effects on high,

Praised be thy name and thine omnipotence
　　By every creature, as befitting is   5
　　To render thanks to thy sweet effluence.

Come unto us the peace of thy dominion,
　　For unto it we cannot of ourselves,
　　If it come not, with all our intellect.

Even as thine own Angels of their will   10
　　Make sacrifice to thee, Hosanna singing,
　　So may all men make sacrifice of theirs.

Give unto us this day our daily manna,
　　Withouten which in this rough wilderness
　　Backward goes he who toils most to advance.   15

And even as we the trespass we have suffered
　　Pardon in one another, pardon thou
　　Benignly, and regard not our desert.

Our virtue, which is easily o'ercome,
　　Put not to proof with the old Adversary,   20
　　But thou from him who spurs it so, deliver.

This last petition verily, dear Lord,
　　Not for ourselves is made, who need it not,
　　But for their sake who have remained behind us."

Thus for themselves and us good furtherance   25
    Those shades imploring, went beneath a weight
    Like unto that of which we sometimes dream,

Unequally in anguish round and round
    And weary all, upon that foremost cornice,
    Purging away the smokestains of the world.   30

If there good words are always said for us,
    What may not here be said and done for them,
    By those who have a good root to their will?

Well may we help them wash away the marks
    That hence they carried, so that clean and light   35
    They may ascend unto the starry wheels!

"Ah! so may pity and justice you disburden
    Soon, that ye may have power to move the wing,
    That shall uplift you after your desire,

Show us on which hand tow'rd the stairs the way   40
    Is shortest, and if more than one the passes,
    Point us out that which least abruptly falls;

For he who cometh with me, through the burden
    Of Adam's flesh wherewith he is invested,
    Against his will is chary of his climbing."   45

The words of theirs which they returned to those
    That he whom I was following had spoken,
    It was not manifest from whom they came,

But it was said: "To the right hand come with us
    Along the bank, and ye shall find a pass   50
    Possible for living person to ascend.

And were I not impeded by the stone,
 Which this proud neck of mine doth subjugate,
 Whence I am forced to hold my visage down,

Him, who still lives and does not name himself, 55
 Would I regard, to see if I may know him
 And make him piteous unto this burden.

A Latian was I, and born of a great Tuscan;
 Guglielmo Aldobrandeschi was my father;
 I know not if his name were ever with you. 60

The ancient blood and deeds of gallantry
 Of my progenitors so arrogant made me
 That, thinking not upon the common mother,

All men I held in scorn to such extent
 I died therefor, as know the Sienese, 65
 And every child in Campagnatico.

I am Omberto; and not to me alone
 Has pride done harm, but all my kith and kin
 Has with it dragged into adversity.

And here must I this burden bear for it 70
 Till God be satisfied, since I did not
 Among the living, here among the dead."

Listening I downward bent my countenance;
 And one of them, not this one who was speaking,
 Twisted himself beneath the weight that cramps him, 75

And looked at me, and knew me, and called out,
 Keeping his eyes laboriously fixed
 On me, who all bowed down was going with them.

"O," asked I him, "art thou not Oderisi,
　　Agobbio's honor, and honor of that art   80
　　Which is in Paris called illuminating?"

"Brother," said he, "more laughing are the leaves
　　Touched by the brush of Franco Bolognese;
　　All his the honor now, and mine in part.

In sooth I had not been so courteous   85
　　While I was living, for the great desire
　　Of excellence, on which my heart was bent.

Here of such pride is paid the forfeiture;
　　And yet I should not be here, were it not
　　That, having power to sin, I turned to God.   90

O thou vain glory of the human powers,
　　How little green upon thy summit lingers,
　　If't be not followed by an age of grossness!

In painting Cimabue thought that he
　　Should hold the field, now Giotto has the cry,   95
　　So that the other's fame is growing dim.

So has one Guido from the other taken
　　The glory of our tongue, and he perchance
　　Is born, who from the nest shall chase them both.

Naught is this mundane rumor but a breath   100
　　Of wind, that comes now this way and now that,
　　And changes name, because it changes side.

What fame shalt thou have more, if old peel off
　　From thee thy flesh, than if thou hadst been dead
　　Before thou left the *pappo* and the *dindi*,   105

Ere pass a thousand years? which is a shorter
    Space to the eterne, than twinkling of an eye
    Unto the circle that in heaven wheels slowest.

With him, who takes so little of the road
    In front of me, all Tuscany resounded;   110
    And now he scarce is lisped of in Siena,

Where he was lord, what time was overthrown
    The Florentine delirium, that superb
    Was at that day as now 'tis prostitute.

Your reputation is the color of grass   115
    Which comes and goes, and that discolors it
    By which it issues green from out the earth."

And I: "Thy true speech fills my heart with good
    Humility, and great tumor thou assuagest;
    But who is he, of whom just now thou spakest?"   120

"That," he replied, "is Provenzan Salvani,
    And he is here because he had presumed
    To bring Siena all into his hands.

He has gone thus, and goeth without rest
    E'er since he died; such money renders back   125
    In payment he who is on earth too daring."

And I: "If every spirit who awaits
    The verge of life before that he repent,
    Remains below there and ascends not hither,

(Unless good orison shall him bestead)   130
    Until as much time as he lived be passed,
    How was the coming granted him in largess?"

"When he in greatest splendor lived," said he,
  "Freely upon the Campo of Siena,
    All shame being laid aside, he placed himself;   135

And there to draw his friend from the duress
  Which in the prison-house of Charles he suffered,
    He brought himself to tremble in each vein.

I say no more, and know that I speak darkly;
  Yet little time shall pass before thy neighbors   140
    Will so demean themselves that thou canst gloss it.

This action has released him from those confines."

⊰ CANTO XII ⊱

The Sculptures on the Pavement — Ascent to the Second Circle

Abreast, like oxen going in a yoke,
  I with that heavy-laden soul went on,
As long as the sweet pedagogue permitted;

But when he said, "Leave him, and onward pass,
  For here 'tis good that with the sail and oars,   5
    As much as may be, each push on his barque";

Upright, as walking wills it, I redressed
  My person, notwithstanding that my thoughts
    Remained within me downcast and abashed.

I had moved on, and followed willingly   10
  The footsteps of my Master, and we both
    Already showed how light of foot we were,

Abreast, like oxen going in a yoke,
I with that heavy-laden soul went on

Purgatorio XII, lines 1–2

When unto me he said: "Cast down thine eyes;
 'Twere well for thee, to alleviate the way,
  To look upon the bed beneath thy feet."   15

As, that some memory may exist of them,
 Above the buried dead their tombs in earth
  Bear sculptured on them what they were before;

Whence often there we weep for them afresh,
 From pricking of remembrance, which alone 20
  To the compassionate doth set its spur;

So saw I there, but of a better semblance
 In point of artifice, with figures covered
  Whate'er as pathway from the mount projects.

I saw that one who was created noble   25
 More than all other creatures, down from heaven
  Flaming with lightnings fall upon one side.

I saw Briareus smitten by the dart
 Celestial, lying on the other side,
  Heavy upon the earth by mortal frost.   30

I saw Thymbræus, Pallas saw, and Mars,
 Still clad in armor round about their father,
  Gaze at the scattered members of the giants.

I saw, at foot of his great labor, Nimrod,
 As if bewildered, looking at the people   35
  Who had been proud with him in Sennaar.

O Niobe! with what afflicted eyes
 Thee I beheld upon the pathway traced,
  Between thy seven and seven children slain!

O Saul! how fallen upon thy proper sword   40
    Didst thou appear there lifeless in Gilboa,
    That felt thereafter neither rain nor dew!

O mad Arachne! so I thee beheld
    E'en then half spider, sad upon the shreds
    Of fabric wrought in evil hour for thee!   45

O Rehoboam! no more seems to threaten
    Thine image there; but full of consternation
    A chariot bears it off, when none pursues!

Displayed moreo'er the adamantine pavement
    How unto his own mother made Alcmæon   50
    Costly appear the luckless ornament;

Displayed how his own sons did throw themselves
    Upon Sennacherib within the temple,
    And how, he being dead, they left him there;

Displayed the ruin and the cruel carnage   55
    That Tomyris wrought, when she to Cyrus said,
    "Blood didst thou thirst for, and with blood I glut thee!"

Displayed how routed fled the Assyrians
    After that Holofernes had been slain,
    And likewise the remainder of that slaughter.   60

I saw there Troy in ashes and in caverns;
    O Ilion! thee, how abject and debased,
    Displayed the image that is there discerned!

Whoe'er of pencil master was or stile,
    That could portray the shades and traits which there   65
    Would cause each subtile genius to admire?

O mad Arachne! so I thee beheld
E'en then half-spider

Purgatorio XII, lines 43–44

Dead seemed the dead, the living seemed alive;
    Better than I saw not who saw the truth,
    All that I trod upon while bowed I went.

Now wax ye proud, and on with looks uplifted,   70
    Ye sons of Eve, and bow not down your faces
    So that ye may behold your evil ways!

More of the mount by us was now encompassed,
    And far more spent the circuit of the sun,
    Than had the mind preoccupied imagined,   75

When he, who ever watchful in advance
    Was going on, began: "Lift up thy head,
    'Tis no more time to go thus meditating.

Lo there an Angel who is making haste
    To come towards us; lo, returning is   80
    From service of the day the sixth handmaiden.

With reverence thine acts and looks adorn,
    So that he may delight to speed us upward;
    Think that this day will never dawn again."

I was familiar with his admonition   85
    Ever to lose no time; so on this theme
    He could not unto me speak covertly.

Towards us came the being beautiful
    Vested in white, and in his countenance
    Such as appears the tremulous morning star.   90

His arms he opened, and opened then his wings;
    "Come," said he, "near at hand here are the steps,
    And easy from henceforth is the ascent."

At this announcement few are they who come!
 O human creatures, born to soar aloft,   95
 Why fall ye thus before a little wind?

He led us on to where the rock was cleft;
 There smote upon my forehead with his wings,
 Then a safe passage promised unto me.

As on the right hand, to ascend the mount   100
 Where seated is the church that lordeth it
 O'er the well-guided, above Rubaconte,

The bold abruptness of the ascent is broken
 By stairways that were made there in the age
 When still were safe the ledger and the stave,   105

E'en thus attempered is the bank which falls
 Sheer downward from the second circle there;
 But on this side and that the high rock grazes.

As we were turning thitherward our persons,
 "*Beati pauperes spiritu,*" voices   110
 Sang in such wise that speech could tell it not.

Ah me! how different are these entrances
 From the Infernal! for with anthems here
 One enters, and below with wild laments.

We now were hunting up the sacred stairs,   115
 And it appeared to me by far more easy
 Than on the plain it had appeared before.

Whence I: "My Master, say, what heavy thing
 Has been uplifted from me, so that hardly
 Aught of fatigue is felt by me in walking?"   120

He answered: "When the P's which have remained
    Still on thy face almost obliterate
    Shall wholly, as the first is, be erased,

Thy feet will be so vanquished by good will,
    That not alone they shall not feel fatigue,   125
    But urging up will be to them delight."

Then did I even as they do who are going
    With something on the head to them unknown,
    Unless the signs of others make them doubt,

Wherefore the hand to ascertain is helpful,   130
    And seeks and finds, and doth fulfill the office
    Which cannot be accomplished by the sight;

And with the fingers of the right hand spread
    I found but six the letters, that had carved
    Upon my temples he who bore the keys;   135

Upon beholding which my Leader smiled.

⊰ CANTO XIII ⊱

The Second Circle: The Envious — Sapia of Siena

We were upon the summit of the stairs,
    Where for the second time is cut away
The mountain, which ascending shriveth all.

There in like manner doth a cornice bind
    The hill all round about, as does the first,   5
    Save that its arc more suddenly is curved.

Shade is there none, nor sculpture that appears;
    So seems the bank, and so the road seems smooth,
    With but the livid color of the stone.

"If to inquire we wait for people here,"   10
    The Poet said, "I fear that peradventure
    Too much delay will our election have."

Then steadfast on the sun his eyes he fixed,
    Made his right side the center of his motion,
    And turned the left part of himself about.   15

"O thou sweet light! with trust in whom I enter
    Upon this novel journey, do thou lead us,"
    Said he, "as one within here should be led.

Thou warmest the world, thou shinest over it;
    If other reason prompt not otherwise,   20
    Thy rays should evermore our leaders be!"

As much as here is counted for a mile,
    So much already there had we advanced
    In little time, by dint of ready will;

And tow'rds us there were heard to fly, albeit   25
    They were not visible, spirits uttering
    Unto Love's table courteous invitations,

The first voice that passed onward in its flight,
    "*Vinum non habent*," said in accents loud,
    And went reiterating it behind us.   30

And ere it wholly grew inaudible
    Because of distance, passed another, crying,
    "I am Orestes!" and it also stayed not.

"O," said I, "Father, these, what voices are they?"
   And even as I asked, behold the third,   35
   Saying: "Love those from whom ye have had evil!"

And the good Master said: "This circle scourges
   The sin of envy, and on that account
   Are drawn from love the lashes of the scourge.

The bridle of another sound shall be;   40
   I think that thou wilt hear it, as I judge,
   Before thou comest to the Pass of Pardon.

But fix thine eyes athwart the air right steadfast,
   And people thou wilt see before us sitting,
   And each one close against the cliff is seated."   45

Then wider than at first mine eyes I opened;
   I looked before me, and saw shades with mantles
   Not from the color of the stone diverse.

And when we were a little farther onward,
   I heard a cry of, "Mary, pray for us!"   50
   A cry of, "Michael, Peter, and all Saints!"

I do not think there walketh still on earth
   A man so hard, that he would not be pierced
   With pity at what afterward I saw.

For when I had approached so near to them   55
   That manifest to me their acts became,
   Drained was I at the eyes by heavy grief.

Covered with sackcloth vile they seemed to me,
   And one sustained the other with his shoulder,
   And all of them were by the bank sustained.   60

Covered with sackcloth vile they seemed to me,
And one sustained the other with his shoulder,
And all of them were by the bank sustained.

Purgatorio XIII, lines 58–60

Thus do the blind, in want of livelihood,
   Stand at the doors of churches asking alms,
   And one upon another leans his head,

So that in others pity soon may rise,
   Not only at the accent of their words,   65
   But at their aspect, which no less implores.

And as unto the blind the sun comes not,
   So to the shades, of whom just now I spake,
   Heaven's light will not be bounteous of itself;

For all their lids an iron wire transpierces,   70
   And sews them up, as to a sparhawk wild
   Is done, because it will not quiet stay.

To me it seemed, in passing, to do outrage,
   Seeing the others without being seen;
   Wherefore I turned me to my counsel sage.   75

Well knew he what the mute one wished to say,
   And therefore waited not for my demand,
   But said: "Speak, and be brief, and to the point."

I had Virgilius upon that side
   Of the embankment from which one may fall,   80
   Since by no border 'tis engarlanded;

Upon the other side of me I had
   The shades devout, who through the horrible seam
   Pressed out the tears so that they bathed their cheeks.

To them I turned me, and, "O people, certain,"   85
   Began I, "of beholding the high light,
   Which your desire has solely in its care,

So may grace speedily dissolve the scum
    Upon your consciences, that limpidly
    Through them descend the river of the mind,   90

Tell me, for dear 'twill be to me and gracious,
    If any soul among you here is Latian,
    And 'twill perchance be good for him I learn it."

"O brother mine, each one is citizen
    Of one true city; but thy meaning is,   95
    Who may have lived in Italy a pilgrim."

By way of answer this I seemed to hear
    A little farther on than where I stood,
    Whereat I made myself still nearer heard.

Among the rest I saw a shade that waited   100
    In aspect, and should anyone ask how,
    Its chin it lifted upward like a blind man.

"Spirit," I said, "who stoopest to ascend,
    If thou art he who did reply to me,
    Make thyself known to me by place or name."   105

"Sienese was I," it replied, "and with
    The others here recleanse my guilty life,
    Weeping to Him to lend himself to us.

Sapient I was not, although I Sapìa
    Was called, and I was at another's harm   110
    More happy far than at my own good fortune.

And that thou mayst not think that I deceive thee,
    Hear if I was as foolish as I tell thee.
    The arc already of my years descending,

"Sienese was I," it replied, "and with
The others here recleanse my guilty life"

Purgatorio XIII, lines 106–107

My fellow citizens near unto Colle   115
   Were joined in battle with their adversaries,
   And I was praying God for what he willed.

Routed were they, and turned into the bitter
   Passes of flight; and I, the chase beholding,
   A joy received unequalled by all others;   120

So that I lifted upward my bold face
   Crying to God, 'Henceforth I fear thee not,'
   As did the blackbird at the little sunshine.

Peace I desired with God at the extreme
   Of my existence, and as yet would not   125
   My debt have been by penitence discharged,

Had it not been that in remembrance held me
   Pier Pettignano in his holy prayers,
   Who out of charity was grieved for me.

But who art thou, that into our conditions   130
   Questioning goest, and hast thine eyes unbound
   As I believe, and breathing dost discourse?"

"Mine eyes," I said, "will yet be here ta'en from me,
   But for short space; for small is the offense
   Committed by their being turned with envy.   135

Far greater is the fear, wherein suspended
   My soul is, of the torment underneath,
   For even now the load down there weighs on me."

And she to me: "Who led thee, then, among us
   Up here, if to return below thou thinkest?"   140
   And I: "He who is with me, and speaks not;

And living am I; therefore ask of me,
   Spirit elect, if thou wouldst have me move
   O'er yonder yet my mortal feet for thee."

"O, this is such a novel thing to hear,"   145
   She answered, "that great sign it is God loves thee;
   Therefore with prayer of thine sometimes assist me.

And I implore, by what thou most desirest,
   If e'er thou treadest the soil of Tuscany,
   Well with my kindred reinstate my fame.   150

Them wilt thou see among that people vain
   Who hope in Talamone, and will lose there
   More hope than in discovering the Diana;

But there still more the admirals will lose."

⊰ Canto XIV ⊱

Guido del Duca and Renier da Calboli — Cities of the Arno Valley —
Denunciation of Stubbornesss

"Who is this one that goes about our mountain,
   Or ever Death has given him power of flight,
And opes his eyes and shuts them at his will?"

"I know not who, but know he's not alone;
   Ask him thyself, for thou art nearer to him,   5
   And gently, so that he may speak, accost him."

Thus did two spirits, leaning tow'rds each other,
   Discourse about me there on the right hand;
   Then held supine their faces to address me.

And said the one: "O soul, that, fastened still   10
   Within the body, tow'rds the heaven art going,
   For charity console us, and declare

Whence comest and who art thou; for thou mak'st us
   As much to marvel at this grace of thine
   As must a thing that never yet has been."   15

And I: "Through midst of Tuscany there wanders
   A streamlet that is born in Falterona,
   And not a hundred miles of course suffice it;

From thereupon do I this body bring.
   To tell you who I am were speech in vain,   20
   Because my name as yet makes no great noise."

"If well thy meaning I can penetrate
   With intellect of mine," then answered me
   He who first spake, "thou speakest of the Arno."

And said the other to him: "Why concealed   25
   This one the appellation of that river,
   Even as a man doth of things horrible?"

And thus the shade that questioned was of this
   Himself acquitted: "I know not; but truly
   'Tis fit the name of such a valley perish;   30

For from its fountainhead (where is so pregnant
   The Alpine mountain whence is cleft Peloro
   That in few places it that mark surpasses)

To where it yields itself in restoration
   Of what the heaven doth of the sea dry up,   35
   Whence have the rivers that which goes with them,

Virtue is like an enemy avoided
    By all, as is a serpent, through misfortune
    Of place, or through bad habit that impels them;

On which account have so transformed their nature   40
    The dwellers in that miserable valley,
    It seems that Circe had them in her pasture.

'Mid ugly swine, of acorns worthier
    Than other food for human use created,
    It first directeth its impoverished way.   45

Curs findeth it thereafter, coming downward,
    More snarling than their puissance demands,
    And turns from them disdainfully its muzzle.

It goes on falling, and the more it grows,
    The more it finds the dogs becoming wolves,   50
    This maledict and misadventurous ditch.

Descended then through many a hollow gulf,
    It finds the foxes so replete with fraud,
    They fear no cunning that may master them.

Nor will I cease because another hears me;   55
    And well 'twill be for him, if still he mind him
    Of what a truthful spirit to me unravels.

Thy grandson I behold, who doth become
    A hunter of those wolves upon the bank
    Of the wild stream, and terrifies them all.   60

He sells their flesh, it being yet alive;
    Thereafter slaughters them like ancient beeves;
    Many of life, himself of praise, deprives.

Bloodstained he issues from the dismal forest;
    He leaves it such, a thousand years from now   65
    In its primeval state 'tis not re-wooded."

As at the announcement of impending ills
    The face of him who listens is disturbed,
    From whate'er side the peril seize upon him;

So I beheld that other soul, which stood   70
    Turned round to listen, grow disturbed and sad,
    When it had gathered to itself the word.

The speech of one and aspect of the other
    Had me desirous made to know their names,
    And question mixed with prayers I made thereof,   75

Whereat the spirit which first spake to me
    Began again: "Thou wishest I should bring me
    To do for thee what thou'lt not do for me;

But since God willeth that in thee shine forth
    Such grace of his, I'll not be chary with thee;   80
    Know, then, that I Guido del Duca am.

My blood was so with envy set on fire,
    That if I had beheld a man make merry,
    Thou wouldst have seen me sprinkled o'er with pallor.

From my own sowing such the straw I reap!   85
    O human race! why dost thou set thy heart
    Where interdict of partnership must be?

This is Renier; this is the boast and honor
    Of the house of Calboli, where no one since
    Has made himself the heir of his desert.   90

And not alone his blood is made devoid,
   'Twixt Po and mount, and seashore and the Reno,
   Of good required for truth and for diversion;

For all within these boundaries is full
   Of venomous roots, so that too tardily   95
   By cultivation now would they diminish.

Where is good Lizio, and Arrigo Manardi,
   Pier Traversaro, and Guido di Carpigna,
   O Romagnuoli into bastards turned?

When in Bologna will a Fabbro rise?   100
   When in Faenza a Bernardin di Fosco,
   The noble scion of ignoble seed?

Be not astonished, Tuscan, if I weep,
   When I remember, with Guido da Prata,
   Ugolin d' Azzo, who was living with us,   105

Frederick Tignoso and his company,
   The house of Traversara, and th' Anastagi,
   And one race and the other is extinct;

The dames and cavaliers, the toils and ease
   That filled our souls with love and courtesy,   110
   There where the hearts have so malicious grown!

O Brettinoro! why dost thou not flee,
   Seeing that all thy family is gone,
   And many people, not to be corrupted?

Bagnacaval does well in not begetting   115
   And ill does Castrocaro, and Conio worse,
   In taking trouble to beget such Counts.

Will do well the Pagani, when their Devil
    Shall have departed; but not therefore pure
    Will testimony of them e'er remain.   120

O Ugolin de' Fantoli, secure
    Thy name is, since no longer is awaited
    One who, degenerating, can obscure it!

But go now, Tuscan, for it now delights me
    To weep far better than it does to speak,   125
    So much has our discourse my mind distressed."

We were aware that those beloved souls
    Heard us depart; therefore, by keeping silent,
    They made us of our pathway confident.

When we became alone by going onward,   130
    Thunder, when it doth cleave the air, appeared
    A voice, that counter to us came, exclaiming:

"Shall slay me whosoever findeth me!"
    And fled as the reverberation dies
    If suddenly the cloud asunder bursts.   135

As soon as hearing had a truce from this,
    Behold another, with so great a crash,
    That it resembled thunderings following fast:

"I am Aglaurus, who became a stone!"
    And then, to press myself close to the Poet,   140
    I backward, and not forward, took a step.

Already on all sides the air was quiet;
    And said he to me: "That was the hard curb
    That ought to hold a man within his bounds;

But you take in the bait so that the hook   145
   Of the old Adversary draws you to him,
   And hence availeth little curb or call.

The heavens are calling you, and wheel around you,
   Displaying to you their eternal beauties,
   And still your eye is looking on the ground;   150

Whence He, who all discerns, chastizes you."

⊰ Canto XV ⊱

The Third Circle: The Irascible — Dante's Visions — The Smoke

As much as 'twixt the close of the third hour
   And dawn of day appeareth of that sphere
Which aye in fashion of a child is playing,

So much it now appeared, towards the night,
   Was of his course remaining to the sun;   5
   There it was evening, and 'twas midnight here;

And the rays smote the middle of our faces,
   Because by us the mount was so encircled,
   That straight towards the west we now were going

When I perceived my forehead overpowered   10
   Beneath the splendor far more than at first,
   And stupor were to me the things unknown,

Whereat towards the summit of my brow
   I raised my hands, and made myself the visor
   Which the excessive glare diminishes.   15

As when from off the water, or a mirror,
    The sunbeam leaps unto the opposite side,
    Ascending upward in the selfsame measure

That it descends, and deviates as far
    From falling of a stone in line direct,   20
    (As demonstrate experiment and art)

So it appeared to me that by a light
    Refracted there before me I was smitten;
    On which account my sight was swift to flee.

"What is that, Father sweet, from which I cannot   25
    So fully screen my sight that it avail me,"
    Said I, "and seems towards us to be moving?"

"Marvel thou not, if dazzle thee as yet
    The family of heaven," he answered me;
    "An angel 'tis, who comes to invite us upward.   30

Soon will it be, that to behold these things
    Shall not be grievous, but delightful to thee
    As much as nature fashioned thee to feel."

When we had reached the Angel benedight,
    With joyful voice he said: "Here enter in   35
    To stairway far less steep than are the others."

We mounting were, already thence departed,
    And *"Beati misericordes"* was
    Behind us sung, "Rejoice, thou that o'ercomest!"

My Master and myself, we two alone   40
    Were going upward, and I thought, in going,
    Some profit to acquire from words of his;

And I to him directed me, thus asking:
  "What did the spirit of Romagna mean,
    Mentioning interdict and partnership?"   45

Whence he to me: "Of his own greatest failing
  He knows the harm; and therefore wonder not
    If he reprove us, that we less may rue it.

Because are thither pointed your desires
  Where by companionship each share is lessened,   50
    Envy doth ply the bellows to your sighs.

But if the love of the supernal sphere
  Should upwardly direct your aspiration,
    There would not be that fear within your breast;

For there, as much the more as one says *Our*,   55
  So much the more of good each one possesses,
    And more of charity in that cloister burns."

"I am more hungering to be satisfied,"
  I said, "than if I had before been silent,
    And more of doubt within my mind I gather.   60

How can it be, that boon distributed
  The more possessors can more wealthy make
    Therein, than if by few it be possessed?"

And he to me: "Because thou fixest still
  Thy mind entirely upon earthly things,   65
    Thou pluckest darkness from the very light.

That goodness infinite and ineffable
  Which is above there, runneth unto love,
    As to a lucid body comes the sunbeam.

So much it gives itself as it finds ardor,   70
    So that as far as charity extends,
    O'er it increases the eternal valor.

And the more people thitherward aspire,
    More are there to love well, and more they love there,
    And, as a mirror, one reflects the other.   75

And if my reasoning appease thee not,
    Thou shalt see Beatrice; and she will fully
    Take from thee this and every other longing.

Endeavor, then, that soon may be extinct,
    As are the two already, the five wounds   80
    That close themselves again by being painful."

Even as I wished to say, "Thou dost appease me,"
    I saw that I had reached another circle,
    So that my eager eyes made me keep silence.

There it appeared to me that in a vision   85
    Ecstatic on a sudden I was rapt,
    And in a temple many persons saw;

And at the door a woman, with the sweet
    Behavior of a mother, saying: "Son,
    Why in this manner hast thou dealt with us?   90

Lo, sorrowing, thy father and myself
    Were seeking for thee"—and as here she ceased,
    That which appeared at first had disappeared.

Then I beheld another with those waters
    Adown her cheeks which grief distils whenever   95
    From great disdain of others it is born,

And saying: "If of that city thou art lord,
　　For whose name was such strife among the gods,
　　And whence doth every science scintillate,

Avenge thyself on those audacious arms　　　　　100
　　That clasped our daughter, O Pisistratus";
　　And the lord seemed to me benign and mild

To answer her with aspect temperate:
　　"What shall we do to those who wish us ill,
　　If he who loves us be by us condemned?"　　　105

Then saw I people hot in fire of wrath,
　　With stones a young man slaying, clamorously
　　Still crying to each other, "Kill him! kill him!"

And him I saw bow down, because of death
　　That weighed already on him, to the earth,　　110
　　But of his eyes made ever gates to heaven,

Imploring the high Lord, in so great strife,
　　That he would pardon those his persecutors,
　　With such an aspect as unlocks compassion.

Soon as my soul had outwardly returned　　　　115
　　To things external to it which are true,
　　Did I my not false errors recognize.

My Leader, who could see me bear myself
　　Like to a man that rouses him from sleep,
　　Exclaimed: "What ails thee, that thou canst not
　　　　stand?　　　　　　　　　　　　　　　120

But hast been coming more than half a league
　　Veiling thine eyes, and with thy legs entangled,
　　In guise of one whom wine or sleep subdues?"

Then saw I people hot in fire of wrath,
With stones a young man slaying, clamorously
Still crying to each other, "Kill him! kill him!"

Purgatorio XV, lines 106–108

"O my sweet Father, if thou listen to me,
    I'll tell thee," said I, "what appeared to me,   125
    When thus from me my legs were ta'en away."

And he: "If thou shouldst have a hundred masks
    Upon thy face, from me would not be shut
    Thy cogitations, howsoever small.

What thou hast seen was that thou mayst not fail   130
    To ope thy heart unto the waters of peace,
    Which from the eternal fountain are diffused.

I did not ask, 'What ails thee?' as he does
    Who only looketh with the eyes that see not
    When of the soul bereft the body lies,   135

But asked it to give vigor to thy feet;
    Thus must we needs urge on the sluggards, slow
    To use their wakefulness when it returns."

We passed along, athwart the twilight peering
    Forward as far as ever eye could stretch   140
    Against the sunbeams serotine and lucent;

And lo! by slow degrees a smoke approached
    In our direction, somber as the night,
    Nor was there place to hide one's self therefrom.

This of our eyes and the pure air bereft us.   145

⫷ CANTO XVI ⫸

Marco Lombardo—Lament over the State of the World

Darkness of hell, and of a night deprived
  Of every planet under a poor sky,
As much as may be tenebrous with cloud,

Ne'er made unto my sight so thick a veil,
  As did that smoke which there enveloped us,   5
  Nor to the feeling of so rough a texture;

For not an eye it suffered to stay open;
  Whereat mine escort, faithful and sagacious,
  Drew near to me and offered me his shoulder.

E'en as a blind man goes behind his guide,   10
  Lest he should wander, or should strike against
  Aught that may harm or peradventure kill him,

So went I through the bitter and foul air,
  Listening unto my Leader, who said only,
  "Look that from me thou be not separated."   15

Voices I heard, and every one appeared
  To supplicate for peace and misericord
  The Lamb of God who takes away our sins.

Still *"Agnus Dei"* their exordium was;
  One word there was in all, and metre one,   20
  So that all harmony appeared among them.

"Master," I said, "are spirits those I hear?"
  And he to me: "Thou apprehendest truly,
  And they the knot of anger go unloosing."

"Now who art thou, that cleavest through our smoke   25
   And art discoursing of us even as though
   Thou didst by calends still divide the time?"

After this manner by a voice was spoken;
   Whereon my Master said: "Do thou reply,
   And ask if on this side the way go upward."   30

And I: "O creature that dost cleanse thyself
   To return beautiful to Him who made thee,
   Thou shalt hear marvels if thou follow me."

"Thee will I follow far as is allowed me,"
   He answered; "and if smoke prevent our seeing,   35
   Hearing shall keep us joined instead thereof."

Thereon began I: "With that swathing band
   Which death unwindeth am I going upward,
   And hither came I through the infernal anguish.

And if God in his grace has me infolded,   40
   So that he wills that I behold his court
   By method wholly out of modern usage,

Conceal not from me who ere death thou wast,
   But tell it me, and tell me if I go
   Right for the pass, and be thy words our escort."   45

"Lombard was I, and I was Marco called;
   The world I knew, and loved that excellence,
   At which has each one now unbent his bow.

For mounting upward, thou art going right."
   Thus he made answer, and subjoined: "I pray thee   50
   To pray for me when thou shalt be above."

"Now who art thou, that cleavest through our smoke
And art discoursing of us even as though
Thou didst by calends still divide the time?"

Purgatorio XVI, lines 25–27

"Thee will I follow far as is allowed me,"
He answered; "and if smoke prevent our seeing,
Hearing shall keep us joined instead thereof."

Purgatorio XVI, lines 34–36

And I to him: "My faith I pledge to thee
    To do what thou dost ask me; but am bursting
    Inly with doubt, unless I rid me of it.

First it was simple, and is now made double   55
    By thy opinion, which makes certain to me,
    Here and elsewhere, that which I couple with it.

The world forsooth is utterly deserted
    By every virtue, as thou tellest me,
    And with iniquity is big and covered;   60

But I beseech thee point me out the cause,
    That I may see it, and to others show it;
    For one in the heavens, and here below one puts it."

A sigh profound, that grief forced into Ai!
    He first sent forth, and then began he: "Brother,   65
    The world is blind, and sooth thou comest from it!

Ye who are living every cause refer
    Still upward to the heavens, as if all things
    They of necessity moved with themselves.

If this were so, in you would be destroyed   70
    Free will, nor any justice would there be
    In having joy for good, or grief for evil.

The heavens your movements do initiate,
    I say not all; but granting that I say it,
    Light has been given you for good and evil,   75

And free volition; which, if some fatigue
    In the first battles with the heavens it suffers,
    Afterwards conquers all, if well 'tis nurtured.

To greater force and to a better nature,
    Though free, ye subject are, and that creates   80
    The mind in you the heavens have not in charge.

Hence, if the present world doth go astray,
    In you the cause is, be it sought in you;
    And I therein will now be thy true spy.

Forth from the hand of Him, who fondles it   85
    Before it is, like to a little girl
    Weeping and laughing in her childish sport,

Issues the simple soul, that nothing knows,
    Save that, proceeding from a joyous Maker,
    Gladly it turns to that which gives it pleasure.   90

Of trivial good at first it tastes the savor;
    Is cheated by it, and runs after it,
    If guide or rein turn not aside its love.

Hence it behoved laws for a rein to place,
    Behoved a king to have, who at the least   95
    Of the true city should discern the tower.

The laws exist, but who sets hand to them?
    No one; because the shepherd who precedes
    Can ruminate, but cleaveth not the hoof;

Wherefore the people that perceives its guide   100
    Strike only at the good for which it hankers,
    Feeds upon that, and farther seeketh not.

Clearly canst thou perceive that evil guidance
    The cause is that has made the world depraved,
    And not that nature is corrupt in you.   105

Rome, that reformed the world, accustomed was
    Two suns to have, which one road and the other,
    Of God and of the world, made manifest.

One has the other quenched, and to the crosier
    The sword is joined, and ill beseemeth it   110
    That by main force one with the other go,

Because, being joined, one feareth not the other;
    If thou believe not, think upon the grain,
    For by its seed each herb is recognized.

In the land laved by Po and Adige,   115
    Valor and courtesy used to be found,
    Before that Frederick had his controversy;

Now in security can pass that way
    Whoever will abstain, through sense of shame,
    From speaking with the good, or drawing near them. 120

True, three old men are left, in whom upbraids
    The ancient age the new, and late they deem it
    That God restore them to the better life:

Currado da Palazzo, and good Gherardo,
    And Guido da Castel, who better named is,   125
    In fashion of the French, the simple Lombard:

Say thou henceforward that the Church of Rome,
    Confounding in itself two governments,
    Falls in the mire, and soils itself and burden."

"O Marco mine," I said, "thou reasonest well;   130
    And now discern I why the sons of Levi
    Have been excluded from the heritage.

But what Gherardo is it, who, as sample
    Of a lost race, thou sayest has remained
    In reprobation of the barbarous age?"   135

"Either thy speech deceives me, or it tempts me,"
    He answered me; "for speaking Tuscan to me,
    It seems of good Gherardo naught thou knowest.

By other surname do I know him not,
    Unless I take it from his daughter Gaia.   140
    May God be with you, for I come no farther.

Behold the dawn, that through the smoke rays out,
    Already whitening; and I must depart—
    Yonder the Angel is—ere he appear."

Thus did he speak, and would no farther hear me.   145

⊰ CANTO XVII ⊱

Dante's Dream of Anger—The Fourth Circle: The Slothful—
Virgil's Discourse of Love

Remember, Reader, if e'er in the Alps
    A mist o'ertook thee, through which thou couldst see
Not otherwise than through its membrane mole,

How, when the vapors humid and condensed
    Begin to dissipate themselves, the sphere   5
    Of the sun feebly enters in among them,

And thy imagination will be swift
    In coming to perceive how I re-saw
    The sun at first, that was already setting.

Thus, to the faithful footsteps of my Master   10
    Mating mine own, I issued from that cloud
    To rays already dead on the low shores.

O thou, Imagination, that dost steal us
    So from without sometimes, that man perceives not,
    Although around may sound a thousand trumpets,   15

Who moveth thee, if sense impel thee not?
    Moves thee a light, which in the heaven takes form,
    By self, or by a will that downward guides it.

Of her impiety, who changed her form
    Into the bird that most delights in singing,   20
    In my imagining appeared the trace;

And hereupon my mind was so withdrawn
    Within itself, that from without there came
    Nothing that then might be received by it.

Then reigned within my lofty fantasy   25
    One crucified, disdainful and ferocious
    In countenance, and even thus was dying.

Around him were the great Ahasuerus,
    Esther his wife, and the just Mordecai,
    Who was in word and action so entire.   30

And even as this image burst asunder
    Of its own self, in fashion of a bubble
    In which the water it was made of fails,

There rose up in my vision a young maiden
    Bitterly weeping, and she said: "O queen,   35
    Why hast thou wished in anger to be naught?

Thou'st slain thyself, Lavinia not to lose;
  Now hast thou lost me; I am she who mourns,
  Mother, at thine ere at another's ruin."

As sleep is broken, when upon a sudden   40
  New light strikes in upon the eyelids closed,
  And broken quivers ere it dieth wholly,

So this imagining of mine fell down
  As soon as the effulgence smote my face,
  Greater by far than what is in our wont.   45

I turned me round to see where I might be,
  When said a voice, "Here is the passage up";
  Which from all other purposes removed me,

And made my wish so full of eagerness
  To look and see who was it that was speaking,   50
  It never rests till meeting face to face;

But as before the sun, which quells the sight,
  And in its own excess its figure veils,
  Even so my power was insufficient here.

"This is a spirit divine, who in the way   55
  Of going up directs us without asking,
  And who with his own light himself conceals.

He does with us as man doth with himself;
  For he who sees the need, and waits the asking,
  Malignly leans already tow'rds denial.   60

Accord we now our feet to such inviting,
  Let us make haste to mount ere it grow dark;
  For then we could not till the day return."

Thus my Conductor said; and I and he
    Together turned our footsteps to a stairway;   65
    And I, as soon as the first step I reached,

Near me perceived a motion as of wings,
    And fanning in the face, and saying, *"Beati*
    Pacifici, who are without ill anger."

Already over us were so uplifted   70
    The latest sunbeams, which the night pursues,
    That upon many sides the stars appeared.

"O manhood mine, why dost thou vanish so?"
    I said within myself; for I perceived
    The vigor of my legs was put in truce.   75

We at the point were where no more ascends
    The stairway upward, and were motionless,
    Even as a ship, which at the shore arrives;

And I gave heed a little, if I might hear
    Aught whatsoever in the circle new;   80
    Then to my Master turned me round and said:

"Say, my sweet Father, what delinquency
    Is purged here in the circle where we are?
    Although our feet may pause, pause not thy speech."

And he to me: "The love of good, remiss   85
    In what it should have done, is here restored;
    Here plied again the ill-belated oar;

But still more openly to understand,
    Turn unto me thy mind, and thou shalt gather
    Some profitable fruit from our delay.   90

Neither Creator nor a creature ever,
   Son," he began, "was destitute of love
   Natural or spiritual; and thou knowest it.

The natural was ever without error;
   But err the other may by evil object,   95
   Or by too much, or by too little vigor.

While in the first it well directed is,
   And in the second moderates itself,
   It cannot be the cause of sinful pleasure;

But when to ill it turns, and, with more care   100
   Or lesser than it ought, runs after good,
   'Gainst the Creator works his own creation.

Hence thou mayst comprehend that love must be
   The seed within yourselves of every virtue,
   And every act that merits punishment.   105

Now inasmuch as never from the welfare
   Of its own subject can love turn its sight,
   From their own hatred all things are secure;

And since we cannot think of any being
   Standing alone, nor from the First divided,   110
   Of hating Him is all desire cut off.

Hence if, discriminating, I judge well,
   The evil that one loves is of one's neighbor,
   And this is born in three modes in your clay.

There are, who, by abasement of their neighbor,   115
   Hope to excel, and therefore only long
   That from his greatness he may be cast down;

There are, who power, grace, honor, and renown
    Fear they may lose because another rises,
    Thence are so sad that the reverse they love;   120

And there are those whom injury seems to chafe,
    So that it makes them greedy for revenge,
    And such must needs shape out another's harm.

This threefold love is wept for down below;
    Now of the other will I have thee hear,   125
    That runneth after good with measure faulty.

Each one confusedly a good conceives
    Wherein the mind may rest, and longeth for it;
    Therefore to overtake it each one strives.

If languid love to look on this attract you,   130
    Or in attaining unto it, this cornice,
    After just penitence, torments you for it.

There's other good that does not make man happy;
    'Tis not felicity, 'tis not the good
    Essence, of every good the fruit and root.   135

The love that yields itself too much to this
    Above us is lamented in three circles;
    But how tripartite it may be described,

I say not, that thou seek it for thyself."

⊰ Canto XVIII ⊱

Virgil Further Discourses of Love and Free Will—The Abbot of San Zeno

An end had put unto his reasoning
The lofty Teacher, and attent was looking
Into my face, if I appeared content;

And I, whom a new thirst still goaded on,
Without was mute, and said within: "Perchance   5
The too much questioning I make annoys him."

But that true Father, who had comprehended
The timid wish, that opened not itself,
By speaking gave me hardihood to speak.

Whence I: "My sight is, Master, vivified   10
So in thy light, that clearly I discern
Whate'er thy speech importeth or describes.

Therefore I thee entreat, sweet Father dear,
To teach me love, to which thou dost refer
Every good action and its contrary."   15

"Direct," he said, "towards me the keen eyes
Of intellect, and clear will be to thee
The error of the blind, who would be leaders.

The soul, which is created apt to love,
Is mobile unto everything that pleases,   20
Soon as by pleasure she is waked to action.

Your apprehension from some real thing
An image draws, and in yourselves displays it
So that it makes the soul turn unto it.

And if, when turned, towards it she incline,   25
    Love is that inclination; it is nature,
    Which is by pleasure bound in you anew

Then even as the fire doth upward move
    By its own form, which to ascend is born,
    Where longest in its matter it endures,   30

So comes the captive soul into desire,
    Which is a motion spiritual, and ne'er rests
    Until she doth enjoy the thing beloved.

Now may apparent be to thee how hidden
    The truth is from those people, who aver   35
    All love is in itself a laudable thing;

Because its matter may perchance appear
    Aye to be good; but yet not each impression
    Is good, albeit good may be the wax."

"Thy words, and my sequacious intellect,"   40
    I answered him, "have love revealed to me;
    But that has made me more impregned with doubt;

For if love from without be offered us,
    And with another foot the soul go not,
    If right or wrong she go, 'tis not her merit."   45

And he to me: "What reason seeth here,
    Myself can tell thee; beyond that await
    For Beatrice, since 'tis a work of faith.

Every substantial form, that segregate
    From matter is, and with it is united,   50
    Specific power has in itself collected,

Which without act is not perceptible,
    Nor shows itself except by its effect,
    As life does in a plant by the green leaves.

But still, whence cometh the intelligence   55
    Of the first notions, man is ignorant,
    And the affection for the first allurements,

Which are in you as instinct in the bee
    To make its honey; and this first desire
    Merit of praise or blame containeth not.   60

Now, that to this all others may be gathered,
    Innate within you is the power that counsels,
    And it should keep the threshold of assent.

This is the principle, from which is taken
    Occasion of desert in you, according   65
    As good and guilty loves it takes and winnows.

Those who, in reasoning, to the bottom went,
    Were of this innate liberty aware,
    Therefore bequeathed they Ethics to the world.

Supposing, then, that from necessity   70
    Springs every love that is within you kindled,
    Within yourselves the power is to restrain it.

The noble virtue Beatrice understands
    By the free will; and therefore see that thou
    Bear it in mind, if she should speak of it."   75

The moon, belated almost unto midnight,
    Now made the stars appear to us more rare,
    Formed like a bucket, that is all ablaze,

And counter to the heavens ran through those paths
 Which the sun sets aflame, when he of Rome   80
 Sees it 'twixt Sardes and Corsicans go down;

And that patrician shade, for whom is named
 Pietola more than any Mantuan town,
 Had laid aside the burden of my lading;

Whence I, who reason manifest and plain   85
 In answer to my questions had received,
 Stood like a man in drowsy reverie.

But taken from me was this drowsiness
 Suddenly by a people, that behind
 Our backs already had come round to us.   90

And as, of old, Ismenus and Asopus
 Beside them saw at night the rush and throng,
 If but the Thebans were in need of Bacchus,

So they along that circle curve their step,
 From what I saw of those approaching us,   95
 Who by goodwill and righteous love are ridden.

Full soon they were upon us, because running
 Moved onward all that mighty multitude,
 And two in the advance cried out, lamenting,

"Mary in haste unto the mountain ran,   100
 And Cæsar, that he might subdue Ilerda,
 Thrust at Marseilles, and then ran into Spain."

"Quick! quick! so that the time may not be lost
 By little love!" forthwith the others cried,
 "For ardor in well-doing freshens grace!"   105

But taken from me was this drowsiness
Suddenly by a people, that behind
Our backs already had come round to us.

Purgatorio XVIII, lines 88–90

"O folk, in whom an eager fervor now
    Supplies perhaps delay and negligence,
    Put by you in well-doing, through lukewarmness,

This one who lives, and truly I lie not,
    Would fain go up, if but the sun relight us;   110
    So tell us where the passage nearest is."

These were the words of him who was my Guide;
    And someone of those spirits said: "Come on
    Behind us, and the opening shalt thou find;

So full of longing are we to move onward,   115
    That stay we cannot; therefore pardon us,
    If thou for churlishness our justice take.

I was San Zeno's Abbot at Verona,
    Under the empire of good Barbarossa,
    Of whom still sorrowing Milan holds discourse;   120

And he has one foot in the grave already,
    Who shall erelong lament that monastery,
    And sorry be of having there had power,

Because his son, in his whole body sick,
    And worse in mind, and who was evil-born,   125
    He put into the place of its true pastor."

If more he said, or silent was, I know not,
    He had already passed so far beyond us;
    But this I heard, and to retain it pleased me.

And he who was in every need my succor   130
    Said: "Turn thee hitherward; see two of them
    Come fastening upon slothfulness their teeth."

In rear of all they shouted: "Sooner were
    The people dead to whom the sea was opened,
    Than their inheritors the Jordan saw;   135

And those who the fatigue did not endure
    Unto the issue, with Anchises's son,
    Themselves to life withouten glory offered."

Then when from us so separated were
    Those shades, that they no longer could be seen,   140
    Within me a new thought did entrance find,

Whence others many and diverse were born;
    And so I lapsed from one into another,
    That in a reverie mine eyes I closed,

And meditation into dream transmuted.   145

⊰ Canto XIX ⊱

Dante's Dream of the Siren—The Fifth Circle: The Avaricious and Prodigal—
Pope Adrian V

It was the hour when the diurnal heat
    No more can warm the coldness of the moon,
Vanquished by earth, or peradventure Saturn,

When geomancers their Fortuna Major
    See in the orient before the dawn   5
    Rise by a path that long remains not dim,

There came to me in dreams a stammering woman,
    Squint in her eyes, and in her feet distorted,
    With hands disseuered, and of sallow hue.

I looked at her; and as the sun restores   10
    The frigid members, which the night benumbs,
    Even thus my gaze did render voluble

Her tongue, and made her all erect thereafter
    In little while, and the lost countenance
    As love desires it so in her did color.   15

When in this wise she had her speech unloosed,
    She 'gan to sing so, that with difficulty
    Could I have turned my thoughts away from her.

"I am," she sang, "I am the Siren sweet
    Who mariners amid the main unman,   20
    So full am I of pleasantness to hear.

I drew Ulysses from his wandering way
    Unto my song, and he who dwells with me
    Seldom departs, so wholly I content him."

Her mouth was not yet closed again, before   25
    Appeared a Lady saintly and alert
    Close at my side to put her to confusion.

"Virgilius, O Virgilius! who is this?"
    Sternly she said; and he was drawing near
    With eyes still fixed upon that modest one.   30

She seized the other and in front laid open,
    Rending her garments, and her belly showed me;
    This waked me with the stench that issued from it.

I turned mine eyes, and good Virgilius said:
    "At least thrice have I called thee; rise and come;   35
    Find we the opening by which thou mayst enter."

I rose; and full already of high day
  Were all the circles of the Sacred Mountain,
  And with the new sun at our back we went.

Following behind him, I my forehead bore   40
  Like unto one who has it laden with thought,
  Who makes himself the half arch of a bridge,

When I heard say, "Come, here the passage is,"
  Spoken in a manner gentle and benign,
  Such as we hear not in this mortal region.   45

With open wings, which of a swan appeared,
  Upward he turned us who thus spake to us,
  Between the two walls of the solid granite.

He moved his pinions afterwards and fanned us,
  Affirming those *qui lugent* to be blessed,   50
  For they shall have their souls with comfort filled.

"What aileth thee, that aye to earth thou gazest?"
  To me my Guide began to say, we both
  Somewhat beyond the Angel having mounted.

And I: "With such misgiving makes me go   55
  A vision new, which bends me to itself,
  So that I cannot from the thought withdraw me."

"Didst thou behold," he said, "that old enchantress,
  Who sole above us henceforth is lamented?
  Didst thou behold how man is freed from her?   60

Suffice it thee, and smite earth with thy heels,
  Thine eyes lift upward to the lure, that whirls
  The Eternal King with revolutions vast."

"What aileth thee, that aye to earth thou gazest?"
To me my Guide began to say, we both
Somewhat beyond the Angel having mounted.

Purgatorio XIX, lines 52–54

Even as the hawk, that first his feet surveys,
 Then turns him to the call and stretches forward, 65
 Through the desire of food that draws him thither,

Such I became, and such, as far as cleaves
 The rock to give a way to him who mounts,
 Went on to where the circling doth begin.

On the fifth circle when I had come forth, 70
 People I saw upon it who were weeping,
 Stretched prone upon the ground, all downward turncd.

"Adhæsit pavimento anima mea,"
 I heard them say with sighings so profound,
 That hardly could the words be understood. 75

"O ye elect of God, whose sufferings
 Justice and Hope both render less severe,
 Direct ye us towards the high ascents."

"If ye are come secure from this prostration,
 And wish to find the way most speedily, 80
 Let your right hands be evermore outside."

Thus did the Poet ask, and thus was answered
 By them somewhat in front of us; whence I
 In what was spoken divined the rest concealed,

And unto my Lord's eyes mine eyes I turned; 85
 Whence he assented with a cheerful sign
 To what the sight of my desire implored.

When of myself I could dispose at will,
 Above that creature did I draw myself,
 Whose words before had caused me to take note, 90

Saying: "O Spirit, in whom weeping ripens
  That without which to God we cannot turn,
  Suspend awhile for me thy greater care.

Who wast thou, and why are your backs turned upwards,
  Tell me, and if thou wouldst that I procure thee   95
  Anything there whence living I departed."

And he to me: "Wherefore our backs the heaven
  Turns to itself, know shalt thou; but beforehand
  Scias quod ego fui successor Petri.

Between Siestri and Chiaveri descends   100
  A river beautiful, and of its name
  The title of my blood its summit makes.

A month and little more essayed I how
  Weighs the great cloak on him from mire who keeps it;
  For all the other burdens seem a feather.   105

Tardy, ah woe is me! was my conversion;
  But when the Roman Shepherd I was made,
  Then I discovered life to be a lie.

I saw that there the heart was not at rest,
  Nor farther in that life could one ascend;   110
  Whereby the love of this was kindled in me.

Until that time a wretched soul and parted
  From God was I, and wholly avaricious;
  Now, as thou seest, I here am punished for it.

What avarice does is here made manifest   115
  In the purgation of these souls converted,
  And no more bitter pain the Mountain has.

Even as our eye did not uplift itself
    Aloft, being fastened upon earthly things,
    So justice here has merged it in the earth.   120

As avarice had extinguished our affection
    For every good, whereby was action lost,
    So justice here doth hold us in restraint,

Bound and imprisoned by the feet and hands;
    And so long as it pleases the just Lord   125
    Shall we remain immovable and prostrate."

I on my knees had fallen, and wished to speak;
    But even as I began, and he was 'ware,
    Only by listening, of my reverence,

"What cause," he said, "has downward bent thee thus?" 130
    And I to him: "For your own dignity,
    Standing, my conscience stung me with remorse."

"Straighten thy legs, and upward raise thee, brother,"
    He answered: "Err not, fellow-servant am I
    With thee and with the others to one power.   135

If e'er that holy, evangelic sound,
    Which sayeth *neque nubent*, thou hast heard,
    Well canst thou see why in this wise I speak.

Now go; no longer will I have thee linger,
    Because thy stay doth incommode my weeping,   140
    With which I ripen that which thou hast said.

On earth I have a grandchild named Alagia,
    Good in herself, unless indeed our house
    Malevolent may make her by example,

And she alone remains to me on earth."   145

"What cause," he said, "has downward bent thee thus?"
And I to him: "For your own dignity,
Standing, my conscience stung me with remorse."

Purgatorio XIX, lines 130–132

⊰ CANTO XX ⊱

Hugh Capet—Corruption of the French Crown—Prophecy of the Abduction of Pope Boniface VIII and the Sacrilege of Philip the Fair—The Earthquake

Ill strives the will against a better will;
    Therefore, to pleasure him, against my pleasure
I drew the sponge not saturate from the water.

Onward I moved, and onward moved my Leader,
    Through vacant places, skirting still the rock,   5
    As on a wall close to the battlements;

For they that through their eyes pour drop by drop
    The malady which all the world pervades,
    On the other side too near the verge approach.

Accursed mayst thou be, thou old she-wolf,   10
    That more than all the other beasts hast prey,
    Because of hunger infinitely hollow!

O heaven, in whose gyrations some appear
    To think conditions here below are changed,
    When will he come through whom she shall depart?   15

Onward we went with footsteps slow and scarce,
    And I attentive to the shades I heard
    Piteously weeping and bemoaning them;

And I by peradventure heard "Sweet Mary!"
    Uttered in front of us amid the weeping   20
    Even as a woman does who is in childbirth;

Onward we went with footsteps slow and scarce,
And I attentive to the shades I heard
Piteously weeping and bemoaning them

Purgatorio XX, lines 16–18

And in continuance: "How poor thou wast
   Is manifested by that hostelry
   Where thou didst lay thy sacred burden down."

Thereafterward I heard: "O good Fabricius,   25
   Virtue with poverty didst thou prefer
   To the possession of great wealth with vice."

So pleasurable were these words to me
   That I drew farther onward to have knowledge
   Touching that spirit whence they seemed to come.   30

He furthermore was speaking of the largess
   Which Nicholas unto the maidens gave,
   In order to conduct their youth to honor.

"O soul that dost so excellently speak,
   Tell me who wast thou," said I, "and why only   35
   Thou dost renew these praises well deserved?

Not without recompense shall be thy word,
   If I return to finish the short journey
   Of that life which is flying to its end."

And he: "I'll tell thee, not for any comfort   40
   I may expect from earth, but that so much
   Grace shines in thee or ever thou art dead.

I was the root of that malignant plant
   Which overshadows all the Christian world,
   So that good fruit is seldom gathered from it;   45

But if Douay and Ghent, and Lille and Bruges
   Had Power, soon vengeance would be taken on it;
   And this I pray of Him who judges all.

Hugh Capet was I called upon the earth;
    From me were born the Louises and Philips,   50
    By whom in later days has France been governed.

I was the son of a Parisian butcher,
    What time the ancient kings had perished all,
    Excepting one, contrite in cloth of gray.

I found me grasping in my hands the rein   55
    Of the realm's government, and so great power
    Of new acquest, and so with friends abounding,

That to the widowed diadem promoted
    The head of mine own offspring was, from whom
    The consecrated bones of these began.   60

So long as the great dowry of Provence
    Out of my blood took not the sense of shame,
    'Twas little worth, but still it did no harm.

Then it began with falsehood and with force
    Its rapine; and thereafter, for amends,   65
    Took Ponthieu, Normandy, and Gascony.

Charles came to Italy, and for amends
    A victim made of Conradin, and then
    Thrust Thomas back to heaven, for amends.

A time I see, not very distant now,   70
    Which draweth forth another Charles from France,
    The better to make known both him and his.

Unarmed he goes, and only with the lance
    That Judas jousted with; and that he thrusts
    So that he makes the paunch of Florence burst.   75

He thence not land, but sin and infamy,
    Shall gain, so much more grievous to himself
    As the more light such damage he accounts.

The other, now gone forth, ta'en in his ship,
    See I his daughter sell, and chaffer for her   80
    As corsairs do with other female slaves.

What more, O Avarice, canst thou do to us,
    Since thou my blood so to thyself hast drawn,
    It careth not for its own proper flesh?

That less may seem the future ill and past,   85
    I see the flower-de-luce Alagna enter,
    And Christ in his own Vicar captive made.

I see him yet another time derided;
    I see renewed the vinegar and gall,
    And between living thieves I see him slain.   90

I see the modern Pilate so relentless,
    This does not sate him, but without decretal
    He to the temple bears his sordid sails!

When, O my Lord! shall I be joyful made
    By looking on the vengeance which, concealed,   95
    Makes sweet thine anger in thy secrecy?

What I was saying of that only bride
    Of the Holy Ghost, and which occasioned thee
    To turn towards me for some commentary,

So long has been ordained to all our prayers   100
    As the day lasts; but when the night comes on,
    Contrary sound we take instead thereof.

At that time we repeat Pygmalion,
  Of whom a traitor, thief, and parricide
  Made his insatiable desire of gold;   105

And the misery of avaricious Midas,
  That followed his inordinate demand,
  At which forevermore one needs but laugh.

The foolish Achan each one then records,
  And how he stole the spoils; so that the wrath   110
  Of Joshua still appears to sting him here.

Then we accuse Sapphira with her husband,
  We laud the hoofbeats Heliodorus had,
  And the whole mount in infamy encircles

Polymnestor who murdered Polydorus.   115
  Here finally is cried: 'O Crassus, tell us,
  For thou dost know, what is the taste of gold?'

Sometimes we speak, one loud, another low,
  According to desire of speech, that spurs us
  To greater now and now to lesser pace.   120

But in the good that here by day is talked of,
  Erewhile alone I was not; yet nearby
  No other person lifted up his voice."

From him already we departed were,
  And made endeavor to o'ercome the road   125
  As much as was permitted to our power,

When I perceived, like something that is falling,
  The mountain tremble, whence a chill seized on me,
  As seizes him who to his death is going.

Certes so violently shook not Delos,   130
    Before Latona made her nest therein
    To give birth to the two eyes of the heaven.

Then upon all sides there began a cry,
    Such that the Master drew himself towards me,
    Saying, "Fear not, while I am guiding thee."   135

"Gloria in excelsis Deo," all
    Were saying, from what near I comprehended,
    Where it was possible to hear the cry.

We paused immovable and in suspense,
    Even as the shepherds who first heard that song,   140
    Until the trembling ceased, and it was finished.

Then we resumed again our holy path,
    Watching the shades that lay upon the ground,
    Already turned to their accustomed plaint.

No ignorance ever with so great a strife   145
    Had rendered me importunate to know,
    If erreth not in this my memory,

As meditating then I seemed to have;
    Nor out of haste to question did I dare,
    Nor of myself I there could aught perceive;   150

So I went onward timorous and thoughtful.

⇥ CANTO XXI ⇤

The Poet Statius — Praise of Virgil

The natural thirst, that ne'er is satisfied
    Excepting with the water for whose grace
The woman of Samaria besought,

Put me in travail, and haste goaded me
    Along the encumbered path behind my Leader   5
    And I was pitying that righteous vengeance;

And lo! in the same manner as Luke writeth
    That Christ appeared to two upon the way
    From the sepulchral cave already risen,

A shade appeared to us, and came behind us,   10
    Down gazing on the prostrate multitude,
    Nor were we ware of it, until it spake,

Saying, "My brothers, may God give you peace!"
    We turned us suddenly, and Virgilius rendered
    To him the countersign thereto conforming.   15

Thereon began he: "In the blessed council,
    Thee may the court veracious place in peace,
    That me doth banish in eternal exile!"

"How," said he, and the while we went with speed,
    "If ye are shades whom God deigns not on high,   20
    Who up his stairs so far has guided you?"

And said my Teacher: "If thou note the marks
    Which this one bears, and which the Angel traces
    Well shalt thou see he with the good must reign.

But because she who spinneth day and night   25
    For him had not yet drawn the distaff off,
    Which Clotho lays for each one and compacts,

His soul, which is thy sister and my own,
    In coming upwards could not come alone,
    By reason that it sees not in our fashion.   30

Whence I was drawn from out the ample throat
    Of Hell to be his guide, and I shall guide him
    As far on as my school has power to lead.

But tell us, if thou knowest, why such a shudder
    Erewhile the mountain gave, and why together   35
    All seemed to cry, as far as its moist feet?"

In asking he so hit the very eye
    Of my desire, that merely with the hope
    My thirst became the less unsatisfied.

"Naught is there," he began, "that without order   40
    May the religion of the mountain feel,
    Nor aught that may be foreign to its custom.

Free is it here from every permutation;
    What from itself heaven in itself receiveth
    Can be of this the cause, and naught beside;   45

Because that neither rain, nor hail, nor snow,
    Nor dew, nor hoarfrost any higher falls
    Than the short, little stairway of three steps.

Dense clouds do not appear, nor rarefied,
    Nor coruscation, nor the daughter of Thaumas,   50
    That often upon earth her region shifts;

No arid vapour any farther rises
>   Than to the top of the three steps I spake of,
>   Whereon the Vicar of Peter has his feet.

Lower down perchance it trembles less or more,   55
>   But, for the wind that in the earth is hidden
>   I know not how, up here it never trembled.

It trembles here, whenever any soul
>   Feels itself pure, so that it soars, or moves
>   To mount aloft, and such a cry attends it.   60

Of purity the will alone gives proof,
>   Which, being wholly free to change its convent,
>   Takes by surprise the soul, and helps it fly.

First it wills well; but the desire permits not,
>   Which divine justice with the selfsame will   65
>   There was to sin, upon the torment sets.

And I, who have been lying in this pain
>   Five hundred years and more, but just now felt
>   A free volition for a better seat.

Therefore thou heardst the earthquake, and the pious   70
>   Spirits along the mountain rendering praise
>   Unto the Lord, that soon he speed them upwards."

So said he to him; and since we enjoy
>   As much in drinking as the thirst is great,
>   I could not say how much it did me good.   75

And the wise Leader: "Now I see the net
>   That snares you here, and how ye are set free,
>   Why the earth quakes, and wherefore ye rejoice.

Now who thou wast be pleased that I may know;
　　And why so many centuries thou hast here   80
　　Been lying, let me gather from thy words."

"In days when the good Titus, with the aid
　　Of the supremest King, avenged the wounds
　　Whence issued forth the blood by Judas sold,

Under the name that most endures and honors,   85
　　Was I on earth," that spirit made reply,
　　"Greatly renowned, but not with faith as yet.

My vocal spirit was so sweet, that Rome
　　Me, a Thoulousian, drew unto herself,
　　Where I deserved to deck my brows with myrtle.   90

Statius the people name me still on earth;
　　I sang of Thebes, and then of great Achilles;
　　But on the way fell with my second burden.

The seeds unto my ardor were the sparks
　　Of that celestial flame which heated me,   95
　　Whereby more than a thousand have been fired;

Of the *Æneid* speak I, which to me
　　A mother was, and was my nurse in song;
　　Without this weighed I not a drachma's weight.

And to have lived upon the earth what time   100
　　Virgilius lived, I would accept one sun
　　More than I must ere issuing from my ban."

These words towards me made Virgilius turn
　　With looks that in their silence said, "Be silent!"
　　But yet the power that wills cannot do all things;   105

For tears and laughter are such pursuivants
    Unto the passion from which each springs forth,
    In the most truthful least the will they follow.

I only smiled, as one who gives the wink;
    Whereat the shade was silent, and it gazed   110
    Into mine eyes, where most expression dwells;

And, "As thou well mayst consummate a labor
    So great," it said, "why did thy face just now
    Display to me the lightning of a smile?"

Now am I caught on this side and on that;   115
    One keeps me silent, one to speak conjures me,
    Wherefore I sigh, and I am understood.

"Speak," said my Master, "and be not afraid
    Of speaking, but speak out, and say to him
    What he demands with such solicitude."   120

Whence I: "Thou peradventure marvelest,
    O antique spirit, at the smile I gave;
    But I will have more wonder seize upon thee.

This one, who guides on high these eyes of mine,
    Is that Virgilius, from whom thou didst learn   125
    To sing aloud of men and of the Gods.

If other cause thou to my smile imputedst,
    Abandon it as false, and trust it was
    Those words which thou hast spoken concerning him."

Already he was stooping to embrace   130
    My Teacher's feet; but he said to him: "Brother,
    Do not; for shade thou art, and shade beholdest."

And he uprising: "Now canst thou the sum
>Of love which warms me to thee comprehend,
>When this our vanity I disremember,   135

Treating a shadow as substantial thing."

⇥ CANTO XXII ⇤

Statius' Denunciation of Avarice—
The Sixth Circle: The Gluttonous—The Mystic Tree

Already was the Angel left behind us,
>The Angel who to the sixth round had turned us,
Having erased one mark from off my face;

And those who have in justice their desire
>Had said to us, *"Beati,"* in their voices,   5
>With *"sitio,"* and without more ended it.

And I, more light than through the other passes,
>Went onward so, that without any labor
>I followed upward the swift-footed spirits;

When thus Virgilius began: "The love   10
>Kindled by virtue aye another kindles,
>Provided outwardly its flame appear.

Hence from the hour that Juvenal descended
>Among us into the infernal Limbo,
>Who made apparent to me thy affection,   15

My kindliness towards thee was as great
>As ever bound one to an unseen person,
>So that these stairs will now seem short to me.

But tell me, and forgive me as a friend,
    If too great confidence let loose the rein,   20
    And as a friend now hold discourse with me;

How was it possible within thy breast
    For avarice to find place, 'mid so much wisdom
    As thou wast filled with by thy diligence?"

These words excited Statius at first   25
    Somewhat to laughter; afterward he answered:
    "Each word of thine is love's dear sign to me.

Verily oftentimes do things appear
    Which give fallacious matter to our doubts,
    Instead of the true causes which are hidden!   30

Thy question shows me thy belief to be
    That I was niggard in the other life,
    It may be from the circle where I was;

Therefore know thou, that avarice was removed
    Too far from me; and this extravagance   35
    Thousands of lunar periods have punished.

And were it not that I my thoughts uplifted,
    When I the passage heard where thou exclaimest,
    As if indignant, unto human nature,

'To what impellest thou not, O cursed hunger   40
    Of gold, the appetite of mortal men?'
    Revolving I should feel the dismal joustings.

Then I perceived the hands could spread too wide
    Their wings in spending, and repented me
    As well of that as of my other sins;   45

How many with shorn hair shall rise again
    Because of ignorance, which from this sin
    Cuts off repentance living and in death!

And know that the transgression which rebuts
    By direct opposition any sin   50
    Together with it here its verdure dries.

Therefore if I have been among that folk
    Which mourns its avarice, to purify me,
    For its opposite has this befallen me."

"Now when thou sangest the relentless weapons   55
    Of the twofold affliction of Jocasta,"
    The singer of the Songs Bucolic said,

"From that which Clio there with thee preludes,
    It does not seem that yet had made thee faithful
    That faith without which no good works suffice.   60

If this be so, what candles or what sun
    Scattered thy darkness so that thou didst trim
    Thy sails behind the Fisherman thereafter?"

And he to him: "Thou first directedst me
    Towards Parnassus, in its grots to drink,   65
    And first concerning God didst me enlighten.

Thou didst as he who walketh in the night,
    Who bears his light behind, which helps him not,
    But wary makes the persons after him,

When thou didst say: 'The age renews itself,   70
    Justice returns, and man's primeval time,
    And a new progeny descends from heaven.'

Through thee I Poet was, through thee a Christian;
    But that thou better see what I design,
    To color it will I extend my hand.   75

Already was the world in every part
    Pregnant with the true creed, disseminated
    By messengers of the eternal kingdom;

And thy assertion, spoken of above,
    With the new preachers was in unison;   80
    Whence I to visit them the custom took.

Then they became so holy in my sight,
    That, when Domitian persecuted them,
    Not without tears of mine were their laments;

And all the while that I on earth remained,   85
    Them I befriended, and their upright customs
    Made me disparage all the other sects.

And ere I led the Greeks unto the rivers
    Of Thebes, in poetry, I was baptized,
    But out of fear was covertly a Christian,   90

For a long time professing paganism;
    And this lukewarmness caused me the fourth circle
    To circuit round more than four centuries.

Thou, therefore, who hast raised the covering
    That hid from me whatever good I speak of,   95
    While in ascending we have time to spare,

Tell me, in what place is our friend Terentius,
    Cæcilius, Plautus, Varro, if thou knowest;
    Tell me if they are damned, and in what alley."

"These, Persius and myself, and others many,"   100
   Replied my Leader, "with that Grecian are
   Whom more than all the rest the Muses suckled,

In the first circle of the prison blind;
   Ofttimes we of the mountain hold discourse
   Which has our nurses ever with itself.   105

Euripides is with us, Antiphon,
   Simonides, Agatho, and many other
   Greeks who of old their brows with laurel decked.

There some of thine own people may be seen,
   Antigone, Deiphile, and Argìa,   110
   And there Ismene mournful as of old.

There she is seen who pointed out Langìa;
   There is Tiresias's daughter, and there Thetis,
   And there Deidamia with her sisters."

Silent already were the poets both,   115
   Attent once more in looking round about,
   From the ascent and from the walls released;

And four handmaidens of the day already
   Were left behind, and at the pole the fifth
   Was pointing upward still its burning horn,   120

What time my Guide: "I think that tow'rds the edge
   Our dexter shoulders it behoves us turn,
   Circling the mount as we are wont to do."

Thus in that region custom was our ensign;
   And we resumed our way with less suspicion   125
   For the assenting of that worthy soul

They in advance went on, and I alone
    Behind them, and I listened to their speech,
    Which gave me lessons in the art of song.

But soon their sweet discourses interrupted   130
    A tree which midway in the road we found,
    With apples sweet and grateful to the smell.

And even as a fir-tree tapers upward
    From bough to bough, so downwardly did that;
    I think in order that no one might climb it.   135

On that side where our pathway was enclosed
    Fell from the lofty rock a limpid water,
    And spread itself abroad upon the leaves.

The Poets twain unto the tree drew near,
    And from among the foliage a voice   140
    Cried: "Of this food ye shall have scarcity."

Then said: "More thoughtful Mary was of making
    The marriage feast complete and honorable,
    Than of her mouth which now for you responds;

And for their drink the ancient Roman women   145
    With water were content; and Daniel
    Disparaged food, and understanding won.

The primal age was beautiful as gold;
    Acorns it made with hunger savorous,
    And nectar every rivulet with thirst.   150

Honey and locusts were the aliments
    That fed the Baptist in the wilderness;
    Whence he is glorious, and so magnified

As by the Evangel is revealed to you."

⊰ Canto XXIII ⊱

Forese—Reproof of Immodest Florentine Women

The while among the verdant leaves mine eyes
    I riveted, as he is wont to do
Who wastes his life pursuing little birds,

My more than Father said unto me: "Son,
    Come now; because the time that is ordained us   5
    More usefully should be apportioned out."

I turned my face and no less soon my steps
    Unto the Sages, who were speaking so
    They made the going of no cost to me;

And lo! were heard a song and a lament,   10
    "Labia mea, Domine," in fashion
    Such that delight and dolence it brought forth.

"O my sweet Father, what is this I hear?"
    Began I; and he answered: "Shades that go
    Perhaps the knot unloosing of their debt."   15

In the same way that thoughtful pilgrims do,
    Who, unknown people on the road o'ertaking,
    Turn themselves round to them, and do not stop,

Even thus, behind us with a swifter motion
    Coming and passing onward, gazed upon us   20
    A crowd of spirits silent and devout.

Each in his eyes was dark and cavernous,
    Pallid in face, and so emaciate
    That from the bones the skin did shape itself.

I do not think that so to merest rind   25
    Could Erisichthon have been withered up
    By famine, when most fear he had of it.

Thinking within myself I said: "Behold,
    This is the folk who lost Jerusalem,
    When Mary made a prey of her own son."   30

Their sockets were like rings without the gems;
    Whoever in the face of men reads *omo*
    Might well in these have recognized the *m*.

Who would believe the odor of an apple,
    Begetting longing, could consume them so,   35
    And that of water, without knowing how?

I still was wondering what so famished them,
    For the occasion not yet manifest
    Of their emaciation and sad squalor;

And lo! from out the hollow of his head   40
    His eyes a shade turned on me, and looked keenly;
    Then cried aloud: "What grace to me is this?"

Never should I have known him by his look;
    But in his voice was evident to me
    That which his aspect had suppressed within it.   45

This spark within me wholly re-enkindled
    My recognition of his altered face,
    And I recalled the features of Forese.

"Ah, do not look at this dry leprosy,"
    Entreated he, "which doth my skin discolor,   50
    Nor at default of flesh that I may have;

"Ah, do not look at this dry leprosy,"
Entreated he, "which doth my skin discolor,
Nor at default of flesh that I may have"

Purgatorio XXIII, lines 49–51

But tell me truth of thee, and who are those
    Two souls, that yonder make for thee an escort;
    Do not delay in speaking unto me."

"That face of thine, which dead I once bewept,   55
    Gives me for weeping now no lesser grief,"
    I answered him, "beholding it so changed!

But tell me, for God's sake, what thus denudes you?
    Make me not speak while I am marveling,
    For ill speaks he who's full of other longings."   60

And he to me: "From the eternal council
    Falls power into the water and the tree
    Behind us left, whereby I grow so thin.

All of this people who lamenting sing,
    For following beyond measure appetite   65
    In hunger and thirst are here re-sanctified.

Desire to eat and drink enkindles in us
    The scent that issues from the appletree,
    And from the spray that sprinkles o'er the verdure;

And not a single time alone, this ground   70
    Encompassing, is refreshed our pain—
    I say our pain, and ought to say our solace—

For the same wish doth lead us to the tree
    Which led the Christ rejoicing to say "Eli,"
    When with his veins he liberated us."   75

And I to him: "Forese, from that day
    When for a better life thou changedst worlds,
    Up to this time five years have not rolled round.

If sooner were the power exhausted in thee
    Of sinning more, than thee the hour surprised   80
    Of that good sorrow which to God rewed us,

How hast thou come up hitherward already?
    I thought to find thee down there underneath,
    Where time for time doth restitution make."

And he to me: "Thus speedily has led me   85
    To drink of the sweet wormwood of these torments,
    My Nella with her overflowing tears;

She with her prayers devout and with her sighs
    Has drawn me from the coast where one awaits,
    And from the other circles set me free.   90

So much more dear and pleasing is to God
    My little widow, whom so much I loved,
    As in good works she is the more alone;

For the Barbagia of Sardinia
    By far more modest in its women is   95
    Than the Barbagia I have left her in.

O brother sweet, what wilt thou have me say?
    A future time is in my sight already,
    To which this hour will not be very old,

When from the pulpit shall be interdicted   100
    To the unblushing womankind of Florence
    To go about displaying breast and paps.

What savages were e'er, what Saracens,
    Who stood in need, to make them covered go,
    Of spiritual or other discipline?   105

But if the shameless women were assured
    Of what swift Heaven prepares for them, already
    Wide open would they have their mouths to howl;

For if my foresight here deceive me not,
    They shall be sad ere he has bearded cheeks   110
    Who now is hushed to sleep with lullaby.

O brother, now no longer hide thee from me;
    See that not only I, but all these people
    Are gazing there, where thou dost veil the sun."

Whence I to him: "If thou bring back to mind   115
    What thou with me hast been and I with thee,
    The present memory will be grievous still.

Out of that life he turned me back who goes
    In front of me, two days agone when round
    The sister of him yonder showed herself,"   120

And to the sun I pointed. "Through the deep
    Night of the truly dead has this one led me,
    With this true flesh, that follows after him.

Thence his encouragements have led me up,
    Ascending and still circling round the mount   125
    That you doth straighten, whom the world made crooked.

He says that he will bear me company,
    Till I shall be where Beatrice will be;
    There it behoves me to remain without him.

This is Virgilius, who thus says to me,"   130
    And him I pointed at; "the other is
    That shade for whom just now shook every slope

Your realm, that from itself discharges him."

⊰ CANTO XXIV ⊱

Buonagiunta da Lucca—Pope Martin IV, and Others—
Inquiry into the State of Poetry

Nor speech the going, nor the going that
 Slackened; but talking we went bravely on,
Even as a vessel urged by a good wind.

And shadows, that appeared things doubly dead,
 From out the sepulchres of their eyes betrayed   5
 Wonder at me, aware that I was living.

And I, continuing my colloquy,
 Said: "Peradventure he goes up more slowly
 Than he would do, for other people's sake.

But tell me, if thou knowest, where is Piccarda;   10
 Tell me if anyone of note I see
 Among this folk that gazes at me so."

"My sister, who, 'twixt beautiful and good,
 I know not which was more, triumphs rejoicing
 Already in her crown on high Olympus."   15

So said he first, and then: "'Tis not forbidden
 To name each other here, so milked away
 Is our resemblance by our dieting.

This," pointing with his finger, "is Buonagiunta,
 Buonagiunta, of Lucca; and that face   20
 Beyond him there, more peaked than the others,

And shadows, that appeared things doubly dead,
From out the sepulchers of their eyes betrayed
Wonder at me, aware that I was living.

Purgatorio XXIV, lines 4–6

Has held the holy Church within his arms;
    From Tours was he, and purges by his fasting
    Bolsena's eels and the Vernaccia wine."

He named me many others one by one;   25
    And all contented seemed at being named,
    So that for this I saw not one dark look.

I saw for hunger bite the empty air
    Ubaldin dalla Pila, and Boniface,
    Who with his crook had pastured many people.   30

I saw Messer Marchese, who had leisure
    Once at Forlì for drinking with less dryness,
    And he was one who ne'er felt satisfied.

But as he does who scans, and then doth prize
    One more than others, did I him of Lucca,   35
    Who seemed to take most cognizance of me.

He murmured, and I know not what Gentucca
    From that place heard I, where he felt the wound
    Of justice, that doth macerate them so.

"O soul," I said, "that seemest so desirous   40
    To speak with me, do so that I may hear thee,
    And with thy speech appease thyself and me."

"A maid is born, and wears not yet the veil,"
    Began he, "who to thee shall pleasant make
    My city, howsoever men may blame it.   45

Thou shalt go on thy way with this prevision;
    If by my murmuring thou hast been deceived,
    True things hereafter will declare it to thee.

But say if him I here behold, who forth
    Evoked the new-invented rhymes, beginning,   50
    'Ladies, that have intelligence of love?' "

And I to him: "One am I, who, whenever
    Love doth inspire me, note, and in that measure
    Which he within me dictates, singing go."

"O brother, now I see," he said, "the knot   55
    Which me, the Notary, and Guittone held
    Short of the sweet new style that now I hear.

I do perceive full clearly how your pens
    Go closely following after him who dictates,
    Which with our own forsooth came not to pass;   60

And he who sets himself to go beyond,
    No difference sees from one style to another";
    And as if satisfied, he held his peace.

Even as the birds, that winter tow'rds the Nile,
    Sometimes into a phalanx form themselves,   65
    Then fly in greater haste, and go in file;

In such wise all the people who were there,
    Turning their faces, hurried on their steps,
    Both by their leanness and their wishes light.

And as a man, who weary is with trotting,   70
    Lets his companions onward go, and walks,
    Until he vents the panting of his chest;

So did Forese let the holy flock
    Pass by, and came with me behind it, saying,
    "When will it be that I again shall see thee?"   75

"How long," I answered, "I may live, I know not;
   Yet my return will not so speedy be,
   But I shall sooner in desire arrive;

Because the place where I was set to live
   From day to day of good is more depleted,   80
   And unto dismal ruin seems ordained."

"Now go," he said, "for him most guilty of it
   At a beast's tail behold I dragged along
   Towards the valley where is no repentance.

Faster at every step the beast is going,   85
   Increasing evermore until it smites him,
   And leaves the body vilely mutilated.

Not long those wheels shall turn," and he uplifted
   His eyes to heaven, "ere shall be clear to thee
   That which my speech no farther can declare.   90

Now stay behind; because the time so precious
   Is in this kingdom, that I lose too much
   By coming onward thus abreast with thee."

As sometimes issues forth upon a gallop
   A cavalier from out a troop that ride,   95
   And seeks the honor of the first encounter,

So he with greater strides departed from us;
   And on the road remained I with those two,
   Who were such mighty marshals of the world.

And when before us he had gone so far   100
   Mine eyes became to him such pursuivants
   As was my understanding to his words,

Appeared to me with laden and living boughs
    Another appletree, and not far distant,
    From having but just then turned thitherward.   105

People I saw beneath it lift their hands,
    And cry I know not what towards the leaves,
    Like little children eager and deluded,

Who pray, and he they pray to doth not answer,
    But, to make very keen their appetite,   110
    Holds their desire aloft, and hides it not.

Then they departed as if undeceived;
    And now we came unto the mighty tree
    Which prayers and tears so manifold refuses.

"Pass farther onward without drawing near;   115
    The tree of which Eve ate is higher up,
    And out of that one has this tree been raised."

Thus said I know not who among the branches;
    Whereat Virgilius, Statius, and myself
    Went crowding forward on the side that rises.   120

"Be mindful," said he, "of the accursed ones
    Formed of the cloud-rack, who inebriate
    Combated Theseus with their double breasts;

And of the Jews who showed them soft in drinking,
    Whence Gideon would not have them for
        companions   125
    When he tow'rds Midian the hills descended."

Thus, closely pressed to one of the two borders,
    On passed we, hearing sins of gluttony,
    Followed forsooth by miserable gains;

People I saw beneath it lift their hands,
And cry I know not what towards the leaves

Purgatorio XXIV, lines 106–107

Then set at large upon the lonely road,   130
    A thousand steps and more we onward went,
    In contemplation, each without a word.

"What go ye thinking thus, ye three alone?"
    Said suddenly a voice, whereat I started
    As terrified and timid beasts are wont.   135

I raised my head to see who this might be,
    And never in a furnace was there seen
    Metals or glass so lucent and so red

As one I saw who said: "If it may please you
    To mount aloft, here it behoves you turn;   140
    This way goes he who goeth after peace."

His aspect had bereft me of my sight,
    So that I turned me back unto my Teachers,
    Like one who goeth as his hearing guides him.

And as, the harbinger of early dawn,   145
    The air of May doth move and breathe out fragrance,
    Impregnate all with herbage and with flowers,

So did I feel a breeze strike in the midst
    My front, and felt the moving of the plumes
    That breathed around an odor of ambrosia;   150

And heard it said: "Blessed are they whom grace
    So much illumines, that the love of taste
    Excites not in their breasts too great desire,

Hungering at all times so far as is just."

⊰ Canto XXV ⊱

Discourse of Statius on Generation—The Seventh Circle: The Wanton

Now was it the ascent no hindrance brooked,
    Because the sun had his meridian circle
To Taurus left, and night to Scorpio;

Wherefore as doth a man who tarries not,
    But goes his way, whate'er to him appear,   5
    If of necessity the sting transfix him,

In this wise did we enter through the gap,
    Taking the stairway, one before the other,
    Which by its narrowness divides the climbers.

And as the little stork that lifts its wing   10
    With a desire to fly, and does not venture
    To leave the nest, and lets it downward droop,

Even such was I, with the desire of asking
    Kindled and quenched, unto the motion coming
    He makes who doth address himself to speak.   15

Not for our pace, though rapid it might be,
    My father sweet forbore, but said: "Let fly
    The bow of speech thou to the barb hast drawn."

With confidence I opened then my mouth,
    And I began: "How can one meager grow   20
    There where the need of nutriment applies not?"

"If thou wouldst call to mind how Meleager
    Was wasted by the wasting of a brand,
    This would not," said he, "be to thee so sour;

And wouldst thou think how at each tremulous motion   25
 Trembles within a mirror your own image;
 That which seems hard would mellow seem to thee.

But that thou mayst content thee in thy wish
 Lo Statius here; and him I call and pray
 He now will be the healer of thy wounds."   30

"If I unfold to him the eternal vengeance,"
 Responded Statius, "where thou present art,
 Be my excuse that I can naught deny thee."

Then he began: "Son, if these words of mine
 Thy mind doth contemplate and doth receive,   35
 They'll be thy light unto the How thou sayest.

The perfect blood, which never is drunk up
 Into the thirsty veins, and which remaineth
 Like food that from the table thou removest,

Takes in the heart for all the human members   40
 Virtue informative, as being that
 Which to be changed to them goes through the veins

Again digest, descends it where 'tis better
 Silent to be than say; and then drops thence
 Upon another's blood in natural vase.   45

There one together with the other mingles,
 One to be passive meant, the other active
 By reason of the perfect place it springs from;

And being conjoined, begins to operate,
 Coagulating first, then vivifying   50
 What for its matter it had made consistent.

The active virtue, being made a soul
    As of a plant (in so far different,
    This on the way is, that arrived already)

Then works so much, that now it moves and feels   55
    Like a sea-fungus, and then undertakes
    To organize the powers whose seed it is.

Now, Son, dilates and now distends itself
    The virtue from the generator's heart,
    Where nature is intent on all the members.   60

But how from animal it man becomes
    Thou dost not see as yet; this is a point
    Which made a wiser man than thou once err

So far, that in his doctrine separate
    He made the soul from possible intellect,   65
    For he no organ saw by this assumed.

Open thy breast unto the truth that's coming,
    And know that, just as soon as in the fœtus
    The articulation of the brain is perfect,

The primal Motor turns to it well pleased   70
    At so great art of nature, and inspires
    A spirit new with virtue all replete,

Which what it finds there active doth attract
    Into its substance, and becomes one soul,
    Which lives, and feels, and on itself revolves.   75

And that thou less may wonder at my word,
    Behold the sun's heat, which becometh wine,
    Joined to the juice that from the vine distils.

Whenever Lachesis has no more thread,
    It separates from the flesh, and virtually   80
    Bears with itself the human and divine;

The other faculties are voiceless all;
    The memory, the intelligence, and the will
    In action far more vigorous than before.

Without a pause it falleth of itself   85
    In marvelous way on one shore or the other;
    There of its roads it first is cognizant.

Soon as the place there circumscribeth it,
    The virtue informative rays round about,
    As, and as much as, in the living members.   90

And even as the air, when full of rain,
    By alien rays that are therein reflected,
    With divers colors shows itself adorned,

So there the neighboring air doth shape itself
    Into that form which doth impress upon it   95
    Virtually the soul that has stood still.

And then in manner of the little flame,
    Which followeth the fire where'er it shifts,
    After the spirit followeth its new form.

Since afterwards it takes from this its semblance,   100
    It is called shade; and thence it organizes
    Thereafter every sense, even to the sight.

Thence is it that we speak, and thence we laugh;
    Thence is it that we form the tears and sighs,
    That on the mountain thou mayhap hast heard.   105

According as impress us our desires
    And other affections, so the shade is shaped,
    And this is cause of what thou wonderest at."

And now unto the last of all the circles
    Had we arrived, and to the right hand turned,   110
    And were attentive to another care.

There the embankment shoots forth flames of fire,
    And upward doth the cornice breathe a blast
    That drives them back, and from itself sequesters.

Hence we must needs go on the open side,   115
    And one by one; and I did fear the fire
    On this side, and on that the falling down.

My Leader said: "Along this place one ought
    To keep upon the eyes a tightened rein,
    Seeing that one so easily might err."   120

"*Summæ Deus clementiæ,*" in the bosom
    Of the great burning chanted then I heard,
    Which made me no less eager to turn round;

And spirits saw I walking through the flame;
    Wherefore I looked, to my own steps and theirs   125
    Apportioning my sight from time to time.

After the close which to that hymn is made,
    Aloud they shouted, "*Virum non cognosco*";
    Then recommenced the hymn with voices low.

This also ended, cried they: "To the wood   130
    Diana ran, and drove forth Helice
    Therefrom, who had of Venus felt the poison."

There the embankment shoots forth flames of fire,
And upward doth the cornice breathe a blast
That drives them back, and from itself sequesters.

Purgatorio XXV, lines 112–114

"*Summæ Deus clementiæ,*" in the bosom
Of the great burning chanted then I heard,
Which made me no less eager to turn round

Purgatorio XXV, lines 121–123

And spirits saw I walking through the flame;
Wherefore I looked, to my own steps and theirs
Apportioning my sight from time to time.

Purgatorio XXV, lines 124–126

Then to their song returned they; then the wives
    They shouted, and the husbands who were chaste,
    As virtue and the marriage vow imposes.   135

And I believe that them this mode suffices,
    For all the time the fire is burning them;
    With such care is it needful, and such food,

That the last wound of all should be closed up.

⊰ CANTO XXVI ⊱

Sodomites — Guido Guinicelli and Arnaldo Daniello

While on the brink thus one before the other
    We went upon our way, oft the good Master
Said: "Take thou heed! suffice it that I warn thee."

On the right shoulder smote me now the sun,
    That, raying out, already the whole west   5
    Changed from its azure aspect into white.

And with my shadow did I make the flame
    Appear more red; and even to such a sign
    Shades saw I many, as they went, give heed.

This was the cause that gave them a beginning   10
    To speak of me; and to themselves began they
    To say: "That seems not a factitious body!"

Then towards me, as far as they could come,
    Came certain of them, always with regard
    Not to step forth where they would not be burned.   15

"O thou who goest, not from being slower
    But reverent perhaps, behind the others,
    Answer me, who in thirst and fire am burning.

Nor to me only is thine answer needful;
    For all of these have greater thirst for it   20
    Than for cold water Ethiop or Indian.

Tell us how is it that thou makest thyself
    A wall unto the sun, as if thou hadst not
    Entered as yet into the net of death."

Thus one of them addressed me, and I straight   25
    Should have revealed myself, were I not bent
    On other novelty that then appeared.

For through the middle of the burning road
    There came a people face to face with these,
    Which held me in suspense with gazing at them.   30

There see I hastening upon either side
    Each of the shades, and kissing one another
    Without a pause, content with brief salute.

Thus in the middle of their brown battalions
    Muzzle to muzzle one ant meets another   35
    Perchance to spy their journey or their fortune.

No sooner is the friendly greeting ended,
    Or ever the first footstep passes onward,
    Each one endeavors to outcry the other;

The newcome people: "Sodom and Gomorrah!"   40
    The rest: "Into the cow Pasiphae enters,
    So that the bull unto her lust may run!"

Then as the cranes, that to Riphæan mountains
    Might fly in part, and part towards the sands,
    These of the frost, those of the sun avoidant,   45

One folk is going, and the other coming,
    And weeping they return to their first songs,
    And to the cry that most befitteth them;

And close to me approached, even as before,
    The very same who had entreated me,   50
    Attent to listen in their countenance.

I, who their inclination twice had seen,
    Began: "O souls secure in the possession,
    Whene'er it may be, of a state of peace,

Neither unripe nor ripened have remained   55
    My members upon earth, but here are with me
    With their own blood and their articulations.

I go up here to be no longer blind;
    A Lady is above, who wins this grace,
    Whereby the mortal through your world I bring.   60

But as your greatest longing satisfied
    May soon become, so that the Heaven may house you
    Which full of love is, and most amply spreads,

Tell me, that I again in books may write it,
    Who are you, and what is that multitude   65
    Which goes upon its way behind your backs?"

Not otherwise with wonder is bewildered
    The mountaineer, and staring round is dumb,
    When rough and rustic to the town he goes,

Than every shade became in its appearance;   70
    But when they of their stupor were disburdened,
    Which in high hearts is quickly quieted,

"Blessed be thou, who of our borderlands,"
    He recommenced who first had questioned us,
    "Experience freightest for a better life.   75

The folk that comes not with us have offended
    In that for which once Cæsar, triumphing,
    Heard himself called in contumely, 'Queen.'

Therefore they separate, exclaiming, 'Sodom!'
    Themselves reproving, even as thou hast heard,   80
    And add unto their burning by their shame.

Our own transgression was hermaphrodite;
    But because we observed not human law,
    Following like unto beasts our appetite,

In our opprobrium by us is read,   85
    When we part company, the name of her
    Who bestialized herself in bestial wood.

Now knowest thou our acts, and what our crime was;
    Wouldst thou perchance by name know who we are,
    There is not time to tell, nor could I do it.   90

Thy wish to know me shall in sooth be granted;
    I'm Guido Guinicelli, and now purge me,
    Having repented ere the hour extreme."

The same that in the sadness of Lycurgus
    Two sons became, their mother re-beholding,   95
    Such I became, but rise not to such height,

The moment I heard name himself the father
    Of me and of my betters, who had ever
    Practiced the sweet and gracious rhymes of love;

And without speech and hearing thoughtfully   100
    For a long time I went, beholding him,
    Nor for the fire did I approach him nearer.

When I was fed with looking, utterly
    Myself I offered ready for his service,
    With affirmation that compels belief.   105

And he to me: "Thou leavest footprints such
    In me, from what I hear, and so distinct,
    Lethe cannot efface them, nor make dim.

But if thy words just now the truth have sworn,
    Tell me what is the cause why thou displayest   110
    In word and look that dear thou holdest me?"

And I to him: "Those dulcet lays of yours
    Which, long as shall endure our modern fashion,
    Shall make forever dear their very ink!"

"O brother," said he, "he whom I point out,"   115
    And here he pointed at a spirit in front,
    "Was of the mother tongue a better smith.

Verses of love and proses of romance,
    He mastered all; and let the idiots talk,
    Who think the Lemosin surpasses him.   120

To clamor more than truth they turn their faces,
    And in this way establish their opinion,
    Ere art or reason has by them been heard.

Thus many ancients with Guittone did,
    From cry to cry still giving him applause,   125
    Until the truth has conquered with most persons.

Now, if thou hast such ample privilege
  'Tis granted thee to go unto the cloister
    Wherein is Christ the abbot of the college,

To him repeat for me a Paternoster,   130
    So far as needful to us of this world,
    Where power of sinning is no longer ours."

Then, to give place perchance to one behind,
    Whom he had near, he vanished in the fire
    As fish in water going to the bottom.   135

I moved a little tow'rds him pointed out,
    And said that to his name my own desire
    An honorable place was making ready.

He of his own free will began to say:
    Tan m' abellis vostre cortes deman,   140
    Que jeu nom' puesc ni vueill a vos cobrire;

Jeu sui Arnaut, que plor e vai chantan;
    Consiros vei la passada folor,
    E vei jauzen lo jorn qu' esper denan.

Ara vus prec per aquella valor,   145
    Que vus condus al som de la scalina,
    *Sovenga vus a temprar ma dolor.**

Then hid him in the fire that purifies them.

---

*So pleases me your courteous demand,
  I cannot and I will not hide me from you.

I am Arnaut, who weep and singing go;
  Contrite I see the folly of the past,
  And joyous see the hoped-for day before me.

Therefore do I implore you, by that power
  Which guides you to the summit of the stairs,
  Be mindful to assuage my suffering!

ᴥ Canto XXVII ᴦ

The Wall of Fire and the Angel of God—
Dante's Sleep upon the Stairway,
and His Dream of Leah and Rachel—
Arrival at the Terrestrial Paradise

As when he vibrates forth his earliest rays,
  In regions where his Maker shed his blood,
(The Ebro falling under lofty Libra,

And waters in the Ganges burnt with noon)
  So stood the Sun; hence was the day departing,   5
  When the glad Angel of God appeared to us.

Outside the flame he stood upon the verge,
  And chanted forth, *"Beati mundo corde,"*
  In voice by far more living than our own.

Then: "No one farther goes, souls sanctified,   10
  If first the fire bite not; within it enter,
  And be not deaf unto the song beyond."

When we were close beside him thus he said;
  Wherefore e'en such became I, when I heard him,
  As he is who is put into the grave.   15

Upon my claspëd hands I straightened me,
  Scanning the fire, and vividly recalling
  The human bodies I had once seen burned.

Towards me turned themselves my good Conductors,
  And unto me Virgilius said: "My son,   20
  Here may indeed be torment, but not death.

Remember thee, remember! and if I
   On Geryon have safely guided thee,
   What shall I do now I am nearer God?

Believe for certain, shouldst thou stand a full   25
   Millennium in the bosom of this flame,
   It could not make thee bald a single hair.

And if perchance thou think that I deceive thee,
   Draw near to it, and put it to the proof
   With thine own hands upon thy garment's hem.   30

Now lay aside, now lay aside all fear,
   Turn hitherward, and onward come securely";
   And I still motionless, and 'gainst my conscience!

Seeing me stand still motionless and stubborn,
   Somewhat disturbed he said: "Now look thou, Son, 35
   'Twixt Beatrice and thee there is this wall."

As at the name of Thisbe oped his lids
   The dying Pyramus, and gazed upon her,
   What time the mulberry became vermilion,

Even thus, my obduracy being softened,   40
   I turned to my wise Guide, hearing the name
   That in my memory evermore is welling.

Whereat he wagged his head, and said: "How now?
   Shall we stay on this side?" then smiled as one
   Does at a child who's vanquished by an apple.   45

Then into the fire in front of me he entered,
   Beseeching Statius to come after me,
   Who a long way before divided us.

When I was in it, into molten glass
    I would have cast me to refresh myself,   50
    So without measure was the burning there!

And my sweet Father, to encourage me,
    Discoursing still of Beatrice went on,
    Saying: "Her eyes I seem to see already!"

A voice, that on the other side was singing,   55
    Directed us, and we, attent alone
    On that, came forth where the ascent began.

"*Venite, benedicti Patris mei,*"
    Sounded within a splendor, which was there
    Such it o'ercame me, and I could not look.   60

"The sun departs," it added, "and night cometh;
    Tarry ye not, but onward urge your steps,
    So long as yet the west becomes not dark."

Straight forward through the rock the path ascended
    In such a way that I cut off the rays   65
    Before me of the sun, that now was low.

And of few stairs we yet had made assay,
    Ere by the vanished shadow the sun's setting
    Behind us we perceived, I and my Sages.

And ere in all its parts immeasurable   70
    The horizon of one aspect had become,
    And Night her boundless dispensation held,

Each of us of a stair had made his bed;
    Because the nature of the mount took from us
    The power of climbing, more than the delight.   75

Even as in ruminating passive grow
    The goats, who have been swift and venturesome
    Upon the mountaintops ere they were fed,

Hushed in the shadow, while the sun is hot,
    Watched by the herdsman, who upon his staff   80
    Is leaning, and in leaning tendeth them;

And as the shepherd, lodging out of doors,
    Passes the night beside his quiet flock,
    Watching that no wild beast may scatter it,

Such at that hour were we, all three of us,   85
    I like the goat, and like the herdsmen they,
    Begirt on this side and on that by rocks.

Little could there be seen of things without;
    But through that little I beheld the stars
    More luminous and larger than their wont.   90

Thus ruminating, and beholding these,
    Sleep seized upon me—sleep, that oftentimes
    Before a deed is done has tidings of it.

It was the hour, I think, when from the East
    First on the mountain Citherea beamed,   95
    Who with the fire of love seems always burning;

Youthful and beautiful in dreams methought
    I saw a lady walking in a meadow,
    Gathering flowers; and singing she was saying:

"Know whosoever may my name demand   100
    That I am Leah, and go moving round
    My beauteous hands to make myself a garland.

Youthful and beautiful in dreams methought
I saw a lady walking in a meadow,
Gathering flowers

Purgatorio XXVII, lines 97–99

To please me at the mirror, here I deck me,
But never does my sister Rachel leave
Her looking glass, and sitteth all day long.   105

To see her beauteous eyes as eager is she,
As I am to adorn me with my hands;
Her, seeing, and me, doing satisfies."

And now before the antelucan splendors
That unto pilgrims the more grateful rise,   110
As, home-returning, less remote they lodge,

The darkness fled away on every side,
And slumber with it; whereupon I rose,
Seeing already the great Masters risen.

"That apple sweet, which through so many branches   115
The care of mortals goeth in pursuit of,
Today shall put in peace thy hungerings."

Speaking to me, Virgilius of such words
As these made use; and never were there guerdons
That could in pleasantness compare with these.   120

Such longing upon longing came upon me
To be above, that at each step thereafter
For flight I felt in me the pinions growing.

When underneath us was the stairway all
Run o'er, and we were on the highest step,   125
Virgilius fastened upon me his eyes,

And said: "The temporal fire and the eternal,
Son, thou hast seen, and to a place art come
Where of myself no farther I discern.

By intellect and art I here have brought thee;   130
   Take thine own pleasure for thy guide henceforth;
   Beyond the steep ways and the narrow art thou.

Behold the sun, that shines upon thy forehead;
   Behold the grass, the flowerets, and the shrubs
   Which of itself alone this land produces.   135

Until rejoicing come the beauteous eyes
   Which weeping caused me to come unto thee,
   Thou canst sit down, and thou canst walk among them.

Expect no more or word or sign from me;
   Free and upright and sound is thy free will,   140
   And error were it not to do its bidding;

Thee o'er thyself I therefore crown and mitre!"

⚜ Canto XXVIII ⚜

The River Lethe—Matilda—The Nature of the Terrestrial Paradise

Eager already to search in and round
   The heavenly forest, dense and living-green,
Which tempered to the eyes the newborn day,

Withouten more delay I left the bank,
   Taking the level country slowly, slowly   5
   Over the soil that everywhere breathes fragrance.

A softly breathing air, that no mutation
   Had in itself, upon the forehead smote me
   No heavier blow than of a gentle wind,

Whereat the branches, lightly tremulous,   10
    Did all of them bow downward toward that side
    Where its first shadow casts the Holy Mountain;

Yet not from their upright direction swayed,
    So that the little birds upon their tops
    Should leave the practice of each art of theirs;   15

But with full ravishment the hours of prime,
    Singing, received they in the midst of leaves,
    That ever bore a burden to their rhymes,

Such as from branch to branch goes gathering on
    Through the pine forest on the shore of Chiassi,   20
    When Eolus unlooses the Sirocco.

Already my slow steps had carried me
    Into the ancient wood so far, that I
    Could not perceive where I had entered it.

And lo! my further course a stream cut off,   25
    Which tow'rd the left hand with its little waves
    Bent down the grass that on its margin sprang.

All waters that on earth most limpid are
    Would seem to have within themselves some mixture
    Compared with that which nothing doth conceal,   30

Although it moves on with a brown, brown current
    Under the shade perpetual, that never
    Ray of the sun lets in, nor of the moon.

With feet I stayed, and with mine eyes I passed
    Beyond the rivulet, to look upon   35
    The great variety of the fresh may.

Already my slow steps had carried me
Into the ancient wood so far, that I
Could not perceive where I had entered it.

Purgatorio XXVIII, lines 22–24

And there appeared to me (even as appears
    Suddenly something that doth turn aside
    Through very wonder every other thought)

A lady all alone, who went along   40
    Singing and culling floweret after floweret,
    With which her pathway was all painted over.

"Ah, beauteous lady, who in rays of love
    Dost warm thyself, if I may trust to looks,
    Which the heart's witnesses are wont to be,   45

May the desire come unto thee to draw
    Near to this river's bank," I said to her,
    "So much that I may hear what thou art singing.

Thou makest me remember where and what
    Proserpina that moment was when lost   50
    Her mother her, and she herself the Spring."

As turns herself, with feet together pressed
    And to the ground, a lady who is dancing,
    And hardly puts one foot before the other,

On the vermilion and the yellow flowerets   55
    She turned towards me, not in other wise
    Than maiden who her modest eyes casts down;

And my entreaties made to be content,
    So near approaching, that the dulcet sound
    Came unto me together with its meaning   60

As soon as she was where the grasses are
    Bathed by the waters of the beauteous river,
    To lift her eyes she granted me the boon.

I do not think there shone so great a light
    Under the lids of Venus, when transfixed   65
    By her own son, beyond his usual custom!

Erect upon the other bank she smiled,
    Bearing full many colors in her hands,
    Which that high land produces without seed.

Apart three paces did the river make us;   70
    But Hellespont, where Xerxes passed across,
    (A curb still to all human arrogance)

More hatred from Leander did not suffer
    For rolling between Sestos and Abydos,
    Than that from me, because it oped not then.   75

"Ye are newcomers; and because I smile,"
    Began she, "peradventure, in this place
    Elect to human nature for its nest,

Some apprehension keeps you marveling;
    But the psalm *Delectasti* giveth light   80
    Which has the power to uncloud your intellect.

And thou who foremost art, and didst entreat me,
    Speak, if thou wouldst hear more; for I came ready
    To all thy questionings, as far as needful."

"The water," said I, "and the forest's sound,   85
    Are combating within me my new faith
    In something which I heard opposed to this."

Whence she: "I will relate how from its cause
    Proceedeth that which maketh thee to wonder,
    And purge away the cloud that smites upon thee.   90

The Good Supreme, sole in itself delighting,
 Created man good, and this goodly place
 Gave him as hansel of eternal peace.

By his default short while he sojourned here;
 By his default to weeping and to toil   95
 He changed his innocent laughter and sweet play.

That the disturbance which below is made
 By exhalations of the land and water,
 (Which far as may be follow after heat)

Might not upon mankind wage any war,   100
 This mount ascended tow'rds the heaven so high,
 And is exempt, from there where it is locked.

Now since the universal atmosphere
 Turns in a circuit with the primal motion
 Unless the circle is broken on some side,   105

Upon this height, that all is disengaged
 In living ether, doth this motion strike
 And make the forest sound, for it is dense;

And so much power the stricken plant possesses
 That with its virtue it impregns the air,   110
 And this, revolving, scatters it around;

And yonder earth, according as 'tis worthy
 In self or in its clime, conceives and bears
 Of divers qualities the divers trees;

It should not seem a marvel then on earth,   115
 This being heard, whenever any plant
 Without seed manifest there taketh root.

And thou must know, this holy table-land
  In which thou art is full of every seed,
  And fruit has in it never gathered there.   120

The water which thou seest springs not from vein
  Restored by vapor that the cold condenses,
  Like to a stream that gains or loses breath;

But issues from a fountain safe and certain,
  Which by the will of God as much regains   125
  As it discharges, open on two sides.

Upon this side with virtue it descends,
  Which takes away all memory of sin;
  On that, of every good deed done restores it.

Here Lethe, as upon the other side   130
  Eunoë, it is called; and worketh not
  If first on either side it be not tasted.

This every other savor doth transcend;
  And notwithstanding slaked so far may be
  Thy thirst, that I reveal to thee no more,   135

I'll give thee a corollary still in grace,
  Nor think my speech will be to thee less dear
  If it spread out beyond my promise to thee.

Those who in ancient times have feigned in song
  The Age of Gold and its felicity,   140
  Dreamed of this place perhaps upon Parnassus.

Here was the human race in innocence;
  Here evermore was Spring, and every fruit;
  This is the nectar of which each one speaks."

Then backward did I turn me wholly round   145
    Unto my Poets, and saw that with a smile
    They had been listening to these closing words;

Then to the beautiful lady turned mine eyes.

⊰ CANTO XXIX ⊱

The Triumph of the Church

Singing like unto an enamored lady
    She, with the ending of her words, continued:
"Beati quorum tecta sunt peccata."

And even as Nymphs, that wandered all alone
    Among the sylvan shadows, sedulous   5
    One to avoid and one to see the sun,

She then against the stream moved onward, going
    Along the bank, and I abreast of her,
    Her little steps with little steps attending.

Between her steps and mine were not a hundred,   10
    When equally the margins gave a turn,
    In such a way, that to the East I faced.

Nor even thus our way continued far
    Before the lady wholly turned herself
    Unto me, saying, "Brother, look and listen!"   15

And lo! a sudden luster ran across
    On every side athwart the spacious forest,
    Such that it made me doubt if it were lightning.

But since the lightning ceases as it comes,
   And that continuing brightened more and more,   20
   Within my thought I said, "What thing is this?"

And a delicious melody there ran
   Along the luminous air, whence holy zeal
   Made me rebuke the hardihood of Eve;

For there where earth and heaven obedient were,   25
   The woman only, and but just created,
   Could not endure to stay 'neath any veil;

Underneath which had she devoutly stayed,
   I sooner should have tasted those delights
   Ineffable, and for a longer time.   30

While 'mid such manifold first-fruits I walked
   Of the eternal pleasure all enrapt,
   And still solicitous of more delights,

In front of us like an enkindled fire
   Became the air beneath the verdant boughs,   35
   And the sweet sound as singing now was heard.

O Virgins sacrosanct! if ever hunger,
   Vigils, or cold for you I have endured,
   The occasion spurs me their reward to claim!

Now Helicon must needs pour forth for me,   40
   And with her choir Urania must assist me,
   To put in verse things difficult to think.

A little farther on, seven trees of gold
   In semblance the long space still intervening
   Between ourselves and them did counterfeit;   45

But when I had approached so near to them
    The common object, which the sense deceives,
    Lost not by distance any of its marks,

The faculty that lends discourse to reason
    Did apprehend that they were candlesticks,   50
    And in the voices of the song "Hosanna!"

Above them flamed the harness beautiful,
    Far brighter than the moon in the serene
    Of midnight, at the middle of her month.

I turned me round, with admiration filled,   55
    To good Virgilius, and he answered me
    With visage no less full of wonderment.

Then back I turned my face to those high things,
    Which moved themselves towards us so sedately,
    They had been distanced by new-wedded brides.   60

The lady chid me: "Why dost thou burn only
    So with affection for the living lights,
    And dost not look at what comes after them?"

Then saw I people, as behind their leaders,
    Coming behind them, garmented in white,   65
    And such a whiteness never was on earth.

The water on my left flank was resplendent,
    And back to me reflected my left side,
    E'en as a mirror, if I looked therein.

When I upon my margin had such post   70
    That nothing but the stream divided us,
    Better to see I gave my steps repose;

And I beheld the flamelets onward go,
    Leaving behind themselves the air depicted,
    And they of trailing pennons had the semblance,   75

So that it overhead remained distinct
    With sevenfold lists, all of them of the colors
    Whence the sun's bow is made, and Delia's girdle.

These standards to the rearward longer were
    Than was my sight; and, as it seemed to me,   80
    Ten paces were the outermost apart.

Under so fair a heaven as I describe
    The four and twenty Elders, two by two,
    Came on incoronate with flower-de-luce.

They all of them were singing: "Blessed thou   85
    Among the daughters of Adam art, and blessed
    For evermore shall be thy loveliness."

After the flowers and other tender grasses
    In front of me upon the other margin
    Were disencumbered of that race elect,   90

Even as in heaven star followeth after star,
    There came close after them four animals,
    Incoronate each one with verdant leaf.

Plumed with six wings was every one of them,
    The plumage full of eyes; the eyes of Argus   95
    If they were living would be such as these.

Reader! to trace their forms no more I waste
    My rhymes; for other spendings press me so,
    That I in this cannot be prodigal.

The four and twenty Elders, two by two,
Came on incoronate with flower-de-luce.

Purgatorio XXIX, lines 83–84

But read Ezekiel, who depicteth them   100
    As he beheld them from the region cold
    Coming with cloud, with whirlwind, and with fire;

And such as thou shalt find them in his pages,
    Such were they here; saving that in their plumage
    John is with me, and differeth from him.   105

The interval between these four contained
    A chariot triumphal on two wheels,
    Which by a Griffin's neck came drawn along;

And upward he extended both his wings
    Between the middle list and three and three,   110
    So that he injured none by cleaving it.

So high they rose that they were lost to sight;
    His limbs were gold, so far as he was bird,
    And white the others with vermilion mingled.

Not only Rome with no such splendid car   115
    E'er gladdened Africanus, or Augustus,
    But poor to it that of the Sun would be—

That of the Sun, which swerving was burnt up
    At the importunate orison of Earth,
    When Jove was so mysteriously just.   120

Three maidens at the right wheel in a circle
    Came onward dancing; one so very red
    That in the fire she hardly had been noted.

The second was as if her flesh and bones
    Had all been fashioned out of emerald;   125
    The third appeared as snow but newly fallen.

Came onward dancing; one so very red
That in the fire she hardly had been noted.
The second was as if her flesh and bones
Had all been fashioned out of emerald;
The third appeared as snow but newly fallen.

Purgatorio XXIX, lines 122–126

And now they seemed conducted by the white,
  Now by the red, and from the song of her
  The others took their step, or slow or swift.

Upon the left hand four made holiday   130
  Vested in purple, following the measure
  Of one of them with three eyes in her head.

In rear of all the group here treated of
  Two old men I beheld, unlike in habit,
  But like in gait, each dignified and grave.   135

One showed himself as one of the disciples
  Of that supreme Hippocrates, whom nature
  Made for the animals she holds most dear;

Contrary care the other manifested,
  With sword so shining and so sharp, it caused   140
  Terror to me on this side of the river.

Thereafter four I saw of humble aspect,
  And behind all an aged man alone
  Walking in sleep with countenance acute.

And like the foremost company these seven   145
  Were habited; yet of the flower-de-luce
  No garland round about the head they wore,

But of the rose, and other flowers vermilion;
  At little distance would the sight have sworn
  That all were in a flame above their brows.   150

And when the car was opposite to me
  Thunder was heard; and all that folk august
  Seemed to have further progress interdicted,

There with the vanward ensigns standing still.

◄ CANTO XXX ►

Virgil's Departure — Beatrice — Dante's Shame

When the Septentrion of the highest heaven
 (Which never either setting knew or rising,
Nor veil of other cloud than that of sin,

And which made everyone therein aware
 Of his own duty, as the lower makes   5
 Whoever turns the helm to come to port)

Motionless halted, the veracious people,
 That came at first between it and the Griffin,
 Turned themselves to the car, as to their peace.

And one of them, as if by Heaven commissioned, 10
 Singing, *"Veni, sponsa, de Libano"*
 Shouted three times, and all the others after.

Even as the Blessed at the final summons
 Shall rise up quickened each one from his cavern,
 Uplifting light the reinvested flesh,   15

So upon that celestial chariot
 A hundred rose *ad vocem tanti senis,*
 Ministers and messengers of life eternal.

They all were saying, *"Benedictus qui venis,"*
 And, scattering flowers above and round about, 20
"Manibus o date lilia plenis."

Ere now have I beheld, as day began,
 The eastern hemisphere all tinged with rose,
 And the other heaven with fair serene adorned;

And the sun's face, uprising, overshadowed   25
 So that by tempering influence of vapors
 For a long interval the eye sustained it;

Thus in the bosom of a cloud of flowers
 Which from those hands angelical ascended,
 And downward fell again inside and out,   30

Over her snow-white veil with olive cinct
 Appeared a lady under a green mantle,
 Vested in color of the living flame.

And my own spirit, that already now
 So long a time had been, that in her presence   35
 Trembling with awe it had not stood abashed,

Without more knowledge having by mine eyes,
 Through occult virtue that from her proceeded
 Of ancient love the mighty influence felt.

As soon as on my vision smote the power   40
 Sublime, that had already pierced me through
 Ere from my boyhood I had yet come forth,

To the left hand I turned with that reliance
 With which the little child runs to his mother,
 When he has fear, or when he is afflicted,   45

To say unto Virgilius: "Not a drachm
 Of blood remains in me, that does not tremble;
 I know the traces of the ancient flame."

But us Virgilius of himself deprived
 Had left, Virgilius, sweetest of all fathers,   50
 Virgilius, to whom I for safety gave me:

Appeared a lady under a green mantle,
Vested in color of the living flame.

Purgatorio XXX, lines 32–33

Nor whatsoever lost the ancient mother
    Availed my cheeks now purified from dew,
    That weeping they should not again be darkened.

"Dante, because Virgilius has departed   55
    Do not weep yet, do not weep yet awhile;
    For by another sword thou need'st must weep."

E'en as an admiral, who on poop and prow
    Comes to behold the people that are working
    In other ships, and cheers them to well-doing.   60

Upon the left hand border of the car,
    When at the sound I turned of my own name,
    Which of necessity is here recorded,

I saw the Lady, who erewhile appeared
    Veiled underneath the angelic festival,   65
    Direct her eyes to me across the river.

Although the veil, that from her head descended,
    Encircled with the foliage of Minerva,
    Did not permit her to appear distinctly,

In attitude still royally majestic   70
    Continued she, like unto one who speaks,
    And keeps his warmest utterance in reserve:

"Look at me well; in sooth I'm Beatrice!
    How didst thou deign to come unto the Mountain?
    Didst thou not know that man is happy here?"   75

Mine eyes fell downward into the clear fountain,
    But, seeing myself therein, I sought the grass,
    So great a shame did weigh my forehead down.

As to the son the mother seems superb,
So she appeared to me; for somewhat bitter   80
Tasteth the savor of severe compassion.

Silent became she, and the Angels sang
Suddenly, *"In te, Domine, speravi"*:
But beyond *pedes meos* did not pass.

Even as the snow among the living rafters   85
Upon the back of Italy congeals,
Blown on and drifted by Sclavonian winds,

And then, dissolving, trickles through itself
Whene'er the land that loses shadow breathes,
So that it seems a fire that melts a taper;   90

E'en thus was I without a tear or sigh,
Before the song of those who sing for ever
After the music of the eternal spheres.

But when I heard in their sweet melodies
Compassion for me, more than had they said,   95
"O wherefore, lady, dost thou thus upbraid him?"

The ice, that was about my heart congealed,
To air and water changed, and in my anguish
Through mouth and eyes came gushing from my breast.

She, on the right-hand border of the car   100
Still firmly standing, to those holy beings
Thus her discourse directed afterwards:

"Ye keep your watch in the eternal day,
So that nor night nor sleep can steal from you
One step the ages make upon their path;   105

Therefore my answer is with greater care,
    That he may hear me who is weeping yonder,
    So that the sin and dole be of one measure.

Not only by the work of those great wheels,
    That destine every seed unto some end,   110
    According as the stars are in conjunction,

But by the largess of celestial graces,
    Which have such lofty vapors for their rain
    That near to them our sight approaches not,

Such had this man become in his new life   115
    Potentially, that every righteous habit
    Would have made admirable proof in him;

But so much more malignant and more savage
    Becomes the land untilled and with bad seed,
    The more good earthly vigor it possesses.   120

Some time did I sustain him with my look;
    Revealing unto him my youthful eyes,
    I led him with me turned in the right way.

As soon as ever of my second age
    I was upon the threshold and changed life,   125
    Himself from me he took and gave to others.

When from the flesh to spirit I ascended,
    And beauty and virtue were in me increased,
    I was to him less dear and less delightful;

And into ways untrue he turned his steps,   130
    Pursuing the false images of good,
    That never any promises fulfill;

Nor prayer for inspiration me availed,
By means of which in dreams and otherwise
I called him back, so little did he heed them.   135

So low he fell, that all appliances
For his salvation were already short,
Save showing him the people of perdition.

For this I visited the gates of death,
And unto him, who so far up has led him,   140
My intercessions were with weeping borne.

God's lofty fiat would be violated,
If Lethe should be passed, and if such viands
Should tasted be, withouten any scot

Of penitence, that gushes forth in tears."   145

⊰ CANTO XXXI ⊱

Reproaches of Beatrice and Confession of Dante —
The Passage of Lethe — The Seven Virtues — The Griffon

"O thou who art beyond the sacred river,"
Turning to me the point of her discourse,
That edgewise even had seemed to me so keen,

She recommenced, continuing without pause,
"Say, say if this be true; to such a charge,   5
Thy own confession needs must be conjoined."

My faculties were in so great confusion,
That the voice moved, but sooner was extinct
Than by its organs it was set at large.

Awhile she waited; then she said: "What thinkest?   10
   Answer me; for the mournful memories
   In thee not yet are by the waters injured."

Confusion and dismay together mingled
   Forced such a Yes! from out my mouth, that sight
   Was needful to the understanding of it.   15

Even as a crossbow breaks, when 'tis discharged
   Too tensely drawn the bowstring and the bow,
   And with less force the arrow hits the mark,

So I gave way beneath that heavy burden,
   Outpouring in a torrent tears and sighs,   20
   And the voice flagged upon its passage forth.

Whence she to me: "In those desires of mine
   Which led thee to the loving of that good,
   Beyond which there is nothing to aspire to,

What trenches lying traverse or what chains   25
   Didst thou discover, that of passing onward
   Thou shouldst have thus despoiled thee of the hope?

And what allurements or what vantages
   Upon the forehead of the others showed,
   That thou shouldst turn thy footsteps unto them?"   30

After the heaving of a bitter sigh,
   Hardly had I the voice to make response,
   And with fatigue my lips did fashion it.

Weeping I said: "The things that present were
   With their false pleasure turned aside my steps,   35
   Soon as your countenance concealed itself."

And she: "Shouldst thou be silent, or deny
   What thou confessest, not less manifest
   Would be thy fault, by such a Judge 'tis known.

But when from one's own cheeks comes bursting forth   40
   The accusal of the sin, in our tribunal
   Against the edge the wheel doth turn itself.

But still, that thou mayst feel a greater shame
   For thy transgression, and another time
   Hearing the Sirens thou mayst be more strong,   45

Cast down the seed of weeping and attend;
   So shalt thou hear, how in an opposite way
   My buried flesh should have directed thee.

Never to thee presented art or nature
   Pleasure so great as the fair limbs wherein   50
   I was enclosed, which scattered are in earth.

And if the highest pleasure thus did fail thee
   By reason of my death, what mortal thing
   Should then have drawn thee into its desire?

Thou oughtest verily at the first shaft   55
   Of things fallacious to have risen up
   To follow me, who was no longer such.

Thou oughtest not to have stooped thy pinions downward
   To wait for further blows, or little girl,
   Or other vanity of such brief use.   60

The callow birdlet waits for two or three,
   But to the eyes of those already fledged,
   In vain the net is spread or shaft is shot."

Even as children silent in their shame
    Stand listening with their eyes upon the ground,   65
    And conscious of their fault, and penitent;

So was I standing; and she said: "If thou
    In hearing sufferest pain, lift up thy beard
    And thou shalt feel a greater pain in seeing."

With less resistance is a robust holm   70
    Uprooted, either by a native wind
    Or else by that from regions of Iarbas,

Than I upraised at her command my chin;
    And when she by the beard the face demanded,
    Well I perceived the venom of her meaning.   75

And as my countenance was lifted up,
    Mine eye perceived those creatures beautiful
    Had rested from the strewing of the flowers;

And, still but little reassured, mine eyes
    Saw Beatrice turned round towards the monster,   80
    That is one person only in two natures.

Beneath her veil, beyond the margent green,
    She seemed to me far more her ancient self
    To excel, than others here, when she was here.

So pricked me then the thorn of penitence,   85
    That of all other things the one which turned me
    Most to its love became the most my foe.

Such self-conviction stung me at the heart
    O'erpowered I fell, and what I then became
    She knoweth who had furnished me the cause.   90

Then, when the heart restored my outward sense,
    The lady I had found alone, above me
    I saw, and she was saying, "Hold me, hold me."

Up to my throat she in the stream had drawn me,
    And, dragging me behind her, she was moving   95
    Upon the water lightly as a shuttle.

When I was near unto the blessed shore,
    "*Asperges me,*" I heard so sweetly sung,
    Remember it I cannot, much less write it.

The beautiful lady opened wide her arms,   100
    Embraced my head, and plunged me underneath,
    Where I was forced to swallow of the water.

Then forth she drew me, and all dripping brought
    Into the dance of the four beautiful,
    And each one with her arm did cover me.   105

"We here are Nymphs, and in the Heaven are stars;
    Ere Beatrice descended to the world,
    We as her handmaids were appointed her.

We'll lead thee to her eyes; but for the pleasant
    Light that within them is, shall sharpen thine   110
    The three beyond, who more profoundly look."

Thus singing they began; and afterwards
    Unto the Griffin's breast they led me with them,
    Where Beatrice was standing, turned towards us.

"See that thou dost not spare thine eyes," they said; 115
    "Before the emeralds have we stationed thee,
    Whence Love aforetime drew for thee his weapons."

The beautiful lady opened wide her arms,
Embraced my head, and plunged me underneath,
Where I was forced to swallow of the water.

Purgatorio XXXI, lines 100–102

A thousand longings, hotter than the flame,
    Fastened mine eyes upon those eyes relucent,
    That still upon the Griffin steadfast stayed.   120

As in a glass the sun, not otherwise
    Within them was the twofold monster shining,
    Now with the one, now with the other nature.

Think, Reader, if within myself I marveled,
    When I beheld the thing itself stand still,   125
    And in its image it transformed itself.

While with amazement filled and jubilant,
    My soul was tasting of the food, that while
    It satisfies us makes us hunger for it,

Themselves revealing of the highest rank   130
    In bearing, did the other three advance,
    Singing to their angelic saraband.

"Turn, Beatrice, O turn thy holy eyes,"
    Such was their song, "unto thy faithful one,
    Who has to see thee ta'en so many steps.   135

In grace do us the grace that thou unveil
    Thy face to him, so that he may discern
    The second beauty which thou dost conceal."

O splendor of the living light eternal!
    Who underneath the shadow of Parnassus   140
    Has grown so pale, or drunk so at its cistern,

He would not seem to have his mind encumbered
    Striving to paint thee as thou didst appear,
    Where the harmonious heaven o'ershadowed thee,

When in the open air thou didst unveil?   145

⊰ Canto XXXII ⊱

The Tree of Knowledge—Allegory of the Chariot

So steadfast and attentive were mine eyes
In satisfying their decennial thirst,
That all my other senses were extinct,

And upon this side and on that they had
   Walls of indifference, so the holy smile   5
   Drew them unto itself with the old net

When forcibly my sight was turned away
   Towards my left hand by those goddesses,
   Because I heard from them a "Too intently!"

And that condition of the sight which is   10
   In eyes but lately smitten by the sun
   Bereft me of my vision some short while;

But to the less when sight reshaped itself,
   I say the less in reference to the greater
   Splendor from which perforce I had withdrawn,   15

I saw upon its right wing wheeled about
   The glorious host, returning with the sun
   And with the sevenfold flames upon their faces.

As underneath its shields, to save itself,
   A squadron turns, and with its banner wheels,   20
   Before the whole thereof can change its front,

That soldiery of the celestial kingdom
   Which marched in the advance had wholly passed us
   Before the chariot had turned its pole.

Then to the wheels the maidens turned themselves,   25
 And the Griffin moved his burden benedight,
 But so that not a feather of him fluttered.

The lady fair who drew me through the ford
 Followed with Statius and myself the wheel
 Which made its orbit with the lesser arc.   30

So passing through the lofty forest, vacant
 By fault of her who in the serpent trusted,
 Angelic music made our steps keep time.

Perchance as great a space had in three flights
 An arrow loosened from the string o'erpassed,   35
 As we had moved when Beatrice descended.

I heard them murmur altogether, "Adam!"
 Then circled they about a tree despoiled
 Of blooms and other leafage on each bough.

Its tresses, which so much the more dilate   40
 As higher they ascend, had been by Indians
 Among their forests marveled at for height.

"Blessed art thou, O Griffin, who dost not
 Pluck with thy beak these branches sweet to taste,
 Since appetite by this was turned to evil."   45

After this fashion round the tree robust
 The others shouted; and the twofold creature:
 "Thus is preserved the seed of all the just."

And turning to the pole which he had dragged,
 He drew it close beneath the widowed bough,   50
 And what was of it unto it left bound.

In the same manner as our trees (when downward
  Falls the great light, with that together mingled
  Which after the celestial Lasca shines)

Begin to swell, and then renew themselves,   55
  Each one with its own color, ere the Sun
  Harness his steeds beneath another star:

Less than of rose and more than violet
  A hue disclosing, was renewed the tree
  That had erewhile its boughs so desolate.   60

I never heard, nor here below is sung,
  The hymn which afterward that people sang,
  Nor did I bear the melody throughout.

Had I the power to paint how fell asleep
  Those eyes compassionless, of Syrinx hearing,   65
  Those eyes to which more watching cost so dear,

Even as a painter who from model paints
  I would portray how I was lulled asleep;
  He may, who well can picture drowsihood.

Therefore I pass to what time I awoke,   70
  And say a splendor rent from me the veil
  Of slumber, and a calling: "Rise, what dost thou?"

As to behold the apple tree in blossom
  Which makes the Angels greedy for its fruit,
  And keeps perpetual bridals in the Heaven,   75

Peter and John and James conducted were,
  And, overcome, recovered at the word
  By which still greater slumbers have been broken,

And saw their school diminished by the loss
    Not only of Elias, but of Moses,   80
    And the apparel of their Master changed;

So I revived, and saw that piteous one
    Above me standing, who had been conductress
    Aforetime of my steps beside the river,

And all in doubt I said, "Where's Beatrice?"   85
    And she: "Behold her seated underneath
    The leafage new, upon the root of it.

Behold the company that circles her;
    The rest behind the Griffin are ascending
    With more melodious song, and more profound."   90

And if her speech were more diffuse I know not,
    Because already in my sight was she
    Who from the hearing of aught else had shut me.

Alone she sat upon the very earth,
    Left there as guardian of the chariot   95
    Which I had seen the biform monster fasten.

Encircling her, a cloister made themselves
    The seven Nymphs, with those lights in their hands
    Which are secure from Aquilon and Auster.

"Short while shalt thou be here a forester,   100
    And thou shalt be with me for evermore
    A citizen of that Rome where Christ is Roman.

Therefore, for that world's good which liveth ill,
    Fix on the car thine eyes, and what thou seest,
    Having returned to earth, take heed thou write."   105

Thus Beatrice; and I, who at the feet
   Of her commandments all devoted was,
   My mind and eyes directed where she willed.

Never descended with so swift a motion
   Fire from a heavy cloud, when it is raining   110
   From out the region which is most remote,

As I beheld the bird of Jove descend
   Down through the tree, rending away the bark,
   As well as blossoms and the foliage new,

And he with all his might the chariot smote,   115
   Whereat it reeled, like vessel in a tempest
   Tossed by the waves, now starboard and now larboard.

Thereafter saw I leap into the body
   Of the triumphal vehicle a Fox,
   That seemed unfed with any wholesome food.   120

But for his hideous sins upbraiding him,
   My Lady put him to as swift a flight
   As such a fleshless skeleton could bear.

Then by the way that it before had come,
   Into the chariot's chest I saw the Eagle   125
   Descend, and leave it feathered with his plumes.

And such as issues from a heart that mourns,
   A voice from Heaven there issued, and it said:
   "My little bark, how badly art thou freighted!"

Methought, then, that the earth did yawn between   130
   Both wheels, and I saw rise from it a Dragon,
   Who through the chariot upward fixed his tail,

And as a wasp that draweth back its sting,
    Drawing unto himself his tail malign,
    Drew out the floor, and went his way rejoicing.   135

That which remained behind, even as with grass
    A fertile region, with the feathers, offered
    Perhaps with pure intention and benign,

Reclothed itself, and with them were reclothed
    The pole and both the wheels so speedily,   140
    A sigh doth longer keep the lips apart.

Transfigured thus the holy edifice
    Thrust forward heads upon the parts of it,
    Three on the pole and one at either corner.

The first were horned like oxen; but the four   145
    Had but a single horn upon the forehead;
    A monster such had never yet been seen!

Firm as a rock upon a mountain high,
    Seated upon it, there appeared to me
    A shameless whore, with eyes swift glancing round,   150

And, as if not to have her taken from him,
    Upright beside her I beheld a giant;
    And ever and anon they kissed each other.

But because she her wanton, roving eye
    Turned upon me, her angry paramour   155
    Did scourge her from her head unto her feet.

Then full of jealousy, and fierce with wrath,
    He loosed the monster, and across the forest
    Dragged it so far, he made of that alone

A shield unto the whore and the strange beast.   160

Upright beside her I beheld a giant;
And ever and anon they kissed each other.

Purgatorio XXXII, lines 152–153

⊰ CANTO XXXIII ⊱

Lament over the State of the Church—
Final Reproaches of Beatrice—The River Eunoe

"**D**eus, *venerunt gentes*," alternating
Now three, now four, melodious psalmody
The maidens in the midst of tears began;

And Beatrice, compassionate and sighing,
Listened to them with such a countenance,   5
That scarce more changed was Mary at the cross.

But when the other virgins place had given
For her to speak, uprisen to her feet
With color as of fire, she made response:

"*Modicum, et non videbitis me;*   10
Et iterum, my sisters predilect,
Modicum, et vos videbitis me."

Then all the seven in front of her she placed;
And after her, by beckoning only, moved
Me and the lady and the sage who stayed.   15

So she moved onward; and I do not think
That her tenth step was placed upon the ground,
When with her eyes upon mine eyes she smote,

And with a tranquil aspect, "Come more quickly,"
To me she said, "that, if I speak with thee,   20
To listen to me thou mayst be well placed."

As soon as I was with her as I should be,
    She said to me: "Why, brother, dost thou not
    Venture to question now, in coming with me?"

As unto those who are too reverential,   25
    Speaking in presence of superiors,
    Who drag no living utterance to their teeth,

It me befell, that without perfect sound
    Began I: "My necessity, Madonna,
    You know, and that which thereunto is good."   30

And she to me: "Of fear and bashfulness
    Henceforward I will have thee strip thyself,
    So that thou speak no more as one who dreams.

Know that the vessel which the serpent broke
    Was, and is not; but let him who is guilty   35
    Think that God's vengeance does not fear a sop.

Without an heir shall not forever be
    The Eagle that left his plumes upon the car,
    Whence it became a monster, then a prey;

For verily I see, and hence narrate it,   40
    The stars already near to bring the time,
    From every hindrance safe, and every bar,

Within which a Five-hundred, Ten, and Five,
    One sent from God, shall slay the thievish woman
    And that same giant who is sinning with her.   45

And peradventure my dark utterance,
    Like Themis and the Sphinx, may less persuade thee,
    Since, in their mode, it clouds the intellect;

But soon the facts shall be the Naiades
   Who shall this difficult enigma solve,   50
   Without destruction of the flocks and harvests.

Note thou; and even as by me are uttered
   These words, so teach them unto those who live
   That life which is a running unto death;

And bear in mind, whene'er thou writest them,   55
   Not to conceal what thou hast seen the plant,
   That twice already has been pillaged here.

Whoever pillages or shatters it,
   With blasphemy of deed offendeth God,
   Who made it holy for his use alone.   60

For biting that, in pain and in desire
   Five thousand years and more the firstborn soul
   Craved Him, who punished in himself the bite.

Thy genius slumbers, if it deem it not
   For special reason so preeminent   65
   In height, and so inverted in its summit.

And if thy vain imaginings had not been
   Water of Elsa round about thy mind,
   And Pyramus to the mulberry, their pleasure,

Thou by so many circumstances only   70
   The justice of the interdict of God
   Morally in the tree wouldst recognize.

But since I see thee in thine intellect
   Converted into stone and stained with sin,
   So that the light of my discourse doth daze thee,   75

I will too, if not written, at least painted,
　　Thou bear it back within thee, for the reason
　　That cinct with palm the pilgrim's staff is borne."

And I: "As by a signet is the wax
　　Which does not change the figure stamped upon it,　80
　　My brain is now imprinted by yourself.

But wherefore so beyond my power of sight
　　Soars your desirable discourse, that aye
　　The more I strive, so much the more I lose it?"

"That thou mayst recognize," she said, "the school　85
　　Which thou hast followed, and mayst see how far
　　Its doctrine follows after my discourse,

And mayst behold your path from the divine
　　Distant as far as separated is
　　From earth the heaven that highest hastens on."　90

Whence her I answered: "I do not remember
　　That ever I estranged myself from you,
　　Nor have I conscience of it that reproves me."

"And if thou art not able to remember,"
　　Smiling she answered, "recollect thee now　95
　　That thou this very day hast drunk of Lethe;

And if from smoke a fire may be inferred,
　　Such an oblivion clearly demonstrates
　　Some error in thy will elsewhere intent.

Truly from this time forward shall my words　100
　　Be naked, so far as it is befitting
　　To lay them open unto thy rude gaze."

And more coruscant and with slower steps
    The sun was holding the meridian circle,
    Which, with the point of view, shifts here and there   105

When halted (as he cometh to a halt,
    Who goes before a squadron as its escort,
    If something new he find upon his way)

The ladies seven at a dark shadow's edge,
    Such as, beneath green leaves and branches black,   110
    The Alp upon its frigid border wears.

In front of them the Tigris and Euphrates
    Methought I saw forth issue from one fountain,
    And slowly part, like friends, from one another.

"O light, O glory of the human race!   115
    What stream is this which here unfolds itself
    From out one source, and from itself withdraws?"

For such a prayer, 'twas said unto me, "Pray
    Matilda that she tell thee"; and here answered,
    As one does who doth free himself from blame,   120

The beautiful lady: "This and other things
    Were told to him by me; and sure I am
    The water of Lethe has not hid them from him."

And Beatrice: "Perhaps a greater care,
    Which oftentimes our memory takes away,   125
    Has made the vision of his mind obscure.

But Eunoë behold, that yonder rises;
    Lead him to it, and, as thou art accustomed,
    Revive again the half-dead virtue in him."

If, Reader, I possessed a longer space
For writing it, I yet would sing in part
Of the sweet draught that ne'er would satiate me

Purgatorio **XXXIII**, lines 136–138

Like gentle soul, that maketh no excuse,   130
 But makes its own will of another's will
 As soon as by a sign it is disclosed,

Even so, when she had taken hold of me,
 The beautiful lady moved, and unto Statius
 Said, in her womanly manner, "Come with him."   135

If, Reader, I possessed a longer space
 For writing it, I yet would sing in part
 Of the sweet draught that ne'er would satiate me;

But inasmuch as full are all the leaves
 Made ready for this second canticle,   140
 The curb of art no farther lets me go.

From the most holy water I returned
 Regenerate, in the manner of new trees
 That are renewed with a new foliage,

Pure and disposed to mount unto the stars.   145

⇥ CANTO I ⇤

The Ascent to the First Heaven — The Sphere of Fire

The glory of Him who moveth everything
    Doth penetrate the universe, and shine
In one part more and in another less.

Within that heaven which most his light receives
    Was I, and things beheld which to repeat   5
    Nor knows, nor can, who from above descends;

Because in drawing near to its desire
    Our intellect ingulphs itself so far,
    That after it the memory cannot go.

Truly whatever of the holy realm   10
    I had the power to treasure in my mind
    Shall now become the subject of my song.

O good Apollo, for this last emprise
    Make of me such a vessel of thy power
    As giving the beloved laurel asks!   15

One summit of Parnassus hitherto
    Has been enough for me, but now with both
    I needs must enter the arena left.

Enter into my bosom, thou, and breathe
    As at the time when Marsyas thou didst draw   20
    Out of the scabbard of those limbs of his.

O power divine, lend'st thou thyself to me
    So that the shadow of the blessed realm
    Stamped in my brain I can make manifest,

Thou'lt see me come unto thy darling tree,   25
    And crown myself thereafter with those leaves
    Of which the theme and thou shall make me worthy.

So seldom, Father, do we gather them
    For triumph or of Cæsar or of Poet,
    (The fault and shame of human inclinations)   30

That the Peneian foliage should bring forth
    Joy to the joyous Delphic deity,
    When any one it makes to thirst for it.

A little spark is followed by great flame;
    Perchance with better voices after me   35
    Shall prayer be made that Cyrrha may respond!

To mortal men by passages diverse
    Uprises the world's lamp; but by that one
    Which circles four uniteth with three crosses,

With better course and with a better star   40
    Conjoined it issues, and the mundane wax
    Tempers and stamps more after its own fashion.

Almost that passage had made morning there
    And evening here, and there was wholly white
    That hemisphere, and black the other part,   45

When Beatrice towards the left-hand side
    I saw turned round, and gazing at the sun;
    Never did eagle fasten so upon it!

And even as a second ray is wont
   To issue from the first and reascend,   50
   Like to a pilgrim who would fain return,

Thus of her action, through the eyes infused
   In my imagination, mine I made,
   And sunward fixed mine eyes beyond our wont.

There much is lawful which is here unlawful   55
   Unto our powers, by virtue of the place
   Made for the human species as its own.

Not long I bore it, nor so little while
   But I beheld it sparkle round about
   Like iron that comes molten from the fire;   60

And suddenly it seemed that day to day
   Was added, as if He who has the power
   Had with another sun the heaven adorned.

With eyes upon the everlasting wheels
   Stood Beatrice all intent, and I, on her   65
   Fixing my vision from above removed,

Such at her aspect inwardly became
   As Glaucus, tasting of the herb that made him
   Peer of the other gods beneath the sea.

To represent transhumanise in words   70
   Impossible were; the example, then, suffice
   Him for whom Grace the experience reserves.

If I was merely what of me thou newly
   Createdst, Love who governest the heaven,
   Thou knowest, who didst lift me with thy light!   75

When now the wheel, which thou dost make eternal
  Desiring thee, made me attentive to it
  By harmony thou dost modulate and measure,

Then seemed to me so much of heaven enkindled
  By the sun's flame, that neither rain nor river   80
  E'er made a lake so widely spread abroad.

The newness of the sound and the great light
  Kindled in me a longing for their cause,
  Never before with such acuteness felt;

Whence she, who saw me as I saw myself,   85
  To quiet in me my perturbed mind,
  Opened her mouth, ere I did mine to ask,

And she began: "Thou makest thyself so dull
  With false imagining, that thou seest not
  What thou wouldst see if thou hadst shaken it off.   90

Thou art not upon earth, as thou believest;
  But lightning, fleeing its appropriate site,
  Ne'er ran as thou, who thitherward returnest."

If of my former doubt I was divested
  By these brief little words more smiled than spoken, 95
  I in a new one was the more ensnared;

And said: "Already did I rest content
  From great amazement; but am now amazed
  In what way I transcend these bodies light."

Whereupon she, after a pitying sigh,   100
  Her eyes directed tow'rds me with that look
  A mother casts on a delirious child;

And she began: "All things whate'er they be
    Have order among themselves, and this is form,
    That makes the universe resemble God.   105

Here do the higher creatures see the footprints
    Of the Eternal Power, which is the end
    Whereto is made the law already mentioned.

In the order that I speak of are inclined
    All natures, by their destinies diverse,   110
    More or less near unto their origin;

Hence they move onward unto ports diverse
    O'er the great sea of being; and each one
    With instinct given it which bears it on.

This bears away the fire towards the moon;   115
    This is in mortal hearts the motive power
    This binds together and unites the earth.

Nor only the created things that are
    Without intelligence this bow shoots forth,
    But those that have both intellect and love.   120

The Providence that regulates all this
    Makes with its light the heaven forever quiet,
    Wherein that turns which has the greatest haste.

And thither now, as to a site decreed,
    Bears us away the virtue of that cord   125
    Which aims its arrows at a joyous mark.

True is it, that as oftentimes the form
    Accords not with the intention of the art,
    Because in answering is matter deaf,

So likewise from this course doth deviate   130
   Sometimes the creature, who the power possesses,
   Though thus impelled, to swerve some other way,

(In the same wise as one may see the fire
   Fall from a cloud) if the first impetus
   Earthward is wrested by some false delight.   135

Thou shouldst not wonder more, if well I judge,
   At thine ascent, than at a rivulet
   From some high mount descending to the lowland.

Marvel it would be in thee, if deprived
   Of hindrance, thou wert seated down below,   140
   As if on earth the living fire were quiet."

Thereat she heavenward turned again her face.

⊰ Canto II ⊱

The First Heaven, the Moon: Spirits Who, Having Taken Sacred Vows,
Were Forced to Violate Them — The Lunar Spots

O Ye, who in some pretty little boat,
   Eager to listen, have been following
Behind my ship, that singing sails along,

Turn back to look again upon your shores;
   Do not put out to sea, lest peradventure,   5
   In losing me, you might yourselves be lost.

The sea I sail has never yet been passed;
   Minerva breathes, and pilots me Apollo,
   And Muses nine point out to me the Bears.

Ye other few who have the neck uplifted   10
    Betimes to th' bread of Angels upon which
    One liveth here and grows not sated by it,

Well may you launch upon the deep salt-sea
    Your vessel, keeping still my wake before you
    Upon the water that grows smooth again.   15

Those glorious ones who unto Colchos passed
    Were not so wonder-struck as you shall be,
    When Jason they beheld a plowman made!

The concreated and perpetual thirst
    For the realm deiform did bear us on,   20
    As swift almost as ye the heavens behold.

Upward gazed Beatrice, and I at her;
    And in such space perchance as strikes a bolt
    And flies, and from the notch unlocks itself,

Arrived I saw me where a wondrous thing   25
    Drew to itself my sight; and therefore she
    From whom no care of mine could be concealed,

Towards me turning, blithe as beautiful,
    Said unto me: "Fix gratefully thy mind
    On God, who unto the first star has brought us."   30

It seemed to me a cloud encompassed us,
    Luminous, dense, consolidate and bright
    As adamant on which the sun is striking.

Into itself did the eternal pearl
    Receive us, even as water doth receive   35
    A ray of light, remaining still unbroken.

If I was body (and we here conceive not
    How one dimension tolerates another,
    Which needs must be if body enter body)

More the desire should be enkindled in us   40
    That essence to behold, wherein is seen
    How God and our own nature were united.

There will be seen what we receive by faith,
    Not demonstrated, but self-evident
    In guise of the first truth that man believes.   45

I made reply: "Madonna, as devoutly
    As most I can do I give thanks to Him
    Who has removed me from the mortal world.

But tell me what the dusky spots may be
    Upon this body, which below on earth   50
    Make people tell that fabulous tale of Cain?"

Somewhat she smiled; and then, "If the opinion
    Of mortals be erroneous," she said,
    "Where'er the key of sense doth not unlock,

Certes, the shafts of wonder should not pierce thee   55
    Now, forasmuch as, following the senses,
    Thou seest that the reason has short wings.

But tell me what thou think'st of it thyself."
    And I: "What seems to us up here diverse,
    Is caused, I think, by bodies rare and dense."   60

And she: "Right truly shalt thou see immersed
    In error thy belief, if well thou hearest
    The argument that I shall make against it.

Lights many the eighth sphere displays to you
>Which in their quality and quantity   65
>May noted be of aspects different.

If this were caused by rare and dense alone,
>One only virtue would there be in all
>Or more or less diffused, or equally.

Virtues diverse must be perforce the fruits   70
>Of formal principles; and these, save one,
>Of course would by thy reasoning be destroyed.

Besides, if rarity were of this dimness
>The cause thou askest, either through and through
>This planet thus attenuate were of matter,   75

Or else, as in a body is apportioned
>The fat and lean, so in like manner this
>Would in its volume interchange the leaves.

Were it the former, in the sun's eclipse
>It would be manifest by the shining through   80
>Of light, as through aught tenuous interfused.

This is not so; hence we must scan the other,
>And if it chance the other I demolish,
>Then falsified will thy opinion be.

But if this rarity go not through and through,   85
>There needs must be a limit, beyond which
>Its contrary prevents the further passing,

And thence the foreign radiance is reflected,
>Even as a color cometh back from glass,
>The which behind itself concealeth lead.   90

Now thou wilt say the sunbeam shows itself
  More dimly there than in the other parts,
  By being there reflected farther back.

From this reply experiment will free thee
  If e'er thou try it, which is wont to be   95
  The fountain to the rivers of your arts.

Three mirrors shalt thou take, and two remove
  Alike from thee, the other more remote
  Between the former two shall meet thine eyes.

Turned towards these, cause that behind thy back   100
  Be placed a light, illuming the three mirrors
  And coming back to thee by all reflected.

Though in its quantity be not so ample
  The image most remote, there shalt thou see
  How it perforce is equally resplendent.   105

Now, as beneath the touches of warm rays
  Naked the subject of the snow remains
  Both of its former color and its cold,

Thee thus remaining in thy intellect,
  Will I inform with such a living light,   110
  That it shall tremble in its aspect to thee.

Within the heaven of the divine repose
  Revolves a body, in whose virtue lies
  The being of whatever it contains.

The following heaven, that has so many eyes,   115
  Divides this being by essences diverse,
  Distinguished from it, and by it contained.

The other spheres, by various differences,
    All the distinctions which they have within them
    Dispose unto their ends and their effects.   120

Thus do these organs of the world proceed,
    As thou perceivest now, from grade to grade;
    Since from above they take, and act beneath.

Observe me well, how through this place I come
    Unto the truth thou wishest, that hereafter   125
    Thou mayst alone know how to keep the ford.

The power and motion of the holy spheres,
    As from the artisan the hammer's craft,
    Forth from the blessed motors must proceed.

The heaven, which lights so manifold make fair,   130
    From the Intelligence profound, which turns it,
    The image takes, and makes of it a seal.

And even as the soul within your dust
    Through members different and accommodated
    To faculties diverse expands itself,   135

So likewise this Intelligence diffuses
    Its virtue multiplied among the stars.
    Itself revolving on its unity.

Virtue diverse doth a diverse alloyage
    Make with the precious body that it quickens,   140
    In which, as life in you, it is combined.

From the glad nature whence it is derived,
    The mingled virtue through the body shines,
    Even as gladness through the living pupil.

From this proceeds whate'er from light to light   145
    Appeareth different, not from dense and rare:
    This is the formal principle that produces,

According to its goodness, dark and bright."

⊰ CANTO III ⊱

Piccarda Donati and the Empress Constance

That Sun, which erst with love my bosom warmed,
    Of beauteous truth had unto me discovered,
By proving and reproving, the sweet aspect.

And, that I might confess myself convinced
    And confident, so far as was befitting,   5
    I lifted more erect my head to speak.

But there appeared a vision, which withdrew me
    So close to it, in order to be seen,
    That my confession I remembered not.

Such as through polished and transparent glass,   10
    Or waters crystalline and undisturbed,
    But not so deep as that their bed be lost,

Come back again the outlines of our faces
    So feeble, that a pearl on forehead white
    Comes not less speedily unto our eyes;   15

Such saw I many faces prompt to speak,
    So that I ran in error opposite
    To that which kindled love 'twixt man and fountain.

Saw I many faces prompt to speak

Paradiso III, line 16

As soon as I became aware of them,
 Esteeming them as mirrored semblances, 20
 To see of whom they were, mine eyes I turned,

And nothing saw, and once more turned them forward
 Direct into the light of my sweet Guide,
 Who smiling kindled in her holy eyes.

"Marvel thou not," she said to me, "because 25
 I smile at this thy puerile conceit,
 Since on the truth it trusts not yet its foot,

But turns thee, as 'tis wont, on emptiness.
 True substances are these which thou beholdest,
 Here relegate for breaking of some vow. 30

Therefore speak with them, listen and believe;
 For the true light, which giveth peace to them,
 Permits them not to turn from it their feet."

And I unto the shade that seemed most wishful
 To speak directed me, and I began, 35
 As one whom too great eagerness bewilders:

"O well-created spirit, who in the rays
 Of life eternal dost the sweetness taste
 Which being untasted ne'er is comprehended,

Grateful 'twill be to me, if thou content me 40
 Both with thy name and with your destiny."
 Whereat she promptly and with laughing eyes:

"Our charity doth never shut the doors
 Against a just desire, except as one
 Who wills that all her court be like herself. 45

I was a virgin sister in the world;
    And if thy mind doth contemplate me well,
    The being more fair will not conceal me from thee,

But thou shalt recognise I am Piccarda,
    Who, stationed here among these other blessed,   50
    Myself am blessed in the slowest sphere.

All our affections, that alone inflamed
    Are in the pleasure of the Holy Ghost,
    Rejoice at being of his order formed;

And this allotment, which appears so low,   55
    Therefore is given us, because our vows
    Have been neglected and in some part void."

Whence I to her: "In your miraculous aspects
    There shines I know not what of the divine,
    Which doth transform you from our first
        conceptions.   60

Therefore I was not swift in my remembrance;
    But what thou tellest me now aids me so,
    That the refiguring is easier to me.

But tell me, ye who in this place are happy,
    Are you desirous of a higher place,   65
    To see more or to make yourselves more friends?"

First with those other shades she smiled a little;
    Thereafter answered me so full of gladness,
    She seemed to burn in the first fire of love:

"Brother, our will is quieted by virtue   70
    Of charity, that makes us wish alone
    For what we have, nor gives us thirst for more.

If to be more exalted we aspired,
   Discordant would our aspirations be
   Unto the will of Him who here secludes us;   75

Which thou shalt see finds no place in these circles,
   If being in charity is needful here,
   And if thou lookest well into its nature;

Nay, 'tis essential to this blest existence
   To keep itself within the will divine,   80
   Whereby our very wishes are made one;

So that, as we are station above station
   Throughout this realm, to all the realm 'tis pleasing,
   As to the King, who makes his will our will.

And his will is our peace; this is the sea   85
   To which is moving onward whatsoever
   It doth create, and all that nature makes."

Then it was clear to me how everywhere
   In heaven is Paradise, although the grace
   Of good supreme there rain not in one measure.   90

But as it comes to pass, if one food sates,
   And for another still remains the longing,
   We ask for this, and that decline with thanks,

E'en thus did I, with gesture and with word,
   To learn from her what was the web wherein   95
   She did not ply the shuttle to the end.

"A perfect life and merit high in-heaven
   A lady o'er us," said she, "by whose rule
   Down in your world they vest and veil themselves,

That until death they may both watch and sleep   100
 Beside that Spouse who every vow accepts
 Which charity conformeth to his pleasure.

To follow her, in girlhood from the world
 I fled, and in her habit shut myself,
 And pledged me to the pathway of her sect.   105

Then men accustomed unto evil more
 Than unto good, from the sweet cloister tore me;
 God knows what afterward my life became.

This other splendor, which to thee reveals
 Itself on my right side, and is enkindled   110
 With all the illumination of our sphere,

What of myself I say applies to her;
 A nun was she, and likewise from her head
 Was ta'en the shadow of the sacred wimple.

But when she too was to the world returned   115
 Against her wishes and against good usage,
 Of the heart's veil she never was divested.

Of great Costanza this is the effulgence,
 Who from the second wind of Suabia
 Brought forth the third and latest puissance."   120

Thus unto me she spake, and then began
 "Ave Maria" singing, and in singing
 Vanished, as through deep water something heavy.

My sight, that followed her as long a time
 As it was possible, when it had lost her   125
 Turned round unto the mark of more desire,

And wholly unto Beatrice reverted;
>But she such lightnings flashed into mine eyes,
>That at the first my sight endured it not;

And this in questioning more backward made me.   130

⊰ Canto IV ⊱

Questionings of the Soul and of Broken Vows

Between two viands, equally removed
And tempting, a free man would die of hunger
Ere either he could bring unto his teeth.

So would a lamb between the ravenings
>Of two fierce wolves stand fearing both alike;   5
>And so would stand a dog between two does.

Hence, if I held my peace, myself I blame not,
>Impelled in equal measure by my doubts,
>Since it must be so, nor do I commend.

I held my peace; but my desire was painted   10
>Upon my face, and questioning with that
>More fervent far than by articulate speech.

Beatrice did as Daniel had done
>Relieving Nebuchadnezzar from the wrath
>Which rendered him unjustly merciless,   15

And said: "Well see I how attracteth thee
>One and the other wish, so that thy care
>Binds itself so that forth it does not breathe.

Thou arguest, if good will be permanent,
    The violence of others, for what reason   **20**
    Doth it decrease the measure of my merit?

Again for doubting furnish thee occasion
    Souls seeming to return unto the stars,
    According to the sentiment of Plato.

These are the questions which upon thy wish   **25**
    Are thrusting equally; and therefore first
    Will I treat that which hath the most of gall.

He of the Seraphim most absorbed in God,
    Moses, and Samuel, and whichever John
    Thou mayst select, I say, and even Mary,   **30**

Have not in any other heaven their seats,
    Than have those spirits that just appeared to thee,
    Nor of existence more or fewer years;

But all make beautiful the primal circle,
    And have sweet life in different degrees,   **35**
    By feeling more or less the eternal breath.

They showed themselves here, not because allotted
    This sphere has been to them, but to give sign
    Of the celestial which is least exalted.

To speak thus is adapted to your mind,   **40**
    Since only through the sense it apprehendeth
    What then it worthy makes of intellect.

On this account the Scripture condescends
    Unto your faculties, and feet and hands
    To God attributes, and means something else;   **45**

And Holy Church under an aspect human
   Gabriel and Michael represent to you,
   And him who made Tobias whole again.

That which Timæus argues of the soul
   Doth not resemble that which here is seen,   50
   Because it seems that as he speaks he thinks.

He says the soul unto its star returns,
   Believing it to have been severed thence
   Whenever nature gave it as a form.

Perhaps his doctrine is of other guise   55
   Than the words sound, and possibly may be
   With meaning that is not to be derided.

If he doth mean that to these wheels return
   The honor of their influence and the blame,
   Perhaps his bow doth hit upon some truth.   60

This principle ill understood once warped
   The whole world nearly, till it went astray
   Invoking Jove and Mercury and Mars.

The other doubt which doth disquiet thee
   Less venom has, for its malevolence   65
   Could never lead thee otherwhere from me.

That as unjust our justice should appear
   In eyes of mortals, is an argument
   Of faith, and not of sin heretical.

But still, that your perception may be able   70
   To thoroughly penetrate this verity,
   As thou desirest, I will satisfy thee.

If it be violence when he who suffers
     Cooperates not with him who uses force,
     These souls were not on that account excused;   75

For will is never quenched unless it will,
     But operates as nature doth in fire
     If violence a thousand times distort it.

Hence, if it yieldeth more or less, it seconds
     The force; and these have done so, having power   80
     Of turning back unto the holy place.

If their will had been perfect, like to that
     Which Lawrence fast upon his gridiron held,
     And Mutius made severe to his own hand,

It would have urged them back along the road   85
     Whence they were dragged, as soon as they were free;
     But such a solid will is all too rare.

And by these words, if thou hast gathered them
     As thou shouldst do, the argument is refuted
     That would have still annoyed thee many times.   90

But now another passage runs across
     Before thine eyes, and such that by thyself
     Thou couldst not thread it ere thou wouldst be weary.

I have for certain put into thy mind
     That soul beatified could never lie,   95
     For it is ever near the primal Truth,

And then thou from Piccarda might'st have heard
     Costanza kept affection for the veil,
     So that she seemeth here to contradict me.

Many times, brother, has it come to pass,   100
    That, to escape from peril, with reluctance
    That has been done it was not right to do,

E'en as Alcmæon (who, being by his father
    Thereto entreated, his own mother slew)
    Not to lose pity pitiless became.   105

At this point I desire thee to remember
    That force with will commingles, and they cause
    That the offenses cannot be excused.

Will absolute consenteth not to evil;
    But in so far consenteth as it fears,   110
    If it refrain, to fall into more harm.

Hence when Piccarda uses this expression,
    She meaneth the will absolute, and I
    The other, so that both of us speak truth."

Such was the flowing of the holy river   115
    That issued from the fount whence springs all truth;
    This put to rest my wishes one and all.

"O love of the first lover, O divine,"
    Said I forthwith, "whose speech inundates me
    And warms me so, it more and more revives me,   120

My own affection is not so profound
    As to suffice in rendering grace for grace;
    Let Him, who sees and can, thereto respond.

Well I perceive that never sated is
    Our intellect unless the Truth illume it,   125
    Beyond which nothing true expands itself.

It rests therein, as wild beast in his lair,
 When it attains it; and it can attain it;
 If not, then each desire would frustrate be.

Therefore springs up, in fashion of a shoot,   130
 Doubt at the foot of truth; and this is nature,
 Which to the top from height to height impels us.

This doth invite me, this assurance give me
 With reverence, Lady, to inquire of you
 Another truth, which is obscure to me.   135

I wish to know if man can satisfy you
 For broken vows with other good deeds, so
 That in your balance they will not be light."

Beatrice gazed upon me with her eyes
 Full of the sparks of love, and so divine,   140
 That, overcome my power, I turned my back

And almost lost myself with eyes downcast.

⊰ CANTO V ⊱

Discourse of Beatrice on Vows and Compensations—Ascent to the Second Heaven,
Mercury: Spirits Who for the Love of Fame Achieved Great Deeds

"If in the heat of love I flame upon thee
 Beyond the measure that on earth is seen,
 So that the valor of thine eyes I vanquish,

Marvel thou not thereat; for this proceeds
 From perfect sight, which as it apprehends   5
 To the good apprehended moves its feet.

Well I perceive how is already shining
   Into thine intellect the eternal light,
   That only seen enkindles always love;

And if some other thing your love seduce,   10
   'Tis nothing but a vestige of the same,
   Ill understood, which there is shining through.

Thou fain wouldst know if with another service
   For broken vow can such return be made
   As to secure the soul from further claim."   15

This Canto thus did Beatrice begin;
   And, as a man who breaks not off his speech,
   Continued thus her holy argument:

"The greatest gift that in his largess God
   Creating made, and unto his own goodness   20
   Nearest conformed, and that which he doth prize

Most highly, is the freedom of the will,
   Wherewith the creatures of intelligence
   Both all and only were and are endowed.

Now wilt thou see, if thence thou reasonest,   25
   The high worth of a vow, if it he made
   So that when thou consentest God consents:

For, closing between God and man the compact,
   A sacrifice is of this treasure made,
   Such as I say, and made by its own act.   30

What can be rendered then as compensation?
   Think'st thou to make good use of what thou'st offered,
   With gains ill gotten thou wouldst do good deed.

Now art thou certain of the greater point;
    But because Holy Church in this dispenses,   35
    Which seems against the truth which I have shown thee,

Behoves thee still to sit awhile at table,
    Because the solid food which thou hast taken
    Requireth further aid for thy digestion.

Open thy mind to that which I reveal,   40
    And fix it there within; for 'tis not knowledge,
    The having heard without retaining it.

In the essence of this sacrifice two things
    Convene together; and the one is that
    Of which 'tis made, the other is the agreement.   45

This last for evermore is canceled not
    Unless complied with, and concerning this
    With such precision has above been spoken.

Therefore it was enjoined upon the Hebrews
    To offer still, though sometimes what was offered   50
    Might be commuted, as thou ought'st to know.

The other, which is known to thee as matter,
    May well indeed be such that one errs not
    If it for other matter be exchanged.

But let none shift the burden on his shoulder   55
    At his arbitrament, without the turning
    Both of the white and of the yellow key;

And every permutation deem as foolish,
    If in the substitute the thing relinquished,
    As the four is in six, be not contained.   60

Therefore whatever thing has so great weight
   In value that it drags down every balance,
   Cannot be satisfied with other spending.

Let mortals never take a vow in jest;
   Be faithful and not blind in doing that,   65
   As Jephthah was in his first offering,

Whom more beseemed to say, 'I have done wrong,
   Than to do worse by keeping; and as foolish
   Thou the great leader of the Greeks wilt find,

Whence wept Iphigenia her fair face,   70
   And made for her both wise and simple weep,
   Who heard such kind of worship spoken of.'

Christians, be ye more serious in your movements;
   Be ye not like a feather at each wind,
   And think not every water washes you.   75

Ye have the Old and the New Testament,
   And the Pastor of the Church who guideth you
   Let this suffice you unto your salvation.

If evil appetite cry aught else to you,
   Be ye as men, and not as silly sheep,   80
   So that the Jew among you may not mock you.

Be ye not as the lamb that doth abandon
   Its mother's milk, and frolicsome and simple
   Combats at its own pleasure with itself."

Thus Beatrice to me even as I write it;   85
   Then all desireful turned herself again
   To that part where the world is most alive.

Her silence and her change of countenance
    Silence imposed upon my eager mind,
    That had already in advance new questions;   90

And as an arrow that upon the mark
    Strikes ere the bowstring quiet hath become,
    So did we speed into the second realm.

My Lady there so joyful I beheld,
    As into the brightness of that heaven she entered,   95
    More luminous thereat the planet grew;

And if the star itself was changed and smiled,
    What became I, who by my nature am
    Exceeding mutable in every guise!

As, in a fish-pond which is pure and tranquil,   100
    The fishes draw to that which from without
    Comes in such fashion that their food they deem it;

So I beheld more than a thousand splendors
    Drawing towards us, and in each was heard:
    "Lo, this is she who shall increase our love."   105

And as each one was coming unto us,
    Full of beatitude the shade was seen,
    By the effulgence clear that issued from it.

Think, Reader, if what here is just beginning
    No farther should proceed, how thou wouldst have   110
    An agonizing need of knowing more;

And of thyself thou'lt see how I from these
    Was in desire of hearing their conditions,
    As they unto mine eyes were manifest.

So I beheld more than a thousand splendors
Drawing toward us

Paradiso V, lines 103–104

"O thou well-born, unto whom Grace concedes   115
　　To see the thrones of the eternal triumph,
　　Or ever yet the warfare be abandoned

With light that through the whole of heaven is spread
　　Kindled are we, and hence if thou desirest
　　To know of us, at thine own pleasure sate thee."   120

Thus by someone among those holy spirits
　　Was spoken, and by Beatrice: "Speak, speak
　　Securely, and believe them even as Gods."

"Well I perceive how thou dost nest thyself
　　In thine own light, and drawest it from thine eyes,   125
　　Because they coruscate when thou dost smile,

But know not who thou art, nor why thou hast,
　　Spirit august, thy station in the sphere
　　That veils itself to men in alien rays."

This said I in direction of the light   130
　　Which first had spoken to me; whence it became
　　By far more lucent than it was before.

Even as the sun, that doth conceal himself
　　By too much light, when heat has worn away
　　The tempering influence of the vapors dense,   135

By greater rapture thus concealed itself
　　In its own radiance the figure saintly,
　　And thus close, close enfolded answered me

In fashion as the following Canto sings.

⊰ CANTO VI ⊱

Justinian — The Roman Eagle — The Empire — Romeo

"After that Constantine the eagle turned
Against the course of heaven, which it had followed
Behind the ancient who Lavinia took,

Two hundred years and more the bird of God
In the extreme of Europe held itself,   5
Near to the mountains whence it issued first;

And under shadow of the sacred plumes
It governed there the world from hand to hand,
And, changing thus, upon mine own alighted.

Cæsar I was, and am Justinian,   10
Who, by the will of primal Love I feel,
Took from the laws the useless and redundant;

And ere unto the work I was attent,
One nature to exist in Christ, not more,
Believed, and with such faith was I contented.   15

But blessed Agapetus, he who was
The supreme pastor, to the faith sincere
Pointed me out the way by words of his.

Him I believed, and what was his assertion
I now see clearly, even as thou seest   20
Each contradiction to be false and true.

As soon as with the Church I moved my feet,
God in his grace it pleased with this high task
To inspire me, and I gave me wholly to it,

And to my Belisarius I commended   25
    The arms, to which was heaven's right hand so joined
    It was a signal that I should repose.

Now here to the first question terminates
    My answer; but the character thereof
    Constrains me to continue with a sequel,   30

In order that thou see with how great reason
    Men move against the standard sacrosanct,
    Both who appropriate and who oppose it.

Behold how great a power has made it worthy
    Of reverence, beginning from the hour   35
    When Pallas died to give it sovereignty.

Thou knowest it made in Alba its abode
    Three hundred years and upward, till at last
    The three to three fought for it yet again.

Thou knowest what it achieved from Sabine wrong   40
    Down to Lucretia's sorrow, in seven kings
    O'ercoming round about the neighboring nations;

Thou knowest what it achieved, borne by the Romans
    Illustrious against Brennus, against Pyrrhus,
    Against the other princes and confederates.   45

Torquatus thence and Quinctius, who from locks
    Unkempt was named, Decii and Fabii,
    Received the fame I willingly embalm;

It struck to earth the pride of the Arabians,
    Who, following Hannibal, had passed across   50
    The Alpine ridges, Po, from which thou glidest;

Beneath it triumphed while they yet were young
    Pompey and Scipio, and to the hill
    Beneath which thou wast born it bitter seemed;

Then, near unto the time when heaven had willed   55
    To bring the whole world to its mood serene,
    Did Cæsar by the will of Rome assume it.

What it achieved from Var unto the Rhine,
    Isère beheld and Saône, beheld the Seine,
    And every valley whence the Rhone is filled;   60

What it achieved when it had left Ravenna,
    And leaped the Rubicon, was such a flight
    That neither tongue nor pen could follow it.

Round towards Spain it wheeled its legions; then
    Towards Durazzo, and Pharsalia smote   65
    That to the calid Nile was felt the pain.

Antandros and the Simois, whence it started,
    It saw again, and there where Hector lies,
    And ill for Ptolemy then roused itself.

From thence it came like lightning upon Juba;   70
    Then wheeled itself again into your West,
    Where the Pompeian clarion it heard.

From what it wrought with the next standard-bearer
    Brutus and Cassius howl in Hell together,
    And Modena and Perugia dolent were;   75

Still doth the mournful Cleopatra weep
    Because thereof, who, fleeing from before it,
    Took from the adder sudden and black death.

With him it ran even to the Red Sea shore;
    With him it placed the world in so great peace,   80
    That unto Janus was his temple closed.

But what the standard that has made me speak
    Achieved before, and after should achieve
    Throughout the mortal realm that lies beneath it,

Becometh in appearance mean and dim,   85
    If in the hand of the third Cæsar seen
    With eye unclouded and affection pure,

Because the living Justice that inspires me
    Granted it, in the hand of him I speak of,
    The glory of doing vengeance for its wrath.   90

Now here attend to what I answer thee;
    Later it ran with Titus to do vengeance
    Upon the vengeance of the ancient sin.

And when the tooth of Lombardy had bitten
    The Holy Church, then underneath its wings   95
    Did Charlemagne victorious succor her.

Now hast thou power to judge of such as those
    Whom I accused above, and of their crimes,
    Which are the cause of all your miseries.

To the public standard one the yellow lilies   100
    Opposes, the other claims it for a party,
    So that 'tis hard to see which sins the most.

Let, let the Ghibellines ply their handicraft
    Beneath some other standard; for this ever
    Ill follows he who it and justice parts.   105

And let not this new Charles e'er strike it down,
  He and his Guelfs, but let him fear the talons
  That from a nobler lion stripped the fell.

Already oftentimes the sons have wept
  The father's crime; and let him not believe   110
  That God will change His scutcheon for the lilies.

This little planet doth adorn itself
  With the good spirits that have active been,
  That fame and honor might come after them;

And whensoever the desires mount thither,   115
  Thus deviating, must perforce the rays
  Of the true love less vividly mount upward.

But in commensuration of our wages
  With our desert is portion of our joy,
  Because we see them neither less nor greater.   120

Herein doth living Justice sweeten so
  Affection in us, that for evermore
  It cannot warp to any iniquity.

Voices diverse make up sweet melodies;
  So in this life of ours the seats diverse   125
  Render sweet harmony among these spheres;

And in the compass of this present pearl
  Shineth the sheen of Romeo, of whom
  The grand and beauteous work was ill rewarded.

But the Provençals who against him wrought,   130
  They have not laughed, and therefore ill goes he
  Who makes his hurt of the good deeds of others.

Four daughters, and each one of them a queen,
 Had Raymond Berenger, and this for him
 Did Romeo, a poor man and a pilgrim;   135

And then malicious words incited him
 To summon to a reckoning this just man,
 Who rendered to him seven and five for ten.

Then he departed poor and stricken in years,
 And if the world could know the heart he had,   140
 In begging bit by bit his livelihood,

Though much it laud him, it would laud him more."

⊰ CANTO VII ⊱

Beatrice's Discourse of the Crucifixion, the Incarnation,
the Immortality of the Soul, and the Resurrection of the Body

"O*SANNA sanctus Deus Sabaoth,*
  Superillustrans claritate tua
Felices ignes horum malahoth!"

In this wise, to his melody returning,
 This substance, upon which a double light   5
 Doubles itself, was seen by me to sing,

And to their dance this and the others moved,
 And in the manner of swift-hurrying sparks
 Veiled themselves from me with a sudden distance.

Doubting was I, and saying, "Tell her, tell her,"   10
 Within me, "tell her," saying, "tell my Lady,"
 Who slakes my thirst with her sweet effluences;

And yet that reverence which doth lord it over
　　The whole of me only by B and ICE,
　　Bowed me again like unto one who drowses.   15

Short while did Beatrice endure me thus;
　　And she began, lighting me with a smile
　　Such as would make one happy in the fire:

"According to infallible advisement,
　　After what manner a just vengeance justly   20
　　Could be avenged has put thee upon thinking,

But I will speedily thy mind unloose;
　　And do thou listen, for these words of mine
　　Of a great doctrine will a present make thee.

By not enduring on the power that wills   25
　　Curb for his good, that man who ne'er was born,
　　Damning himself damned all his progeny;

Whereby the human species down below
　　Lay sick for many centuries in great error,
　　Till to descend it pleased the Word of God   30

To where the nature, which from its own Maker
　　Estranged itself, he joined to him in person
　　By the sole act of his eternal love.

Now unto what is said direct thy sight;
　　This nature when united to its Maker,   35
　　Such as created, was sincere and good;

But by itself alone was banished forth
　　From Paradise, because it turned aside
　　Out of the way of truth and of its life.

Therefore the penalty the cross held out,   40
    If measured by the nature thus assumed,
    None ever yet with so great justice stung,

And none was ever of so great injustice,
    Considering who the Person was that suffered,
    Within whom such a nature was contracted.   45

From one act therefore issued things diverse;
    To God and to the Jews one death was pleasing;
    Earth trembled at it and the Heaven was opened.

It should no longer now seem difficult
    To thee, when it is said that a just vengeance   50
    By a just court was afterward avenged.

But now do I behold thy mind entangled
    From thought to thought within a knot, from which
    With great desire it waits to free itself.

Thou sayest, 'Well discern I what I hear;   55
    But it is hidden from me why God willed
    For our redemption only this one mode.'

Buried remaineth, brother, this decree
    Unto the eyes of every one whose nature
    Is in the flame of love not yet adult.   60

Verily, inasmuch as at this mark
    One gazes long and little is discerned,
    Wherefore this mode was worthiest will I say.

Goodness Divine, which from itself doth spurn
    All envy, burning in itself so sparkles   65
    That the eternal beauties it unfolds.

Whate'er from this immediately distils
    Has afterwards no end, for ne'er removed
    Is its impression when it sets its seal.

Whate'er from this immediately rains down   70
    Is wholly free, because it is not subject
    Unto the influences of novel things.

The more conformed thereto, the more it pleases;
    For the blest ardor that irradiates all things
    In that most like itself is most vivacious.   75

With all of these things has advantaged been
    The human creature; and if one be wanting,
    From his nobility he needs must fall.

'Tis sin alone which doth disfranchise him,
    And render him unlike the Good Supreme,   80
    So that he little with its light is blanched,

And to his dignity no more returns,
    Unless he fill up where transgression empties
    With righteous pains for criminal delights.

Your nature when it sinned so utterly   85
    In its own seed, out of these dignities
    Even as out of Paradise was driven,

Nor could itself recover, if thou notest
    With nicest subtilty, by any way,
    Except by passing one of these two fords: 90

Either that God through clemency alone
    Had pardon granted, or that man himself
    Had satisfaction for his folly made.

Fix now thine eye deep into the abyss
   Of the eternal counsel, to my speech   95
   As far as may be fastened steadfastly!

Man in his limitations had not power
   To satisfy, not having power to sink
   In his humility obeying then,

Far as he disobeying thought to rise;   100
   And for this reason man has been from power
   Of satisfying by himself excluded.

Therefore it God behoved in his own ways
   Man to restore unto his perfect life,
   I say in one, or else in both of them.   105

But since the action of the doer is
   So much more grateful, as it more presents
   The goodness of the heart from which it issues,

Goodness Divine, that doth imprint the world,
   Has been contented to proceed by each   110
   And all its ways to lift you up again;

Nor 'twixt the first day and the final night
   Such high and such magnificent proceeding
   By one or by the other was or shall be;

For God more bounteous was himself to give   115
   To make man able to uplift himself,
   Than if he only of himself had pardoned;

And all the other modes were insufficient
   For justice, were it not the Son of God
   Himself had humbled to become incarnate.   120

Now, to fill fully each desire of thine,
    Return I to elucidate one place,
    In order that thou there mayst see as I do.

Thou sayst: 'I see the air, I see the fire,
    The water, and the earth, and all their mixtures   125
    Come to corruption, and short while endure;

And these things notwithstanding were created';
    Therefore if that which I have said were true,
    They should have been secure against corruption.

The Angels, brother, and the land sincere   130
    In which thou art, created may be called
    Just as they are in their entire existence;

But all the elements which thou hast named,
    And all those things which out of them are made,
    By a created virtue are informed.   135

Created was the matter which they have;
    Created was the informing influence
    Within these stars that round about them go.

The soul of every brute and of the plants
    By its potential temperament attracts   140
    The ray and motion of the holy lights;

But your own life immediately inspires
    Supreme Beneficence, and enamours it
    So with herself, it evermore desires her.

And thou from this mayst argue furthermore   145
    Your resurrection, if thou think again
    How human flesh was fashioned at that time

When the first parents both of them were made."

⊰ CANTO VIII ⊱

Ascent to the Third Heaven, Venus: Lovers —
Charles Martel — Discourse on Diverse Natures

The world used in its peril to believe
 That the fair Cypria delirious love
Rayed out, in the third epicycle turning;

Wherefore not only unto her paid honor
 Of sacrifices and of votive cry   5
 The ancient nations in the ancient error,

But both Dione honored they and Cupid,
 That as her mother, this one as her son,
 And said that he had sat in Dido's lap;

And they from her, whence I beginning take,   10
 Took the denomination of the star
 That woos the sun, now following, now in front.

I was not ware of our ascending to it;
 But of our being in it gave full faith
 My Lady whom I saw more beauteous grow.   15

And as within a flame a spark is seen,
 And as within a voice a voice discerned,
 When one is steadfast, and one comes and goes,

Within that light beheld I other lamps
 Move in a circle, speeding more and less,   20
 Methinks in measure of their inward vision.

From a cold cloud descended never winds,
 Or visible or not, so rapidly
 They would not laggard and impeded seem

To anyone who had those lights divine   25
    Seen come towards us, leaving the gyration
    Begun at first in the high Seraphim.

And behind those that most in front appeared
    Sounded *"Osanna!"* so that never since
    To hear again was I without desire.   30

Then unto us more nearly one approached,
    And it alone began: "We all are ready
    Unto thy pleasure, that thou joy in us.

We turn around with the celestial Princes,
    One gyre and one gyration and one thirst,   35
    To whom thou in the world of old didst say,

'Ye who, *intelligent, the third heaven are moving*';
    And are so full of love, to pleasure thee
    A little quiet will not be less sweet."

After these eyes of mine themselves had offered   40
    Unto my Lady reverently, and she
    Content and certain of herself had made them,

Back to the light they turned, which so great promise
    Made of itself, and "Say, who art thou?" was
    My voice, imprinted with a great affection.   45

O how and how much I beheld it grow
    With the new joy that superadded was
    Unto its joys, as soon as I had spoken!

Thus changed, it said to me: "The world possessed me
    Short time below; and, if it had been more,   50
    Much evil will be which would not have been.

My gladness keepeth me concealed from thee,
    Which rayeth round about me, and doth hide me
    Like as a creature swathed in its own silk.

Much didst thou love me, and thou hadst good reason;   55
    For had I been below, I should have shown thee
    Somewhat beyond the foliage of my love.

That left-hand margin, which doth bathe itself
    In Rhone, when it is mingled with the Sorgue,
    Me for its lord awaited in due time,   60

And that horn of Ausonia, which is towned
    With Bari, with Gaeta and Catona,
    Whence Tronto and Verde in the sea disgorge.

Already flashed upon my brow the crown
    Of that dominion which the Danube waters   65
    After the German borders it abandons;

And beautiful Trinacria, that is murky
    'Twixt Pachino and Peloro, (on the gulf
    Which greatest scath from Eurus doth receive)

Not through Typhœus, but through nascent sulphur,   70
    Would have awaited her own monarchs still,
    Through me from Charles descended and from Rudolph,

If evil lordship, that exasperates ever
    The subject populations, had not moved
    Palermo to the outcry of 'Death! death!'   75

And if my brother could but this foresee,
    The greedy poverty of Catalonia
    Straight would he flee, that it might not molest him;

"That left-hand margin, which doth bathe itself
In Rhone, when it is mingled with the Sorgue,
Me for its lord awaited in due time"

Paradiso VIII, lines 58–60

For verily 'tis needful to provide,
    Through him or other, so that on his bark   80
    Already freighted no more freight be placed.

His nature, which from liberal covetous
    Descended, such a soldiery would need
    As should not care for hoarding in a chest."

"Because I do believe the lofty joy   85
    Thy speech infuses into me, my Lord,
    Where every good thing doth begin and end

Thou seest as I see it, the more grateful
    Is it to me; and this too hold I dear,
    That gazing upon God thou dost discern it.   90

Glad hast thou made me; so make clear to me,
    Since speaking thou hast stirred me up to doubt,
    How from sweet seed can bitter issue forth."

This I to him; and he to me: "If I
    Can show to thee a truth, to what thou askest   95
    Thy face thou'lt hold as thou dost hold thy back.

The Good which all the realm thou art ascending
    Turns and contents, maketh its providence
    To be a power within these bodies vast;

And not alone the natures are foreseen   100
    Within the mind that in itself is perfect,
    But they together with their preservation.

For whatsoever thing this bow shoots forth
    Falls foreordained unto an end foreseen,
    Even as a shaft directed to its mark.   105

If that were not, the heaven which thou dost walk
    Would in such manner its effects produce,
    That they no longer would be arts, but ruins.

This cannot be, if the Intelligences
    That keep these stars in motion are not maimed,   110
    And maimed the First that has not made them perfect.

Wilt thou this truth have clearer made to thee?"
    And I: "Not so; for 'tis impossible
    That nature tire, I see, in what is needful."

Whence he again: "Now say, would it be worse   115
    For men on earth were they not citizens?"
    "Yes," I replied; "and here I ask no reason."

"And can they be so, if below they live not
    Diversely unto offices diverse?
    No, if your master writeth well for you."   120

So came he with deductions to this point;
    Then he concluded: "Therefore it behoves
    The roots of your effects to be diverse.

Hence one is Solon born, another Xerxes,
    Another Melchisedec, and another he   125
    Who, flying through the air, his son did lose.

Revolving Nature, which a signet is
    To mortal wax, doth practice well her art,
    But not one inn distinguish from another;

Thence happens it that Esau differeth   130
    In seed from Jacob; and Quirinus comes
    From sire so vile that he is given to Mars.

A generated nature its own way
    Would always make like its progenitors,
    If Providence divine were not triumphant. 135

Now that which was behind thee is before thee;
    But that thou know that I with thee am pleased,
    With a corollary will I mantle thee.

Evermore nature, if it fortune find
    Discordant to it, like each other seed 140
    Out of its region, maketh evil thrift;

And if the world below would fix its mind
    On the foundation which is laid by nature,
    Pursuing that, 'twould have the people good.

But you unto religion wrench aside 145
    Him who was born to gird him with the sword,
    And make a king of him who is for sermons;

Therefore your footsteps wander from the road."

⊰ CANTO IX ⊱

Cunizza da Romano, Folco of Marseilles, and Rahab —
Neglect of the Holy Land

Beautiful Clemence, after that thy Charles
    Had me enlightened, he narrated to me
The treacheries his seed should undergo;

But said: "Be still and let the years roll round";
    So I can only say, that lamentation 5
    Legitimate shall follow on your wrongs.

And of that holy light the life already
    Had to the Sun which fills it turned again,
    As to that good which for each thing sufficeth.

Ah, souls deceived, and creatures impious,   10
    Who from such good do turn away your hearts,
    Directing upon vanity your foreheads!

And now, behold, another of those splendors
    Approached me, and its will to pleasure me
    It signified by brightening outwardly.   15

The eyes of Beatrice, that fastened were
    Upon me, as before, of dear assent
    To my desire assurance gave to me.

"Ah, bring swift compensation to my wish,
    Thou blessed spirit," I said, "and give me proof   20
    That what I think in thee I can reflect!"

Whereat the light, that still was new to me,
    Out of its depths, whence it before was singing,
    As one delighted to do good, continued:

"Within that region of the land depraved   25
    Of Italy, that lies between Rialto
    And fountainheads of Brenta and of Piava,

Rises a hill, and mounts not very high,
    Wherefrom descended formerly a torch
    That made upon that region great assault.   30

Out of one root were born both I and it;
    Cunizza was I called, and here I shine
    Because the splendor of this star o'ercame me.

But gladly to myself the cause I pardon
    Of my allotment, and it does not grieve me;   35
    Which would perhaps seem strong unto your vulgar.

Of this so luculent and precious jewel,
    Which of our heaven is nearest unto me,
    Great fame remained; and ere it die away

This hundredth year shall yet quintupled be.   40
    See if man ought to make him excellent,
    So that another life the first may leave!

And thus thinks not the present multitude
    Shut in by Adige and Tagliamento,
    Nor yet for being scourged is penitent.   45

But soon 'twill be that Padua in the marsh
    Will change the water that Vicenza bathes,
    Because the folk are stubborn against duty;

And where the Sile and Cagnano join
    One lordeth it, and goes with lofty head,   50
    For catching whom e'en now the net is making.

Feltro moreover of her impious pastor
    Shall weep the crime, which shall so monstrous be
    That for the like none ever entered Malta.

Ample exceedingly would be the vat   55
    That of the Ferrarese could hold the blood,
    And weary who should weigh it ounce by ounce,

Of which this courteous priest shall make a gift
    To show himself a partisan; and such gifts
    Will to the living of the land conform.   60

Above us there are mirrors, Thrones you call them,
   From which shines out on us God Judicant,
   So that this utterance seems good to us."

Here it was silent, and it had the semblance
   Of being turned elsewhither, by the wheel   65
   On which it entered as it was before.

The other joy, already known to me,
   Became a thing transplendent in my sight,
   As a fine ruby smitten by the sun.

Through joy effulgence is acquired above,   70
   As here a smile; but down below, the shade
   Outwardly darkens, as the mind is sad.

"God seeth all things, and in Him, blest spirit,
   Thy sight is," said I, "so that never will
   Of his can possibly from thee be hidden;   75

Thy voice, then, that forever makes the heavens
   Glad, with the singing of those holy fires
   Which of their six wings make themselves a cowl,

Wherefore does it not satisfy my longings?
   Indeed, I would not wait thy questioning   80
   If I in thee were as thou art in me."

"The greatest of the valleys where the water
   Expands itself," forthwith its words began,
   "That sea excepted which the earth engarlands,

Between discordant shores against the sun   85
   Extends so far, that it meridian makes
   Where it was wont before to make the horizon.

I was a dweller on that valley's shore
    'Twixt Ebro and Magra that with journey short
    Doth from the Tuscan part the Genoese.   90

With the same sunset and same sunrise nearly
    Sit Buggia and the city whence I was,
    That with its blood once made the harbor hot.

Folco that people called me unto whom
    My name was known; and now with me this heaven   95
    Imprints itself, as I did once with it;

For more the daughter of Belus never burned,
    Offending both Sichæus and Creusa,
    Than I, so long as it became my locks,

Nor yet that Rodophean, who deluded   100
    was by Demophoön, nor yet Alcides,
    When Iole he in his heart had locked.

Yet here is no repenting, but we smile,
    Not at the fault, which comes not back to mind,
    But at the power which ordered and foresaw.   105

Here we behold the art that doth adorn
    With such affection, and the good discover
    Whereby the world above turns that below.

But that thou wholly satisfied mayst bear
    Thy wishes hence which in this sphere are born,   110
    Still farther to proceed behoveth me.

Thou fain wouldst know who is within this light
    That here beside me thus is scintillating,
    Even as a sunbeam in the limpid water.

Then know thou, that within there is at rest   115
   Rahab, and being to our order joined,
   With her in its supremest grade 'tis sealed.

Into this heaven, where ends the shadowy cone
   Cast by your world, before all other souls
   First of Christ's triumph was she taken up.   120

Full meet it was to leave her in some heaven,
   Even as a palm of the high victory
   Which he acquired with one palm and the other,

Because she favored the first glorious deed
   Of Joshua upon the Holy Land,   125
   That little stirs the memory of the Pope.

Thy city, which an offshoot is of him
   Who first upon his Maker turned his back,
   And whose ambition is so sorely wept,

Brings forth and scatters the accursed flower   130
   Which both the sheep and lambs hath led astray,
   Since it has turned the shepherd to a wolf.

For this the Evangel and the mighty Doctors
   Are derelict, and only the Decretals
   So studied that it shows upon their margins.   135

On this are Pope and Cardinals intent;
   Their meditations reach not Nazareth,
   There where his pinions Gabriel unfolded;

But Vatican and the other parts elect
   Of Rome, which have a cemetery been   140
   Unto the soldiery that followed Peter,

Shall soon be free from this adultery."

⊰ CANTO X ⊱

*The Fourth Heaven, the Sun: Theologians and Fathers of the Church —
The First Circle — St. Thomas of Aquinas*

Looking into his Son with all the Love
　　Which each of them eternally breathes forth,
The Primal and unutterable Power

Whate'er before the mind or eye revolves
　　With so much order made, there can be none　　5
　　Who this beholds without enjoying Him.

Lift up then, Reader, to the lofty wheels
　　With me thy vision straight unto that part
　　Where the one motion on the other strikes,

And there begin to contemplate with joy　　10
　　That Master's art, who in himself so loves it
　　That never doth his eye depart therefrom.

Behold how from that point goes branching off
　　The oblique circle, which conveys the planets,
　　To satisfy the world that calls upon them;　　15

And if their pathway were not thus inflected,
　　Much virtue in the heavens would be in vain,
　　And almost every power below here dead.

If from the straight line distant more or less
　　Were the departure, much would wanting be　　20
　　Above and underneath of mundane order.

Remain now, Reader, still upon thy bench,
　　In thought pursuing that which is foretasted,
　　If thou wouldst jocund be instead of weary.

I've set before thee; henceforth feed thyself,   25
    For to itself diverteth all my care
    That theme whereof I have been made the scribe.

The greatest of the ministers of nature,
    Who with the power of heaven the world imprints
    And measures with his light the time for us,   30

With that part which above is called to mind
    Conjoined, along the spirals was revolving,
    Where each time earlier he presents himself;

And I was with him; but of the ascending
    I was not conscious, saving as a man   35
    Of a first thought is conscious ere it come;

And Beatrice, she who is seen to pass
    From good to better, and so suddenly
    That not by time her action is expressed,

How lucent in herself must she have been!   40
    And what was in the sun, wherein I entered,
    Apparent not by color but by light,

I, though I call on genius, art, and practice,
    Cannot so tell that it could be imagined;
    Believe one can, and let him long to see it.   45

And if our fantasies too lowly are
    For altitude so great, it is no marvel,
    Since o'er the sun was never eye could go.

Such in this place was the fourth family
    Of the high Father, who forever sates it,   50
    Showing how he breathes forth and how begets.

And Beatrice began: "Give thanks, give thanks
   Unto the Sun of Angels, who to this
   Sensible one has raised thee by his grace!"

Never was heart of mortal so disposed   55
   To worship, nor to give itself to God
   With all its gratitude was it so ready,

As at those words did I myself become;
   And all my love was so absorbed in Him,
   That in oblivion Beatrice was eclipsed.   60

Nor this displeased her; but she smiled at it
   So that the splendor of her laughing eyes
   My single mind on many things divided.

Lights many saw I, vivid and triumphant,
   Make us a center and themselves a circle,   65
   More sweet in voice than luminous in aspect.

Thus girt about the daughter of Latona
   We sometimes see, when pregnant is the air,
   So that it holds the thread which makes her zone.

Within the court of Heaven, whence I return,   70
   Are many jewels found, so fair and precious
   They cannot be transported from the realm;

And of them was the singing of those lights.
   Who takes not wings that he may fly up thither,
   The tidings thence may from the dumb await!   75

As soon as singing thus those burning suns
   Had round about us whirled themselves three times,
   Like unto stars neighboring the steadfast poles,

Ladies they seemed, not from the dance released,
    But who stop short, in silence listening   80
    Till they have gathered the new melody.

And within one I heard beginning: "When
    The radiance of grace, by which is kindled
    True love, and which thereafter grows by loving,

Within thee multiplied is so resplendent   85
    That it conducts thee upward by that stair,
    Where without reascending none descends,

Who should deny the wine out of his vial
    Unto thy thirst, in liberty were not
    Except as water which descends not seaward.   90

Fain wouldst thou know with what plants is enflowered
    This garland that encircles with delight
    The Lady fair who makes thee strong for heaven.

Of the lambs was I of the holy flock
    Which Dominic conducteth by a road   95
    Where well one fattens if he strayeth not.

He who is nearest to me on the right
    My brother and master was; and he Albertus
    Is of Cologne, I Thomas of Aquinum.

If thou of all the others wouldst be certain,   100
    Follow behind my speaking with thy sight
    Upward along the blessed garland turning.

That next effulgence issues from the smile
    Of Gratian, who assisted both the courts
    In such wise that it pleased in Paradise.   105

The other which nearby adorns our choir
    That Peter was who, e'en as the poor widow,
    Offered his treasure unto Holy Church.

The fifth light, that among us is the fairest,
    Breathes forth from such a love, that all the world   110
    Below is greedy to learn tidings of it.

Within it is the lofty mind, where knowledge
    So deep was put, that, if the true be true,
    To see so much there never rose a second.

Thou seest next the luster of that taper,   115
    Which in the flesh below looked most within
    The angelic nature and its ministry.

Within that other little light is smiling
    The advocate of the Christian centuries,
    Out of whose rhetoric Augustine was furnished.   120

Now if thou trainest thy mind's eye along
    From light to light pursuant of my praise,
    With thirst already of the eighth thou waitest.

By seeing every good therein exults
    The sainted soul, which the fallacious world   125
    Makes manifest to him who listeneth well;

The body whence 'twas hunted forth is lying
    Down in Cieldauro, and from martyrdom
    And banishment it came unto this peace.

See farther onward flame the burning breath   130
    Of Isidore, of Beda, and of Richard
    Who was in contemplation more than man.

This, whence to me returneth thy regard,
    The light is of a spirit unto whom
    In his grave meditations death seemed slow.   135

It is the light eternal of Sigier,
    Who, reading lectures in the Street of Straw,
    Did syllogize invidious verities."

Then, as a horologe that calleth us
    What time the Bride of God is rising up   140
    With matins to her Spouse that he may love her,

Wherein one part the other draws and urges,
    Ting! ting! resounding with so sweet a note,
    That swells with love the spirit well disposed,

Thus I beheld the glorious wheel move round,   145
    And render voice to voice, in modulation
    And sweetness that can not be comprehended,

Excepting there where joy is made eternal.

⊰ CANTO XI ⊱

St. Thomas Recounts the Life of St. Francis —
Lament over the State of the Dominican Order

O Thou insensate care of mortal men,
    How inconclusive are the syllogisms
That make thee beat thy wings in downward flight!

One after laws and one to aphorisms
    Was going, and one following the priesthood,   5
    And one to reign by force or sophistry,

And one in theft, and one in state affairs,
    One in the pleasures of the flesh involved
    Wearied himself, one gave himself to ease;

When I, from all these things emancipate,   10
    With Beatrice above there in the Heavens
    With such exceeding glory was received!

When each one had returned unto that point
    Within the circle where it was before,
    It stood as in a candlestick a candle;   15

And from within the effulgence which at first
    Had spoken unto me, I heard begin
    Smiling while it more luminous became:

"Even as I am kindled in its ray,
    So, looking into the Eternal Light,   20
    The occasion of thy thoughts I apprehend.

Thou doubtest, and wouldst have me to resift
    In language so extended and so open
    My speech, that to thy sense it may be plain,

Where just before I said, 'where well one fattens,'   25
    And where I said, 'there never rose a second';
    And here 'tis needful we distinguish well.

The Providence, which governeth the world
    With counsel, wherein all created vision
    Is vanquished ere it reach unto the bottom   30

(So that towards her own Beloved might go
    The bride of Him who, uttering a loud cry,
    Espoused her with his consecrated blood,

Self-confident and unto Him more faithful)
    Two Princes did ordain in her behoof,   35
    Which on this side and that might be her guide.

The one was all seraphical in ardor;
    The other by his wisdom upon earth
    A splendor was of light cherubical.

One will I speak of, for of both is spoken   40
    In praising one, whichever may be taken,
    Because unto one end their labors were.

Between Tupino and the stream that falls
    Down from the hill elect of blessed Ubald,
    A fertile slope of lofty mountain hangs,   45

From which Perugia feels the cold and heat
    Through Porta Sole, and behind it weep
    Gualdo and Nocera their grievous yoke.

From out that slope, there where it breaketh most
    Its steepness, rose upon the world a sun   50
    As this one does sometimes from out the Ganges;

Therefore let him who speaketh of that place,
    Say not Ascesi, for he would say little,
    But Orient, if he properly would speak.

He was not yet far distant from his rising   55
    Before he had begun to make the earth
    Some comfort from his mighty virtue feel.

For he in youth his father's wrath incurred
    For certain Dame, to whom, as unto death,
    The gate of pleasure no one doth unlock;   60

And was before his spiritual court
    Et coram patre unto her united;
    Then day by day more fervently he loved her.

She, reft of her first husband, scorned, obscure,
    One thousand and one hundred years and more,   65
    Waited without a suitor till he came.

Naught it availed to hear, that with Amyclas
    Found her unmoved at sounding of his voice
    He who struck terror into all the world;

Naught it availed being constant and undaunted,   70
    So that, when Mary still remained below,
    She mounted up with Christ upon the cross.

But that too darkly I may not proceed,
    Francis and Poverty for these two lovers
    Take thou henceforward in my speech diffuse.   75

Their concord and their joyous semblances,
    The love, the wonder, and the sweet regard,
    They made to be the cause of holy thoughts;

So much so that the venerable Bernard
    First bared his feet, and after so great peace   80
    Ran, and, in running, thought himself too slow.

O wealth unknown! O veritable good!
    Giles bares his feet, and bares his feet Sylvester
    Behind the bridegroom, so doth please the bride!

Then goes his way that father and that master,   85
    He and his Lady and that family
    Which now was girding on the humble cord;

Nor cowardice of heart weighed down his brow
    At being son of Peter Bernardone,
    Nor for appearing marvelously scorned;   90

But regally his hard determination
    To Innocent he opened, and from him
    Received the primal seal upon his Order.

After the people mendicant increased
    Behind this man, whose admirable life   95
    Better in glory of the heavens were sung,

Incoronated with a second crown
    Was through Honorius by the Eternal Spirit
    The holy purpose of this Archimandrite.

And when he had, through thirst of martyrdom,   100
    In the proud presence of the Sultan preached
    Christ and the others who came after him,

And, finding for conversion too unripe
    The folk, and not to tarry there in vain,
    Returned to fruit of the Italic grass,   105

On the rude rock 'twixt Tiber and the Arno
    From Christ did he receive the final seal,
    Which during two whole years his members bore.

When He, who chose him unto so much good,
    Was pleased to draw him up to the reward   110
    That he had merited by being lowly,

Unto his friars, as to the rightful heirs,
    His most dear Lady did he recommend,
    And bade that they should love her faithfully;

And from her bosom the illustrious soul   115
   Wished to depart, returning to its realm,
   And for its body wished no other bier.

Think now what man was he, who was a fit
   Companion over the high seas to keep
   The bark of Peter to its proper bearings.   120

And this man was our Patriarch; hence whoever
   Doth follow him as he commands can see
   That he is laden with good merchandise.

But for new pasturage his flock has grown
   So greedy, that it is impossible   125
   They be not scattered over fields diverse;

And in proportion as his sheep remote
   And vagabond go farther off from him,
   More void of milk return they to the fold.

Verily some there are that fear a hurt,   130
   And keep close to the shepherd; but so few,
   That little cloth doth furnish forth their hoods.

Now if my utterance be not indistinct,
   If thine own hearing hath attentive been,
   If thou recall to mind what I have said,   135

In part contented shall thy wishes be;
   For thou shalt see the plant that's chipped away,
   And the rebuke that lieth in the words,

'Where well one fattens, if he strayeth not.' "

⊰ CANTO XII ⊱

*St. Buonaventura Recounts the Life of St. Dominic—Lament over the State
of the Franciscan Order—The Second Circle*

Soon as the blessed flame had taken up
  The final word to give it utterance,
Began the holy millstone to revolve,

And in its gyre had not turned wholly round,
  Before another in a ring enclosed it,   5
  And motion joined to motion, song to song;

Song that as greatly doth transcend our Muses,
  Our Sirens, in those dulcet clarions,
  As primal splendor that which is reflected.

And as are spanned athwart a tender cloud   10
  Two rainbows parallel and like in color,
  When Juno to her handmaid gives command

(The one without born of the one within,
  Like to the speaking of that vagrant one
  Whom love consumed as doth the sun the vapors)   15

And make the people here, through covenant
  God set with Noah, presageful of the world
  That shall no more be covered with a flood,

In such wise of those sempiternal roses
  The garlands twain encompassed us about,   20
  And thus the outer to the inner answered.

In such wise of those sempiternal roses
The garlands twain encompassed us about,
And thus the outer to the inner answered.

Paradiso XII, lines 19–21

After the dance, and other grand rejoicings,
    Both of the singing, and the flaming forth
    Effulgence with effulgence blithe and tender,

Together, at once, with one accord had stopped   25
    (Even as the eyes, that, as volition moves them,
    Must needs together shut and lift themselves)

Out of the heart of one of the new lights
    There came a voice, that needle to the star
    Made me appear in turning thitherward.   30

And it began: "The love that makes me fair
    Draws me to speak about the other leader,
    By whom so well is spoken here of mine.

'Tis right, where one is, to bring in the other,
    That, as they were united in their warfare,   35
    Together likewise may their glory shine.

The soldiery of Christ, which it had cost
    So dear to arm again, behind the standard
    Moved slow and doubtful and in numbers few,

When the Emperor who reigneth evermore   40
    Provided for the host that was in peril,
    Through grace alone and not that it was worthy;

And, as was said, he to his Bride brought succor
    With champions twain, at whose deed, at whose word
    The straggling people were together drawn.   45

Within that region where the sweet west wind
    Rises to open the new leaves, wherewith
    Europe is seen to clothe herself afresh,

Not far off from the beating of the waves,
    Behind which in his long career the sun   50
    Sometimes conceals himself from every man,

Is situate the fortunate Calahorra,
    Under protection of the mighty shield
    In which the Lion subject is and sovereign.

Therein was born the amorous paramour   55
    Of Christian Faith, the athlete consecrate,
    Kind to his own and cruel to his foes;

And when it was created was his mind
    Replete with such a living energy,
    That in his mother her it made prophetic.   60

As soon as the espousals were complete
    Between him and the Faith at holy font,
    Where they with mutual safety dowered each other,

The woman, who for him had given assent,
    Saw in a dream the admirable fruit   65
    That issue would from him and from his heirs;

And that he might be construed as he was,
    A spirit from this place went forth to name him
    With His possessive whose he wholly was.

Dominic was he called; and him I speak of   70
    Even as of the husbandman whom Christ
    Elected to his garden to assist him.

Envoy and servant sooth he seemed of Christ,
    For the first love made manifest in him
    Was the first counsel that was given by Christ.   75

Silent and wakeful many a time was he
   Discovered by his nurse upon the ground,
   As if he would have said, 'For this I came.'

O thou his father, Felix verily!
   O thou his mother, verily Joanna,   80
   If this, interpreted, means as is said!

Not for the world which people toil for now
   In following Ostiense and Taddeo,
   But through his longing after the true manna,

He in short time became so great a teacher,   85
   That he began to go about the vineyard,
   Which fadeth soon, if faithless be the dresser;

And of the See (that once was more benignant
   Unto the righteous poor, not through itself,
   But him who sits there and degenerates)   90

Not to dispense or two or three for six,
   Not any fortune of first vacancy,
   Non decimas quæ sunt pauperum Dei,

He asked for, but against the errant world
   Permission to do battle for the seed,   95
   Of which these four and twenty plants surround thee.

Then with the doctrine and the will together,
   With office apostolical he moved,
   Like torrent which some lofty vein out-presses;

And in among the shoots heretical   100
   His impetus with greater fury smote,
   Wherever the resistance was the greatest.

Of him were made thereafter divers runnels,
    Whereby the garden catholic is watered,
    So that more living its plantations stand.   105

If such the one wheel of the Biga was,
    In which the Holy Church itself defended
    And in the field its civic battle won,

Truly full manifest should be to thee
    The excellence of the other, unto whom   110
    Thomas so courteous was before my coming.

But still the orbit, which the highest part
    Of its circumference made, is derelict,
    So that the mould is where was once the crust.

His family, that had straight forward moved   115
    With feet upon his footprints, are turned round
    So that they set the point upon the heel.

And soon aware they will be of the harvest
    Of this bad husbandry, when shall the tares
    Complain the granary is taken from them.   120

Yet say I, he who searcheth leaf by leaf
    Our volume through, would still some page discover
    Where he could read, 'I am as I am wont.'

'Twill not be from Casal nor Acquasparta,
    From whence come such unto the written word   125
    That one avoids it, and the other narrows.

Bonaventura of Bagnoregio's life
    Am I, who always in great offices
    Postponed considerations sinister.

Here are Illuminato and Agostino,   130
    Who of the first barefooted beggars were
    That with the cord the friends of God became.

Hugh of Saint Victor is among them here,
    And Peter Mangiador, and Peter of Spain,
    Who down below in volumes twelve is shining;   135

Nathan the seer, and metropolitan
    Chrysostom, and Anselmus, and Donatus
    Who deigned to lay his hand to the first art;

Here is Rabanus, and beside me here
    Shines the Calabrian Abbot Joachim,   140
    He with the spirit of prophecy endowed.

To celebrate so great a paladin
    Have moved me the impassioned courtesy
    And the discreet discourses of Friar Thomas,

And with me they have moved this company."   145

⇥ CANTO XIII ⇤

Of the Wisdom of Solomon — St. Thomas Reproaches Dante's Judgment

Let him imagine, who would well conceive
    What now I saw, and let him while I speak
Retain the image as a steadfast rock,

The fifteen stars, that in their divers regions
    The sky enliven with a light so great   5
    That it transcends all clusters of the air;

Let him the Wain imagine unto which
    Our vault of heaven sufficeth night and day,
    So that in turning of its pole it fails not;

Let him the mouth imagine of the horn   10
    That in the point beginneth of the axis
    Round about which the primal wheel revolves—

To have fashioned of themselves two signs in heaven,
    Like unto that which Minos's daughter made,
    The moment when she felt the frost of death;   15

And one to have its rays within the other,
    And both to whirl themselves in such a manner
    That one should forward go, the other backward;

And he will have some shadowing forth of that
    True constellation and the double dance   20
    That circled round the point at which I was;

Because it is as much beyond our wont,
    As swifter than the motion of the Chiana
    Moveth the heaven that all the rest outspeeds.

There sang they neither Bacchus, nor Apollo,   25
    But in the divine nature Persons three,
    And in one person the divine and human.

The singing and the dance fulfilled their measure,
    And unto us those holy lights gave need,
    Growing in happiness from care to care.   30

Then broke the silence of those saints concordant
    The light in which the admirable life
    Of God's own mendicant was told to me,

And said: "Now that one straw is trodden out
    Now that its seed is garnered up already,   35
    Sweet love invites me to thresh out the other.

Into that bosom, thou believest, whence
    Was drawn the rib to form the beauteous cheek
    Whose taste to all the world is costing dear,

And into that which, by the lance transfixed,   40
    Before and since, such satisfaction made
    That it weighs down the balance of all sin,

Whate'er of light it has to human nature
    Been lawful to possess was all infused
    By the same power that both of them created;   45

And hence at what I said above dost wonder,
    When I narrated that no second had
    The good which in the fifth light is enclosed.

Now ope thine eyes to what I answer thee,
    And thou shalt see thy creed and my discourse   50
    Fit in the truth as center in a circle.

That which can die, and that which dieth not,
    Are nothing but the splendor of the idea
    Which by his love our Lord brings into being;

Because that living Light, which from its fount   55
    Effulgent flows, so that it disunites not
    From Him nor from the Love in them intrined,

Through its own goodness reunites its rays
    In nine subsistences, as in a mirror,
    Itself eternally remaining One.   60

Thence it descends to the last potencies,
　　Downward from act to act becoming such
　　That only brief contingencies it makes;

And these contingencies I hold to be
　　Things generated, which the heaven produces　　65
　　By its own motion, with seed and without.

Neither their wax, nor that which tempers it,
　　Remains immutable, and hence beneath
　　The ideal signet more and less shines through;

Therefore it happens, that the selfsame tree　　70
　　After its kind bears worse and better fruit,
　　And ye are born with characters diverse.

If in perfection tempered were the wax,
　　And were the heaven in its supremest virtue,
　　The brilliance of the seal would all appear;　　75

But nature gives it evermore deficient,
　　In the like manner working as the artist,
　　Who has the skill of art and hand that trembles.

If then the fervent Love, the Vision clear,
　　Of primal Virtue do dispose and seal,　　80
　　Perfection absolute is there acquired.

Thus was of old the earth created worthy
　　Of all and every animal perfection;
　　And thus the Virgin was impregnate made;

So that thine own opinion I commend,　　85
　　That human nature never yet has been,
　　Nor will be, what it was in those two persons.

Now if no farther forth I should proceed,
    'Then in what way was he without a peer?'
    Would be the first beginning of thy words.   90

But, that may well appear what now appears not,
    Think who he was, and what occasion moved him
    To make request, when it was told him, 'Ask.'

I've not so spoken that thou canst not see
    Clearly he was a king who asked for wisdom,   95
    That he might be sufficiently a king;

'Twas not to know the number in which are
    The motors here above, or if *necesse*
    With a contingent e'er *necesse* make,

Non si est dare primum motum esse,   100
    Or if in semicircle can be made
    Triangle so that it have no right angle.

Whence, if thou notest this and what I said,
    A regal prudence is that peerless seeing
    In which the shaft of my intention strikes.   105

And if on 'rose' thou turnest thy clear eyes,
    Thou'lt see that it has reference alone
    To kings who're many, and the good are rare.

With this distinction take thou what I said,
    And thus it can consist with thy belief   110
    Of the first father and of our Delight.

And lead shall this be always to thy feet,
    To make thee, like a weary man, move slowly
    Both to the Yes and No thou seest not;

For very low among the fools is he   115
    Who affirms without distinction, or denies,
    As well in one as in the other case;

Because it happens that full often bends
    Current opinion in the false direction,
    And then the feelings bind the intellect.   120

Far more than uselessly he leaves the shore,
    (Since he returneth not the same he went)
    Who fishes for the truth, and has no skill;

And in the world proofs manifest thereof
    Parmenides, Melissus, Brissus are,   125
    And many who went on and knew not whither;

Thus did Sabellius, Arius, and those fools
    Who have been even as swords unto the Scriptures
    In rendering distorted their straight faces.

Nor yet shall people be too confident   130
    In judging, even as he is who doth count
    The corn in field or ever it be ripe.

For I have seen all winter long the thorn
    First show itself intractable and fierce,
    And after bear the rose upon its top;   135

And I have seen a ship direct and swift
    Run o'er the sea throughout its course entire,
    To perish at the harbor's mouth at last.

Let not Dame Bertha nor Ser Martin think,
    Seeing one steal, another offering make,   140
    To see them in the arbitrament divine;

For one may rise, and fall the other may."

ᵈᴴ Canto XIV ᵉᴴ

The Third Circle—Discourse on the Resurrection of the Flesh—
The Fifth Heaven, Mars: Martyrs and Crusaders Who Died
Fighting for the True Faith—The Celestial Cross

From center unto rim, from rim to center,
  In a round vase the water moves itself,
As from without 'tis struck or from within.

Into my mind upon a sudden dropped
  What I am saying, at the moment when   5
  Silent became the glorious life of Thomas,

Because of the resemblance that was born
  Of his discourse and that of Beatrice,
  Whom, after him, it pleased thus to begin:

"This man has need (and does not tell you so,   10
  Nor with the voice, nor even in his thought)
  Of going to the root of one truth more.

Declare unto him if the light wherewith
  Blossoms your substance shall remain with you
  Eternally the same that it is now;   15

And if it do remain, say in what manner,
  After ye are again made visible,
  It can be that it injure not your sight."

As by a greater gladness urged and drawn
  They who are dancing in a ring sometimes   20
  Uplift their voices and their motions quicken;

So, at that orison devout and prompt,
    The holy circles a new joy displayed
    In their revolving and their wondrous song.

Whoso lamenteth him that here we die   25
    That we may live above, has never there
    Seen the refreshment of the eternal rain.

The One and Two and Three who ever liveth,
    And reigneth ever in Three and Two and One,
    Not circumscribed and all things circumscribing,   30

Three several times was chanted by each one
    Among those spirits, with such melody
    That for all merit it were just reward;

And, in the luster most divine of all
    The lesser ring, I heard a modest voice,   35
    Such as perhaps the Angel's was to Mary,

Answer: "As long as the festivity
    Of Paradise shall be, so long our love
    Shall radiate round about us such a vesture.

Its brightness is proportioned to the ardor,   40
    The ardor to the vision; and the vision
    Equals what grace it has above its worth.

When, glorious and sanctified, our flesh
    Is reassumed, then shall our persons be
    More pleasing by their being all complete;   45

For will increase whate'er bestows on us
    Of light gratuitous the Good Supreme,
    Light which enables us to look on Him;

Therefore the vision must perforce increase,
 Increase the ardor which from that is kindled,   50
 Increase the radiance which from this proceeds.

But even as a coal that sends forth flame,
 And by its vivid whiteness overpowers it
 So that its own appearance it maintains,

Thus the effulgence that surrounds us now   55
 Shall be o'erpowered in aspect by the flesh,
 Which still today the earth doth cover up;

Nor can so great a splendor weary us,
 For strong will be the organs of the body
 To everything which hath the power to please us."   60

So sudden and alert appeared to me
 Both one and the other choir to say Amen,
 That well they showed desire for their dead bodies;

Nor sole for them perhaps, but for the mothers,
 The fathers, and the rest who had been dear   65
 Or ever they became eternal flames.

And lo! all round about of equal brightness
 Arose a luster over what was there,
 Like an horizon that is clearing up.

And as at rise of early eve begin   70
 Along the welkin new appearances,
 So that the sight seems real and unreal,

It seemed to me that new subsistences
 Began there to be seen, and make a circle
 Outside the other two circumferences.   75

O very sparkling of the Holy Spirit,
How sudden and incandescent it became
Unto mine eyes, that vanquished bore it not!

But Beatrice so beautiful and smiling
Appeared to me, that with the other sights   80
That followed not my memory I must leave her.

Then to uplift themselves mine eyes resumed
The power, and I beheld myself translated
To higher salvation with my Lady only.

Well was I ware that I was more uplifted   85
By the enkindled smiling of the star,
That seemed to me more ruddy than its wont.

With all my heart, and in that dialect
Which is the same in all, such holocaust
To God I made as the new grace beseemed;   90

And not yet from my bosom was exhausted
The ardor of sacrifice, before I knew
This offering was accepted and auspicious;

For with so great a luster and so red
Splendors appeared to me in twofold rays,   95
I said: "O Helios who dost so adorn them!"

Even as distinct with less and greater lights
Glimmers between the two poles of the world
The Galaxy that maketh wise men doubt,

Thus constellated in the depths of Mars,   100
Those rays described the venerable sign
That quadrants joining in a circle make.

Well was I ware that I was more uplifted
By the enkindled smiling of the star,
That seemed to me more ruddy than its wont.

Paradiso XIV, lines 85–87

Here doth my memory overcome my genius;
    For on that cross as levin gleamed forth Christ,
    So that I cannot find ensample worthy;   105

But he who takes his cross and follows Christ
    Again will pardon me what I omit,
    Seeing in that aurora lighten Christ.

From horn to horn, and 'twixt the top and base,
    Lights were in motion, brightly scintillating   110
    As they together met and passed each other;

Thus level and aslant and swift and slow
    We here behold, renewing still the sight,
    The particles of bodies long and short,

Across the sunbeam move, wherewith is listed   115
    Sometimes the shade, which for their own defense
    People with cunning and with art contrive.

And as a lute and harp, accordant strung
    With many strings, a dulcet tinkling make
    To him by whom the notes are not distinguished,   120

So from the lights that there to me appeared
    Upgathered through the cross a melody,
    Which rapt me, not distinguishing the hymn.

Well was I ware it was of lofty laud,
    Because there came to me, "Arise and conquer!"   125
    As unto him who hears and comprehends not.

So much enamored I became therewith,
    That until then there was not anything
    That e'er had fettered me with such sweet bonds.

Here doth my memory overcome my genius;
For on that cross as levin gleamed forth Christ,
So that I cannot find ensample worthy

Paradiso XIV, lines 103–105

Perhaps my word appears somewhat too bold,   130
    Postponing the delight of those fair eyes,
    Into which gazing my desire has rest;

But who bethinks him that the living seals
    Of every beauty grow in power ascending,
    And that I there had not turned round to those,   135

Can me excuse, if I myself accuse
    To excuse myself, and see that I speak truly:
    For here the holy joy is not disclosed,

Because ascending it becomes more pure.

⊰ CANTO XV ⊱

Cacciaguida—Florence in the Olden Time

A will benign, in which reveals itself
    Ever the love that righteously inspires,
As in the iniquitous, cupidity,

Silence imposed upon that dulcet lyre,
    And quieted the consecrated chords,   5
    That Heaven's right hand doth tighten and relax.

How unto just entreaties shall be deaf
    Those substances, which, to give me desire
    Of praying them, with one accord grew silent?

'Tis well that without end he should lament,   10
    Who for the love of thing that doth not last
    Eternally despoils him of that love!

As through the pure and tranquil evening air
    There shoots from time to time a sudden fire,
    Moving the eyes that steadfast were before,   15

And seems to be a star that changeth place,
    Except that in the part where it is kindled
    Nothing is missed, and this endureth little;

So from the horn that to the right extends
    Unto that cross's foot there ran a star   20
    Out of the constellation shining there;

Nor was the gem dissevered from its ribbon,
    But down the radiant fillet ran along,
    So that fire seemed it behind alabaster.

Thus piteous did Anchises' shade reach forward,   25
    If any faith our greatest Muse deserve,
    When in Elysium he his son perceived.

"*O sanguis meus, O super infusa*
    Gratia Dei, sicut tibi, cui
    Bis unquam Cœli janua reclusa?"   30

Thus that effulgence; whence I gave it heed;
    Then round unto my Lady turned my sight,
    And on this side and that was stupefied;

For in her eyes was burning such a smile
    That with mine own methought I touched the
        bottom   35
    Both of my grace and of my Paradise!

Then, pleasant to the hearing and the sight,
    The spirit joined to its beginning things
    I understood not, so profound it spake;

Nor did it hide itself from me by choice,   40
    But by necessity; for its conception
    Above the mark of mortals set itself.

And when the bow of burning sympathy
    Was so far slackened, that its speech descended
    Towards the mark of our intelligence,   45

The first thing that was understood by me
    Was "Benedight be Thou, O Trine and One,
    Who hast unto my seed so courteous been!"

And it continued: "Hunger long and grateful,
    Drawn from the reading of the mighty volume   50
    Wherein is never changed the white nor dark,

Thou hast appeased, my son, within this light
    In which I speak to thee, by grace of her
    Who to this lofty flight with plumage clothed thee.

Thou thinkest that to me thy thought doth pass   55
    From Him who is the first, as from the unit,
    If that be known, ray out the five and six;

And therefore who I am thou askest not,
    And why I seem more joyous unto thee
    Than any other of this gladsome crowd.   60

Thou think'st the truth; because the small and great
    Of this existence look into the mirror
    Wherein, before thou think'st, thy thought thou showest.

But that the sacred love, in which I watch
    With sight perpetual, and which makes me thirst   65
    With sweet desire, may better be fulfilled,

Now let thy voice secure and frank and glad
   Proclaim the wishes, the desire proclaim,
   To which my answer is decreed already."

To Beatrice I turned me, and she heard   70
   Before I spake, and smiled to me a sign,
   That made the wings of my desire increase;

Then in this wise began I: "Love and knowledge,
   When on you dawned the first Equality,
   Of the same weight for each of you became;   75

For in the Sun, which lighted you and burned
   With heat and radiance, they so equal are,
   That all similitudes are insufficient.

But among mortals will and argument,
   For reason that to you is manifest,   80
   Diversely feathered in their pinions are.

Whence I, who mortal am, feel in myself
   This inequality; so give not thanks,
   Save in my heart, for this paternal welcome.

Truly do I entreat thee, living topaz!   85
   Set in this precious jewel as a gem,
   That thou wilt satisfy me with thy name."

"O leaf of mine, in whom I pleasure took
   E'en while awaiting, I was thine own root!"
   Such a beginning he in answer made me.   90

Then said to me: "That one from whom is named
   Thy race, and who a hundred years and more
   Has circled round the mount on the first cornice,

A son of mine and thy great-grandsire was;
  Well it behoves thee that the long fatigue   95
  Thou shouldst for him make shorter with thy works.

Florence, within the ancient boundary
  From which she taketh still her tierce and nones,
  Abode in quiet, temperate and chaste.

No golden chain she had, nor coronal,   100
  Nor ladies shod with sandal shoon, nor girdle
  That caught the eye more than the person did.

Not yet the daughter at her birth struck fear
  Into the father, for the time and dower
  Did not o'errun this side or that the measure.   105

No houses had she void of families,
  Not yet had thither come Sardanapalus
  To show what in a chamber can be done;

Not yet surpassed had Montemalo been
  By your Uccellatojo, which surpassed   110
  Shall in its downfall be as in its rise.

Bellincion Berti saw I go begirt
  With leather and with bone, and from the mirror
  His dame depart without a painted face;

And him of Nerli saw, and him of Vecchio,   115
  Contented with their simple suits of buff
  And with the spindle and the flax their dames.

O fortunate women! and each one was certain
  Of her own burial-place, and none as yet
  For sake of France was in her bed deserted.   120

One o'er the cradle kept her studious watch,
　　And in her lullaby the language used
　　That first delights the fathers and the mothers;

Another, drawing tresses from her distaff,
　　Told o'er among her family the tales　　125
　　Of Trojans and of Fesole and Rome.

As great a marvel then would have been held
　　A Lapo Salterello, a Cianghella,
　　As Cincinnatus or Cornelia now.

To such a quiet, such a beautiful　　130
　　Life of the citizen, to such a safe
　　Community, and to so sweet an inn,

Did Mary give me, with loud cries invoked,
　　And in your ancient Baptistery at once
　　Christian and Cacciaguida I became.　　135

Moronto was my brother, and Eliseo;
　　From Val di Pado came to me my wife,
　　And from that place thy surname was derived.

I followed afterward the Emperor Conrad,
　　And he begirt me of his chivalry,　　140
　　So much I pleased him with my noble deeds.

I followed in his train against that law's
　　Iniquity, whose people doth usurp
　　Your just possession, through your Pastor's fault.

There by that execrable race was I　　145
　　Released from bonds of the fallacious world,
　　The love of which defileth many souls,

And came from martyrdom unto this peace."

⊰ CANTO XVI ⊱

Dante's Noble Ancestry—Cacciaguida's Discourse of the Great Florentines

O thou our poor nobility of blood,
If thou dost make the people glory in thee
Down here where our affection languishes,

A marvellous thing it ne'er will be to me;
For there where appetite is not perverted,   5
I say in Heaven, of thee I made a boast!

Truly thou art a cloak that quickly shortens,
So that unless we piece thee day by day
Time goeth round about thee with his shears!

With *You*, which Rome was first to tolerate,   10
(Wherein her family less perseveres)
Yet once again my words beginning made;

Whence Beatrice, who stood somewhat apart,
Smiling, appeared like unto her who coughed
At the first failing writ of Guenever.   15

And I began: "You are my ancestor,
You give to me all hardihood to speak,
You lift me so that I am more than I.

So many rivulets with gladness fill
My mind, that of itself it makes a joy   20
Because it can endure this and not burst.

Then tell me, my beloved root ancestral,
Who were your ancestors, and what the years
That in your boyhood chronicled themselves?

"You are my ancestor,
You give to me all hardihood to speak,
You lift me so that I am more than I."

Paradiso XVI, lines 16–18

Tell me about the sheepfold of Saint John,   25
　　How large it was, and who the people were
　　Within it worthy of the highest seats."

As at the blowing of the winds a coal
　　Quickens to flame, so I beheld that light
　　Become resplendent at my blandishments.   30

And as unto mine eyes it grew more fair,
　　With voice more sweet and tender, but not in
　　This modern dialect, it said to me:

"From uttering of the *Ave*, till the birth
　　In which my mother, who is now a saint,   35
　　Of me was lightened who had been her burden,

Unto its Lion had this fire returned
　　Five hundred fifty times and thirty more,
　　To reinflame itself beneath his paw.

My ancestors and I our birthplace had   40
　　Where first is found the last ward of the city
　　By him who runneth in your annual game.

Suffice it of my elders to hear this;
　　But who they were, and whence they thither came,
　　Silence is more considerate than speech.   45

All those who at that time were there between
　　Mars and the Baptist, fit for bearing arms,
　　Were a fifth part of those who now are living;

But the community, that now is mixed
　　With Campi and Certaldo and Figghine,   50
　　Pure in the lowest artisan was seen.

O how much better 'twere to have as neighbors
   The folk of whom I speak, and at Galluzzo
   And at Trespiano have your boundary,

Than have them in the town, and bear the stench   55
   Of Aguglione's churl, and him of Signa
   Who has sharp eyes for trickery already.

Had not the folk, which most of all the world
   Degenerates, been a step-dame unto Cæsar,
   But as a mother to her son benignant,   60

Some who turn Florentines, and trade and discount,
   Would have gone back again to Simifonte
   There where their grandsires went about as beggars.

At Montemurlo still would be the Counts,
   The Cerchi in the parish of Acone,   65
   Perhaps in Valdigrieve the Buondelmonti.

Ever the intermingling of the people
   Has been the source of malady in cities,
   As in the body food it surfeits on;

And a blind bull more headlong plunges down   70
   Than a blind lamb; and very often cuts
   Better and more a single sword than five.

If Luni thou regard, and Urbisaglia,
   How they have passed away, and how are passing
   Chiusi and Sinigaglia after them,   75

To hear how races waste themselves away,
   Will seem to thee no novel thing nor hard,
   Seeing that even cities have an end.

All things of yours have their mortality,
    Even as yourselves; but it is hidden in some   80
    That a long while endure, and lives are short;

And as the turning of the lunar heaven
    Covers and bares the shores without a pause,
    In the like manner fortune does with Florence.

Therefore should not appear a marvellous thing   85
    What I shall say of the great Florentines
    Of whom the fame is hidden in the Past.

I saw the Ughi, saw the Catellini,
    Filippi, Greci, Ormanni, and Alberichi,
    Even in their fall illustrious citizens;   90

And saw, as mighty as they ancient were,
    With him of La Sannella him of Arca,
    And Soldanier, Ardinghi, and Bostichi.

Near to the gate that is at present laden
    With a new felony of so much weight   95
    That soon it shall be jetsam from the bark,

The Ravignani were, from whom descended
    The County Guido, and whoe'er the name
    Of the great Bellincione since hath taken.

He of La Pressa knew the art of ruling   100
    Already, and already Galigajo
    Had hilt and pommel gilded in his house.

Mighty already was the Column Vair,
    Sacchetti, Giuochi, Fifant, and Barucci,
    And Galli, and they who for the bushel blush.   105

The stock from which were the Calfucci born
   Was great already, and already chosen
   To curule chairs the Sizii and Arrigucci.

O how beheld I those who are undone
   By their own pride! and how the Balls of Gold   110
   Florence enflowered in all their mighty deeds!

So likewise did the ancestors of those
   Who evermore, when vacant is your church,
   Fatten by staying in consistory.

The insolent race, that like a dragon follows   115
   Whoever flees, and unto him that shows
   His teeth or purse is gentle as a lamb,

Already rising was, but from low people;
   So that it pleased not Ubertin Donato
   That his wife's father should make him their kin.   120

Already had Caponsacco to the Market
   From Fesole descended, and already
   Giuda and Infangato were good burghers.

I'll tell a thing incredible, but true;
   One entered the small circuit by a gate   125
   Which from the Della Pera took its name!

Each one that bears the beautiful escutcheon
   Of the great baron whose renown and name
   The festival of Thomas keepeth fresh,

Knighthood and privilege from him received;   130
   Though with the populace unites himself
   Today the man who binds it with a border.

Already were Gualterotti and Importuni;
    And still more quiet would the Borgo be
    If with new neighbors it remained unfed.   135

The house from which is born your lamentation,
    Through just disdain that death among you brought
    And put an end unto your joyous life,

Was honored in itself and its companions.
    O Buondelmonte, how in evil hour   140
    Thou fled'st the bridal at another's promptings!

Many would be rejoicing who are sad,
    If God had thee surrendered to the Ema
    The first time that thou camest to the city.

But it behoved the mutilated stone   145
    Which guards the bridge, that Florence should provide
    A victim in her latest hour of peace.

With all these families, and others with them,
    Florence beheld I in so great repose,
    That no occasion had she whence to weep;   150

With all these families beheld so just
    And glorious her people, that the lily
    Never upon the spear was placed reversed,

Nor by division was vermilion made."

⊰ Canto XVII ⊱

Cacciaguida's Prophecy of Dante's Banishment

As came to Clymene, to be made certain
　　Of that which he had heard against himself,
He who makes fathers chary still to children,

Even such was I, and such was I perceived
　　By Beatrice and by the holy light　　　　　　　5
　　That first on my account had changed its place.

Therefore my Lady said to me: "Send forth
　　The flame of thy desire, so that it issue
　　Imprinted well with the internal stamp;

Not that our knowledge may be greater made　　10
　　By speech of thine, but to accustom thee
　　To tell thy thirst, that we may give thee drink."

"O my beloved tree (that so dost lift thee,
　　That even as minds terrestrial perceive
　　No triangle containeth two obtuse,　　　　　　15

So thou beholdest the contingent things
　　Ere in themselves they are, fixing thine eyes
　　Upon the point in which all times are present)

While I was with Virgilius conjoined
　　Upon the mountain that the souls doth heal,　　20
　　And when descending into the dead world,

Were spoken to me of my future life
　　Some grievous words; although I feel myself
　　In sooth foursquare against the blows of chance.

On this account my wish would be content   25
    To hear what fortune is approaching me,
    Because foreseen an arrow comes more slowly."

Thus did I say unto that selfsame light
    That unto me had spoken before; and even
    As Beatrice willed was my own will confessed.   30

Not in vague phrase, in which the foolish folk
    Ensnared themselves of old, ere yet was slain
    The Lamb of God who taketh sins away,

But with clear words and unambiguous
    Language responded that paternal love,   35
    Hid and revealed by its own proper smile:

"Contingency, that outside of the volume
    Of your materiality extends not,
    Is all depicted in the eternal aspect.

Necessity however thence it takes not,   40
    Except as from the eye, in which 'tis mirrored,
    A ship that with the current down descends.

From thence, e'en as there cometh to the ear
    Sweet harmony from an organ, comes in sight
    To me the time that is preparing for thee.   45

As forth from Athens went Hippolytus,
    By reason of his step-dame false and cruel,
    So thou from Florence must perforce depart.

Already this is willed, and this is sought for;
    And soon it shall be done by him who thinks it,   50
    Where every day the Christ is bought and sold.

The blame shall follow the offended party
    In outcry as is usual; but the vengeance
    Shall witness to the truth that doth dispense it.

Thou shalt abandon everything beloved   55
    Most tenderly, and this the arrow is
    Which first the bow of banishment shoots forth.

Thou shalt have proof how savoreth of salt
    The bread of others, and how hard a road
    The going down and up another's stairs.   60

And that which most shall weigh upon thy shoulders
    Will be the bad and foolish company
    With which into this valley thou shalt fall;

For all ingrate, all mad and impious
    Will they become against thee; but soon after   65
    They, and not thou, shall have the forehead scarlet.

Of their bestiality their own proceedings
    Shall furnish proof; so 'twill be well for thee
    A party to have made thee by thyself.

Thine earliest refuge and thine earliest inn   70
    Shall be the mighty Lombard's courtesy,
    Who on the Ladder bears the holy bird,

Who such benign regard shall have for thee
    That 'twixt you twain, in doing and in asking,
    That shall be first which is with others last.   75

With him shalt thou see one who at his birth
    Has by this star of strength been so impressed,
    That notable shall his achievements be.

Not yet the people are aware of him
    Through his young age, since only nine years yet   80
    Around about him have these wheels revolved.

But ere the Gascon cheat the noble Henry,
    Some sparkles of his virtue shall appear
    In caring not for silver nor for toil.

So recognized shall his magnificence   85
    Become hereafter, that his enemies
    Will not have power to keep mute tongues about it.

On him rely, and on his benefits;
    By him shall many people be transformed,
    Changing condition rich and mendicant;   90

And written in thy mind thou hence shalt bear
    Of him, but shalt not say it"—and things said he
    Incredible to those who shall be present.

Then added: "Son, these are the commentaries
    On what was said to thee; behold the snares   95
    That are concealed behind few revolutions;

Yet would I not thy neighbors thou shouldst envy,
    Because thy life into the future reaches
    Beyond the punishment of their perfidies."

When by its silence showed that sainted soul   100
    That it had finished putting in the woof
    Into that web which I had given it warped,

Began I, even as he who yearneth after,
    Being in doubt, some counsel from a person
    Who seeth, and uprightly wills, and loves: 105

"Well see I, father mine, how spurreth on
    The time towards me such a blow to deal me
    As heaviest is to him who most gives way.

Therefore with foresight it is well I arm me,
    That, if the dearest place be taken from me,   110
    I may not lose the others by my songs.

Down through the world of infinite bitterness,
    And o'er the mountain, from whose beauteous summit
    The eyes of my own Lady lifted me,

And afterward through heaven from light to light,   115
    I have learned that which, if I tell again,
    Will be a savor of strong herbs to many.

And if I am a timid friend to truth,
    I fear lest I may lose my life with those
    Who will hereafter call this time the olden."   120

The light in which was smiling my own treasure
    Which there I had discovered, flashed at first
    As in the sunshine doth a golden mirror;

Then made reply: "A conscience overcast
    Or with its own or with another's shame,   125
    Will taste forsooth the tartness of thy word;

But ne'ertheless, all falsehood laid aside,
    Make manifest thy vision utterly,
    And let them scratch wherever is the itch;

For if thine utterance shall offensive be   130
    At the first taste, a vital nutriment
    'Twill leave thereafter, when it is digested.

This cry of thine shall do as doth the wind,
    Which smiteth most the most exalted summits,
    And that is no slight argument of honor.   135

Therefore are shown to thee within these wheels,
    Upon the mount and in the dolorous valley,
    Only the souls that unto fame are known;

Because the spirit of the hearer rests not,
    Nor doth confirm its faith by an example   140
    Which has the root of it unknown and hidden,

Or other reason that is not apparent."

ᕹ Canto XVIII ᕹ

The Sixth Heaven, Jupiter: Righteous Kings and Rulers—
The Celestial Eagle—Dante's Invectives against Ecclesiastical Avarice

Now was alone rejoicing in its word
    That soul beatified, and I was tasting
My own, the bitter tempering with the sweet,

And the Lady who to God was leading me
    Said: "Change thy thought; consider that I am   5
    Near unto Him who every wrong disburdens."

Unto the loving accents of my comfort
    I turned me round, and then what love I saw
    Within those holy eyes I here relinquish;

Not only that my language I distrust,   10
    But that my mind cannot return so far
    Above itself, unless another guide it.

Thus much upon that point can I repeat,
    That, her again beholding, my affection
    From every other longing was released.   15

While the eternal pleasure, which direct
    Rayed upon Beatrice, from her fair face
    Contented me with its reflected aspect,

Conquering me with the radiance of a smile,
    She said to me, "Turn thee about and listen;   20
    Not in mine eyes alone is Paradise."

Even as sometimes here do we behold
    The affection in the look, if it be such
    That all the soul is wrapt away by it,

So, by the flaming of the effulgence holy   25
    To which I turned, I recognized therein
    The wish of speaking to me somewhat farther.

And it began: "In this fifth resting place
    Upon the tree that liveth by its summit,
    And aye bears fruit, and never loses leaf,   30

Are blessed spirits that below, ere yet
    They came to Heaven, were of such great renown
    That every Muse therewith would affluent be.

Therefore look thou upon the cross's horns;
    He whom I now shall name will there enact   35
    What doth within a cloud its own swift fire."

I saw athwart the Cross a splendor drawn
    By naming Joshua, (even as he did it,)
    Nor noted I the word before the deed;

And at the name of the great Maccabee   40
    I saw another move itself revolving,
    And gladness was the whip unto that top.

Likewise for Charlemagne and for Orlando,
    Two of them my regard attentive followed
    As followeth the eye its falcon flying.   45

William thereafterward, and Renouard,
    And the Duke Godfrey, did attract my sight
    Along upon that Cross, and Robert Guiscard.

Then, moved and mingled with the other lights,
    The soul that had addressed me showed how great   50
    An artist 'twas among the heavenly singers.

To my right side I turned myself around,
    My duty to behold in Beatrice
    Either by words or gesture signified;

And so translucent I beheld her eyes,   55
    So full of pleasure, that her countenance
    Surpassed its other and its latest wont.

And as, by feeling greater delectation,
    A man in doing good from day to day
    Becomes aware his virtue is increasing,   60

So I became aware that my gyration
    With heaven together had increased its arc,
    That miracle beholding more adorned.

And such as is the change, in little lapse
    Of time, in a pale woman, when her face   65
    Is from the load of bashfulness unladen,

Such was it in mine eyes, when I had turned,
    Caused by the whiteness of the temperate star,
    The sixth, which to itself had gathered me.

Within that Jovial torch did I behold   70
    The sparkling of the love which was therein
    Delineate our language to mine eyes.

And even as birds uprisen from the shore,
    As in congratulation o'er their food,
    Make squadrons of themselves, now round, now long, 75

So from within those lights the holy creatures
    Sang flying to and fro, and in their figures
    Made of themselves now D, now I, now L.

First singing they to their own music moved;
    Then one becoming of these characters,   80
    A little while they rested and were silent.

O divine Pegasea, thou who genius
    Dost glorious make, and render it long-lived,
    And this through thee the cities and the kingdoms,

Illume me with thyself, that I may bring   85
    Their figures out as I have them conceived!
    Apparent be thy power in these brief verses!

Themselves then they displayed in five times seven
    Vowels and consonants; and I observed
    The parts as they seemed spoken unto me.   90

Diligite justitiam, these were
    First verb and noun of all that was depicted;
    Qui judicatis terram were the last.

The holy creatures
Sang flying to and fro

Paradiso XVIII, lines 76–77

Thereafter in the M of the fifth word
    Remained they so arranged, that Jupiter   95
    Seemed to be silver there with gold inlaid.

And other lights I saw descend where was
    The summit of the M, and pause there singing
    The good, I think, that draws them to itself.

Then, as in striking upon burning logs   100
    Upward there fly innumerable sparks,
    Whence fools are wont to look for auguries,

More than a thousand lights seemed thence to rise,
    And to ascend, some more, and others less,
    Even as the Sun that lights them had allotted;   105

And, each one being quiet in its place,
    The head and neck beheld I of an eagle
    Delineated by that inlaid fire.

He who there paints has none to be his guide;
    But Himself guides; and is from Him remembered   110
    That virtue which is form unto the nest.

The other beatitude, that contented seemed
    At first to bloom a lily on the M,
    By a slight motion followed out the imprint.

O gentle star! what and how many gems   115
    Did demonstrate to me, that all our justice
    Effect is of that heaven which thou ingemmest!

Wherefore I pray the Mind, in which begin
    Thy motion and thy virtue, to regard
    Whence comes the smoke that vitiates thy rays;   120

So that a second time it now be wroth
   With buying and with selling in the temple
   Whose walls were built with signs and martyrdoms!

O soldiery of heaven, whom I contemplate,
   Implore for those who are upon the earth   125
   All gone astray after the bad example!

Once 'twas the custom to make war with swords;
   But now 'tis made by taking here and there
   The bread the pitying Father shuts from none.

Yet thou, who writest but to cancel, think   130
   That Peter and that Paul, who for this vineyard
   Which thou art spoiling died, are still alive!

Well canst thou say: "So steadfast my desire
   Is unto him who willed to live alone,
   And for a dance was led to martyrdom,   135

That I know not the Fisherman nor Paul."

⊰ CANTO XIX ⊱

*The Eagle Discourses of Salvation, Faith, and Virtue—
Condemnation of the Vile Kings of A.D. 1300*

Appeared before me with its wings outspread
   The beautiful image that in sweet fruition
Made jubilant the interwoven souls;

Appeared a little ruby each, wherein
   Ray of the sun was burning so enkindled   5
   That each into mine eyes refracted it.

O soldiery of heaven, whom I contemplate,
Implore for those who are upon the earth
All gone astray after the bad example!

Paradiso XVIII, lines 124–126

Appeared before me with its wings outspread
The beautiful image that in sweet fruition
Made jubilant the interwoven souls

Paradiso XIX, lines 1–3

And what it now behoves me to retrace
   Nor voice has e'er reported, nor ink written,
   Nor was by fantasy e'er comprehended;

For speak I saw, and likewise heard, the beak,   10
   And utter with its voice both *I* and *My*,
   When in conception it was *We* and *Our*.

And it began: "Being just and merciful
   Am I exalted here unto that glory
   Which cannot be exceeded by desire;   15

And upon earth I left my memory
   Such, that the evil-minded people there
   Commend it, but continue not the story."

So doth a single heat from many embers
   Make itself felt, even as from many loves   20
   Issued a single sound from out that image.

Whence I thereafter: "O perpetual flowers
   Of the eternal joy, that only one
   Make me perceive your odors manifold,

Exhaling, break within me the great fast   25
   Which a long season has in hunger held me,
   Not finding for it any food on earth.

Well do I know, that if in heaven its mirror
   Justice Divine another realm doth make,
   Yours apprehends it not through any veil.   30

You know how I attentively address me
   To listen; and you know what is the doubt
   That is in me so very old a fast."

Even as a falcon, issuing from his hood,
    Doth move his head, and with his wings applaud
        him,   35
    Showing desire, and making himself fine,

Saw I become that standard, which of lauds
    Was interwoven of the grace divine,
    With such songs as he knows who there rejoices.

Then it began: "He who a compass turned   40
    On the world's outer verge, and who within it
    Devised so much occult and manifest,

Could not the impress of his power so make
    On all the universe, as that his Word
    Should not remain in infinite excess.   45

And this makes certain that the first proud being,
    Who was the paragon of every creature,
    By not awaiting light fell immature.

And hence appears it, that each minor nature
    Is scant receptacle unto that good   50
    Which has no end, and by itself is measured.

In consequence our vision, which perforce
    Must be some ray of that intelligence
    With which all things whatever are replete,

Cannot in its own nature be so potent,   55
    That it shall not its origin discern
    Far beyond that which is apparent to it.

Therefore into the justice sempiternal
    The power of vision that your world receives,
    As eye into the ocean, penetrates;   60

Which, though it see the bottom near the shore,
   Upon the deep perceives it not, and yet
   'Tis there, but it is hidden by the depth.

There is no light but comes from the serene
   That never is o'ercast, nay, it is darkness   65
   Or shadow of the flesh, or else its poison.

Amply to thee is opened now the cavern
   Which has concealed from thee the living justice
   Of which thou mad'st such frequent questioning.

For saidst thou: 'Born a man is on the shore   70
   Of Indus, and is none who there can speak
   Of Christ, nor who can read, nor who can write;

And all his inclinations and his actions
   Are good, so far as human reason sees,
   Without a sin in life or in discourse: 75

He dieth unbaptised and without faith;
   Where is this justice that condemneth him?
   Where is his fault, if he do not believe?'

Now who art thou, that on the bench wouldst sit
   In judgment at a thousand miles away,   80
   With the short vision of a single span?

Truly to him who with me subtilizes,
   If so the Scripture were not over you,
   For doubting there were marvellous occasion.

O animals terrene, O stolid minds,   85
   The primal will, that in itself is good,
   Ne'er from itself, the Good Supreme, has moved.

So much is just as is accordant with it;
   No good created draws it to itself,
   But it, by raying forth, occasions that."   90

Even as above her nest goes circling round
   The stork when she has fed her little ones,
   And he who has been fed looks up at her,

So lifted I my brows, and even such
   Became the blessed image, which its wings   95
   Was moving, by so many counsels urged.

Circling around it sang, and said: "As are
   My notes to thee, who dost not comprehend them,
   Such is the eternal judgment to you mortals."

Those lucent splendors of the Holy Spirit   100
   Grew quiet then, but still within the standard
   That made the Romans reverend to the world.

It recommenced: "Unto this kingdom never
   Ascended one who had not faith in Christ,
   Before or since he to the tree was nailed.   105

But look thou, many crying are, 'Christ, Christ!'
   Who at the judgment shall be far less near
   To him than some shall be who knew not Christ.

Such Christians shall the Ethiop condemn,
   When the two companies shall be divided,   110
   The one forever rich, the other poor.

What to your kings may not the Persians say,
   When they that volume opened shall behold
   In which are written down all their dispraises?

There shall be seen, among the deeds of Albert,   115
    That which ere long shall set the pen in motion,
    For which the realm of Prague shall be deserted.

There shall be seen the woe that on the Seine
    He brings by falsifying of the coin,
    Who by the blow of a wild boar shall die.   120

There shall be seen the pride that causes thirst,
    Which makes the Scot and Englishman so mad
    That they within their boundaries cannot rest;

Be seen the luxury and effeminate life
    Of him of Spain, and the Bohemian,   125
    Who valor never knew and never wished;

Be seen the Cripple of Jerusalem,
    His goodness represented by an I,
    While the reverse an M shall represent;

Be seen the avarice and poltroonery   130
    Of him who guards the Island of the Fire,
    Wherein Anchises finished his long life;

And to declare how pitiful he is
    Shall be his record in contracted letters
    Which shall make note of much in little space.   135

And shall appear to each one the foul deeds
    Of uncle and of brother who a nation
    So famous have dishonored, and two crowns.

And he of Portugal and he of Norway
    Shall there be known, and he of Rascia too,   140
    Who saw in evil hour the coin of Venice.

O happy Hungary, if she let herself
    Be wronged no farther! and Navarre the happy,
    If with the hills that gird her she be armed!

And each one may believe that now, as hansel   145
    Thereof, do Nicosìa and Famagosta
    Lament and rage because of their own beast,

Who from the others' flank departeth not."

⊰ CANTO XX ⊱

The Eagle Praises the Righteous Kings of Old—Benevolence of the Divine Will

When he who all the world illuminates
    Out of our hemisphere so far descends
That on all sides the daylight is consumed,

The heaven, that erst by him alone was kindled,
    Doth suddenly reveal itself again   5
    By many lights, wherein is one resplendent.

And came into my mind this act of heaven,
    When the ensign of the world and of its leaders
    Had silent in the blessed beak become;

Because those living luminaries all,   10
    By far more luminous, did songs begin
    Lapsing and falling from my memory.

O gentle Love, that with a smile dost cloak thee,
    How ardent in those sparks didst thou appear,
    That had the breath alone of holy thoughts!   15

Because those living luminaries all,
By far more luminous, did songs begin
Lapsing and falling from my memory.

Paradiso XX, lines 10–12

After the precious and pellucid crystals,
    With which begemmed the sixth light I beheld,
    Silence imposed on the angelic bells,

I seemed to hear the murmuring of a river
    That clear descendeth down from rock to rock,   20
    Showing the affluence of its mountaintop.

And as the sound upon the cithern's neck
    Taketh its form, and as upon the vent
    Of rustic pipe the wind that enters it,

Even thus, relieved from the delay of waiting,   25
    That murmuring of the eagle mounted up
    Along its neck, as if it had been hollow.

There it became a voice, and issued thence
    From out its beak, in such a form of words
    As the heart waited for wherein I wrote them.   30

"The part in me which sees and bears the sun
    In mortal eagles," it began to me,
    "Now fixedly must needs be looked upon;

For of the fires of which I make my figure,
    Those whence the eye doth sparkle in my head   35
    Of all their orders the supremest are.

He who is shining in the midst as pupil
    Was once the singer of the Holy Spirit,
    Who bore the ark from city unto city;

Now knoweth he the merit of his song,   40
    Insofar as effect of his own counsel,
    By the reward which is commensurate.

Of five, that make a circle for my brow,
   He that approacheth nearest to my beak
   Did the poor widow for her son console;   45

Now knoweth he how dearly it doth cost
   Not following Christ, by the experience
   Of this sweet life and of its opposite.

He who comes next in the circumference
   Of which I speak, upon its highest arc,   50
   Did death postpone by penitence sincere;

Now knoweth he that the eternal judgment
   Suffers no change, albeit worthy prayer
   Maketh below tomorrow of today.

The next who follows, with the laws and me,   55
   Under the good intent that bore bad fruit
   Became a Greek by ceding to the pastor;

Now knoweth he how all the ill deduced
   From his good action is not harmful to him,
   Although the world thereby may be destroyed.   60

And he, whom in the downward arc thou seest,
   Guglielmo was, whom the same land deplores
   That weepeth Charles and Frederick yet alive;

Now knoweth he how heaven enamored is
   With a just king; and in the outward show   65
   Of his effulgence he reveals it still.

Who would believe, down in the errant world,
   That e'er the Trojan Ripheus in this round
   Could be the fifth one of the holy lights?

Now knoweth he enough of what the world   70
    Has not the power to see of grace divine,
    Although his sight may not discern the bottom."

Like as a lark that in the air expatiates,
    First singing and then silent with content
    Of the last sweetness that doth satisfy her,   75

Such seemed to me the image of the imprint
    Of the eternal pleasure, by whose will
    Doth everything become the thing it is.

And notwithstanding to my doubt I was
    As glass is to the color that invests it,   80
    To wait the time in silence it endured not,

But forth from out my mouth, "What things are these?"
    Extorted with the force of its own weight;
    Whereat I saw great joy of coruscation.

Thereafterward with eye still more enkindled   85
    The blessed standard made to me reply,
    To keep me not in wonderment suspended:

"I see that thou believest in these things
    Because I say them, but thou seest not how;
    So that, although believed in, they are hidden.   90

Thou doest as he doth who a thing by name
    Well apprehendeth, but its quiddity
    Cannot perceive, unless another show it.

Regnum cœlorum suffereth violence
    From fervent love, and from that living hope   95
    That overcometh the Divine volition;

Not in the guise that man o'ercometh man,
  But conquers it because it will be conquered,
  And conquered conquers by benignity.

The first life of the eyebrow and the fifth   100
  Cause thee astonishment, because with them
  Thou seest the region of the angels painted.

They passed not from their bodies, as thou thinkest,
  Gentiles, but Christians in the steadfast faith
  Of feet that were to suffer and had suffered.   105

For one from Hell, where no one e'er turns back
  Unto good will, returned unto his bones,
  And that of living hope was the reward—

Of living hope, that placed its efficacy
  In prayers to God made to resuscitate him,   110
  So that 'twere possible to move his will.

The glorious soul concerning which I speak,
  Returning to the flesh, where brief its stay,
  Believed in Him who had the power to aid it;

And, in believing, kindled to such fire   115
  Of genuine love, that at the second death
  Worthy it was to come unto this joy.

The other one, through grace, that from so deep
  A fountain wells that never hath the eye
  Of any creature reached its primal wave,   120

Set all his love below on righteousness;
  Wherefore from grace to grace did God unclose
  His eye to our redemption yet to be,

Whence he believed therein, and suffered not
    From that day forth the stench of paganism,   125
    And he reproved therefor the folk perverse.

Those Maidens three, whom at the right-hand wheel
    Thou didst behold, were unto him for baptism
    More than a thousand years before baptizing.

O thou predestination, how remote   130
    Thy root is from the aspect of all those
    Who the First Cause do not behold entire!

And you, O mortals! hold yourselves restrained
    In judging; for ourselves, who look on God,
    We do not know as yet all the elect;   135

And sweet to us is such a deprivation,
    Because our good in this good is made perfect,
    That whatsoe'er God wills, we also will."

After this manner by that shape divine,
    To make clear in me my short-sightedness,   140
    Was given to me a pleasant medicine;

And as good singer a good lutanist
    Accompanies with vibrations of the chords,
    Whereby more pleasantness the song acquires,

So, while it spake, do I remember me   145
    That I beheld both of those blessed lights,
    Even as the winking of the eyes concords,

Moving unto the words their little flames.

⊰ CANTO XXI ⊱

The Seventh Heaven, Saturn: The Contemplative — The Celestial Stairway —
St. Peter Damiano — His Invectives against the Luxury of the Prelates

Already on my Lady's face mine eyes
   Again were fastened, and with these my mind,
And from all other purpose was withdrawn;

And she smiled not; but "If I were to smile,"
   She unto me began, "thou wouldst become   5
   Like Semele, when she was turned to ashes.

Because my beauty, that along the stairs
   Of the eternal palace more enkindles,
   As thou hast seen, the farther we ascend,

If it were tempered not, is so resplendent   10
   That all thy mortal power in its effulgence
   Would seem a leaflet that the thunder crushes.

We are uplifted to the seventh splendor,
   That underneath the burning Lion's breast
   Now radiates downward mingled with his power.   15

Fix in direction of thine eyes the mind,
   And make of them a mirror for the figure
   That in this mirror shall appear to thee."

He who could know what was the pasturage
   My sight had in that blessed countenance,   20
   When I transferred me to another care,

Already on my Lady's face mine eyes
Again were fastened

Paradiso XXI, lines 1–2

Would recognize how grateful was to me
    Obedience unto my celestial escort,
    By counterpoising one side with the other.

Within the crystal which, around the world   25
    Revolving, bears the name of its dear leader,
    Under whom every wickedness lay dead,

Colored like gold, on which the sunshine gleams,
    A stairway I beheld to such a height
    Uplifted, that mine eye pursued it not.   30

Likewise beheld I down the steps descending
    So many splendors, that I thought each light
    That in the heaven appears was there diffused.

And as accordant with their natural custom
    The rooks together at the break of day   35
    Bestir themselves to warm their feathers cold;

Then some of them fly off without return,
    Others come back to where they started from,
    And others, wheeling round, still keep at home;

Such fashion it appeared to me was there   40
    Within the sparkling that together came,
    As soon as on a certain step it struck,

And that which nearest unto us remained
    Became so clear, that in my thought I said,
    "Well I perceive the love thou showest me;   45

But she, from whom I wait the how and when
    Of speech and silence, standeth still; whence I
    Against desire do well if I ask not."

A stairway I beheld to such a height
Uplifted, that mine eye pursued it not.

Paradiso XXI, lines 29–30

She thereupon, who saw my silentness
    In the sight of Him who seeth everything,   50
    Said unto me, "Let loose thy warm desire."

And I began: "No merit of my own
    Renders me worthy of response from thee;
    But for her sake who granteth me the asking,

Thou blessed life that dost remain concealed   55
    In thy beatitude, make known to me
    The cause which draweth thee so near my side;

And tell me why is silent in this wheel
    The dulcet symphony of Paradise,
    That through the rest below sounds so devoutly."   60

"Thou hast thy hearing mortal as thy sight,"
    It answer made to me; "they sing not here,
    For the same cause that Beatrice has not smiled.

Thus far adown the holy stairway's steps
    Have I descended but to give thee welcome   65
    With words, and with the light that mantles me;

Nor did more love cause me to be more ready,
    For love as much and more up there is burning,
    As doth the flaming manifest to thee.

But the high charity, that makes us servants   70
    Prompt to the counsel which controls the world,
    Allotteth here, even as thou dost observe."

"I see full well," said I, "O sacred lamp!
    How love unfettered in this court sufficeth
    To follow the eternal Providence;   75

But this is what seems hard for me to see,
    Wherefore predestinate wast thou alone
    Unto this office from among thy consorts."

No sooner had I come to the last word,
    Than of its middle made the light a center,   80
    Whirling itself about like a swift millstone.

When answer made the love that was therein:
    "On me directed is a light divine,
    Piercing through this in which I am embosomed,

Of which the virtue with my sight conjoined   85
    Lifts me above myself so far, I see
    The supreme essence from which this is drawn.

Hence comes the joyfulness with which I flame,
    For to my sight, as far as it is clear,
    The clearness of the flame I equal make.   90

But that soul in the heaven which is most pure,
    That seraph which his eye on God most fixes,
    Could this demand of thine not satisfy;

Because so deeply sinks in the abyss
    Of the eternal statute what thou askest,   95
    From all created sight it is cut off.

And to the mortal world, when thou returnest,
    This carry back, that it may not presume
    Longer tow'rd such a goal to move its feet.

The mind, that shineth here, on earth doth smoke;   100
    From this observe how can it do below
    That which it cannot though the heaven assume it?"

Such limit did its words prescribe to me,
    The question I relinquished, and restricted
    Myself to ask it humbly who it was.   105

"Between two shores of Italy rise cliffs,
    And not far distant from thy native place,
    So high, the thunders far below them sound,

And form a ridge that Catria is called,
    'Neath which is consecrate a hermitage   110
    Wont to be dedicate to worship only."

Thus unto me the third speech recommenced,
    And then, continuing, it said: "Therein
    Unto God's service I became so steadfast,

That feeding only on the juice of olives   115
    Lightly I passed away the heats and frosts,
    Contented in my thoughts contemplative.

That cloister used to render to these heavens
    Abundantly, and now is empty grown,
    So that perforce it soon must be revealed.   120

I in that place was Peter Damiano;
    And Peter the Sinner was I in the house
    Of Our Lady on the Adriatic shore.

Little of mortal life remained to me,
    When I was called and dragged forth to the hat   125
    Which shifteth evermore from bad to worse.

Came Cephas, and the mighty Vessel came
    Of the Holy Spirit, meager and barefooted,
    Taking the food of any hostelry.

Now someone to support them on each side   130
    The modern shepherds need, and some to lead them,
    So heavy are they, and to hold their trains.

They cover up their palfreys with their cloaks,
    So that two beasts go underneath one skin;
    O Patience, that dost tolerate so much!"   135

At this voice saw I many little flames
    From step to step descending and revolving,
    And every revolution made them fairer.

Round about this one came they and stood still,
    And a cry uttered of so loud a sound,   140
    It here could find no parallel, nor I

Distinguished it, the thunder so o'ercame me.

⊰ CANTO XXII ⊱

St. Benedict—His Lamentation over the Corruption of Monks—
The Eighth Heaven, the Fixed Stars

Oppressed with stupor, I unto my guide
    Turned like a little child who always runs
For refuge there where he confideth most;

And she, even as a mother who straightway
    Gives comfort to her pale and breathless boy   5
    With voice whose wont it is to reassure him,

Said to me: "Knowest thou not thou art in heaven,
    And knowest thou not that heaven is holy all
    And what is done here cometh from good zeal?

After what wise the singing would have changed thee   10
    And I by smiling, thou canst now imagine,
    Since that the cry has startled thee so much,

In which if thou hadst understood its prayers
    Already would be known to thee the vengeance
    Which thou shalt look upon before thou diest.   15

The sword above here smiteth not in haste
    Nor tardily, howe'er it seem to him
    Who fearing or desiring waits for it.

But turn thee round towards the others now,
    For very illustrious spirits shalt thou see,   20
    If thou thy sight directest as I say."

As it seemed good to her mine eyes I turned,
    And saw a hundred spherules that together
    With mutual rays each other more embellished.

I stood as one who in himself represses   25
    The point of his desire, and ventures not
    To question, he so feareth the too much.

And now the largest and most luculent
    Among those pearls came forward, that it might
    Make my desire concerning it content.   30

Within it then I heard: "If thou couldst see
    Even as myself the charity that burns
    Among us, thy conceits would be expressed;

But, that by waiting thou mayst not come late
    To the high end, I will make answer even   35
    Unto the thought of which thou art so chary.

That mountain on whose slope Cassino stands
    Was frequented of old upon its summit
    By a deluded folk and ill-disposed;

And I am he who first up thither bore   40
    The name of Him who brought upon the earth
    The truth that so much sublimateth us.

And such abundant grace upon me shone
    That all the neighboring towns I drew away
    From the impious worship that seduced the world.   45

These other fires, each one of them, were men
    Contemplative, enkindled by that heat
    Which maketh holy flowers and fruits spring up.

Here is Macarius, here is Romualdus,
    Here are my brethren, who within the cloisters   50
    Their footsteps stayed and kept a steadfast heart."

And I to him: "The affection which thou showest
    Speaking with me, and the good countenance
    Which I behold and note in all your ardors,

In me have so my confidence dilated   55
    As the sun doth the rose, when it becomes
    As far unfolded as it hath the power.

Therefore I pray, and thou assure me, father,
    If I may so much grace receive, that I
    May thee behold with countenance unveiled."   60

He thereupon: "Brother, thy high desire
    In the remotest sphere shall be fulfilled,
    Where are fulfilled all others and my own.

There perfect is, and ripened, and complete,
    Every desire; within that one alone   65
    Is every part where it has always been;

For it is not in space, nor turns on poles,
    And unto it our stairway reaches up,
    Whence thus from out thy sight it steals away.

Up to that height the Patriarch Jacob saw it   70
    Extending its supernal part, what time
    So thronged with angels it appeared to him.

But to ascend it now no one uplifts
    His feet from off the earth, and now my Rule
    Below remaineth for mere waste of paper.   75

The walls that used of old to be an Abbey
    Are changed to dens of robbers, and the cowls
    Are sacks filled full of miserable flour.

But heavy usury is not taken up
    So much against God's pleasure as that fruit   80
    Which maketh so insane the heart of monks;

For whatsoever hath the Church in keeping
    Is for the folk that ask it in God's name,
    Not for one's kindred or for something worse.

The flesh of mortals is so very soft,   85
    That good beginnings down below suffice not
    From springing of the oak to bearing acorns.

Peter began with neither gold nor silver,
    And I with orison and abstinence,
    And Francis with humility his convent.   90

And if thou lookest at each one's beginning,
    And then regardest whither he has run,
    Thou shalt behold the white changed into brown.

In verity the Jordan backward turned,
    And the sea's fleeing, when God willed were more   95
    A wonder to behold, than succor here. "

Thus unto me he said; and then withdrew
    To his own band, and the band closed together;
    Then like a whirlwind all was upward rapt.

The gentle Lady urged me on behind them   100
    Up o'er that stairway by a single sign,
    So did her virtue overcome my nature;

Nor here below, where one goes up and down
    By natural law, was motion e'er so swift
    That it could be compared unto my wing.   105

Reader, as I may unto that devout
    Triumph return, on whose account I often
    For my transgressions weep and beat my breast—

Thou hadst not thrust thy finger in the fire
    And drawn it out again, before I saw   110
    The sign that follows Taurus, and was in it.

O glorious stars, O light impregnated
    With mighty virtue, from which I acknowledge
    All of my genius, whatsoe'er it be,

With you was born, and hid himself with you,   115
    He who is father of all mortal life,
    When first I tasted of the Tuscan air;

And then when grace was freely given to me
 To enter the high wheel which turns you round,
 Your region was allotted unto me.   120

To you devoutly at this hour my soul
 Is sighing, that it virtue may acquire
 For the stern pass that draws it to itself.

"Thou art so near unto the last salvation,"
 Thus Beatrice began, "thou oughtest now   125
 To have thine eves unclouded and acute;

And therefore, ere thou enter farther in,
 Look down once more, and see how vast a world
 Thou hast already put beneath thy feet;

So that thy heart, as jocund as it may,   130
 Present itself to the triumphant throng
 That comes rejoicing through this rounded ether."

I with my sight returned through one and all
 The sevenfold spheres, and I beheld this globe
 Such that I smiled at its ignoble semblance;   135

And that opinion I approve as best
 Which doth account it least; and he who thinks
 Of something else may truly be called just.

I saw the daughter of Latona shining
 Without that shadow, which to me was cause   140
 That once I had believed her rare and dense.

The aspect of thy son, Hyperion,
 Here I sustained, and saw how move themselves
 Around and near him Maia and Dione.

Thence there appeared the temperateness of Jove   145
    'Twixt son and father, and to me was clear
    The change that of their whereabout they make;

And all the seven made manifest to me
    How great they are, and eke how swift they are,
    And how they are in distant habitations.   150

The threshing-floor that maketh us so proud,
    To me revolving with the eternal Twins,
    Was all apparent made from hill to harbor!

Then to the beauteous eyes mine eyes I turned.

⇥ CANTO XXIII ⇤

The Triumph of Christ — The Virgin Mary — The Apostles — Gabriel

Even as a bird, 'mid the beloved leaves,
    Quiet upon the nest of her sweet brood
Throughout the night, that hideth all things from us,

Who, that she may behold their longed-for looks
    And find the food wherewith to nourish them,   5
    In which, to her, grave labors grateful are,

Anticipates the time on open spray
    And with an ardent longing waits the sun,
    Gazing intent as soon as breaks the dawn:

Even thus my Lady standing was, erect   10
    And vigilant, turned round towards the zone
    Underneath which the sun displays less haste;

So that beholding her distraught and wistful,
    Such I became as he is who desiring
    For something yearns, and hoping is appeased.   15

But brief the space from one When to the other;
    Of my awaiting, say I, and the seeing
    The welkin grow resplendent more and more.

And Beatrice exclaimed: "Behold the hosts
    Of Christ's triumphal march, and all the fruit   20
    Harvested by the rolling of these spheres!"

It seemed to me her face was all aflame;
    And eyes she had so full of ecstasy
    That I must needs pass on without describing.

As when in nights serene of the full moon   25
    Smiles Trivia among the nymphs eternal
    Who paint the firmament through all its gulfs,

Saw I, above the myriads of lamps,
    A Sun that one and all of them enkindled,
    E'en as our own doth the supernal sights,   30

And through the living light transparent shone
    The lucent substance so intensely clear
    Into my sight, that I sustained it not.

O Beatrice, thou gentle guide and dear!
    To me she said: "What overmasters thee   35
    A virtue is from which naught shields itself.

There are the wisdom and the omnipotence
    That oped the thoroughfares 'twixt heaven and earth,
    For which there erst had been so long a yearning."

As fire from out a cloud unlocks itself,   40
   Dilating so it finds not room therein,
   And down, against its nature, falls to earth,

So did my mind, among those aliments
   Becoming larger, issue from itself,
   And that which it became cannot remember.   45

"Open thine eyes, and look at what I am:
   Thou hast beheld such things, that strong enough
   Hast thou become to tolerate my smile."

I was as one who still retains the feeling
   Of a forgotten vision, and endeavors   50
   In vain to bring it back into his mind,

When I this invitation heard, deserving
   Of so much gratitude, it never fades
   Out of the book that chronicles the past.

If at this moment sounded all the tongues   55
   That Polyhymnia and her sisters made
   Most lubrical with their delicious milk,

To aid me, to a thousandth of the truth
   It would not reach, singing the holy smile
   And how the holy aspect it illumed.   60

And therefore, representing Paradise,
   The sacred poem must perforce leap over,
   Even as a man who finds his way cut off;

But whoso thinketh of the ponderous theme,
   And of the mortal shoulder laden with it,   65
   Should blame it not, if under this it tremble.

It is no passage for a little boat
    This which goes cleaving the audacious prow,
    Nor for a pilot who would spare himself.

"Why doth my face so much enamor thee,   70
    That to the garden fair thou turnest not,
    Which under the rays of Christ is blossoming?

There is the Rose in which the Word Divine
    Became incarnate; there the lilies are
    By whose perfume the good way was discovered."   75

Thus Beatrice; and I, who to her counsels
    Was wholly ready, once again betook me
    Unto the battle of the feeble brows.

As in the sunshine, that unsullied streams
    Through fractured cloud, ere now a meadow of
        flowers   80
    Mine eyes with shadow covered o'er have seen,

So troops of splendors manifold I saw
    Illumined from above with burning rays,
    Beholding not the source of the effulgence.

O power benignant that dost so imprint them!   85
    Thou didst exalt thyself to give more scope
    There to mine eyes, that were not strong enough.

The name of that fair flower I e'er invoke
    Morning and evening utterly enthralled
    My soul to gaze upon the greater fire.   90

And when in both mine eyes depicted were
    The glory and greatness of the living star
    Which there excelleth, as it here excelled,

Athwart the heavens a little torch descended
  Formed in a circle like a coronal,   95
  And cinctured it, and whirled itself about it.

Whatever melody most sweetly soundeth
  On earth, and to itself most draws the soul,
  Would seem a cloud that, rent asunder, thunders,

Compared unto the sounding of that lyre   100
  Wherewith was crowned the sapphire beautiful,
  Which gives the clearest heaven its sapphire hue.

"I am Angelic Love, that circle round
  The joy sublime which breathes from out the womb
  That was the hostelry of our Desire;   105

And I shall circle, Lady of Heaven, while
  Thou followest thy Son, and mak'st diviner
  The sphere supreme, because thou enterest there."

Thus did the circulated melody
  Seal itself up; and all the other lights   110
  Were making to resound the name of Mary.

The regal mantle of the volumes all
  Of that world, which most fervid is and living
  With breath of God and with his works and ways,

Extended over us its inner border,   115
  So very distant, that the semblance of it
  There where I was not yet appeared to me.

Therefore mine eyes did not possess the power
  Of following the incoronated flame,
  Which mounted upward near to its own seed.   120

And as a little child, that towards its mother
    Stretches its arms, when it the milk has taken,
    Through impulse kindled into outward flame,

Each of those gleams of whiteness upward reached
    So with its summit, that the deep affection   125
    They had for Mary was revealed to me.

Thereafter they remained there in my sight,
    Regina cœli singing with such sweetness,
    That ne'er from me has the delight departed.

O, what exuberance is garnered up   130
    Within those richest coffers, which had been
    Good husbandmen for sowing here below!

There they enjoy and live upon the treasure
    Which was acquired while weeping in the exile
    Of Babylon, wherein the gold was left.   135

There triumpheth, beneath the exalted Son
    Of God and Mary, in his victory,
    Both with the ancient council and the new,

He who doth keep the keys of such a glory.

⊰ Canto XXIV ⊱

The Radiant Wheel—St. Peter Examines Dante on Faith

"O company elect to the great supper
    Of the Lamb benedight, who feedeth you
So that forever full is your desire,

If by the grace of God this man foretaste
    Something of that which falleth from your table,   5
    Or ever death prescribe to him the time,

Direct your mind to his immense desire,
    And him somewhat bedew; ye drinking are
    Forever at the fount whence comes his thought."

Thus Beatrice; and those souls beatified   10
    Transformed themselves to spheres on steadfast poles,
    Flaming intensely in the guise of comets.

And as the wheels in works of horologes
    Revolve so that the first to the beholder
    Motionless seems, and the last one to fly,   15

So in like manner did those carols, dancing
    In different measure, of their affluence
    Give me the gauge, as they were swift or slow.

From that one which I noted of most beauty
    Beheld I issue forth a fire so happy   20
    That none it left there of a greater brightness;

And around Beatrice three several times
    It whirled itself with so divine a song,
    My fantasy repeats it not to me;

Therefore the pen skips, and I write it not,   25
    Since our imagination for such folds,
    Much more our speech, is of a tint too glaring.

"O holy sister mine, who us implorest
    With such devotion, by thine ardent love
    Thou dost unbind me from that beautiful sphere!"   30

Thereafter, having stopped, the blessed fire
    Unto my Lady did direct its breath,
    Which spake in fashion as I here have said.

And she: "O light eterne of the great man
    To whom our Lord delivered up the keys   35
    He carried down of this miraculous joy,

This one examine on points light and grave,
    As good beseemeth thee, about the Faith
    By means of which thou on the sea didst walk.

If he love well, and hope well, and believe,   40
    From thee 'tis hid not; for thou hast thy sight
    There where depicted everything is seen.

But since this kingdom has made citizens
    By means of the true Faith, to glorify it
    'Tis well he have the chance to speak thereof."   45

As baccalaureate arms himself, and speaks not
    Until the master doth propose the question,
    To argue it, and not to terminate it,

So did I arm myself with every reason,
    While she was speaking, that I might be ready   50
    For such a questioner and such profession.

"Say, thou good Christian; manifest thyself;
    What is the Faith?" Whereat I raised my brow
    Unto that light wherefrom was this breathed forth.

Then turned I round to Beatrice, and she   55
    Prompt signals made to me that I should pour
    The water forth from my internal fountain.

"May grace, that suffers me to make confession,"
    Began I, "to the great centurion,
    Cause my conceptions all to be explicit!"   60

And I continued: "As the truthful pen,
    Father, of thy dear brother wrote of it,
    Who put with thee Rome into the good way,

Faith is the substance of the things we hope for,
    And evidence of those that are not seen;   65
    And this appears to me its quiddity."

Then heard I: "Very rightly thou perceivest,
    If well thou understandest why he placed it
    With substances and then with evidences."

And I thereafterward: "The things profound,   70
    That here vouchsafe to me their apparition,
    Unto all eyes below are so concealed,

That they exist there only in belief,
    Upon the which is founded the high hope,
    And hence it takes the nature of a substance.   75

And it behoveth us from this belief
    To reason without having other sight,
    And hence it has the nature of evidence."

Then heard I: "If whatever is acquired
    Below by doctrine were thus understood,   80
    No sophist's subtlety would there find place."

Thus was breathed forth from that enkindled love;
    Then added: "Very well has been gone over
    Already of this coin the alloy and weight;

But tell me if thou hast it in thy purse?"   85
   And I: "Yes, both so shining and so round
   That in its stamp there is no peradventure."

Thereafter issued from the light profound
   That there resplendent was: "This precious jewel,
   Upon the which is every virtue founded,   90

Whence hadst thou it?" And I: "The large outpouring
   Of Holy Spirit, which has been diffused
   Upon the ancient parchments and the new,

A syllogism is, which proved it to me
   With such acuteness, that, compared therewith,   95
   All demonstration seems to me obtuse."

And then I heard: "The ancient and the new
   Postulates, that to thee are so conclusive,
   Why dost thou take them for the word divine?"

And I: "The proofs, which show the truth to me,   100
   Are the works subsequent, whereunto Nature
   Ne'er heated iron yet, nor anvil beat."

'Twas answered me: "Say, who assureth thee
   That those works ever were? the thing itself
   That must be proved, nought else to thee affirms it."   105

"Were the world to Christianity converted,"
   I said, "withouten miracles, this one
   Is such, the rest are not its hundredth part;

Because that poor and fasting thou didst enter
   Into the field to sow there the good plant,   110
   Which was a vine and has become a thorn!"

This being finished, the high, holy Court
    Resounded through the spheres, "One God we praise!"
    In melody that there above is chanted.

And then that Baron, who from branch to branch,   115
    Examining, had thus conducted me,
    Till the extremest leaves we were approaching,

Again began: "The Grace that dallying
    Plays with thine intellect thy mouth has opened,
    Up to this point, as it should opened be,   120

So that I do approve what forth emerged;
    But now thou must express what thou believest,
    And whence to thy belief it was presented."

"O holy father, spirit who beholdest
    What thou believedst so that thou o'ercamest,   125
    Towards the sepulchre, more youthful feet,"

Began I, "thou dost wish me in this place
    The form to manifest of my prompt belief,
    And likewise thou the cause thereof demandest.

And I respond: In one God I believe,   130
    Sole and eterne, who moveth all the heavens
    With love and with desire, himself unmoved;

And of such faith not only have I proofs
    Physical and metaphysical, but gives them
    Likewise the truth that from this place rains down   135

Through Moses, through the Prophets and the Psalms,
    Through the Evangel, and through you, who wrote
    After the fiery Spirit sanctified you;

In Persons three eterne believe, and these
    One essence I believe, so one and trine   140
    They bear conjunction both with *sunt* and *est*.

With the profound condition and divine
    Which now I touch upon, doth stamp my mind
    Ofttimes the doctrine evangelical.

This the beginning is, this is the spark   145
    Which afterwards dilates to vivid flame,
    And, like a star in heaven, is sparkling in me."

Even as a lord who hears what pleaseth him
    His servant straight embraces, gratulating
    For the good news as soon as he is silent;   150

So, giving me its benediction, singing,
    Three times encircled me, when I was silent,
    The apostolic light, at whose command

I spoken had, in speaking I so pleased him.

⇥ Canto XXV ⇤

The Laurel Crown — St. James Examines Dante on Hope — Dante's Blindness

If e'er it happen that the Poem Sacred,
    To which both heaven and earth have set their hand,
So that it many a year hath made me lean,

O'ercome the cruelty that bars me out
    From the fair sheepfold, where a lamb I slumbered,   5
    An enemy to the wolves that war upon it,

With other voice forthwith, with other fleece
    Poet will I return, and at my font
    Baptismal will I take the laurel crown;

Because into the Faith that maketh known   10
    All souls to God there entered I, and then
    Peter for her sake thus my brow encircled.

Thereafterward towards us moved a light
    Out of that band whence issued the first-fruits
    Which of his vicars Christ behind him left,   15

And then my Lady, full of ecstasy,
    Said unto me: "Look, look! behold the Baron
    For whom below Galicia is frequented."

In the same way as, when a dove alights
    Near his companion, both of them pour forth,   20
    Circling about and murmuring, their affection,

So one beheld I by the other grand
    Prince glorified to be with welcome greeted,
    Lauding the food that there above is eaten.

But when their gratulations were complete,   25
    Silently *coram me* each one stood still,
    So incandescent it o'ercame my sight.

Smiling thereafterwards, said Beatrice:
    "Illustrious life, by whom the benefactions
    Of our Basilica have been described,   30

Make Hope resound within this altitude;
    Thou knowest as oft thou dost personify it
    As Jesus to the three gave greater clearness."

"Lift up thy head, and make thyself assured;
    For what comes hither from the mortal world   35
    Must needs be ripened in our radiance."

This comfort came to me from the second fire;
    Wherefore mine eyes I lifted to the hills,
    Which bent them down before with too great weight.

"Since, through his grace, our Emperor wills that thou 40
    Shouldst find thee face to face, before thy death,
    In the most secret chamber, with his Counts,

So that, the truth beholden of this court,
    Hope, which below there rightfully enamors,
    Thereby thou strengthen in thyself and others,   45

Say what it is, and how is flowering with it
    Thy mind, and say from whence it came to thee."
    Thus did the second light again continue.

And the Compassionate, who piloted
    The plumage of my wings in such high flight,   50
    Did in reply anticipate me thus:

"No child whatever the Church Militant
    Of greater hope possesses, as is written
    In that Sun which irradiates all our band;

Therefore it is conceded him from Egypt   55
    To come into Jerusalem to see,
    Or ever yet his warfare be completed.

The two remaining points, that not for knowledge
    Have been demanded, but that he report
    How much this virtue unto thee is pleasing,   60

To him I leave; for hard he will not find them,
    Nor of self-praise; and let him answer them;
    And may the grace of God in this assist him!"

As a disciple, who his teacher follows,
    Ready and willing, where he is expert,   65
    That his proficiency may be displayed,

"Hope," said I, "is the certain expectation
    Of future glory, which is the effect
    Of grace divine and merit precedent.

From many stars this light comes unto me;   70
    But he instilled it first into my heart
    Who was chief singer unto the chief captain.

Sperent in te, in the high Theody
    He sayeth, 'those who know thy name'; and who
    Knoweth it not, if he my faith possess?   75

Thou didst instil me, then, with his instilling
    In the Epistle, so that I am full,
    And upon others rain again your rain."

While I was speaking, in the living bosom
    Of that combustion quivered an effulgence,   80
    Sudden and frequent, in the guise of lightning;

Then breathed: "The love wherewith I am inflamed
    Towards the virtue still which followed me
    Unto the palm and issue of the field,

Wills that I breathe to thee that thou delight   85
    In her; and grateful to me is thy telling
    Whatever things Hope promises to thee."

And I: "The ancient Scriptures and the new
    The mark establish, and this shows it me,
    Of all the souls whom God hath made his friends.   90

Isaiah saith, that each one garmented
    In his own land shall be with twofold garments,
    And his own land is this delightful life.

Thy brother, too, far more explicitly,
    There where he treateth of the robes of white,   95
    This revelation manifests to us."

And first, and near the ending of these words,
    Sperent in te from over us was heard,
    To which responsive answered all the carols.

Thereafterward a light among them brightened,   100
    So that, if Cancer one such crystal had,
    Winter would have a month of one sole day.

And as uprises, goes, and enters the dance
    A winsome maiden, only to do honor
    To the new bride, and not from any failing,   105

Even thus did I behold the brightened splendor
    Approach the two, who in a wheel revolved
    As was beseeming to their ardent love.

Into the song and music there it entered;
    And fixed on them my Lady kept her look,   110
    Even as a bride silent and motionless.

"This is the one who lay upon the breast
    Of him our Pelican; and this is he
    To the great office from the cross elected."

My Lady thus; but therefore none the more   115
    Did move her sight from its attentive gaze
    Before or afterward these words of hers.

Even as a man who gazes, and endeavors
    To see the eclipsing of the sun a little,
    And who, by seeing, sightless doth become,   120

So I became before that latest fire,
    While it was said, "Why dost thou daze thyself
    To see a thing which here hath no existence?

Earth in the earth my body is, and shall be
    With all the others there, until our number   125
    With the eternal proposition tallies.

With the two garments in the blessed cloister
    Are the two lights alone that have ascended:
    And this shalt thou take back into your world."

And at this utterance the flaming circle   130
    Grew quiet, with the dulcet intermingling
    Of sound that by the trinal breath was made,

As to escape from danger or fatigue
    The oars that erst were in the water beaten
    Are all suspended at a whistle's sound.   135

Ah, how much in my mind was I disturbed,
    When I turned round to look on Beatrice,
    That her I could not see, although I was

Close at her side and in the Happy World!

⊰ CANTO XXVI ⊱

St. John Examines Dante on Charity—Dante's Sight—Adam

While I was doubting for my vision quenched,
 Out of the flame refulgent that had quenched it
Issued a breathing, that attentive made me,

Saying: "While thou recoverest the sense
 Of seeing which in me thou hast consumed,   5
 'Tis well that speaking thou shouldst compensate it.

Begin then, and declare to what thy soul
 Is aimed, and count it for a certainty,
 Sight is in thee bewildered and not dead;

Because the Lady, who through this divine   10
 Region conducteth thee, has in her look
 The power the hand of Ananias had."

I said: "As pleaseth her, or soon or late
 Let the cure come to eyes that portals were
 When she with fire I ever burn with entered.   15

The Good, that gives contentment to this Court,
 The Alpha and Omega is of all
 The writing that love reads me low or loud."

The selfsame voice, that taken had from me
 The terror of the sudden dazzlement,   20
 To speak still farther put it in my thought;

And said: "In verity with finer sieve
 Behoveth thee to sift; thee it behoveth
 To say who aimed thy bow at such a target."

"Begin then, and declare to what thy soul
Is aimed, and count it for a certainty,
Sight is in thee bewildered and not dead"

Paradiso XXVI, lines 7–9

And I: "By philosophic arguments,   25
    And by authority that hence descends,
    Such love must needs imprint itself in me;

For Good, so far as good, when comprehended
    Doth straight enkindle love, and so much greater
    As more of goodness in itself it holds;   30

Then to that Essence (whose is such advantage
    That every good which out of it is found
    Is nothing but a ray of its own light)

More than elsewhither must the mind be moved
    Of every one, in loving, who discerns   35
    The truth in which this evidence is founded.

Such truth he to my intellect reveals
    Who demonstrates to me the primal love
    Of all the sempiternal substances.

The voice reveals it of the truthful Author,   40
    Who says to Moses, speaking of Himself,
    'I will make all my goodness pass before thee.'

Thou too revealest it to me, beginning
    The loud Evangel, that proclaims the secret
    Of heaven to earth above all other edict."   45

And I heard say: "By human intellect
    And by authority concordant with it,
    Of all thy loves reserve for God the highest.

But say again if other cords thou feelest,
    Draw thee towards Him, that thou mayst proclaim   50
    With how many teeth this love is biting thee."

The holy purpose of the Eagle of Christ
 Not latent was, nay, rather I perceived
 Whither he fain would my profession lead.

Therefore I recommenced: "All of those bites   55
 Which have the power to turn the heart to God
 Unto my charity have been concurrent.

The being of the world, and my own being,
 The death which He endured that I may live,
 And that which all the faithful hope, as I do, 60

With the forementioned vivid consciousness
 Have drawn me from the sea of love perverse,
 And of the right have placed me on the shore.

The leaves, wherewith embowered is all the garden
 Of the Eternal Gardener, do I love   65
 As much as he has granted them of good."

As soon as I had ceased, a song most sweet
 Throughout the heaven resounded, and my Lady
 Said with the others, "Holy, holy, holy!"

And as at some keen light one wakes from sleep 70
 By reason of the visual spirit that runs
 Unto the splendor passed from coat to coat,

And he who wakes abhorreth what he sees,
 So all unconscious is his sudden waking,
 Until the judgment cometh to his aid,   75

So from before mine eyes did Beatrice
 Chase every mote with radiance of her own,
 That cast its light a thousand miles and more.

Whence better after than before I saw,
   And in a kind of wonderment I asked   80
   About a fourth light that I saw with us.

And said my Lady: "There within those rays
   Gazes upon its Maker the first soul
   That ever the first virtue did create."

Even as the bough that downward bends its top   85
   At transit of the wind, and then is lifted
   By its own virtue, which inclines it upward,

Likewise did I, the while that she was speaking,
   Being amazed, and then I was made bold
   By a desire to speak wherewith I burned.   90

And I began: "O apple, that mature
   Alone hast been produced, O ancient father,
   To whom each wife is daughter and daughter-in-law,

Devoutly as I can I supplicate thee
   That thou wouldst speak to me; thou seest my wish; 95
   And I, to hear thee quickly, speak it not."

Sometimes an animal, when covered, struggles
   So that his impulse needs must be apparent,
   By reason of the wrappage following it;

And in like manner the primeval soul   100
   Made clear to me athwart its covering
   How jubilant it was to give me pleasure.

Then breathed: "Without thy uttering it to me,
   Thine inclination better I discern
   Than thou whatever thing is surest to thee;   105

For I behold it in the truthful mirror,
    That of Himself all things parhelion makes,
    And none makes Him parhelion of itself.

Thou fain wouldst hear how long ago God placed me
    Within the lofty garden, where this Lady   110
    Unto so long a stairway thee disposed.

And how long to mine eyes it was a pleasure,
    And of the great disdain the proper cause,
    And the language that I used and that I made.

Now, son of mine, the tasting of the tree   115
    Not in itself was cause of so great exile,
    But solely the o'erstepping of the bounds.

There, whence thy Lady moved Virgilius,
    Four thousand and three hundred and two circuits
    Made by the sun, this Council I desired;   120

And him I saw return to all the lights
    Of his highway nine hundred times and thirty,
    Whilst I upon the earth was tarrying.

The language that I spake was quite extinct
    Before that in the work interminable   125
    The people under Nimrod were employed;

For nevermore result of reasoning
    (Because of human pleasure that doth change,
    Obedient to the heavens) was durable.

A natural action is it that man speaks;   130
    But whether thus or thus, doth nature leave
    To your own art, as seemeth best to you.

Ere I descended to the infernal anguish,
    El was on earth the name of the Chief Good,
    From whom comes all the joy that wraps me round   135

Eli he then was called, and that is proper,
    Because the use of men is like a leaf
    On bough, which goeth and another cometh.

Upon the mount that highest o'er the wave
    Rises was I, in life or pure or sinful,   140
    From the first hour to that which is the second,

As the sun changes quadrant, to the sixth."

⊰ Canto XXVII ⊱

St. Peter's Reproof of Bad Popes —
The Ascent to the Ninth Heaven, the Primum Mobile

"Glory be to the Father, to the Son,
    And Holy Ghost!" all Paradise began,
So that the melody inebriate made me.

What I beheld seemed unto me a smile
    Of the universe; for my inebriation   5
    Found entrance through the hearing and the sight.

O joy! O gladness inexpressible!
    O perfect life of love and peacefulness!
    O riches without hankering secure!

Before mine eyes were standing the four torches   10
    Enkindled, and the one that first had come
    Began to make itself more luminous;

"Glory be to the Father, to the Son,
And Holy Ghost!" all Paradise began,
So that the melody inebriate made me.

Paradiso XXVII, lines 1–3

And even such in semblance it became
   As Jupiter would become, if he and Mars
   Were birds, and they should interchange their
      feathers.   15

That Providence, which here distributeth
   Season and service, in the blessed choir
   Had silence upon every side imposed.

When I heard say: "If I my color change,
   Marvel not at it; for while I am speaking   20
   Thou shalt behold all these their color change.

He who usurps upon the earth my place,
   My place, my place, which vacant has become
   Before the presence of the Son of God,

Has of my cemetery made a sewer   25
   Of blood and stench, whereby the Perverse One,
   Who fell from here, below there is appeased!"

With the same color which, through sun adverse,
   Painteth the clouds at evening or at morn,
   Beheld I then the whole of heaven suffused.   30

And as a modest woman, who abides
   Sure of herself, and at another's failing,
   From listening only, timorous becomes,

Even thus did Beatrice change countenance;
   And I believe in heaven was such eclipse,   35
   When suffered the supreme Omnipotence;

Thereafterward proceeded forth his words
   With voice so much transmuted from itself,
   The very countenance was not more changed.

"The spouse of Christ has never nurtured been   40
  On blood of mine, of Linus and of Cletus,
  To be made use of in acquest of gold;

But in acquest of this delightful life
  Sixtus and Pius, Urban and Calixtus,
  After much lamentation, shed their blood.   45

Our purpose was not, that on the right hand
  Of our successors should in part be seated
  The Christian folk, in part upon the other;

Nor that the keys which were to me confided
  Should e'er become the escutcheon on a banner,   50
  That should wage war on those who are baptized;

Nor I be made the figure of a seal
  To privileges venal and mendacious,
  Whereat I often redden and flash with fire.

In garb of shepherds the rapacious wolves   55
  Are seen from here above o'er all the pastures!
  O wrath of God, why dost thou slumber still?

To drink our blood the Caorsines and Gascons
  Are making ready. O thou good beginning,
  Unto how vile an end must thou needs fall!   60

But the high Providence, that with Scipio
  At Rome the glory of the world defended,
  Will speedily bring aid, as I conceive;

And thou, my son, who by thy mortal weight
  Shalt down return again, open thy mouth;   65
  What I conceal not, do not thou conceal."

As with its frozen vapors downward falls
   In flakes our atmosphere, what time the horn
   Of the celestial Goat doth touch the sun,

Upward in such array saw I the ether   70
   Become, and flaked with the triumphant vapors,
   Which there together with us had remained.

My sight was following up their semblances,
   And followed till the medium, by excess,
   The passing farther onward took from it;   75

Whereat the Lady, who beheld me freed
   From gazing upward, said to me: "Cast down
   Thy sight, and see how far thou art turned round."

Since the first time that I had downward looked,
   I saw that I had moved through the whole arc   80
   Which the first climate makes from midst to end;

So that I saw the mad track of Ulysses
   Past Gades, and this side, well nigh the shore
   Whereon became Europa a sweet burden.

And of this threshing-floor the site to me   85
   Were more unveiled, but the sun was proceeding
   Under my feet, a sign and more removed.

My mind enamored, which is dallying
   At all times with my Lady, to bring back
   To her mine eyes was more than ever ardent.   90

And if or Art or Nature has made bait
   To catch the eyes and so possess the mind,
   In human flesh or in its portraiture,

All joined together would appear as nought
    To the divine delight which shone upon me   95
    When to her smiling face I turned me round.

The virtue that her look endowed me with
    From the fair nest of Leda tore me forth,
    And up into the swiftest heaven impelled me.

Its parts exceeding full of life and lofty   100
    Are all so uniform, I cannot say
    Which Beatrice selected for my place.

But she, who was aware of my desire,
    Began, the while she smiled so joyously
    That God seemed in her countenance to rejoice: 105

"The nature of that motion, which keeps quiet
    The center, and all the rest about it moves,
    From hence begins as from its starting point.

And in this heaven there is no other Where
    Than in the Mind Divine, wherein is kindled   110
    The love that turns it, and the power it rains.

Within a circle light and love embrace it,
    Even as this doth the others, and that precinct
    He who encircles it alone controls.

Its motion is not by another meted,   115
    But all the others measured are by this,
    As ten is by the half and by the fifth.

And in what manner time in such a pot
    May have its roots, and in the rest its leaves,
    Now unto thee can manifest be made.   120

O Covetousness, that mortals dost ingulf
  Beneath thee so, that no one hath the power
  Of drawing back his eyes from out thy waves!

Full fairly blossoms in mankind the will;
  But the uninterrupted rain converts   125
  Into abortive wildings the true plums.

Fidelity and innocence are found
  Only in children; afterwards they both
  Take flight or e'er the cheeks with down are covered.

One, while he prattles still, observes the fasts,   130
  Who, when his tongue is loosed, forthwith devours
  Whatever food under whatever moon;

Another, while he prattles, loves and listens
  Unto his mother, who when speech is perfect
  Forthwith desires to see her in her grave.   135

Even thus is swarthy made the skin so white
  In its first aspect of the daughter fair
  Of him who brings the morn, and leaves the night.

Thou, that it may not be a marvel to thee,
  Think that on earth there is no one who governs;   140
  Whence goes astray the human family.

Ere January be unwintered wholly
  By the centesimal on earth neglected,
  Shall these supernal circles roar so loud

The tempest that has been so long awaited   145
  Shall whirl the poops about where are the prows;
  So that the fleet shall run its course direct,

And the true fruit shall follow on the flower."

⊰ Canto XXVIII ⊱

God and the Angelic Hierarchies

A fter the truth against the present life
　　Of miserable mortals was unfolded
By her who doth imparadise my mind,

As in a looking-glass a taper's flame
　　He sees who from behind is lighted by it,　　　　5
　　Before he has it in his sight or thought,

And turns him round to see if so the glass
　　Tell him the truth, and sees that it accords
　　Therewith as doth a music with its meter,

In similar wise my memory recollecteth　　　　　10
　　That I did, looking into those fair eyes,
　　Of which Love made the springes to ensnare me.

And as I turned me round, and mine were touched
　　By that which is apparent in that volume,
　　Whenever on its gyre we gaze intent,　　　　　15

A point beheld I, that was raying out
　　Light so acute, the sight which it enkindles
　　Must close perforce before such great acuteness.

And whatsoever star seems smallest here
　　Would seem to be a moon, if placed beside it.　　20
　　As one star with another star is placed.

Perhaps at such a distance as appears
　　A halo cincturing the light that paints it,
　　When densest is the vapor that sustains it,

Thus distant round the point a circle of fire   25
    So swiftly whirled, that it would have surpassed
    Whatever motion soonest girds the world;

And this was by another circumcinct,
    That by a third, the third then by a fourth,
    By a fifth the fourth, and then by a sixth the fifth;   30

The seventh followed thereupon in width
    So ample now, that Juno's messenger
    Entire would be too narrow to contain it.

Even so the eighth and ninth; and every one
    More slowly moved, according as it was   35
    In number distant farther from the first.

And that one had its flame most crystalline
    From which less distant was the stainless spark,
    I think because more with its truth imbued.

My Lady, who in my anxiety   40
    Beheld me much perplexed, said: "From that point
    Dependent is the heaven and nature all.

Behold that circle most conjoined to it,
    And know thou, that its motion is so swift
    Through burning love whereby it is spurred on."   45

And I to her: "If the world were arranged
    In the order which I see in yonder wheels,
    What's set before me would have satisfied me;

But in the world of sense we can perceive
    That evermore the circles are diviner   50
    As they are from the center more remote

Wherefore if my desire is to be ended
   In this miraculous and angelic temple,
   That has for confines only love and light,

To hear behoves me still how the example   55
   And the exemplar go not in one fashion,
   Since for myself in vain I contemplate it."

"If thine own fingers unto such a knot
   Be insufficient, it is no great wonder,
   So hard hath it become for want of trying."   60

My Lady thus; then said she: "Do thou take
   What I shall tell thee, if thou wouldst be sated,
   And exercise on that thy subtlety.

The circles corporal are wide and narrow
   According to the more or less of virtue   65
   Which is distributed through all their parts.

The greater goodness works the greater weal,
   The greater weal the greater body holds,
   If perfect equally are all its parts.

Therefore this one which sweeps along with it   70
   The universe sublime, doth correspond
   Unto the circle which most loves and knows.

On which account, if thou unto the virtue
   Apply thy measure, not to the appearance
   Of substances that unto thee seem round,   75

Thou wilt behold a marvellous agreement,
   Of more to greater, and of less to smaller,
   In every heaven, with its Intelligence."

Even as remaineth splendid and serene
    The hemisphere of air, when Boreas   80
    Is blowing from that cheek where he is mildest,

Because is purified and resolved the rack
    That erst disturbed it, till the welkin laughs
    With all the beauties of its pageantry;

Thus did I likewise, after that my Lady   85
    Had me provided with her clear response,
    And like a star in heaven the truth was seen.

And soon as to a stop her words had come,
    Not otherwise does iron scintillate
    When molten, than those circles scintillated.   90

Their coruscation all the sparks repeated,
    And they so many were, their number makes
    More millions than the doubling of the chess.

I heard them sing hosanna choir by choir
    To the fixed point which holds them at the *Ubi,*   95
    And ever will, where they have ever been.

And she, who saw the dubious meditations
    Within my mind, "The primal circles," said,
    "Have shown thee Seraphim and Cherubim.

Thus rapidly they follow their own bonds,   100
    To be as like the point as most they can,
    And can as far as they are high in vision.

Those other Loves, that round about them go,
    Thrones of the countenance divine are called,
    Because they terminate the primal Triad.   105

Not otherwise does iron scintillate
When molten, than those circles scintillated.

Paradiso **XXVIII**, lines 89–90

And thou shouldst know that they all have delight
    As much as their own vision penetrates
    The Truth, in which all intellect finds rest.

From this it may be seen how blessedness
    Is founded in the faculty which sees,   110
    And not in that which loves, and follows next;

And of this seeing merit is the measure,
    Which is brought forth by grace, and by good will;
    Thus on from grade to grade doth it proceed.

The second Triad, which is germinating   115
    In such wise in this sempiternal spring,
    That no nocturnal Aries despoils,

Perpetually hosanna warbles forth
    With threefold melody, that sounds in three
    Orders of joy, with which it is intrined.   120

The three Divine are in this hierarchy,
    First the Dominions, and the Virtues next;
    And the third order is that of the Powers.

Then in the dances twain penultimate
    The Principalities and Archangels wheel;   125
    The last is wholly of angelic sports.

These orders upward all of them are gazing,
    And downward so prevail, that unto God
    They all attracted are and all attract.

And Dionysius with so great desire   130
    To contemplate these Orders set himself,
    He named them and distinguished them as I do.

But Gregory afterwards dissented from him;
    Wherefore, as soon as he unclosed his eyes
    Within this heaven, he at himself did smile.   135

And if so much of secret truth a mortal
    Proffered on earth, I would not have thee marvel,
    For he who saw it here revealed it to him,

With much more of the truth about these circles."

⊰ CANTO XXIX ⊱

Beatrice's Discourse of the Creation of the Angels, and of the Fall of Lucifer—
Her Reproof of Foolish and Avaricious Preachers

At what time both the children of Latona,
    Surmounted by the Ram and by the Scales,
Together make a zone of the horizon,

As long as from the time the zenith holds them
    In equipoise, till from that girdle both   5
    Changing their hemisphere disturb the balance,

So long, her face depicted with a smile,
    Did Beatrice keep silence while she gazed
    Fixedly at the point which had o'ercome me.

Then she began: "I say, and I ask not   10
    What thou dost wish to hear, for I have seen it
    Where centers every When and every *Ubi.*

Not to acquire some good unto himself,
    Which is impossible, but that his splendor
    In its resplendency may say, *Subsisto,*   15

In his eternity outside of time,
    Outside all other limits, as it pleased him,
    Into new Loves the Eternal Love unfolded.

Nor as if torpid did he lie before;
    For neither after nor before proceeded   20
    The going forth of God upon these waters.

Matter and Form unmingled and conjoined
    Came into being that had no defect,
    E'en as three arrows from a three-stringed bow.

And as in glass, in amber, or in crystal   25
    A sunbeam flashes so, that from its coming
    To its full being is no interval,

So from its Lord did the triform effect
    Ray forth into its being all together,
    Without discrimination of beginning.   30

Order was concreated and constructed
    In substances, and summit of the world
    Were those wherein the pure act was produced.

Pure potentiality held the lowest part;
    Midway bound potentiality with act   35
    Such bond that it shall never be unbound.

Jerome has written unto you of angels
    Created a long lapse of centuries
    Or ever yet the other world was made;

But written is this truth in many places   40
    By writers of the Holy Ghost, and thou
    Shalt see it, if thou lookest well thereat.

And even reason seeth it somewhat,
    For it would not concede that for so long
    Could be the motors without their perfection.   45

Now dost thou know both where and when these Loves
    Created were, and how; so that extinct
    In thy desire already are three fires.

Nor could one reach, in counting, unto twenty
    So swiftly, as a portion of these angels   50
    Disturbed the subject of your elements.

The rest remained, and they began this art
    Which thou discernest, with so great delight
    That never from their circling do they cease.

The occasion of the fall was the accursed   55
    Presumption of that One, whom thou hast seen
    By all the burden of the world constrained.

Those whom thou here beholdest modest were
    To recognise themselves as of that goodness
    Which made them apt for so much understanding;   60

On which account their vision was exalted
    By the enlightening grace and their own merit,
    So that they have a full and steadfast will.

I would not have thee doubt, but certain be,
    'Tis meritorious to receive this grace,   65
    According as the affection opens to it.

Now round about in this consistory
    Much mayst thou contemplate, if these my words
    Be gathered up, without all further aid.

But since upon the earth, throughout your schools,   70
    They teach that such is the angelic nature
    That it doth hear, and recollect, and will,

More will I say, that thou mayst see unmixed
    The truth that is confounded there below,
    Equivocating in such like prelections.   75

These substances, since in God's countenance
    They jocund were, turned not away their sight
    From that wherefrom not anything is hidden;

Hence they have not their vision intercepted
    By object new, and hence they do not need   80
    To recollect, through interrupted thought.

So that below, not sleeping, people dream,
    Believing they speak truth, and not believing;
    And in the last is greater sin and shame.

Below you do not journey by one path   85
    Philosophising; so transporteth you
    Love of appearance and the thought thereof.

And even this above here is endured
    With less disdain, than when is set aside
    The Holy Writ, or when it is distorted.   90

They think not there how much of blood it costs
    To sow it in the world, and how he pleases
    Who in humility keeps close to it.

Each striveth for appearance, and doth make
    His own inventions; and these treated are   95
    By preachers, and the Evangel holds its peace.

One sayeth that the moon did backward turn,
    In the Passion of Christ, and interpose herself
    So that the sunlight reached not down below;

And lies; for of its own accord the light   100
    Hid itself; whence to Spaniards and to Indians,
    As to the Jews, did such eclipse respond.

Florence has not so many Lapi and Bindi
    As fables such as these, that every year
    Are shouted from the pulpit back and forth,   105

In such wise that the lambs, who do not know,
    Come back from pasture fed upon the wind,
    And not to see the harm doth not excuse them.

Christ did not to his first disciples say,
    'Go forth, and to the world preach idle tales,'   110
    But unto them a true foundation gave;

And this so loudly sounded from their lips,
    That, in the warfare to enkindle Faith,
    They made of the Evangel shields and lances.

Now men go forth with jests and drolleries   115
    To preach, and if but well the people laugh,
    The hood puffs out, and nothing more is asked.

But in the cowl there nestles such a bird,
    That, if the common people were to see it,
    They would perceive what pardons they confide in,   120

For which so great on earth has grown the folly,
    That, without proof of any testimony,
    To each indulgence they would flock together.

By this Saint Anthony his pig doth fatten,
>
> And many others, who are worse than pigs,   125
>
> Paying in money without mark of coinage.

But since we have digressed abundantly,
>
> Turn back thine eyes forthwith to the right path,
>
> So that the way be shortened with the time.

This nature doth so multiply itself   130
>
> In numbers, that there never yet was speech
>
> Nor mortal fancy that can go so far.

And if thou notest that which is revealed
>
> By Daniel, thou wilt see that in his thousands
>
> Number determinate is kept concealed.   135

The primal light, that all irradiates it,
>
> By modes as many is received therein,
>
> As are the splendors wherewith it is mated.

Hence, inasmuch as on the act conceptive
>
> The affection followeth, of love the sweetness   140
>
> Therein diversely fervid is or tepid.

The height behold now and the amplitude
>
> Of the eternal power, since it hath made
>
> Itself so many mirrors, where 'tis broken,

One in itself remaining as before."   145

⊰ CANTO XXX ⊱

The Tenth Heaven, or Empyrean—The River of Light—
The Two Courts of Heaven—The White Rose of Paradise—The Great Throne

Perchance six thousand miles remote from us
  Is glowing the sixth hour, and now this world
Inclines its shadow almost to a level,

When the mid-heaven begins to make itself
  So deep to us, that here and there a star   5
  Ceases to shine so far down as this depth,

And as advances bright exceedingly
  The handmaid of the sun, the heaven is closed
  Light after light to the most beautiful;

Not otherwise the Triumph, which forever   10
  Plays round about the point that vanquished me,
  Seeming enclosed by what itself encloses,

Little by little from my vision faded;
  Whereat to turn mine eyes on Beatrice
  My seeing nothing and my love constrained me.   15

If what has hitherto been said of her
  Were all concluded in a single praise,
  Scant would it be to serve the present turn.

Not only does the beauty I beheld
  Transcend ourselves, but truly I believe   20
  Its Maker only may enjoy it all.

Vanquished do I confess me by this passage
    More than by problem of his theme was ever
    O'ercome the comic or the tragic poet;

For as the sun the sight that trembles most,   25
    Even so the memory of that sweet smile
    My mind depriveth of its very self.

From the first day that I beheld her face
    In this life, to the moment of this look,
    The sequence of my song has ne'er been severed;   30

But now perforce this sequence must desist
    From following her beauty with my verse,
    As every artist at his uttermost.

Such as I leave her to a greater fame
    Than any of my trumpet, which is bringing   35
    Its arduous matter to a final close,

With voice and gesture of a perfect leader
    She recommenced: "We from the greatest body
    Have issued to the heaven that is pure light;

Light intellectual replete with love,   40
    Love of true good replete with ecstasy,
    Ecstasy that transcendeth every sweetness.

Here shalt thou see the one host and the other
    Of Paradise, and one in the same aspects
    Which at the final judgment thou shalt see."   45

Even as a sudden lightning that disperses
    The visual spirits, so that it deprives
    The eye of impress from the strongest objects,

Thus round about me flashed a living light,
    And left me swathed around with such a veil   50
    Of its effulgence, that I nothing saw.

"Ever the Love which quieteth this heaven
    Welcomes into itself with such salute,
    To make the candle ready for its flame."

No sooner had within me these brief words   55
    An entrance found, than I perceived myself
    To be uplifted over my own power,

And I with vision new rekindled me,
    Such that no light whatever is so pure
    But that mine eyes were fortified against it.   60

And light I saw in fashion of a river
    Fulvid with its effulgence, 'twixt two banks
    Depicted with an admirable Spring.

Out of this river issued living sparks,
    And on all sides sank down into the flowers,   65
    Like unto rubies that are set in gold;

And then, as if inebriate with the odors,
    They plunged again into the wondrous torrent,
    And as one entered issued forth another.

"The high desire, that now inflames and moves thee   70
    To have intelligence of what thou seest,
    Pleaseth me all the more, the more it swells.

But of this water it behoves thee drink
    Before so great a thirst in thee be slaked."
    Thus said to me the sunshine of mine eyes;   75

And added: "The river and the topazes
    Going in and out, and the laughing of the herbage,
    Are of their truth foreshadowing prefaces;

Not that these things are difficult in themselves,
    But the deficiency is on thy side,   80
    For yet thou hast not vision so exalted."

There is no babe that leaps so suddenly
    With face towards the milk, if he awake
    Much later than his usual custom is,

As I did, that I might make better mirrors   85
    Still of mine eyes, down stooping to the wave
    Which flows that we therein be better made.

And even as the penthouse of mine eyelids
    Drank of it, it forthwith appeared to me
    Out of its length to be transformed to round.   90

Then as a folk who have been under masks
    Seem other than before, if they divest
    The semblance not their own they disappeared in,

Thus into greater pomp were changed for me
    The flowerets and the sparks, so that I saw   95
    Both of the Courts of Heaven made manifest.

O splendor of God! by means of which I saw
    The lofty triumph of the realm veracious,
    Give me the power to say how it I saw!

There is a light above, which visible   100
    Makes the Creator unto every creature,
    Who only in beholding Him has peace,

And it expands itself in circular form
    To such extent, that its circumference
    Would be too large a girdle for the sun.   105

The semblance of it is all made of rays
    Reflected from the top of Primal Motion,
    Which takes therefrom vitality and power.

And as a hill in water at its base
    Mirrors itself, as if to see its beauty   110
    When affluent most in verdure and in flowers,

So, ranged aloft all round about the light,
    Mirrored I saw in more ranks than a thousand
    All who above there have from us returned.

And if the lowest row collect within it   115
    So great a light, how vast the amplitude
    Is of this Rose in its extremest leaves!

My vision in the vastness and the height
    Lost not itself, but comprehended all
    The quantity and quality of that gladness.   120

There near and far nor add nor take away;
    For there where God immediately doth govern,
    The natural law in naught is relevant.

Into the yellow of the Rose Eternal
    That spreads, and multiplies, and breathes an odor   125
    Of praise unto the ever-vernal Sun,

As one who silent is and fain would speak,
    Me Beatrice drew on, and said: "Behold
    Of the white stoles how vast the convent is!

Behold how vast the circuit of our city!   130
    Behold our seats so filled to overflowing,
    That here henceforward are few people wanting!

On that great throne whereon thine eyes are fixed
    For the crown's sake already placed upon it,
    Before thou suppest at this wedding feast   135

Shall sit the soul (that is to be Augustus
    On earth) of noble Henry, who shall come
    To redress Italy ere she be ready.

Blind covetousness, that casts its spell upon you,
    Has made you like unto the little child,   140
    Who dies of hunger and drives off the nurse.

And in the sacred forum then shall be
    A Prefect such, that openly or covert
    On the same road he will not walk with him.

But long of God he will not be endured   145
    In holy office; he shall be thrust down
    Where Simon Magus is for his deserts,

And make him of Alagna lower go!"

⊰ Canto XXXI ⊱

The Glory of Paradise — Departure of Beatrice — St. Bernard

In fashion then as of a snow-white rose
    Displayed itself to me the saintly host,
Whom Christ in his own blood had made his bride,

In fashion then as of a snow-white rose
Displayed itself to me the saintly host

Paradiso XXXI, lines 1–2

But the other host, that flying sees and sings
    The glory of Him who doth enamor it,   5
    And the goodness that created it so noble,

Even as a swarm of bees, that sinks in flowers
    One moment, and the next returns again
    To where its labor is to sweetness turned,

Sank into the great flower, that is adorned   10
    With leaves so many, and thence reascended
    To where its love abideth evermore.

Their faces had they all of living flame,
    And wings of gold, and all the rest so white
    No snow unto that limit doth attain.   15

From bench to bench, into the flower descending,
    They carried something of the peace and ardor
    Which by the fanning of their flanks they won.

Nor did the interposing 'twixt the flower
    And what was o'er it of such plenitude   20
    Of flying shapes impede the sight and splendor;

Because the light divine so penetrates
    The universe, according to its merit,
    That naught can be an obstacle against it.

This realm secure and full of gladsomeness,   25
    Crowded with ancient people and with modern,
    Unto one mark had all its look and love.

O Trinal Light, that in a single star
    Sparkling upon their sight so satisfies them,
    Look down upon our tempest here below!   30

If the barbarians, coming from some region
    That every day by Helice is covered,
    Revolving with her son whom she delights in,

Beholding Rome and all her noble works,
    Were wonder-struck, what time the Lateran   35
    Above all mortal things was eminent—

I who to the divine had from the human,
    From time unto eternity, had come,
    From Florence to a people just and sane,

With what amazement must I have been filled!   40
    Truly between this and the joy, it was
    My pleasure not to hear, and to be mute.

And as a pilgrim who delighteth him
    In gazing round the temple of his vow,
    And hopes some day to retell how it was,   45

So through the living light my way pursuing
    Directed I mine eyes o'er all the ranks,
    Now up, now down, and now all round about.

Faces I saw of charity persuasive,
    Embellished by His light and their own smile,   50
    And attitudes adorned with every grace.

The general form of Paradise already
    My glance had comprehended as a whole,
    In no part hitherto remaining fixed,

And round I turned me with rekindled wish   55
    My Lady to interrogate of things
    Concerning which my mind was in suspense.

One thing I meant, another answered me;
   I thought I should see Beatrice, and saw
   An Old Man habited like the glorious people.   60

O'erflowing was he in his eyes and cheeks
   With joy benign, in attitude of pity
   As to a tender father is becoming.

And "She, where is she?" instantly I said;
   Whence he: "To put an end to thy desire,   65
   Me Beatrice hath sent from mine own place.

And if thou lookest up to the third round
   Of the first rank, again shalt thou behold her
   Upon the throne her merits have assigned her."

Without reply I lifted up mine eyes,   70
   And saw her, as she made herself a crown
   Reflecting from herself the eternal rays.

Not from that region which the highest thunders
   Is any mortal eye so far removed,
   In whatsoever sea it deepest sinks,   75

As there from Beatrice my sight; but this
   Was nothing unto me; because her image
   Descended not to me by medium blurred.

"O Lady, thou in whom my hope is strong,
   And who for my salvation didst endure   80
   In Hell to leave the imprint of thy feet,

Of whatsoever things I have beheld,
   As coming from thy power and from thy goodness
   I recognise the virtue and the grace.

Thou from a slave hast brought me unto freedom,   85
    By all those ways, by all the expedients,
    Whereby thou hadst the power of doing it.

Preserve towards me thy magnificence,
    So that this soul of mine, which thou hast healed,
    Pleasing to thee be loosened from the body."   90

Thus I implored; and she, so far away,
    Smiled, as it seemed, and looked once more at me;
    Then unto the eternal fountain turned.

And said the Old Man holy: "That thou mayst
    Accomplish perfectly thy journeying,   95
    Whereunto prayer and holy love have sent me,

Fly with thine eyes all round about this garden;
    For seeing it will discipline thy sight
    Farther to mount along the ray divine.

And she, the Queen of Heaven, for whom I burn   100
    Wholly with love, will grant us every grace,
    Because that I her faithful Bernard am."

As he who peradventure from Croatia
    Cometh to gaze at our Veronica,
    Who through its ancient fame is never sated,   105

But says in thought, the while it is displayed,
    "My Lord, Christ Jesus, God of very God,
    Now was your semblance made like unto this?"

Even such was I while gazing at the living
    Charity of the man, who in this world   110
    By contemplation tasted of that peace.

"Thou son of grace, this jocund life," began he,
   "Will not be known to thee by keeping ever
   Thine eyes below here on the lowest place;

But mark the circles to the most remote,   115
   Until thou shalt behold enthroned the Queen
   To whom this realm is subject and devoted."

I lifted up mine eyes, and as at morn
   The oriental part of the horizon
   Surpasses that wherein the sun goes down,   120

Thus, as if going with mine eyes from vale
   To mount, I saw a part in the remoteness
   Surpass in splendor all the other front.

And even as there where we await the pole
   That Phaeton drove badly, blazes more   125
   The light, and is on either side diminished,

So likewise that pacific oriflamme
   Gleamed brightest in the center, and each side
   In equal measure did the flame abate.

And at that center, with their wings expanded,   130
   More than a thousand jubilant Angels saw I,
   Each differing in effulgence and in kind.

I saw there at their sports and at their songs
   A beauty smiling, which the gladness was
   Within the eyes of all the other saints;   135

And if I had in speaking as much wealth
   As in imagining, I should not dare
   To attempt the smallest part of its delight.

"Until thou shalt behold enthroned the Queen
To whom this realm is subject and devoted."

Paradiso **XXXI**, lines 116–117

Bernard, as soon as he beheld mine eyes
  Fixed and intent upon its fervid fervor,   140
  His own with such affection turned to her

That it made mine more ardent to behold.

⊰ Canto XXXII ⊱

St. Bernard Points out the Saints in the White Rose

Absorbed in his delight, that contemplator
  Assumed the willing office of a teacher,
And gave beginning to these holy words:

"The wound that Mary closed up and anointed,
  She at her feet who is so beautiful,   5
  She is the one who opened it and pierced it.

Within that order which the third seats make
  Is seated Rachel, lower than the other,
  With Beatrice, in manner as thou seest.

Sarah, Rebecca, Judith, and her who was   10
  Ancestress of the Singer, who for dole
  Of the misdeed said, *Miserere mei,*

Canst thou behold from seat to seat descending
  Down in gradation, as with each one's name
  I through the Rose go down from leaf to leaf.   15

And downward from the seventh row, even as
  Above the same, succeed the Hebrew women,
  Dividing all the tresses of the flower;

Because, according to the view which Faith
    In Christ had taken, these are the partition   20
    By which the sacred stairways are divided.

Upon this side, where perfect is the flower
    With each one of its petals, seated are
    Those who believed in Christ who was to come.

Upon the other side, where intersected   25
    With vacant spaces are the semicircles,
    Are those who looked to Christ already come.

And as, upon this side, the glorious seat
    Of the Lady of Heaven, and the other seats
    Below it, such a great division make,   30

So opposite doth that of the great John,
    Who, ever holy, desert and martyrdom
    Endured, and afterwards two years in Hell.

And under him thus to divide were chosen
    Francis, and Benedict, and Augustine,   35
    And down to us the rest from round to round.

Behold now the high providence divine;
    For one and other aspect of the Faith
    In equal measure shall this garden fill.

And know that downward from that rank which
    cleaves   40
    Midway the sequence of the two divisions,
    Not by their proper merit are they seated;

But by another's under fixed conditions;
    For these are spirits one and all assoiled
    Before they any true election had.   45

Well canst thou recognise it in their faces,
   And also in their voices puerile,
   If thou regard them well and hearken to them.

Now doubtest thou, and doubting thou art silent;
   But I will loosen for thee the strong bond   50
   In which thy subtile fancies hold thee fast.

Within the amplitude of this domain
   No casual point can possibly find place,
   No more than sadness can, or thirst, or hunger;

For by eternal law has been established   55
   Whatever thou beholdest, so that closely
   The ring is fitted to the finger here.

And therefore are these people, festinate
   Unto true life, not *sine causa* here
   More and less excellent among themselves.   60

The King, by means of whom this realm reposes
   In so great love and in so great delight
   That no will ventureth to ask for more,

In his own joyous aspect every mind
   Creating, at his pleasure dowers with grace   65
   Diversely; and let here the effect suffice.

And this is clearly and expressly noted
   For you in Holy Scripture, in those twins
   Who in their mother had their anger roused.

According to the color of the hair,   70
   Therefore, with such a grace the light supreme
   Consenteth that they worthily be crowned.

Without, then, any merit of their deeds,
    Stationed are they in different gradations,
    Differing only in their first acuteness.   75

'Tis true that in the early centuries,
    With innocence, to work out their salvation
    Sufficient was the faith of parents only.

After the earlier ages were completed,
    Behoved it that the males by circumcision   80
    Unto their innocent wings should virtue add;

But after that the time of grace had come
    Without the baptism absolute of Christ,
    Such innocence below there was retained.

Look now into the face that unto Christ   85
    Hath most resemblance; for its brightness only
    Is able to prepare thee to see Christ."

On her did I behold so great a gladness
    Rain down, borne onward in the holy minds
    Created through that altitude to fly,   90

That whatsoever I had seen before
    Did not suspend me in such admiration,
    Nor show me such similitude of God.

And the same Love that first descended there,
    "Ave Maria, gratia plena," singing,   95
    In front of her his wings expanded wide.

Unto the canticle divine responded
    From every part the court beatified,
    So that each sight became serener for it.

"O holy father, who for me endurest   100
   To be below here, leaving the sweet place
   In which thou sittest by eternal lot,

Who is the Angel that with so much joy
   Into the eyes is looking of our Queen,
   Enamored so that he seems made of fire?"   105

Thus I again recourse had to the teaching
   Of that one who delighted him in Mary
   As doth the star of morning in the sun.

And he to me: "Such gallantry and grace
   As there can be in Angel and in soul,   110
   All is in him; and thus we fain would have it;

Because he is the one who bore the palm
   Down unto Mary, when the Son of God
   To take our burden on himself decreed.

But now come onward with thine eyes, as I   115
   Speaking shall go, and note the great patricians
   Of this most just and merciful of empires.

Those two that sit above there most enrapture
   As being very near unto Augusta,
   Are as it were the two roots of this Rose.   120

He who upon the left is near her placed
   The father is, by whose audacious taste
   The human species so much bitter tastes.

Upon the right thou seest that ancient father
   Of Holy Church, into whose keeping Christ   125
   The keys committed of this lovely flower.

And he who all the evil days beheld,
   Before his death, of her the beauteous bride
   Who with the spear and with the nails was won,

Beside him sits, and by the other rests   130
   That leader under whom on manna lived
   The people ingrate, fickle, and stiff-necked.

Opposite Peter seest thou Anna seated,
   So well content to look upon her daughter,
   Her eyes she moves not while she sings Hosanna.   135

And opposite the eldest household father
   Lucìa sits, she who thy Lady moved
   When to rush downward thou didst bend thy brows.

But since the moments of thy vision fly,
   Here will we make full stop, as a good tailor   140
   Who makes the gown according to his cloth,

And unto the first Love will turn our eyes,
   That looking upon Him thou penetrate
   As far as possible through his effulgence.

Truly, lest peradventure thou recede,   145
   Moving thy wings believing to advance,
   By prayer behoves it that grace be obtained;

Grace from that one who has the power to aid thee;
   And thou shalt follow me with thy affection
   That from my words thy heart turn not aside."   150

And he began this holy orison.

⊰ Canto XXXIII ⊱

Prayer to the Virgin—The Threefold Circle of the Trinity—
Mystery of the Divine and Human Nature

"Thou Virgin Mother, daughter of thy Son,
  Humble and high beyond all other creature,
The limit fixed of the eternal counsel,

Thou art the one who such nobility
  To human nature gave, that its Creator   5
  Did not disdain to make himself its creature.

Within thy womb rekindled was the love,
  By heat of which in the eternal peace
  After such wise this flower has germinated.

Here unto us thou art a noonday torch   10
  Of charity, and below there among mortals
  Thou art the living fountainhead of hope.

Lady, thou art so great, and so prevailing,
  That he who wishes grace, nor runs to thee,
  His aspirations without wings would fly.   15

Not only thy benignity gives succor
  To him who asketh it, but oftentimes
  Forerunneth of its own accord the asking.

In thee compassion is, in thee is pity,
  In thee magnificence; in thee unites   20
  Whate'er of goodness is in any creature.

Now doth this man, who from the lowest depth
  Of the universe as far as here has seen
  One after one the spiritual lives,

Supplicate thee through grace for so much power   25
 That with his eyes he may uplift himself
 Higher towards the uttermost salvation.

And I, who never burned for my own seeing
 More than I do for his, all of my prayers
 Proffer to thee, and pray they come not short,   30

That thou wouldst scatter from him every cloud
 Of his mortality so with thy prayers,
 That the Chief Pleasure be to him displayed.

Still farther do I pray thee, Queen, who canst
 Whate'er thou wilt, that sound thou mayst preserve   35
 After so great a vision his affections.

Let thy protection conquer human movements;
 See Beatrice and all the blessed ones
 My prayers to second clasp their hands to thee!"

The eyes beloved and revered of God,   40
 Fastened upon the speaker, showed to us
 How grateful unto her are prayers devout;

Then unto the Eternal Light they turned,
 On which it is not credible could be
 By any creature bent an eye so clear.   45

And I, who to the end of all desires
 Was now approaching, even as I ought
 The ardor of desire within me ended.

Bernard was beckoning unto me, and smiling,
 That I should upward look; but I already   50
 Was of my own accord such as he wished;

Because my sight, becoming purified,
   Was entering more and more into the ray
   Of the High Light which of itself is true.

From that time forward what I saw was greater   55
   Than our discourse, that to such vision yields,
   And yields the memory unto such excess.

Even as he is who seeth in a dream,
   And after dreaming the imprinted passion
   Remains, and to his mind the rest returns not,   60

Even such am I, for almost utterly
   Ceases my vision, and distilleth yet
   Within my heart the sweetness born of it;

Even thus the snow is in the sun unsealed,
   Even thus upon the wind in the light leaves   65
   Were the soothsayings of the Sibyl lost.

O Light Supreme, that dost so far uplift thee
   From the conceits of mortals, to my mind
   Of what thou didst appear relend a little,

And make my tongue of so great puissance,   70
   That but a single sparkle of thy glory
   It may bequeath unto the future people;

For by returning to my memory somewhat,
   And by a little sounding in these verses,
   More of thy victory shall be conceived!   75

I think the keenness of the living ray
   Which I endured would have bewildered me,
   If but mine eyes had been averted from it;

And I remember that I was more bold
   On this account to bear, so that I joined   80
   My aspect with the Glory Infinite.

O grace abundant, by which I presumed
   To fix my sight upon the Light Eternal,
   So that the seeing I consumed therein!

I saw that in its depth far down is lying   85
   Bound up with love together in one volume,
   What through the universe in leaves is scattered;

Substance, and accident, and their operations,
   All interfused together in such wise
   That what I speak of is one simple light.   90

The universal fashion of this knot
   Methinks I saw, since more abundantly
   In saying this I feel that I rejoice.

One moment is more lethargy to me,
   Than five and twenty centuries to the emprise   95
   That startled Neptune with the shade of Argo!

My mind in this wise wholly in suspense,
   Steadfast, immovable, attentive gazed,
   And evermore with gazing grew enkindled.

In presence of that light one such becomes,   100
   That to withdraw therefrom for other prospect
   It is impossible he e'er consent;

Because the good, which object is of will,
   Is gathered all in this, and out of it
   That is defective which is perfect there.   105

Shorter henceforward will my language fall
    Of what I yet remember, than an infant's
    Who still his tongue doth moisten at the breast.

Not because more than one unmingled semblance
    Was in the living light on which I looked,   110
    For it is always what it was before;

But through the sight, that fortified itself
    In me by looking, one appearance only
    To me was ever changing as I changed.

Within the deep and luminous subsistence   115
    Of the High Light appeared to me three circles,
    Of threefold color and of one dimension,

And by the second seemed the first reflected
    As Iris is by Iris, and the third
    Seemed fire that equally from both is breathed.   120

O how all speech is feeble and falls short
    Of my conceit, and this to what I saw
    Is such, 'tis not enough to call it little!

O Light Eterne, sole in thyself that dwellest,
    Sole knowest thyself, and, known unto thyself   125
    And knowing, lovest and smilest on thyself!

That circulation, which being thus conceived
    Appeared in thee as a reflected light,
    When somewhat contemplated by mine eyes,

Within itself, of its own very color   130
    Seemed to me painted with our effigy,
    Wherefore my sight was all absorbed therein.

As the geometrician, who endeavors
   To square the circle, and discovers not,
   By taking thought, the principle he wants,   135

Even such was I at that new apparition;
   I wished to see how the image to the circle
   Conformed itself, and how it there finds place;

But my own wings were not enough for this,
   Had it not been that then my mind there smote   140
   A flash of lightning, wherein came its wish.

Here vigour failed the lofty fantasy:
   But now was turning my desire and will,
   Even as a wheel that equally is moved,

The Love which moves the sun and the other stars.   145

About the Author

DANTE ALIGHIERI WAS BORN IN FLORENCE, ITALY IN 1265, THE OLDEST SON of a prominent Florentine family. At the age of twelve he was promised in marriage to Gemma di Manetto Donati. Three years earlier, however, he had met Beatrice Portinari, the woman whom he would look to in his adult years as his literary inspiration and muse. Dante studied both Tuscan and Latin poetry in his youth and befriended several future poets with whom he would become a leading exponent of *Dolce Stil Nuovo*, a literary movement devoted to the themes of nobility, love, and feminine beauty. He fought in the Battle of Campaldino in 1289 with the calvalry of the Guelphs, a political faction that supported the papacy. Afterwards, Dante enrolled in the guild of physicians and apothecaries, which helped to further his ambitions in Florentine politics. In 1293 he published *La Vita Nuova*, a book of poems on the theme of courtly love. It was followed by *Convivio*, a book on his philosophical beliefs. A dispute between the White and Black factions of the Guelphs in 1301 lead to Dante's exile from Florence for life. Over the next few years he made his home in Verona, Lucca, and other cities, and occasionally assisted attempts to overthrow Florence's ruling Guelph party. By 1310 he had written *Inferno* and *Purgatorio*, the first two books of his *Divine Comedy*. He wrote the third and concluding book, *Paradiso*, in the years after he found sanctuary in Ravenna in 1318. An allegorical account of his wanderings in a spiritual wilderness and eventual salvation under the guidance of his beloved Beatrice, the *Divine Comedy* is recognized as Dante's masterwork and a landmark of world literature. Although Dante was offered amnesty by the rulers of Florence on several occasions, he did not consider the terms honorable and never returned to his hometown. He died in 1321 and was buried in Ravenna.